THE MINIATURE PINSCHER
KING OF TOYS

Patricia F. Lehman

The Miniature Pinscher: King of Toys

First edition, first printing 2009

PFL Publications
Wilmington, Delaware, USA
DOGBOOKAUTHOR@aol.com

Title: The Miniature Pinscher: King of Toys
Author: Patricia F. Lehman

ISBN 978-0-9816444-0-0

Copyright ©2009 Patricia F. Lehman
All rights reserved. No part of this book may be used, reproduced or transmitted in any form without written permission of the publisher, except in the case of brief quotations embodied in critical essays and reviews.

Printed in China.

The veterinary information outlined in this book, including the names of medications and possible treatments, is provided to encourage informed dialogue between the Miniature Pinscher owner and veterinarian. It is not meant as a substitute for the dog's thorough physical examination by his local veterinarian. The author and publisher disclaim any liability associated with this information.

**In case of illness or other emergency,
contact your Min Pin's veterinarian or emergency clinic at once.**

Every effort has been made to ensure the accuracy of dogs' names and titles, and breeders' and owners' names. Any errors or omissions are purely unintentional.

Front Cover: ©Photo courtesy of Sandra J. Mestyanek. Bluehen's Little Miss Mesty (black and rust) and Bluehen's Yellowribbonfortodd (red). Bred by Norma D. Cacka.
Back Cover, Top Left: ©Chris Halvorson of DogAds. Ch. Kimro's Toy Soldier, bred by Robin Greenslade, Kimberly Pastella, and Howard Schwell, and owned by his breeders along with Anthony Calvacca and Mary Curtin.
Back Cover, Top Right: ©Chris Halvorson of DogAds. Ch. Kimro's Rocket Man, bred by Robin Greenslade and Kimberly Pastella, and owned by Howard Schwell.
Back Cover, Bottom: ©Mark Raycroft. Dogs are owned by Ms. Heather Nicol of Pinache Miniature Pinschers (Ontario, Canada).
Poem Illustration: ©Earl Sherwan. Illustration may not be reproduced without specific written permission from Earl Sherwan and/or Lakeshore Artisans, Inc.

TABLE OF CONTENTS

1 KING OF TOYS..1
EARLY HISTORY *1* • PINSCHER-KLUB *5* • THE DOBERMAN PINSCHER *6* • JUDGE BERTA *6* • THE GOLDEN AGE *7*

2 AMERICAN INTEREST...9
NOTABLE OWNERS *9* • IN THE SHOW RING *11* • HISTORICAL KENNELS *12* • A LOOK AHEAD *17*

3 CANINE COMPANION...19
WHERE TO OBTAIN YOUR MINIATURE PINSCHER *21* • HOW TO CHOOSE A MIN PIN *22* • ADOPTING AN ADULT *24* • PREPARING FOR YOUR MIN PIN'S ARRIVAL *25* • VISITING THE VETERINARIAN *26* • AKC REGISTRATION: FULL VERSUS LIMITED *26* • IDENTIFICATION *26* • HOUSEBREAKING *27* • CORRECTING PROBLEM BEHAVIOR *28* • BASIC COMMANDS *29* • AKC CANINE GOOD CITIZEN® (CGC) PROGRAM *32*

4 GROOMING BASICS..35
BRUSHING *35* • BATHING *35* • TOENAIL CLIPPING *35* • ANAL GLANDS *36* • DENTAL CARE *37* • EXTERNAL PARASITES AND THE DISEASES THEY CARRY *38*

5 ON THE ROAD...43
AIRPLANE TRAVEL *43* • CAR TRAVEL *44* • BUS AND TRAIN TRAVEL *44* • RECREATIONAL VEHICLE TRAVEL *45* • SHIP TRAVEL *45* • HOTEL & MOTEL ACCOMMODATIONS *46* • TOURING WITH GROUPS *47* • TRAVEL IN THE UNITED STATES *47* • BOARDING YOUR MIN PIN *47*

6 THE OFFICIAL MIN PIN STANDARD..49
DEVELOPMENT OF THE STANDARD *49* • THE OFFICIAL STANDARD *51*

7 MIN PIN MOTION...59
VIEWPOINTS ON CORRECT MOTION *59*

8 ALL ABOUT EARS...65
COMMON EAR DISORDERS *65* • EAR CROPPING *68* • EAR BRACING *71* • THE NATURAL UNCROPPED EAR *72*

9 FOOD FOR THOUGHT..75
THE SIX NUTRIENT CLASSES *75* • HOW MUCH TO FEED *78* • TYPES OF DOG FOOD *78* • RAW FOOD DIET *80* • SPECIAL NUTRITIONAL NEEDS *80*

10 IN SICKNESS AND HEALTH..85
BASIC CARE *85* • INFECTIOUS DISEASES *86* • NEUTERING *88* • NONSURGICAL STERILIZATION *89* • TREATING COMMON AILMENTS *90* • FIRST AID FOR SERIOUS CONDITIONS *92*

11 SENIOR CARE..95
PREVENTIVE CARE *95* • PROBLEMS AFFECTING OLDER DOGS *97*

12 READY, SET, SHOW..105
CLUBS AND CLASSES *106* • CHAMPIONSHIP POINTS *108* • NONREGULAR CLASSES *109* • JUNIOR SHOWMANSHIP *111*

13 THE SHOW PUPPY..113
EVALUATING PUPPIES FOR SHOW POTENTIAL *113* • LOCATING YOUR SHOW PUPPY *115* • GROOMING FOR THE SHOW RING *116* • EARLY SHOW TRAINING *117*

14 THE JUDGE'S VIEW..121
JUDGING BASICS *121* • EVALUATING THE MINIATURE PINSCHER *122* • JUDGES' OPINIONS *124* • IT'S ABOUT ATTITUDE! *126*

15 UNDERSTANDING GENETICS..129
CHROMOSOMES AND GENES *130* • INCOMPLETE DOMINANCE *131* • POLYGENIC INHERITANCE *132* • CELL DIVISION (MITOSIS) *132* • REPRODUCTIVE CELL DIVISION (MEIOSIS) *132* • GENETICS TERMINOLOGY *132* • PUPPIES: MALE OR FEMALE? *133* • GENETIC DISORDERS *133* • THE CANINE GENOME: DNA CODE OF THE DOG *136*

16 IN LIVING COLOR..139
GENES THAT CONTROL COLOR IN THE MINIATURE PINSCHER *139* • STANDARD MIN PIN COLORS *141* • OTHER COLORS *142* • COLOR DILUTION ALOPECIA *147*

17 BREEDING BASICS..155
THE FOUNDATION BITCH *155* • UNDERSTANDING PEDIGREES *159* • CHOOSING THE STUD *160* • BREEDING PROGRAMS *160*

18 THE STUD DOG..165
CRYPTORCHIDISM *166* • RESPONSIBILITIES OF THE STUD DOG OWNER *166* • PLANNING THE FIRST MATING *168* • ASSISTING WITH THE MATING *168* • ARTIFICIAL INSEMINATION *171* • HALL OF FAME SIRES *171*

19 THE BROOD BITCH..173
THE ESTROUS CYCLE *174* • THE RIGHT AGE TO BREED *176* • THE PRE-BREEDING EXAMINATION *178* • CANINE BRUCELLOSIS *178* • THE BEST TIME TO BREED *179* • CANINE BIRTH CONTROL *179* • PSEUDOPREGNANCY *180* • MISALLIANCE *180* • HALL OF FAME DAMS *181*

20   THE EXPECTANT MIN PIN..183
METHODS TO DETECT PREGNANCY *183* • FEEDING AND EXERCISE *184* • PREPARING FOR THE PUPPIES' ARRIVAL *185* • THE NORMAL DELIVERY *185* • DIFFICULT DELIVERIES *188* • POSTWHELPING CARE OF THE DAM *190* • FEEDING THE NEWBORN *191* • DEWCLAW REMOVAL AND TAIL DOCKING *195*

21   THE OBEDIENT MIN PIN...197
THE ORIGIN OF OBEDIENCE COMPETITION *197* • OBEDIENCE ACHIEVEMENTS *197* • CONFORMATION VERSUS OBEDIENCE TRAINING *198* • GETTING STARTED *199* • RULES & REGULATIONS *201* • REGULAR CLASSES *202* • OBEDIENCE TRIAL CHAMPION *206* • NONREGULAR CLASSES *206* • AGILITY *206* • TRACKING *213* • OBEDIENCE TITLES *216*

22   THE MINIATURE PINSCHER IN CANADA..219
FOUNDING KENNELS *219* • CURRENT KENNELS *221* • SHOWING YOUR DOG *222* • BREED STANDARD *224*

23   HISTORICAL DEVELOPMENT AROUND THE WORLD..229
AUSTRALIA *229* • COLOMBIA *233* • DENMARK *236* • NORWAY *236* • SOUTH AFRICA *237* • SWEDEN *239*

24   WINNERS' GALLERY..241
MPCA SPECIALTY SHOW BEST OF BREED WINNERS *242* • WESTMINSTER KENNEL CLUB BEST OF BREED WINNERS *250* • ALL-BREED BEST IN SHOW WINNERS *251*

A POEM BY PENNY KRAFT..259

APPENDICES:

1929 MINIATURE PINSCHER BREED STANDARD... 263
1935 MINIATURE PINSCHER BREED STANDARD... 265
UKC MINIATURE PINSCHER BREED STANDARD 267
FCI MINIATURE PINSCHER STANDARD 271
CANINE TERMINOLOGY 275
BIBLIOGRAPHY 281
REFERENCES... 287
ACKNOWLEDGMENTS 296
INDEX 299
ABOUT THE AUTHOR 303

THE MINIATURE PINSCHER
KING OF TOYS

This 1901 painting by German dog breed expert, Richard Strebel, shows the black-and-tan (upper left) and harlequin (lower right) Miniature Pinscher varieties. Also pictured are the Affenpinscher (lower left) and German Silk-Spitz (upper right). Photo courtesy of the American Kennel Club.

KING OF TOYS
1

The Miniature Pinscher is an ideal family pet. He is a healthy, long-lived dog, whose small size and spirited personality allow him to maintain his youthful appearance throughout his lifetime. Intelligent and trainable, he also enjoys all forms of competition, from basic obedience exercises to advanced Utility, Tracking, and Agility. In fact, in 1937, a Min Pin became the first toy breed to earn the American Kennel Club's Companion Dog degree.

Physically, the Min Pin is a large dog in a small package. Standing 10 to 12½ inches from withers to ground, he is sturdy and compact, yet graceful and well balanced. His short, easy-care coat—which can be red, stag red (red with intermingling of black hairs), black and rust, or chocolate and rust—enhances his dynamic, clean-cut appearance.

In the show ring, the Min Pin is characterized by his high-stepping, hackney-like gait, fearless animation, and complete self-possession. He can't hide his faults under a long, glamorous coat. Every element must fit together harmoniously, creating the impression of a working dog in miniature. Moving out at the end of the lead, he prances with assurance, head and tail held high. The Miniature Pinscher, by his bold and flashy "look at me" attitude, challenges all to recognize he is the "King of Toys."

EARLY HISTORY

As it is for many ancient breeds, the precise beginning of the Miniature Pinscher is difficult to trace. Although researchers have developed different theories to explain the dog's background, all agree on two facts: the Min Pin originated in Germany, and he is not a descendant, or miniaturized version, of the Doberman Pinscher.

Painting by Edwin Megargee.

Born for success he seemed,
With grace to win, with heart to hold,
With shining gifts that took all eyes.
Ralph Waldo Emerson

Stone Age Origin

A forerunner of the Miniature Pinscher, the medium-sized German pinscher traces his history to one of the oldest canine families: the *Torfspitzgrupe*, or turf terrier group, of the Stone Age period. This canine variety may have existed as early as 3000 B.C. Pinscher-type canine skulls from this time have been found in locations throughout Europe and Asia, and may have found their way to Great Britain, possibly contributing to the development of several terrier varieties. The dogs that evolved in Germany were the ancestors of the modern Pinschers, Schnauzers, and Affenpinscher.

Manchester Roots

During the late 1930s, Hertha von der Kammer-Brugger, a breeder, co-founder, and life member of the Miniature Pinscher Club of America (MPCA), conducted extensive research into the origin of this breed. She concluded that the Min Pin evolved from the old world black-and-tan terrier, later known in England as the Manchester Terrier.

Edward C. Ash, author of *The Practical Dog Book* and *The New Book of the Dog*, believed that dogs resembling the black-and-tan terrier had existed for nearly 500 years in Europe. The first visual record was the illuminated manuscript, *Hours of the Virgin*, which dates to the year 1500. Early dog writers also described a short-legged, smooth-coated terrier and a long-legged, shaggy type. A number of breeds were crossed with the black and tan, creating entirely new varieties. Many were attractive and much sought after by prospective owners. Around 1800, a well-built, smooth-coated dog resembling the Fox Terrier emerged. These dogs were extraordinary ratters, a trait also evident in today's Miniature Pinscher.

The Manchester Terrier and German Pinscher may both trace their origins to the European black-and-tan terrier, yet historians deny a direct link between the two breeds. Jean Bungartz, a German animal artist and author, wrote in 1884,

Above: *Angelo*, signed by Angelo P. Lenordez.
Photo courtesy of F. Turner Reuter, Red Fox Fine Art, Middleburg, Virginia.

Left: A small black-and-tan dog resembling a Miniature Pinscher was featured in the 1891 painting, *Lady with a Dog*, by Henri de Toulouse-Lautrec.
Photo courtesy of the National Gallery of Art, Washington, D.C. Gift of the W. Averell Harriman Foundation, in memory of Marie N. Harriman.

"The pinscher varieties were by no means developed from the English black-and-tan terrier." He claimed that breeders in Germany's Württemberg province had a much longer history than did England's Manchester Terrier breeders. He also believed that the geographical isolation of southern Germany made any connection between the two breeds impossible.

In his 1905 book, *Die Deutschen Hunde und Ihre Leistung* (The German Dog Breeds and Their Achievements), Richard Strebel quoted a portion of the 1880 pinscher standard, which stated, "It should prove to be an extremely difficult task, if not utterly impossible, to determine whether our pinscher varieties originated in Germany, or whether they are only descendants of the old English black-and-tan terrier, whose old ancestral form was modified or changed by us here in Germany during the course of time. At any rate, our pinscher varieties are entirely different from the present day black-and-tan Manchester Terrier, and our pinscher has been bred long enough as a constant form here in Germany to justify its being regarded and classified as a German breed."

To ensure that the German pinscher varieties remained pure and would never be crossed with the Manchester, "thumb marks"—black spots surrounded by rust coloring on the forelegs—were deemed a serious fault and now are a disqualification. Required in the Manchester Terrier, these marks immediately reveal a cross between the two breeds.

Italian Greyhound and Dachshund Crosses

Another theory has it that the Miniature Pinscher resulted from crosses involving the Italian Greyhound and the Dachshund. Many researchers, as well as breeders, agree that these two dogs figured prominently in the background of the breed. Min Pin puppies often exhibit the sleek head, flat skull, small folded ears, and slender build of the Italian Greyhound, whose prancing gait resembles the Miniature Pinscher's flashy action.

Above: The larger *Glatthaariger Deutscher Pinscher* weighed about 20 pounds. The smaller variety, called *Glatthaariger Deutscher Zwergpinscher*, weighed a mere 2 to 5 pounds.

Left: *Dog Life*. Great Dane and Toy Terrier, by Raphael Tuck & Sons, circa 1921.
Author's collection.

Miss Phyllis Dare with a small pinscher puppy.

Early post card, from the author's collection.

An "ideal" Miniature Pinscher, shown with a Maltese.

Miniature Pinscher, circa 1913.

Post cards from the author's collection.

In addition, white patches—a disqualifying fault in the Min Pin—could have been introduced into the bloodline by the Italian Greyhound.

The Dachshund, also a native of Germany, may have contributed his coat colors to the breed. According to a standard from the 1930s, permissible colors for Min Pins included red, solid yellow, stag red, brown, or blue or black with rust or tan markings. This early standard also allowed a harlequin pattern, favored in the United States by Hertha von der Kammer-Brugger. The standard described this color as "spotted on a white body, flecked, mostly gray, with black spots and red or yellow markings." These colors closely resemble

Smooth-coated pinschers, from *The New Book of the Dog.*

the Dachshund's colors of red, red-yellow, yellow, brindle (stag red in the Min Pin), and black, chocolate, or gray (blue) with tan markings. Even the Min Pin's harlequin color, which has been linked with the Italian Greyhound or an early solid-white pinscher, could have developed from crosses with the "dappled" Dachshund. A modern Dachshund standard refers to this color as a brown, gray, or white ground, with dark irregular patches of dark-gray, brown, red-yellow, or black.

Zwerg Pinscher

As early as 1850, German writers described medium-sized and miniature pinscher-type dogs in both wire-haired and smooth-coated varieties. The larger smooth-haired breed, known as *Glatthaariger Deutscher Pinscher* (German pinscher with straight hair), or *Rehpinscher*, measured 40 to 50 centimeters from withers to ground and weighed about 20 pounds. The smaller variety, called *Glatthaariger Deutscher Zwergpinscher*, or *Zwergrehpinscher*, weighed a mere two to five pounds. The correct German term for the Miniature Pinscher is Zwerg Pinscher (dwarf terrier). Reh Pinscher (deer terrier) technically refers to dogs of the stag-red color—the color of the small red deer inhabiting German forests.

PINSCHER-KLUB

Regardless of which branch of the ancestral tree the Miniature Pinscher comes from, his development did not begin in earnest until the Pinscher-Klub, later known as the Pinscher-Schnauzer-Klub, was formed in 1895. One of the club's first tasks was the identification and separation of the two sizes and coat types. Before 1880, when the German Genealogical Register published the first pinscher standard, these varieties frequently were crossed with one another.

In his 1895 book, *Buch von den Hunden* (Book on Dogs), Bernardt Wolphofer recognized the four pinscher types that then existed:

1. The rough-haired German pinscher [which later became the Giant and Standard Schnauzers].
2. The rough-haired dwarf pinscher [Miniature Schnauzer and/or Affenpinscher].
3. The smooth-haired German pinscher [German Pinscher, a forerunner of the Doberman Pinscher, which joined the AKC's Working Group in 2003].
4. The short-haired dwarf pinscher [Miniature Pinscher].

These four types are described in greater detail in the following translation from the Brockhaus *Konversation Lexikon*, 1905:

The Pinscher Dog

"A truly German breed which occurs in four types: (1) The smooth-haired pinscher, characterized by a lively, bold carriage and disposition; head and neck carried well up; ears constantly erect and alert; the very short tail stub (these dogs are always docked) curves directly upwards from its base. Of compact body build and standing well up on graceful and rather longish legs; the head somewhat shorter and the skull wider and more arched than in the English terrier types. The tips of the ears, which break over, are always cropped to give them a smarter appearance. Eyes are of medium size and of marked attentive expression. Neck is free of pouches or wattles; well-rounded back and neck. Thorax full and deep, more flat than convex laterally. Abdominal underlines rising moderately toward the rear; legs clean-boned and straight from every viewpoint. Toes are well arched and foot round and small. Hair short, close and smooth. Color mostly shiny black with yellowish markings. Less desirable coloring is brown with yellow markings. Still less desirable—solid red or yellow. Regarded as serious defects are weak and too extremely pointed nose; overshot or undershot lower jaw; protruding or bulging eyeballs with a tendency to lachrymation [teariness]; uncropped ears; oversoft hair coating; black spots within yellow markings and any and all white markings.

"Other types of the breed are (2) the smooth-haired Miniature Pinscher which, with the exception of size and weight, must meet all of the qualifications of the standard type, but may have slightly shorter and silkier hair than the standard; (3) the long-haired (wire) pinscher, of standard size, also called 'rat catcher'; (4) the miniature long-haired (wire) pinscher."

Figurine from the collection of Ruth H. Norwood.

THE DOBERMAN PINSCHER

The Doberman Pinscher was named in honor of Louis Dobermann who lived in Germany from 1834 to 1894. Working with his friend, Herr Stegmann, Dobermann crossed the standard-sized, smooth German pinscher with various powerful shepherd dogs found in the region of Thuringia, Germany. The first black-and-tan Doberman Pinscher evolved around 1865, and by 1899 the Dobermann Pinscher Klub was founded in Apolda, Germany. These two breeds are both related to the German pinscher. However, the Miniature Pinscher—a much older dog—is not a descendant, or smaller version, of the Doberman Pinscher.

JUDGE BERTA

While the Pinscher-Schnauzer-Klub worked to define the four pinscher types, one man—a dog judge named Josef Berta—led the fight to create a sound, sturdy, well-moving Miniature Pinscher. Although his views were considered controversial by early breeders, Berta was the first toy dog judge to insist that the Min Pin move on the ground to prove his soundness. According to Judge Berta, from 1880 to around 1900, the Min Pin had been a tiny lap dog, usually owned by dignified, aristocratic ladies of upperclass German society. These women bred their tiny pets with much devotion, yet they had neither a plan nor an ideal, except to breed the smallest possible specimen. However, Berta did have a vision of the ideal Min Pin, which he described in a 1906 issue of the Frankfurt *Sportblatt*:

"I consider as ideal the Miniature Pinscher head which fits with the foursquare body, with the strong, upright forequarters, with the sinewy back, with the neck which flows alert and sinewy out of the shoulder and which carries the lines of breeding art; which, as a whole, fits in harmoniously and presents a fitting and aesthetic effect. I want a whole head and not merely a skull with a pair of ugly eyes; I want a head with a well-developed muzzle which works itself strongly out of the skull, and if these two, muzzle and skull, fit together to create a head of beautiful lines, then a uniform and harmonious unity is formed, a perfect picture of the breed is created."

Although the Berlin Toy Dog Club feuded openly with Berta, a few breeders already had been working to create the type of dog favored by Berta and an increasing number of German judges. Among these dedicated individuals were Ernst Kniss, whose Klein Paris kennel showed winner after winner, and Georg Mohr's Rheingold kennel, which specialized in red-colored pinschers.

THE GOLDEN AGE

The period from 1918 to 1925 is considered the "Golden Age" for Miniature Pinschers in Germany. The breed had successfully overcome all the opposition and resistance that characterized its growth from 1880 to 1918. During this time, the Pinscher-Schnauzer-Klub registered more than 1,300 dogs annually, whereas today that number is below 400. The first Miniature Pinscher Specialty Show, held at Stuttgart in 1900, boasted an entry of 93 dogs. By the end of World War I, both judges and breeders believed that the Min Pin had achieved a high degree of perfection. Many of these well-built dogs were exported to other countries, including Holland, Denmark, Sweden, and the United States, where they formed the foundation behind today's outstanding Miniature Pinschers.

Sieger Prinz Hans and Siegerin Cora, owned by Georg Mohr, Wiesbaden, Germany. Mohr's Rheingold kennel specialized in breeding red-coated Miniature Pinschers.

International and German champion of 1936 and 1937, Asta v Wettin.

The AMERICAN KENNEL GAZETTE

Vol. 49, No. 3
Per Year $4

March 1, 1932
Per Copy 50 Cents

CH. PRINZ-HEINZ
(Miniature Pinscher)
Owned by
MRS. HENRIETTA PROCTOR DONNELL
Larchmont, New York

PUBLISHED OFFICIALLY by the AMERICAN KENNEL CLUB

AMERICAN INTEREST
2

The earliest Miniature Pinschers to arrive in the United States were family pets, brought by German immigrants at the beginning of the 20th century. These small yet stylish dogs, whose sporty appearance and flashy attitude attracted many newcomers to the breed, continued to gain favor among both pet owners and show exhibitors, who imported dogs directly from Germany's top kennels.

The first Min Pin registered with the American Kennel Club (AKC), in March 1925, was a black-and-rust female, Asta von Sandreuth, owned by Mrs. B. Seyschab. Before the Miniature Pinscher Club of America (MPCA) was founded, in 1929, the breed was exhibited in the Miscellaneous Class. After the parent club gained AKC recognition, dogs competed for a brief period in the Terrier Group. By 1930, the Min Pin was reclassified to the Toy Group, where it remains today.

NOTABLE OWNERS

As the breed became established, several well-known individuals discovered the charms of the little Min Pin, including Mae Marsh (an early movie actress), Lee Olwell (publisher of the *New York Evening Journal*), and newspaper columnist Sheilah Graham. Miss Graham, who once wrote "Why I Hate Dogs" for the *New York Evening Journal*, was given a Min Pin by a friend who had never read her article. Miss Graham later apologized for the column, writing: "I want you to meet Ilka. Pretty isn't she? But her outer beauty is nothing compared to the loveliness of her little soul. She's loyal and affectionate and courageous. Her intelligence rates higher than that of most human beings. The companionship she gives me so generously is more satisfying than any I have yet received." Respected dog judge and author during the 1920s and 1930s, Dr. William A. Bruette also favored the Min Pin. After judging the breed at the Morris and Essex Dog Show, held on Mrs. M. Hartley Dodge's Giralda Farms in Madison, New Jersey, he stated, "A fancier of Miniature Pinschers will always be a fancier of the breed. They get under your skin."

Mr. Charles Healy Day, a prominent airplane designer and engineer who circled the globe during the 1930s, owned a Miniature Pinscher named Ericka von Heinzelmennchen. According to Mrs. Day, Ericka traveled by air more often than any other dog, almost always in an open plane. "When Ericka is tired of the scenery, she settles herself down in her basket, which I always bring along," Mrs. Day was quoted in a 1933 column in *Pure-Bred Dogs/American Kennel Gazette*. Born in Hamburg, Germany, in 1922, Ericka was unable to accompany the Days on their round-the-world trip because of Great Britain's quarantine restrictions.

The beginnings of all things are small.
Cicero

Ch. Prinz v Warnowtal, owned by Mrs. H. D. Sims, shown in a 1935 photo.

Ch. Freya v Rochsburg, owned by Dr. F. W. Hartman.

Ch. Barbele v Wurzburger Glockle, a German import owned by Mrs. Owen A. West. Barbele won several Group placements and a Best in Show during her distinguished career.

Ch. Lulabel von Rochsburg was a top show dog during the late 1940s. Rochsburg kennel, founded by Dr. and Mrs. F. W. Hartman, produced more than 80 champions.

Ch. Asta v Montgomery II was owned by K. J. Hedengren, a founder of the Miniature Pinscher Club of America.

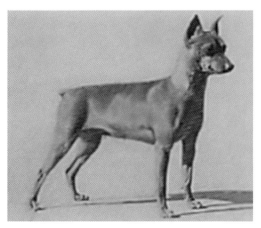
Ch. Red Lady of Cocoland, owned by Marshall C. Barth, shown in a 1941 photo.

Ch. Count Otto v Montgomery, owned by Dr. Harry A. Shier.

Ch. Marlene's Rajah was the son of Ch. Rajah v Siegenburg and grandson of Ch. King Eric v Konigsbach. Owned by Mrs. William O. Bagshaw.

Perhaps the breed's best-known enthusiast was Mrs. Cornelius Vanderbilt. Her son, Cornelius Vanderbilt, Jr., mentioned these dogs several times in his biography, *Queen of the Golden Age, The Fabulous Story of Grace Wilson Vanderbilt*. He wrote, "Mother often had a fire in her bedroom and beside the fireplace slept her little brown dog (she had a long succession of these) in a little canopied wooden box with silk brocade cushions. Her dogs were all champion rae [reh] pinschers, purchased in Germany, where they were well-known as the favored breed of Emperor Wilhelm."

In her later years, Mrs. Vanderbilt was so devoted to her dogs that she allowed them to sit on her lap at lunch and nibble at her plate. "During one particular luncheon," wrote her son, "little Teepee, as her dog was called, jumped down and soon sounds came from beneath the long gleaming mahogany table. The guests, greatly surprised, peered under the tablecloth. There was Teepee, savagely tearing to bits Mrs. Van Alen's new mink cape."

Cornelius purchased Jarl Ivar von Montgomery for his mother after the death of one of her Min Pins at 14 years. Mrs. Vanderbilt showed Jarl Ivar several times in Rhode Island and displayed his winning ribbons in a glass frame.

IN THE SHOW RING
First Champion

In 1931, Mona av Assarstorp earned the required points to become the American Kennel Club's first Miniature Pinscher champion of record. Mr. K. J. Hedengren, a founder and secretary of the MPCA, and his wife imported Mona in 1927 from Mrs. Ellen Lindeblad's kennel in Sweden.

Toy Group First

Mrs. Henrietta Proctor Donnell imported Konig Heinzelmennchen, the German sieger (champion) of 1930, from Professor Walther's kennel in Germany. Mrs. Donnell, the first president of the MPCA, exhibited Konig throughout the eastern United States, quickly finishing his championship. Konig's impressive accomplishments include being the first Miniature Pinscher to win the Toy Group (Miami-Biltmore) and, in 1937, winning Best of Breed (BOB) at the Westminster Kennel Club dog show when he was eight years old. Described by K. J. Hedengren as "an eminent example of a Miniature Pinscher...well built with almost perfect skeleton formation," his portrait graced the Miniature Pinscher breed column of *Pure-Bred Dogs/American Kennel Gazette* from 1931 until 1955.

First Best in Show

Less than a decade after the MPCA was founded, Fritz von Arnowtal surpassed all entries to win the breed's first all-breed Best in Show. Fritz, a 9-month-old puppy competing at his second show, took the prize in 1938 at Fort Worth, Texas. Among the group finalists were

Ch. Konig Heinzelmennchen, owned by Henrietta Proctor Donnell, of Larchmont, New York. Konig was bred by W. Walther's kennel in Germany.

Ch. King Eric v Konigsbach was a leading competitor for Mr. and Mrs. William O. Bagshaw's Canyon Crest kennel, in Beverly Hills, California. According to his owners, King Eric always was aware of what was going on in the ring and frequently would locate the trophies on the table or in the judge's hands. Once he spied the trophy, his eyes became glued to it and he followed it wherever it was moved.

three eastern champions with Best in Show honors to their credit. Owned by Miss Betty Lois Celaya, Fritz won 15 Toy Group firsts before his brilliant career was cut short by his death at the age of 20 months.

Champion Of Champions

Ch. King Eric v Konigsbach, born in 1938 at Eunice Wentker's kennel in Wisconsin, dominated the show ring during the late 1930s and early 1940s. His record-breaking achievements include 10 Bests in Show, 71 Toy Group firsts, and 77 Bests of Breed. King Eric also was the first Miniature Pinscher to win the Toy Group at Westminster (1941). In 1949, his son, Ch. Rajah v Siegenburg, became the second Min Pin to earn the honor. An elegant little dog and a tremendous showman, King Eric was so outgoing and animated that his owner, William O. Bagshaw, often needed to walk him around the show grounds to calm him down before going into the ring. King Eric continued to set records as a producer, siring 36 champion offspring.

Today's Miniature Pinscher owes his heritage to many dedicated individuals, too numerous to mention in this book. Readers interested in learning more about the breed's early supporters are encouraged to obtain Dr. Buris R. Boshell's *Your Miniature Pinscher* or Viva Leone Ricketts' *The Complete Miniature Pinscher*.

HISTORICAL KENNELS
Bel-Roc

Established in 1950 by Forrest P. and Maisie Booher (now Summers), Bel-Roc kennel has produced some of the breed's most famous sires. Ch. Bel-Roc's Dobe von Enztal passed on his racy, elegant appearance to many champion offspring, including Ch. Bel-Roc's Sugar von Enztal, Ch. Shieldcrest Cinnamon Toast, Ch. Bo-Mar's Pepper Pot von Enztal, and Ch. Sergeant Fritz von Enztal. Dobe was a 12½-inch black and rust that dominated both the show ring and pedigrees during the 1950s. Although he was at the top of the height limit, he showed no trace of coarseness. Dobe was very short-backed, with correct high tail set. His greatest contribution was to refine and improve the short, thick necks

Ch. Rajah v Siegenburg, bred and owned by Capt. and Mrs. A. C. Berry, compiled an outstanding record during the 1950s.

seen in many early Miniature Pinschers. Dobe had the overall balance that Bel-Roc kennel was striving for.

"Dobe was a ham," said Mrs. Booher. "He was a scene stealer. Once, when he was very young and not as mature-looking as he should have been, he won the Toy Group at Mansfield, Ohio by judging every other dog in the group right along with the judge. As each dog gaited, he would look at the judge, then bark at the dog until he stole the audience and the judge, too. When it was his turn, he hackneyed as though he knew he was the winner, which he was."

Other show winners and producers raised by the Boohers include Ch. Rusty von Enztal (Dobe's sire), Bel-Roc's Snicklefritz von Enztal, Ch. Bel-Roc's Buster Brown, and Bel-Roc's Krissie von Enztal.

Bo-Mar

Dr. and Mrs. Buris R. Boshell started Bo-Mar kennel in 1956 with Ch. Rebel Roc's Cora von Kurt. Von Enztal, Bel-Roc, Rebel Roc, and Alema bloodlines played an important role in achieving such outstanding examples as Best in Show and National Specialty Best of Breed winners Ch. Bo-Mar's Drummer Boy and Ch. Rebel Roc's Star Boarder. The late Dr. Boshell, who trained as a veterinarian before becoming a medical doctor, has raised more than 100 champions, including Ch. Bo-Mar's Johnny Come Lately, Ch. Bo-Mar's Ballet Dancer, Ch. Bo-Mar's Drum Call, Ch. Bo-Mar's Brandy of Jay Mac, and Ch. Bo-Mar's Drum Song. One of the most influential Bo-Mar dogs was top producer, and for many years number one Hall of Fame Sire, Ch. Bo-Mar's Road Runner. Owned by Mr. and Mrs. William Kleinmanns, Roadie sired an impressive 73 champions in his lifetime.

Carlee

Beauty, elegance, and soundness of body and mind characterized the late Carol Garrison's Carlee bloodline. From her first Miniature Pinscher, Ch. Shajawn Free Love, to her kennel's many top producers, Mrs. Garrison sought always to improve the breed and perfect her Carlee line. A thorough study of genetics, extensive planning, patience, and attention to detail underscored each Carlee breeding. The result: more than 35 champions, many of them top producers, in 10 years.

Among Mrs. Garrison's winners are Ch. Carlee Southern Prancer (Hall of Fame Sire); Ch. Carlee Southern Exposure, Ch. Carlee Cover Me In Silk, Ch. Carlee Satin Sachet, Ch. Carlee Classie Chassie, and Ch. Carlee Careless Love (Hall of Fame Dams); Ch. Carlee Braggin Again; Ch. Carlee Fancy Free; and Ch. Carlee Color Perfect. The most outstanding record, though, is held by all-time top producer and 3-time National Specialty Best of Breed winner, Ch. Carlee Nubby Silk. Nubby sired more than 100 champions in his 9½-year lifespan. His prizewinning offspring include Ch. Pevensey's Cash Dividend, Ch. Milebet's Nubby Star, Ch. Sunsprite Sparkle Plenty, and Ch. Pevenseys Winsome Sadie.

Hall of Fame Sire, Ch. Bo-Mar's Road Runner.

Jay-Mac

Jay-Mac kennel began in 1960, with foundation dogs from Rebel Roc and Bo-Mar. Mr. John McNamara, whose family had been involved in breeding saddle horses for more than 100 years, felt that the ideal Miniature Pinscher should have the same clean lines and silhouette as a fine saddle mare. Many dogs of the past tended to be short and cobby, with heavy heads and short, thick necks. Jay-Mac breeding introduced a sleeker, more elegant dog with a long, graceful neck, thin chiseled head with alert ears, good topline, high tail set, and structurally sound, well-moving legs.

Although the late John McNamara's dogs have not been favored by all judges, Jay-Mac has amassed an exceptional record of 110-plus champions. Outstanding examples include Ch. Jay-Mac's Silk Stockings and Ch. Jay-Mac's Ramblin Rose (Hall of Fame Dams), National Specialty winners Ch. Jay-Mac's Jacqueline, Ch. Jay-Mac's Candy Man, Ch. Jay-Mac's Pat Hand (Hall of Fame Sire), Ch. Jay-Mac's Dream Walking, and 3-time Specialty winner Ch. Jay-Mac's Impossible Dream, known as Impy. Owned by Dorothy DeMaria and handled by Joe Waterman, Impy earned 45 Bests in Show, 175 Toy Group firsts (winning the Group at Westminster), and was Top Toy Dog in 1975 and 1976.

Onlyone

Mr. Thomas W. Baldwin, a licensed dog judge, began his interest in breeding and showing with Irish Setters. His first Setter litter produced only one puppy, hence the "Onlyone" kennel name. In 1966, Mr. Baldwin added three Miniature Pinschers from Vera Halpin Bistrim's Halrok line. Ch. Halrok Headliner, sired by Ch. Rebel Roc's Casanova von Kurt, became a Hall of Fame Sire, contributing to Onlyone's 30-plus Min Pin champions.

A particular interest of Onlyone is the improvement of the chocolate-and-rust color. By the mid-1970s, the quality had deterio-

Ch. Jay-Mac's Impossible Dream dominated the show ring during the early 1970s.

Ch. Sunsprite Sparkle Plenty, the Number 2 Miniature Pinscher bitch of 1986, competed at the Purina Invitational in 1987 and 1988. Owned by Juanita L. Kean.

rated so much that some breeders suggested the color be removed from the standard. Farrell's Ballerine and Ch. K-Box Lord Dexter Of Rigadoon became the foundation of Onlyone's chocolate breeding program. Among Onlyone's chocolate-colored champions are Ch. Onlyone Chocolate Pudding, Ch. Onlyone Chocolate Mocha, Ch. Onlyone Chocolate Kisses, and Ch. Onlyone Chocolate Ripple. Ch. Onlyone Chocolate Bon Bon holds two distinctions: she was the chocolate champion in the breed's only 3-color (red, black-and-rust, and chocolate-and-rust), all-champion litter. She also was the breed's first, and to date only, chocolate MPCA National Specialty Best of Breed winner (1980). Mr. Baldwin, along with Marcia Tucker, also owned National Specialty BOB winner Ch. Sunsprite Saxon Of Carlee, who took the honor in 1985.

Rebel Roc

One of the finest and best known Miniature Pinschers of all time is Ch. Rebel Roc's Casanova von Kurt. Handled by his owner, the late Mr. E. W. Tipton, Jr., a respected dog judge, Little Daddy dominated the show ring during the early 1960s. His unsurpassed record includes 75 Bests in Show, 146 Toy Group firsts (including Group at Westminster), and 140 *consecutive* Bests of Breed. He won the Quaker Oats Award for Top Toy Dog, as well as Popular Dog's Top Dog Award. Named for a character in *Cat on a Hot Tin Roof*, Little Daddy also is a Hall of Fame Sire, producing 47 champions during his 17-year lifespan.

Founded with dogs from the Bel-Roc line, Rebel Roc's 35 champions include Ch. Rebel Roc's Cover Girl, Ch. Rebel Roc's Living Doll, Ch. Rebel Roc's Vanguard von Kurt, and Ch.

Ch. Onlyone Chocolate Fudge was the second chocolate-and-rust Miniature Pinscher to earn a championship. He was the first champion in an all-champion litter of three. Owned and handled by Norma D. Cacka.

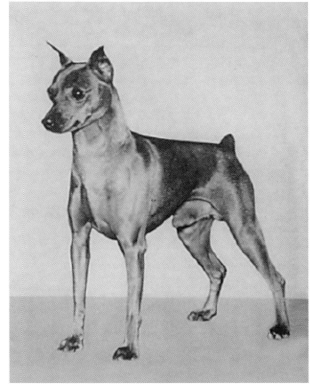

Ch. Rebel Roc's Casanova von Kurt, the top-winning Miniature Pinscher of all time, was bred, owned, and handled by E. W. Tipton, Jr.

Since 1978, the Kettle Moraine Kennel Club has offered a commemorative medallion to honor a past judge for his or her contribution to the sport of dog showing. Mr. E. W. Tipton, Jr. was honored in 1988. Club members vote on the individual to be honored, and a professional engraver works from a photograph to create the design.
Medallion courtesy of Charles Prager, Kettle Moraine Kennel Club.
Photo by Eric Crossan.

Rebel Roc's Fiesta von Kurt. Ch. Rebel Roc's Jackpot and Ch. Rebel Roc's Star Boarder proved their merits as National Specialty BOB winners.

Sanbrook

Mrs. Ann Dutton's Sanbrook kennel, established in 1961, has bred more than 130 Min Pin champions to date. Her best-known foundation sires were Ch. Mudhen Acres Red Snapper (bred by Mr. and Mrs. Hank Hearn) and Bel-Roc's Juno von Enztal (bred by the Boohers). Slats (Mudhen Acres) was an 11¼-inch red dog that excelled in almost every detail: neck, topline, tail set, rear, and feet. He was a showman, always alert and performing, never letting down, yet under perfect control. Born in 1952, Slats produced many champions, especially when bred to bitches of the Bel-Roc line. One of the most famous of these is Rolling Greens Sparkle. Although not a champion herself, Sparkle was the dam of all-time show winner, Ch. Rebel Roc's Casanova von Kurt.

Ch. Sanbrook Silk Electric, bred by Ann Dutton, was the MPCA National Specialty Best of Breed winner in 1988, 1989, and 1991. Owned and handled by Armando Angelbello.

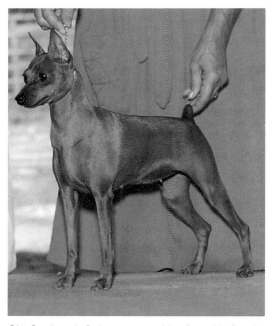

Ch. Sanbrook Sahara, owned by Sara McCutchen and Ann Walker, was the Fall 1984 MPCA National Specialty Best of Breed winner.

Additional Sanbrook winners are Ch. Sanbrook Impossible Scheme (Hall of Fame Sire), Ch. Sanbrook Star Topaz, Ch. Sanbrook Dancing In Silk, Ch. Sanbrook Silk Trader, and Ch. Sanbrook Smooth Operator. National Specialty BOB winners include Ch. Sanbrook Sahara, Ch. Sanbrook Simplicity, and Ch. Sanbrook Silk Electric (Hall of Fame Sire).

Sunsprite

Mrs. Marcia Tucker founded Sunsprite kennel in 1980, with foundation bitch Ch. Carlee Satin Sachet, bred by Carol Garrison. A year later, Sunsprite welcomed the dog that was to change Miniature Pinscher history—Ch. Carlee Nubby Silk. Nubby proved to be a top show competitor, winning Best of Breed at Westminster in 1982 and 1983. He also won an all-breed Best in Show, many Group placements, and three MPCA National Specialty Bests of Breed. His show record is outstanding, yet Nubby's greatest distinction was his ability to pass on his qualities to future generations. Nubby currently is the top Hall of Fame Sire, with more than 100 champions and many other pointed offspring to his credit.

One example of the depth of this kennel's breeding was the 1985 MPCA Fall National Specialty, where the four top prizes went to Sunsprite dogs: Best of Breed, Ch. Sunsprite Saxon Of Carlee; Best of Opposite Sex, Ch. Sunsprite Silk Delight; Winners Bitch, Best of Winners, and Sweepstakes, Sunsprite Sparkle Plenty; and Winners Dog, Sunsprite Grand Larceny.

A LOOK AHEAD

No breed can survive, let alone flourish, without the involvement of new, dedicated enthusiasts. Although the Miniature Pinscher has not yet reached the point of overpopularity, the breed steadily is gaining in annual registrations. To maintain the quality of today's dogs and guard against future deterioration in soundness or temperament, fanciers must continue to carry the torch of quality established by Germany's Judge Berta and America's pioneer breeders.

Ch. Carlee Nubby Silk (far left) is shown winning the Stud Dog Class at the Spring 1986 MPCA National Specialty in Louisville, Kentucky, under judge E. W. Tipton, Jr. Also shown: Ch. Pevensey's Cash Dividend, 1987 National Specialty Best of Breed winner, with owner Pamella Ruggie (standing left); Ch. Sunsprite Traces of Silk, with owner Gloria Knapp (standing right); Ch. Fillpin's Red Raider, a Best in Show winner, with owner Paulann Phelan (seated center); and Ch. Sunsprite Sparkle Plenty, with handler Debbie Butt (seated right).

Ch. Haycoss Hynote Kaaba, with Nicole Towell, of Australia.

CANINE COMPANION
3

Are you considering adding a Miniature Pinscher to your family? As a member of the Toy Group—bred for centuries to serve mankind as a true companion—this lively little fellow thrives on love, care, and attention. Unlike certain breeds that tend to be "one-person" dogs, the Min Pin gets along with all members of his family. He especially enjoys the companionship of children and often shows a unique protectiveness toward his young charges. Highly sensitive to his environment, he adapts his behavior to the special needs of those around him, snuggling quietly on the lap of a senior citizen, cheering up a teenager with his energetic antics, or playing a vigorous game of "chase-the-ball" with youngsters.

Mark Fiorentino, who became involved with the breed while stationed at Elmendorf Air Force Base, Alaska, related the following story: "One evening near Christmas, my friend Lance and I arrived home from shopping. The house was quiet and only the Christmas tree lights were on. My wife was asleep on one couch, while Lance's 6-month-old daughter, Nicole, slept nearby with our Miniature Pinscher, Buddy (Ch. Easy Street's Midnite Express). Although my friend had known Buddy since puppyhood, when Lance went to kiss his daughter the dog flew at him growling and showing his teeth. Perhaps it was too dark for Buddy to recognize Lance, but he was not going to let anyone or anything hurt that baby!"

Ch. Kimro's Rocket Man, bred by Robin Greenslade and Kimberly Pastella, and owned by Howard Schwell. Photo by DogAds.

My dog was about my only friend,
and I told my wife that a man needs at least two friends.
She bought me another dog.
Pepper Rogers, former football coach of the UCLA Bruins

Rockin' L's My Miss Holly, owned by Judy Smay. "When Holly looks into my face with her trusting eyes," said Judy Smay, "I realize how important she is to me, and I to her. She is everything I dreamed a little house dog could be. I am so glad that I found the perfect dog... especially for me."

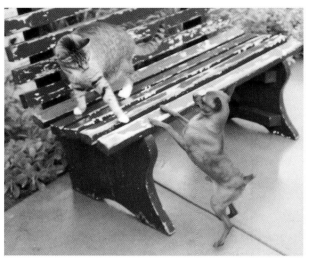

Miniature Pinschers are curious, inquisitive, and energetic little dogs. Here, Midnite's For Pete's Sake, owned by Mark and Karen Fiorentino, plays with his feline roommate, Kit.

Gail Freisinger, whose canine family members nap in tiny individual bed sacks, told this amusing anecdote of the time she "lost" one of her cuddlers: "When I made a head count of my Min Pins one evening, I found that one of the dogs was missing. I looked everywhere—in the bathroom, the closets, the cellar, and the dog run. My worst fear was that somehow he had got out of the house and was loose outside. Finally, as I raced upstairs to dress, I noticed one of the pillows on my bed moving. Sure enough, on closer inspection, I found a small, sleepy body under the pillow, wedged inside the pillowcase. I'm sure he wondered what all the fuss was about."

This inquisitive, ever-curious nature, coupled with an extremely high activity level—even into adulthood—led one breeder to caution, "The Min Pin is guaranteed to keep you laughing or cussing." According to Norma Cacka, whose special interest is preserving and promoting the blue-coated variety, "Miniature Pinschers are happy, inventive little dogs that love to play with children, other dogs, or cats. They even play with the pony and sheep that 'mow' our grass."

Lorraine Lyons, of western Canada, also noted the vitality of the "little beasts" as she affectionately calls them. "They can out-jump any dog I've seen, grab whatever they are after, and run like the dickens. Often, we are able to retrieve the stolen object only because the puppy tries to carry it out the pet door and the item won't go through the hole."

Perhaps the most distinctive characteristic of the breed is his keen intelligence. Min Pins excel at all forms of competitive obedience, from Novice to Utility, Tracking to Agility. They have served as therapy dogs, signal dogs for the hearing impaired, and a few have been trained by police as drug-detecting dogs.

Is the Min Pin right for you? If you're looking for a canine companion that is active and alert, vigorous and versatile, whose mischievous capers only are hampered by your ability to out-think him, you'll be rewarded with a lifetime of loyalty, devotion, and love. Perhaps the phrase, "a large dog in a small package," best describes the distinguished "gentleman" known to admirers as the King of Toys. Could you ask for anything more?

WHERE TO OBTAIN YOUR MINIATURE PINSCHER

To ensure that your new puppy is healthy and has been raised with love, gentleness, and plenty of human companionship, it's important to deal only with reputable breeders. The first step in locating that special youngster is to contact the Miniature Pinscher Club of America (MPCA) or a local kennel club for a list of breeders in your area. Though not all MPCA members are actively involved in breeding, the organization requires those who are to adhere to specific guidelines to assure that the welfare of the breed is always the top priority.

Another method of finding a puppy is to attend dog shows, either all-breed events with Miniature Pinscher entries or, better yet, a specialty show sponsored by the MPCA. By observing the dogs competing for points, as well as finished champions, you can begin to notice subtle differences in the types of dogs that various kennels are producing. Always purchase the show catalog so that you can identify the dogs and their breeders by their handlers' armband numbers. After a handler has completed his part of the competition, you may feel free to approach him with your questions and ask whether he knows of any breeders who might have puppies available.

Be extremely cautious when looking for a puppy on the Internet. Although many fine breeders showcase their kennels online, it's nearly impossible to determine which breeders adhere to ethical breeding practices based on the caliber of their Web sites alone. If you do find a puppy that looks promising, be sure to ask for references from satisfied puppy buyers and, if possible, obtain a referral from a local breeder or the MPCA. Make an appointment to visit the breeder's home and see the puppy in person. This will allow you to better assess the suitability of the puppy and the conditions under which he was raised.

When you have narrowed your list of possible kennels, you then can start to contact breeders with specific information about the kind of Min Pin you're looking for. Do you want a dog primarily as a family companion, or for showing or breeding purposes? Male or female? Puppy

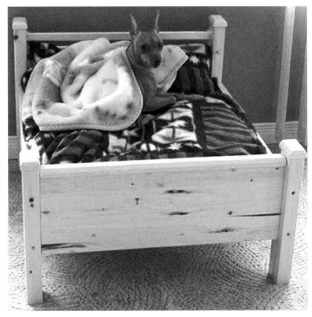
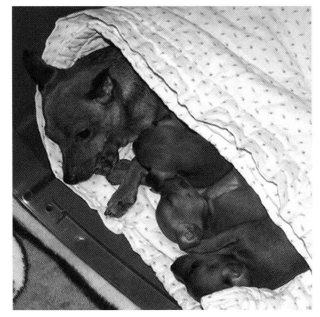

Can. Ch. Patapin Next Episode (left) rests in her own bed while Ch. Islands Yaquina (right) snuggles with her puppies under a blanket. Both live with Judy Bohnert in their British Columbia home.

Be sure to purchase your puppy from a reputable breeder. These adorable seven week olds, owned by Valerie Edwards and Joan Krumm, were sired by Ch. Redwing's On The Cutting Edge, an all-breed Best in Show and MPCA National Specialty Best of Breed winner.

or adult? Do you prefer a certain coat color? Pet buyers often choose black-and-rust puppies because they resemble tiny Doberman Pinschers. However, those interested in showing generally favor dogs with solid red coloring. Will you accept a puppy that might be larger or smaller than the standard permits? Always ask to see the dam and at least a photograph of the sire, if he is not on the premises. Although the dam might not have regained her youthful figure soon after giving birth, you should have some idea of what your puppy will look like as an adult.

It's also important to ask breeders whether they regularly have their breeding stock tested for known hereditary disorders, such as patellar luxation (a knee disorder), hip dysplasia, Legg-Calvé-Perthes disease (a hip disease that occurs mainly in small breeds), progressive retinal atrophy (an eye disorder that leads to blindness), and congenital deafness. Test results are registered with the Orthopedic Foundation for Animals (OFA) and the Canine Eye Registration Foundation (CERF) and may be viewed at the organizations' Web sites. For more information on genetic disorders in Min Pins, see Chapter 15 "Understanding Genetics."

Be patient when seeking that perfect puppy. Min Pins often have small litters—three or four puppies on average—and it's not uncommon for all the puppies to be the color or sex opposite to that requested by potential buyers. If you are set on a female puppy, keep in mind that breeders rarely part with an especially nice specimen. These are kept for showing and breeding, or are sold to individuals actively involved in showing. Many breeders don't produce a litter every year and usually have waiting lists for their puppies. Most ethical breeders do not accept a deposit until the litter has been born and evaluated for show potential. After the breeder has determined which puppies will be available to pet homes, he may then request a deposit to hold a particular puppy. Be sure you understand the terms of any contract you sign, including whether you can get your deposit back if a health problem later is found.

HOW TO CHOOSE A MIN PIN

Can you think of a more difficult task than choosing your favorite puppy from a litter of adorable babies? If more than one puppy is available for purchase, have the breeder remove all puppies that don't meet your preferences for color, sex, or other characteristics. If you plan to show your Miniature Pinscher, any puppies with breed faults also should be removed. Now you can begin to evaluate both the physical health and personality of the puppies.

Go over each puppy slowly, examining him from head to tail. Are his eyes clear and bright, with no teariness or discharge? His ears clean and odor free? If he scratches or shakes his head, this could indicate the presence of ear mites or a possible infection. Do his teeth meet in the correct scissors bite—the upper front teeth just overlapping the lowers? Are his teeth clean and white, gums pink and firm? Is his coat thick, smooth, and glossy? Dandruff, dryness, or bald patches suggest several problems, including ringworm, allergies, mites, or even a poor diet. Also, check to make certain the dewclaws (the extra toes near the ankles) have been removed and his tail has been docked to the proper length. Depending on his age, and the breeder from whom you're purchasing him, his ears may have been cropped, as well.

An important consideration, whether you're selecting a family pet or prospective show stopper, is temperament. The puppy should be friendly, lively, alert, interested in his surroundings (especially kennel visitors), and playful (except directly after mealtime). Avoid any puppy that runs and hides, and never choose one that growls or snaps. This is not acceptable behavior in any companion breed. If none of the puppies at a particular kennel appeals to you, don't feel pressured into making a purchase. Your Min Pin will be part of your family for many years, so you'll be happier if you wait a bit longer for that special youngster.

After you have selected the puppy that you want to take home, it's time to discuss the terms of sale with the breeder. The first consideration, of course, is price. This will depend on several factors, including whether the puppy has potential as a show or breeding prospect, the age of the puppy, the breeder's experience and reputation, and the caliber of ancestors in the puppy's pedigree. The breeder will expect full payment before releasing the puppy; some accept credit cards or allow time payments. A few will refund part of the price for a show or obedience title, or for spaying or neutering.

At the time of purchase, be sure to obtain the AKC registration, pedigree, diet instructions and small bag of food, blanket or favorite toy, and health certificate listing previous inoculations, wormings, and other medications or procedures. Reputable breeders typically provide written guarantees on their puppies. Make certain you understand exactly what the

Marykins' Hamilton CD and Buckeye Butter Cup CDX, owned by Paula A. Lacker, celebrate holiday festivities.

agreement covers: Is the puppy guaranteed to be free of disease only at the time of purchase, or does it cover future problems as well? Remember, depending on the specific disorder, most genetic defects don't appear until the dog is at least six months of age—sometimes well beyond. Will the breeder pay the veterinary bills, refund all or part of the price, or offer a replacement puppy? What if you're already attached to your dog? To avoid unpleasant surprises, be sure both you and the breeder agree on the various points of the guarantee before you take the puppy home.

ADOPTING AN ADULT

Don't overlook an older puppy or even an adult in your search for the ideal Min Pin. Both have advantages over a young pup, including greater reliability in housetraining, being past the teething (chewing) stage, and a more settled nature. Older puppies may be available from breeders who had originally kept them as show prospects. The puppy may have turned out to be over or under the size requirements, or simply may not have enjoyed showing. These Min Pins make wonderful pets and already have undergone considerable training. Typically, they have learned the basic commands and walk nicely on lead. Breeders may have adults available to pet homes, as well. Because breeders limit the number of dogs they own to those they can readily care for, you may be able to obtain a healthy, sound, well-trained adult—possibly even a retired champion. Contact breeders to let them know you would be interested in an adult Min Pin.

Rescue organizations, too, should be considered in your search for a canine companion. Unfortunately, through no fault of their own, Min Pins become homeless due to the death of their owners, divorce, relocation, or financial hardships. Since 1998, the Internet Miniature Pinscher Service, Inc. (IMPS) has provided foster homes, transport, training, and veterinary care in its mission to improve the lives of homeless Min Pins. All dogs

Choosing the right puppy is a difficult decision, so be sure to take your time. In this litter, from Winnifred Wartnow's Airlane kennel, the two red puppies became Canadian champions.

Karlee and Tipper, owned by Hal and Patsy Pawley, love to snuggle in their comfortable fleece bed.

placed by IMPS have been spayed or neutered, vaccinated, and tested for heartworms. In addition, they have been evaluated for temperament and training needs. IMPS carefully screens prospective adopters and works closely with families before and after the adoption. Dogs that have faced difficulties in their early lives often become exceptionally loving and loyal pets when given a second chance in their forever homes.

PREPARING FOR YOUR MIN PIN'S ARRIVAL

Living harmoniously with your new Min Pin starts with "puppy proofing" your home. As soon as you have selected the room in which your youngster will spend most of his time, cover the floor with a thick layer of newspapers and block the doorways with dog gates. (If you use a commercial gate, make certain your puppy can't crawl through the bars.) Keep chewable items out of reach and unplug all electrical cords. Pay special attention to household poisons, such as pesticides, detergent, bleach, antifreeze, and poisonous house plants.

The best time to introduce your puppy to his new home is over a weekend or vacation (but not a busy holiday), when you have plenty of time to spend with him. Allow him to make his own advances in greeting or playing with family members. He may feel insecure or anxious apart from his mother and littermates and prefer the quiet of his own bed for a day or two. Adult dogs also need time to warm up to their new owners, but usually come around quickly once they have had a chance to size up the situation.

Always talk to your puppy in a soft, reassuring voice. When he decides to play, avoid rough handling and don't allow him to become overtired. Even active Min Pins need frequent naps to recoup their energy. If you have young children, be sure they understand that the puppy is not a toy to be dealt with carelessly, but a living creature whose developing personality requires kindness and love in order to flourish. Although some controversy exists about whether small breeds face a greater risk of injury—from rough play or other accidents—in homes with small children, numerous examples show that with the involvement and supervision of parents both Min Pins and their young owners thrive on the loyalty and devotion fostered by their relationship.

PUPPY SUPPLIES

When you find out that your puppy is on the way, you can begin to assemble the following supplies:

- Food and water bowls, small yet heavy enough so that they won't tip over.
- Puppy food (the breeder may send a small bag of the food the puppy currently is eating).
- Brush, comb, toenail clippers.
- Crate or pen; don't buy a fancy bed until your puppy is past the teething (chewing) stage.
- Safe chew toys, such as Nylabones.
- Newspapers, paper towels, urine cleaner (odor neutralizer).
- Old blankets or cotton towels for bedding.
- Collar (after you measure your puppy's neck), lightweight leash, and ID tag (after you have chosen his name).

This 6-week-old puppy, Rødkildes Tango, is owned by Inge Hansen, of Denmark.

VISITING THE VETERINARIAN

Because most breeders allow only 48 to 72 hours to return a puppy found to have health problems, you must take your Miniature Pinscher to the veterinarian as soon as possible for a thorough examination. During this initial visit, the doctor will record your puppy's medical history, including the vaccinations he has received, dates of previous wormings, and other treatments. The veterinarian also will evaluate your puppy's overall health and check for any apparent physical abnormalities.

Be sure to find out what additional puppy shots are needed and feel free to ask any questions about your Min Pin's care. The veterinarian can suggest an appropriate diet and feeding schedule, as well as discuss the benefits or drawbacks of future procedures, such as ear cropping, tattooing or microchipping for identification purposes, teeth cleaning, and spaying or neutering. For basic information, it's a good idea to invest in a comprehensive home veterinary manual.

AKC REGISTRATION: FULL VERSUS LIMITED

When you pick up your puppy from the breeder, make certain you receive an AKC Dog Registration Application. If you're interested in entering conformation events, you'll need to obtain full registration. This allows your dog to compete in dog shows, as well as enables any litters from future breedings to be registered with the AKC. However, most breeders sell their pet puppies with limited registration privileges. By preventing registration of future puppies, Limited Registration helps to protect breeders from having their dogs fall into the hands of unscrupulous breeders who may not have the welfare of the breed as a top priority. With Limited Registration, your dog is registered with the AKC and may compete in all obedience, tracking, agility, and other performance events. If your Min Pin should turn out to be show quality at a later date, the breeder may convert his Limited Registration status to Full Registration. After you have selected your puppy's name, fill out the form and mail it to the AKC with the proper fee. If you plan to show your Miniature Pinscher, you or the breeder may want the kennel name included as part of your dog's name. If the kennel name is registered with the AKC, the breeder must sign the appropriate place on the application, giving permission to use the name. After the AKC processes the application, you'll receive your dog's formal registration certificate by mail.

IDENTIFICATION

Few things strike greater fear in the hearts of owners than discovering an open gate and realizing their pets are missing. Because Min Pins are noted "escape artists," able to squeeze through the tiniest crevices, it's important to properly identify your dog as soon as you bring him home. Currently, three methods are available: ID tags, tattoos, and microchips. All dogs need basic tags, even when they have permanent forms of identification. People who find stray animals usually check first for collar tags. Information on the tag can include your name and address, or the telephone number of a national lost pet registry service. Using a third-party listing, instead of your own, protects your privacy and avoids nuisance calls from those who prey on peoples' misfortunes.

However, because collars can break and ID tags be lost, many owners prefer to use tattoos or microchips to distinguish their Min Pins. In fact, your puppy already may have one of these forms of identification when he comes from the breeder. Both methods are safe, easy to perform, and well tolerated. Veterinarians can tattoo code numbers on a pet's inner thigh or abdomen in less than 15 minutes, usually without anesthesia. They also can insert microchips, which resemble grains of rice, with a syringe in an area between the shoulder blades. After the tattoo or microchip is in place, be sure to enroll your dog with one of the registry organizations. Most offer round-the-clock phone monitoring, so if someone finds a pet with the special tag, he or she calls the center and gives the identification number. The registry then contacts the owner with the finder's location. Because scanners are needed to read microchips, manufacturers have provided them free of charge to all humane organizations.

With the minimal effort and modest cost involved, why not make certain your furry friend carries permanent identification? Remember, your Min Pin cannot ask for help or give his address if he gets lost. A collar tag, combined with a tattoo or microchip, is vital in helping him to find his way back home.

HOUSEBREAKING

The first lesson your puppy must learn is where to go to the bathroom—on newspapers or outdoors. Or, perhaps, as several owners suggest, a litter box. If you have access to a backyard and are available during the day to take the puppy out at least every two hours, you can start with outdoor training. However, for puppies under 12 weeks of age some form of paper training usually is necessary.

> **HOUSEBREAKING TIPS**
>
> - Establish a regular feeding and walking schedule.
> - Don't give water later than two or three hours before bedtime.
> - Watch your puppy closely. Place him on the papers or take him out immediately when he signals that he needs to go.
> - Praise lavishly when he performs correctly.
> - When you're not with him, keep him confined in a secure area until he performs reliably.
> - Never give an untrained puppy the run of the house.
> - Give the same command each time he eliminates.
> - Never scold him unless you catch him in the act.
> - Never use harsh punishment under any circumstances.
> - If your adult (already trained) dog starts to soil in the house, have him thoroughly checked by the veterinarian for health problems.

Indoor Training

Choose a room with a washable floor, where the family likes to gather, such as the kitchen. This is where your puppy will spend most of his time until he performs reliably. Put down a training pad and encourage your puppy to use it. The key to successful training—from housebreaking to top-level obedience—is to prevent mistakes from occurring rather than correct them after the fact. Be observant; if your puppy appears anxious, or is sniffing the floor or circling, quickly place him on the pad. Always praise him enthusiastically when he performs correctly. A number of owners who have limited access to outdoor exercise areas keep training pads down in an out-of-the-way place for their adult dogs, as well.

Outdoor Training

By about four months, after he has received his second set of inoculations, your Miniature Pinscher is ready to start outdoor training. As it was with paper training, this involves confining your puppy to a secure area or crate where you can watch him. Don't leave him alone in the type of fold-up exercise pen used by handlers at dog shows; he will soon meet the challenge of climbing over the top. Also, make certain all outdoor runs, if you use them, are designed so that your dog can't dig or tunnel underneath and escape.

To begin housebreaking, remove all papers from the floor and set up a consistent schedule for outdoor walks. Your puppy will need to go out immediately after waking in the morning, after meals and naps, after play or excitement, and just before bedtime. Keep an eye on your youngster and be ready to pick him up and carry him to the proper spot. (Have his leash handy.) During the early stages of training, always return to the same place. His scent will remain and help to remind him of his "business." Choose a special phrase and use it each time your puppy eliminates. Training him to "go" on command will save time when you don't want to dawdle.

Crate Training

Because your puppy instinctively prefers to keep his "den" clean, crate training allows you to determine when, as well as where, he will eliminate. To start training, introduce your Miniature Pinscher to his crate in such a way that he will learn to enjoy having his own quiet area. Place a treat or chew toy inside and leave the door open. Praise your puppy every time he explores inside the crate. As soon as he enters without hesitation, close the door for a minute or two. Continue to offer praise when he settles down.

When your Min Pin becomes accustomed to his crate, you then can begin housetraining. Keep the crate in a room with the family, where you can watch your puppy for signs that he needs to go out. Be ready to take him to the proper spot and praise lavishly when he behaves. (If he doesn't go, take him back to his crate.) Successful training requires careful monitoring. You must take your puppy outside every hour or so, and whenever he appears that he needs to go. As a housebreaking tool, the crate prevents your puppy from making mistakes and allows you to choose the place where he eliminates.

In addition, his scent remains on the preferred spot to reinforce your training. The crate is not a method for locking up a puppy for hours at a time. When you must leave during the day, place him in a confined area with papers on the floor. It's unrealistic to expect a puppy to wait hours to relieve himself.

All puppies have accidents. Don't scold your youngster unless you catch him in the act. He has a short memory span and won't be able to associate your displeasure with his mistake. To prevent future accidents, use a commercial odor neutralizer (available at most pet supply stores and catalogs) to clean the spot and remove all traces of odor.

CORRECTING PROBLEM BEHAVIOR
Barking

Min Pins take their role as family guardian quite seriously. When Judy Smay acquired her puppy, Rockin' L's My Miss Holly, she knew she would be getting an alert, intelligent watchdog. "To capitalize on this aspect of her personality and to help her reach her full potential, I try to

Joanne Wilds' Min Pins enjoy relaxing in their favorite spot on a sunny day. Shown are Ch. Dragonholds Dressed To Kill (front left) with her 14-year-old granddam, Jo-El's Formal Attire (front right), and Ch. Altanero Sharper Image (back).

pay attention to the different signals she gives me," explained Judy. As the family bird watcher, Holly protects her surroundings from her perch inside the sliding glass door. With a quick bark, Holly chases pesky robins and starlings from the bird feeder and the family's strawberry patch.

When your dog barks for good reason—a visitor arriving or someone coming into the yard—praise him. If he continues to bark after alerting you, firmly tell him "Quiet!" or "Enough!" If he won't pay attention to your command, pick him up and gently hold his mouth closed until he calms down. Barking is a difficult habit to break. You must be patient and persistent in training.

Begging

Never give treats from the table! Begging for food comes naturally to most puppies, yet this irritating habit should be broken when your Min Pin is young. Some owners put their dogs in their crates at dinnertime. However, this may create another problem—crying or whining. Perhaps, the most successful technique is to feed your puppy before the family sits down to dinner. He then will feel content and soon be ready for a nap.

Chewing

During the teething stage—from four to six months—puppies usually begin chewing in earnest. To prevent yours from gnawing the leg of your favorite chair or shredding the carpet, always provide safe chew toys, such as Nylabones. Avoid giving squeaky toys and be cautious with rawhide bones; puppies can chew off pieces and swallow them. In fact, one breeder lost a promising 3-month-old when the puppy chewed off the foot of a latex toy. The piece lodged in his intestines and before anyone realized what had happened the puppy died of shock.

If you catch your Min Pin with an unacceptable object, give a firm "Leave It!" command and show him his own toy. For persistent chewers, try using one of the unpleasant-tasting repellents, such as Bitter Apple. If your puppy is destructive when left alone, place him in his crate or a safe,

> **TRAINING TIPS**
> - Train in a confined area with few distractions until your puppy has mastered the command.
> - Start with one family member working with the puppy.
> - Train before meals so that he won't be sleepy or develop an upset stomach.
> - Keep training sessions short, 5 to 10 minutes.
> - Work on one exercise at a time until your puppy has mastered it.
> - When you give the command, wait a few seconds for him to perform before correcting him.
> - Praise enthusiastically and/or give a small treat when your puppy obeys.
> - End each lesson on a successful note and have a short play period afterward.
> - Never get angry or prolong punishment.
> - Above all: Be patient and have a sense of humor. Your Miniature Pinscher certainly does!

confined area where he can't do damage. Never punish your puppy long after the fact. The best way to avoid a chewing problem is to prevent it, by watching your dog closely and providing safe alternatives.

Jumping Up

If you could not see above your owner's knees, you would jump up, too! Although a rambunctious Min Pin doesn't create the problems that an unruly Great Dane might, you still must train him not to jump on people. Choose a command, such as "Off!" (Don't use "Down!," which means to lie down.) Then, either step back from him to make him stand down, or move his front feet to the floor. Always greet your puppy at his level, so that he won't need to jump up to gain your attention.

BASIC COMMANDS

Puppies vary in temperament and learning ability. However, most are ready for simple lessons by about 12 weeks. First, your puppy needs two pieces of equipment: a properly fitting collar and a 6-foot leash. Training manuals often suggest using a choke collar, which tightens momentarily during corrections. For

This father (red dog) and son duo walk nicely on a loose lead. Front dog is Ch. Labell All American, owned by Salina Bailey. Back dog is Ch. Marlex Mister Chips, owned by Armando Angelbello. Photo by Lisa Uhacz.

puppies—especially toy breeds—start with a less-restrictive buckle collar. To determine the proper collar size, measure around your dog's neck and add about 2 to 2½ inches. If the total equals eight inches, for example, you'll need to purchase a size-8 collar. Choose a nylon collar for your puppy; most leather collars are too bulky for tiny dogs. If you decide to try a choke collar, use one made of nylon or fine link chain. Because these collars tighten when the "active" ring is pulled, never leave a choke collar on your dog, except during training sessions. When purchasing a leash, look for ½-inch-wide cotton or nylon fabric. Chain-link leashes are not suitable for training and leather may be too cumbersome. Always look for a leash with a small snap device; you don't want to bump your puppy in the chin with a large bolt! Fasten the leash to the ring provided on the buckle collar. With a choke collar, you must attach the leash to the ring that comes over, not under, his neck. Before you begin training, allow your Min Pin to become accustomed to his leash by attaching it to his collar and letting it drag on the floor during play. Watch your puppy, though, so that the leash doesn't tangle or choke him.

Should you use treats when training? Whereas purists insist that praise is its own reward, a treat is useful in certain situations to get through to the puppy. Be sure to use them only during the learning phase of practice, however. When your youngster understands what you expect, give plenty of praise and offer treats sparingly. You don't want your Miniature Pinscher to become a glutton, so try a plain fat-free snack such as Cheerios.

Sit

This is perhaps the easiest command for Min Pins to learn. Kneel, with your puppy in front of you or at your left side. Place your right hand on his chest to steady him. When you give the "sit" command, gently push down on his rump while pressing back slightly on his chest. When your pup sits, give lots of praise. If he stiffens his rear legs and refuses to sit, run your left hand down his back, over his rump, and press inward behind his knees. If you plan to compete in formal obedience one day, be sure your Min Pin sits straight and doesn't lean sideways on one hip. Crooked sits will result in points off in competition.

Come

For safety's sake, "come" is the most important command your puppy will learn. Always start this exercise on leash or in a confined area. With your dog in a sitting position, step back a couple of feet and call him to you. Use your pup's name as part of the command; for example, "Ricky, come!" Open your arms or pat your hands on your legs to encourage him. Another method of teaching this command is to carefully "reel in" your puppy with his leash while calling and praising him. Pet your dog enthusiastically when he obeys, but never call your dog to you to punish him. When your Min Pin comes reliably on leash or indoors, move to a fenced-in area outdoors where he will face greater distractions. Never allow your dog off leash until he always responds promptly to your command. Min Pins are great scramblers and are difficult to capture when they disobey!

Down

To teach the "down" command, place your dog in a sitting position. While giving the command, press gently on his back with one hand and move his front legs out with the other. You also can pat the floor to encourage him to lie down, or place a treat on the floor in front of him. Praise lavishly when he performs correctly.

Stay

With your puppy sitting or lying down, firmly tell him "Stay!" At the same time, give the hand signal to stay by placing your left hand in front of the dog's face with your palm toward him and fingers pointing down. To begin the exercise, walk one or two steps ahead of your dog, then turn toward him. Hold the stay only a few seconds before returning and releasing him. If he remained in position, praise him. If he moved, have him sit or lie down and try again. You also can practice this exercise with an assistant kneeling behind your dog, ready to steady him if he moves. To achieve the type of sit- or down-stay required in the obedience ring, gradually increase the distance you move away from your dog and the length of time he must stay in position. Should he fail to perform, return to the previous level until he remains still.

Heel

Your Min Pin must learn to walk properly on leash, without racing, pulling, or lagging. Begin with your puppy sitting or standing close to your left hip. This is correct heel position. Allow the leash to run loosely through your left hand, with the excess looped in your right. Give the "heel" command, then step out on your left foot. If your dog forges, repeat the command and give the leash a quick snap. This signals a correction

Can. Ch. Patapin Next Episode shows her athleticism as she jumps for a treat. Bred by Patricia Gauthier and owned by Judy Bohnert.

even if he is wearing a buckle collar. If your Min Pin continues to pull on the leash, cross your right foot in front of him while you're walking and stomp the ground. If he lags, encourage him by patting your leg and calling his name. Give plenty of praise when your dog walks at your side on a loose lead. To improve his skills, begin to alternate your pace between fast and slow. Also, add some right, left, and about turns to your pattern. When he has learned to walk reliably on leash, try off-lead heeling in a confined area. Start with a lightweight line attached to his collar, or a show lead, to maintain control. Try the exercise with his leash dragging on the ground, then remove the lead entirely (still in a safe area). Always use common sense when practicing off-lead heeling. Never let your dog run freely near busy roads, or in other potentially hazardous situations.

AKC CANINE GOOD CITIZEN® (CGC) PROGRAM

When your Min Pin has mastered the basic obedience commands, he may participate in the AKC Canine Good Citizen® Program sponsored by K9 Advantix® to encourage responsible pet ownership. To qualify for the CGC™ Certificate, you and your dog must pass a 2-part test. First, you must sign the Responsible Dog Owner's Pledge. The AKC believes that responsible dog ownership is a key part of the CGC concept, and by signing the pledge owners agree to take care of their dog's health needs, safety, exercise, training, and quality of life. You also must agree to show responsibility by doing things such as cleaning up after your dog in public places and never letting your dog infringe on the rights of others. After signing the pledge, you and your dog are ready to take the CGC Test.

Test 1: Accepting a Friendly Stranger
This test demonstrates that the dog will allow a friendly stranger to approach him and speak to the handler in a natural, everyday situation. The evaluator walks up to the dog and handler and greets the handler in a friendly manner, ignoring the dog. The evaluator and handler shake hands and exchange pleasantries. The dog must show no sign of resentment or shyness, and must not break position or try to go to the evaluator.

Test 2: Sitting Politely for Petting
This test demonstrates that the dog will allow a friendly stranger to touch him while he is out with his handler. With the dog sitting at the handler's side, to begin the exercise, the evaluator pets the dog on the head and body. The handler may talk to his or her dog throughout the exercise. The dog may stand in place as he is petted. The dog must not show shyness or resentment.

Test 3: Appearance and Grooming
This practical test demonstrates that the dog will welcome being groomed and examined and will permit someone, such as a veterinarian, groomer or friend of the owner, to do so. It also demonstrates the owner's care, concern and sense of responsibility. The evaluator inspects the dog to determine if he is clean and groomed. The dog must appear to be in healthy condition (*i.e.*, proper weight, clean, healthy and alert). The handler should supply the comb or brush commonly used on the dog. The evaluator then softly combs or brushes the dog, and in a natural manner, lightly examines the ears and gently picks up each front foot. It is not necessary for the dog to hold a specific position during the examination, and the handler may talk to the dog, praise it and give encouragement throughout.

Test 4: Out for a Walk
This test demonstrates that the handler is in control of the dog. The dog may be on either side of the handler. The dog's position should leave no doubt that the dog is attentive to the handler and is responding to the handler's movements and changes of direction. The dog need not be perfectly aligned with the handler and need not sit when the handler stops. The evaluator may use a pre-plotted course or may direct the handler/dog team by issuing instructions or commands. In either case, there should be a right turn, left turn, and an about turn with at least one stop in between and another at the end. The handler may talk to the dog along the way, praise the dog, or give commands in a normal tone of voice. The handler may sit the dog at the halts if desired.

Test 5: Walking Through a Crowd
This test demonstrates that the dog can move about politely in pedestrian traffic and is under control in public places. The dog and handler walk around and pass close to several people.

The dog may show some interest in the strangers but should continue to walk with the handler, without evidence of overexuberance, shyness, or resentment. The handler may talk to the dog and encourage or praise the dog throughout the test. The dog should not jump on people in the crowd or strain on the leash.

Test 6: Sit and Down on Command/Staying in Place
This test demonstrates that the dog has training, will respond to the handler's commands to sit and down and will remain in the place commanded by the handler (sit or down position, whichever the handler prefers). The dog must do sit AND down on command, then the owner chooses the position for leaving the dog in the stay. Prior to this test, the dog's leash is replaced with a line 20 feet long. The handler may take a reasonable amount of time and use more than one command to get the dog to sit and then down. The evaluator must determine if the dog has responded to the handler's commands. The handler may not force the dog into position but may touch the dog to offer gentle guidance. When instructed by the evaluator, the handler tells the dog to stay and walks forward the length of the line, turns and returns to the dog at a natural pace. The dog must remain in the place in which he was left (he may change position) until the evaluator instructs the handler to release the dog. The dog may be released from the front or the side.

Test 7: Coming When Called
This test demonstrates that the dog will come when called by the handler. The handler will walk 10 feet from the dog, turn to face the dog, and call the dog. The handler may use encouragement to get the dog to come. Handlers may choose to tell dogs to "stay" or "wait" or they may simply walk away, giving no instructions to the dog.

Test 8: Reaction to Another Dog
This test demonstrates that the dog can behave politely around other dogs. Two handlers and their dogs approach each other from a distance of about 20 feet, stop, shake hands and exchange pleasantries, and continue on for about 10 feet. The dogs should show no more than casual interest in each other. Neither dog should go to the other dog or its handler.

Test 9: Reactions to Distractions
This test demonstrates that the dog is confident at all times when faced with common distracting situations. The evaluator will select and present two distractions. Examples of distractions include dropping a chair, rolling a crate dolly past the dog, having a jogger run in front of the dog, or dropping a crutch or cane. The dog may express natural interest and curiosity and/or may appear slightly startled but should not panic, try to run away, show aggressiveness, or bark. The handler may talk to the dog and encourage or praise him throughout the exercise.

Test 10: Supervised Separation
This test demonstrates that a dog can be left with a trusted person, if necessary, and will maintain training and good manners. Evaluators are encouraged to say something like, "Would you like me to watch your dog?" and then take hold of the dog's leash. The owner will go out of sight for three minutes. The dog does not have to stay in position but should not continually bark, whine, or pace unnecessarily, or show anything stronger than mild agitation or nervousness. Evaluators may talk to the dog but should not engage in excessive talking, petting, or management attempts (e.g, "there, there, it's alright").

Reprinted, with permission, from the American Kennel Club and the Canine Good Citizen® Program Sponsored by K9 Advantix®.

The Miniature Pinscher's short, smooth coat makes him a breeze to keep in peak condition.

GROOMING BASICS
4

The Miniature Pinscher's sleek, easy-care coat makes him a popular choice both as a family pet and show dog. Unlike many breeds whose flowing manes require daily attention and professional styling, this short-coated dog thrives on a minimum of grooming. A quick brushing or rubdown with a coarse piece of cloth, occasional bath when he is dirty, and trimming of stray hairs keep the Min Pin looking his regal best.

BRUSHING

Brush your Miniature Pinscher several times a week with a soft bristle brush, rubber brush, or grooming glove. Although his hair doesn't tangle or mat like that of long-coated dogs, brushing is essential to remove dead hair, stimulate the skin, and distribute the natural oils to the ends of the hair shafts. When your Min Pin is a puppy, introduce him to grooming by gently rubbing his coat with a piece of cloth or the cloth side of a grooming mitt. As he gains confidence, start at his rear and brush from back to front, against the natural hair-growth pattern. Then, reverse the procedure, brushing from front to back. Remember his front and rear legs, chest, and head. (If you have more than one dog, clean your combs and brushes before using them on another dog.) You might want to try one of the commercial coat conditioner sprays to prevent dryness and add a deep, rich shine to the coat.

BATHING

Before your dog's bath, thoroughly brush his coat to loosen dead hair and any dandruff flakes. Insert a cotton ball in each ear to prevent water from entering the ear canal, and place a drop of mineral oil in each eye to protect against irritation from the shampoo (or use a tearless puppy shampoo). Wet the coat completely, over the chest, back, and legs, saving the head for last. Apply a dab of shampoo to the back area and massage into his skin. Work up a sudsy lather, adding more water and shampoo if necessary. Finish his bath by soaping the head and face with a wet washcloth (avoiding the eyes), then rinse completely. Be sure to clear away all traces of lather because this can irritate the skin. Most Miniature Pinschers don't require conditioner. However, some owners finish with a rinse of ½-cup Listerine® in a cup of warm water. This mild antiseptic is beneficial if your dog suffers from skin problems. Towel dry; in chilly weather use a blow dryer on a low setting, so that you won't burn your dog's skin.

TOENAIL CLIPPING

When your dog's toenails become too long, they are more likely to break during exercise. Long nails also interfere with his ability to stand well up on his toes. Cut the nails every week or two with a nail clipper designed for small dogs,

---

The Min Pin is the fun breed.
Shirley A. Meyers

SHAMPOOS	
Chlorhexidine	Antiseptic, antimicrobial; good for cleaning wounds.
Flea and Tick	Kills fleas, lice, and ticks.
Hypo-Allergenic	Cleans coat without irritation. Good for dry, itchy skin.
Medicated	Antibacterial, antifungal; for flea allergy dermatitis, hot spots, mange.
Oatmeal	Good for dry, itchy skin.
Protein	For a shiny, thicker, more manageable coat.
Tar/Sulfur	Dandruff, seborrhea, eczema, hot spots.
Tearless	For puppies and dogs with sensitive skin. Rinses quickly.
Waterless	Apply to coat, massage into a lather, towel dry. No rinsing needed.

or grind the tip of the nail with a Dremel Pet Nail Grooming device. Insert the toenail into the opening on the clipper and trim each nail a little at a time. Be careful not to cut the quick, the sensitive area running the length of the nail that contains nerves and blood supply. The quick is difficult to see in dark-colored nails, so trim only the portion of the nail that curves downward.

Can. Ch. Patapin Next Episode gets her weekly pedicure with a Dremel device.
Bred by Patricia Gauthier and owned by Judy Bohnert.

If you accidentally cut the quick and the nail begins to bleed, apply styptic powder, such as Kwik Stop®. A nail cautery device, available from kennel suppliers, also stops bleeding. Finally, smooth any rough edges with an emery board.

ANAL GLANDS

Dogs have a pair of anal glands located on the lower sides of their rectums, at the "4 o'clock" and "8 o'clock" positions. Their exact purpose is not known. However, the fluid produced by the glands may lubricate the rectal area, allowing dogs to pass their bowel movements more easily. The glands also might help dogs determine the sex of other dogs upon meeting, by secreting a distinctive scent. Occasionally, these glands become impacted with matter. Some individuals are more prone to impaction than others. When this occurs, your dog may scoot across the floor or try to lick the anal area. You may notice a strong fishy odor. The glands also may appear swollen. The best time to empty the sacs is during a bath. Stand your dog in the tub and lift his tail out of the way. Place a cotton square over the anus to absorb any fluid that comes out. With your thumb on one side of the opening (under and slightly behind the gland) and index finger on the other, gently press in an upward motion to release the material. Follow with his shampoo. If you notice blood or pus, your dog may have an infection and need antibiotic medication or topical ointment. Rarely, an abscess may form, which needs veterinary attention.

DENTAL CARE

Puppies begin to develop their first set of teeth between three and six weeks of age. This deciduous set consists of the canines, incisors, and premolars. By 12 to 14 weeks, many start to go through the uncomfortable teething stage. During this process, the emerging permanent teeth put pressure on the puppy teeth, causing the first set to loosen and fall out. If your Miniature Pinscher appears to be in pain or his gums are red or swollen, put a teething toy or wet washcloth in the freezer and allow him to chew on it.

Small breeds are prone to retaining puppy teeth even after the permanent teeth appear, so be sure to check your puppy's mouth periodically. It may be necessary for the veterinarian to pull retained teeth in order to ensure proper adult tooth alignment. This procedure should be performed as soon as the tip of the adult tooth has erupted to avoid later problems with the position of the adult teeth.

Min Pins also are susceptible to gum disease and tooth loss without regular dental care. Although cavities are rare in dogs, periodontal (the tissue and structures surrounding and supporting the teeth) disease is common. In fact, as many as 85 percent of dogs over three years of age show signs of periodontal disease. Untreated, this condition can lead to bad breath, inflamed gums, and discomfort. When the pain is severe, dogs often become irritable and stop eating. According to Dr. Edward R. Eisner of the Denver Veterinary Dental Service, Campus Veterinary Clinic, periodontal difficulties even can become critical to an animal's overall health if the problem remains untreated. This is because bacteria that originate in the mouth may travel to other areas of the body where they can do more harm. "For example," said Dr. Eisner, in an article in *Dog World* magazine, "*streptococci* are a common oral bacteria that can spread to the valves of the heart in dogs. In fact, it's not unusual to find heart disease and a chronic oral infection in the same patient. Infection of the kidneys or the joints are two other possible systemic complications caused when oral bacteria are transported through the bloodstream."

GUM DISEASE

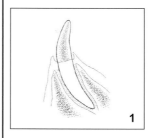
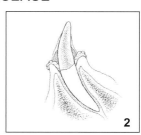

1. The Healthy Tooth: Tissues that support the tooth in the alveolar socket are the gingiva, cementum, periodontal ligament, and alveolar bone.

2. The components that form plaque include mucin from saliva, food particles, bacteria, and exfoliated epithelial cells. Calculus (tartar), which forms when plaque mineralizes, is irritating to the sensitive gum tissues. Inflammation then causes the gums to swell, forming a pocket that traps bacteria under the gum line. This leads to detachment of the gingiva from the tooth.

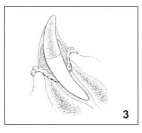
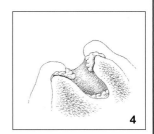

3. As the infection progresses, the periodontal ligament and supporting bone are destroyed. Abscesses may develop where the roots fork on a multirooted tooth, or at the tip of the root, causing the infection to spread via tiny blood vessels to the pulp of the tooth.

4. This progression leads to the eventual loss of the tooth.

Illustrations by Nancy Ross.

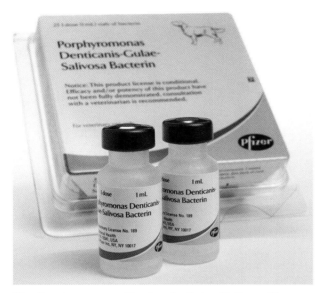

The Porphyromonas Denticanis-Gulae-Salivosa Bacterin is approved for the vaccination of healthy dogs as an aid in preventing periodontitis, as demonstrated by a reduction in bone changes (osteolysis/osteosclerosis). It is the first and only vaccine to aid in the prevention of canine periodontitis, which affects 85 percent of dogs over 3 years of age.
Photo and information courtesy of Pfizer Animal Health.

Because dogs don't experience pain during the early stages of periodontal disease, it's known as the "silent disease." Unfortunately, the condition may advance for years before enough tooth-supporting bone is destroyed to cause the loss of a tooth. To maintain healthy teeth and gums, brush your dog's teeth at least several times a week, or—better yet—daily, with a toothbrush and toothpaste made especially for dogs. Have the veterinarian perform a complete dental exam during your dog's annual checkup. If tartar buildup becomes severe, the doctor can scale the teeth with special instruments while your dog is under a light anesthesia. Following a professional cleaning, the veterinarian may apply a sealant that prevents plaque-forming bacteria from attaching to the teeth. You may continue this protection at home with a weekly application of a prescription plaque preventing gel.

To further guard against periodontitis and its resulting bone loss, in 2006, Pfizer Animal Health developed a vaccine that targets key bacteria responsible for plaque formation. This *porphyromonas* vaccine initially is given in two doses, three weeks apart, and has been tested for safety in puppies, as well as adults. In combination with traditional dental therapies, it promises to give pets extra protection against one of the most common bacterial infections in dogs.

EXTERNAL PARASITES AND THE DISEASES THEY CARRY
Fleas

Of the more than 2,400 types of fleas, the most common variety to affect dogs is *Ctenocephalides felis*, or the cat flea. Adult fleas live between 6 and 12 months (with a 4-week life cycle), and can transmit a number of diseases to humans, including typhus, tularemia, and even plague (carried by the rat flea). When they bite pets, fleas may cause skin irritation, allergic reactions, and anemia, and are intermediate hosts for tapeworms. If your Min Pin swallows an infected flea, he could contract tapeworms. Normally, fleas thrive in warm, humid climates, yet some are known in the arid regions of the southwestern United States. Further, fleas can live in a warm house year-round.

Controlling fleas often seems like a never-ending task to most owners. Although fleas live and feed on dogs, their eggs usually fall off and hatch indoors in bedding, carpets, and furniture, and outdoors in warm, shady areas of the yard. Comprehensive flea control involves treating both your Min Pin and his environment, as well as preventing reinfestation. To eliminate fleas on your dog, you'll need to kill adult fleas and stop immature fleas from developing. Shampoos, dips, collars, and medications, such as CAPSTAR®, kill adult fleas. Products with Insect Growth Regulators (IGRs) affect fleas in the larval stage, as well. These include topical "spot-on" treatments, such as Frontline® Plus and others, which may kill adult fleas, eggs, and larvae; ticks;

and mosquitoes, depending on the formulation. Another weapon in the war on fleas is PROGRAM® Flavor Tabs®, a once-a-month tablet, that contains an insect development inhibitor (IDI). PROGRAM does not kill adult fleas but prevents eggs from developing into adults. It should be used along with one of the products mentioned above for complete flea control.

To eliminate fleas indoors, you'll need to wash your pet's bedding and vacuum thoroughly. Foggers and sprays are effective in hard-to-reach areas. Outdoor treatment includes sprays that kill adults and contain IGRs to interrupt the fleas' life cycle. Because these chemicals may be toxic, follow directions carefully and always check with the veterinarian before combining or "doubling up" on products.

Flea Allergy Dermatitis—Dogs develop flea allergy dermatitis (FAD) from a reaction to proteins in the saliva of biting fleas. Itching and scratching are the most common symptoms, along with scaly, crusty patches on the loin or rump. These patches can spread, covering the entire pelvic region and legs, and may become infected. Treatment of FAD—a lifetime problem for many dog owners—consists of rigorous flea control; medication, such as prednisone, to suppress itching and inflammation; and, in some cases, weekly injections of flea antigen.

Mites

Demodectic Mange—In a 1995 survey by the MPCA's Health and Welfare Committee, almost one third of respondents had encountered the generalized form of demodectic mange, or demodicosis, at least once in their kennels, whereas more than half had encountered the localized form at least once (115 individuals replied to the survey).

Demodicosis is caused by a microscopic mite, *Demodex canis*, that lives in the hair follicles of most dogs. It is transmitted from the dam to her puppies during nursing, but otherwise is not contagious between dogs. The disease may be localized to small, red, hairless patches on the face or forelegs, or may be generalized, involving the entire coat. A third form is limited only to the feet. A skin scraping confirms the diagnosis, as the mites clearly are visible under a microscope.

The main treatment for localized demodicosis is Goodwinol Ointment, applied daily to affected lesions. Bathing your Min Pin with a medicated shampoo will help to reduce any secondary bacterial infection that may develop, as well. This form primarily occurs in young puppies, and most cases clear with or without intervention. Generalized demodicosis, though, is more complicated and difficult to manage. It affects not only puppies but also adults with weakened immune systems. The only drug currently approved by the U.S. Food and Drug Administration (FDA) is Mitaban®, a dip that must be applied every two weeks until skin scrapings return to normal. When this treatment is unsuccessful, or dogs have side effects of sedation, vomiting, or diarrhea, two medications typically used to prevent heartworms—ivermectin and Interceptor®—may be tried. Given daily, by injection or pill, these "off-label" drugs may take up to three months to kill mites. Antibiotics usually are needed to fight skin infections.

The best way to prevent your Min Pin from developing demodicosis is to keep him in peak condition, free of parasites, with optimal nutrition, vaccinations, and regular veterinary care. Because a genetic component may exist, the Academy of Veterinary Dermatology recommends that all dogs with the generalized form of the disease be neutered to eliminate those individuals from the gene pool.

Mosquitoes

Heartworms are responsible for serious illness—even death—in dogs. Transmitted by a mosquito bite, rather than from dog-to-dog contact, the parasites are found throughout the United States and Canada. Mosquitoes become infected with microscopic worms, called microfilariae, when they bite a heartworm-positive dog. Larvae then develop within the mosquito, which later are deposited into other dogs when they are bitten by the mosquito. These larvae travel through the dog's bloodstream to the right chamber of the heart where they grow into adult worms. Between 4 and 12 inches in length, heartworms live in the heart, lungs, and large blood vessels between the heart and lungs. Both adult worms and microfilariae often exist for years without signs of disease. By the time owners notice coughing, difficulty breathing, or other problems, their pets are seriously ill. Treatment, which is aimed at killing adult worms, as well as microfilariae, has many potential complications.

To minimize the number of adult worms that will need to be killed, thereby reducing the risks associated with treatment, circulating microfilariae usually are treated first using a monthly preventive medication. Adult heartworms must be killed by a series of arsenic-based injections. Currently, Merial's Immiticide® is the only approved adulticide. The American Heartworm Society recommends a 3-dose protocol, in which the first dose is given, then followed four to six weeks later by two doses given 24 hours apart. Dogs must be on cage rest during the entire treatment period. The major complication of killing adult worms is obstruction of blood vessels due to dead worms. Sometimes, worms must be removed surgically.

Fortunately, heartworms can be prevented with a monthly pill or chewable tablet, including Heartgard® and Sentinel®, or topical product, such as Revolution®. However, dogs always should be tested before they begin the first dose of the season or when switching preventives. An antigen test finds a specific antigen produced by adult female heartworms. The best age to begin heartworm prevention, especially if you live in a region with a heavy mosquito infestation, is between 9 and 12 weeks. Preventives, may be used year-round or for the duration of mosquito season. Many preventives also help to combat hookworms, roundworms, and whipworms.

West Nile Virus first appeared in the United States, in 1999, in the wild bird population in New York City, and is spreading across the country. As with heartworm disease, West Nile Virus (WNV) is transmitted through the bite of an infected mosquito. Mosquitoes feed on birds that have the virus, then pass it on to both humans and animals. WNV is not spread directly from animal to animal, or from the bite of an infected dog. However, transmission has occurred when animals, such as cats, prey on infected birds or mice.

Whereas people have developed a range of symptoms, from mild to serious, including encephalitis and meningitis, dogs seem to be relatively resistant to showing signs of illness. According to the American Animal Hospital Association, WNV poses a relatively small risk to dogs. Although no preventive vaccine currently exists and no specific treatment is recommended, other than supportive care, most dogs fully recover. The best way to prevent your Min Pin from contracting WNV is to reduce his exposure to mosquitoes. Keep him indoors during early morning and evening hours when mosquitoes are most active, and avoid areas of standing water that serve as breeding grounds for mosquitoes. Several of the spot-on flea control products, mentioned earlier, also repel mosquitoes.

Ticks

The most common ticks that affect dogs are the brown dog tick and the American dog tick. Dogs come in contact with these and other varieties of ticks in wooded or grassy areas. However, birds, mice, deer, and other animals can transport ticks into the dog's own backyard. Because ticks can't jump or fly, they cling to fur and travel upward onto your dog's body to find a place to attach. As they feed on blood, ticks may swell to as much as 10 times their normal size. Ticks are difficult to remove because their barbed mouths become imbedded in the skin as they feed. The best method for

Blacklegged (deer) tick.

Adult female American dog tick.

Photos by Jim Kalisch, Department of Entomology, University of Nebraska-Lincoln.

removal, according to *Pediatrics* magazine, is with forceps or tweezers. Grasp the tick as close as possible to the dog's skin and pull straight up with steady pressure. Disinfect the bite and surrounding area with rubbing alcohol before and after removal. Several products are useful in repelling ticks, including spot-on treatments and the Preventic® collar by Virbac Animal Health. A tick vaccine is being studied, but currently is available only against cattle ticks.

Lyme Disease—Named for the town of Lyme, Connecticut, where an unusual number of children had been diagnosed as having juvenile rheumatoid arthritis (a disease with similar symptoms), Lyme disease affects both humans and pets. Although the disease first was identified in 1975, researchers were unable to confirm the mode of transmission—the tiny deer tick—until 1982. Caused by the bacteria, *Borrelia burgdorferi*, the symptoms of Lyme disease include lameness and swollen joints, loss of appetite, weight loss, fatigue, fever, and occasionally seizures. As with humans, dogs may develop the characteristic round, red "bull's-eye" rash. Early diagnosis and treatment with antibiotics are essential in guarding against serious long-term complications. However, the symptoms may not appear for months or even years after the tick bite. Today, vaccination offers dog owners a promising weapon against this rapidly spreading disease.

Ehrlichiosis is a bacterial infection transmitted by the brown dog tick. The bacteria that affect dogs, *Ehrlichia canis*, are found throughout the United States—most commonly in the southwest and Gulf Coast regions. *E. canis* attacks the white blood cells, and the disease may progress in three stages:

1. Acute phase: This is a mild stage that occurs one to three weeks after a dog is bitten by an infected tick, and may last up to a month. Signs include fatigue and low appetite, fever, enlarged lymph nodes, and bleeding disorders. Platelet destruction begins, and the platelet count on a blood test may be low. Many dogs overcome this infection on their own. However, some progress to the next stage.

2. Subclinical phase: The dog shows no outward signs of infection during this stage, other than a reduced platelet count or an increased globulin (a blood protein) level on a blood test. This "silent" phase may last months or even years.

3. Chronic phase: Dogs with the chronic form of Ehrlichiosis may not survive. Symptoms include anemia and bleeding disorders, infection, kidney disease, and brain and eye disorders.

Ehrlichiosis, if suspected, is diagnosed through a blood test that looks for antibodies against *E. canis* bacteria. IDEXX Laboratories has developed the SNAP® 3Dx® test that enables the veterinarian to detect *E. canis*, heartworms, and Lyme disease with a single blood sample. Most cases, when found in the acute phase, successfully resolve by giving antibiotics. The best way to prevent Ehrlichiosis is to minimize your Min Pin's exposure to ticks. Dogs at very high risk of exposure may take a maintenance dose of the antibiotic tetracycline for the duration of tick season.

The "mail" will always get through with these Miniature Pinschers, owned and trained by Rae Galea, of Australia, at the helm! Shown left to right: Ch. Whypin Little Bitaluck CDX AD, Ch. Whypin Lawson Lad CDX AD, Ch. Whypin Kute Ketti CD, Ch. Wentari Lady Minnie, and Ch. Whypin Tommison CD.

ON THE ROAD
5

Whether your dream vacation includes pink-tinted beaches, snow-covered mountain slopes, or exotic foreign ports, your Miniature Pinscher's small size and lively nature make him an ideal travel companion. If you're planning a trip with your pet, begin preparations well in advance of your departure date. Start with a complete veterinary exam—a health certificate is required for most destinations—and make certain your dog's inoculations are up to date. Book your stay through a travel agent who can choose accommodations that accept pets, or obtain one of the canine travel directories that list hotels and motels with favorable pet policies. Be aware that a number of countries have quarantine requirements of up to six months.

AIRPLANE TRAVEL

Since the 1930s, when aviator Charles Healy Day's dog, Ericka von Heinzelmennchen, accompanied her family in an open plane, Min Pins have joined their globe-trotting owners as "jet set" pets. Today, commercial airlines transport thousands of dogs annually, with relatively few complications. Because each flight can handle only a limited number of pets, make your reservations early. This especially is important if you want your dog to accompany you in the passenger cabin, where only one pet is allowed in each section of the plane. Try to book a direct midweek flight and avoid, if possible, weekend or holiday travel. (Few travelers realize that mail has first priority as cargo, an additional consideration during holidays, when both travel and mail volume are heavy.)

According to the U.S. Department of Agriculture (USDA), all dogs traveling by air must be at least eight weeks old and fully weaned. In addition, under the Animal Welfare Act, shipments are restricted when the temperature in holding areas falls below 45°F. or exceeds 85°F. During warm weather, try to book a morning or evening flight when holding areas are cooler. If you must travel during the winter, reserve space for your Min Pin in the passenger cabin.

To transport your pet by air, use only crates marked "airline approved." These meet Animal and Plant Health Inspection Service (APHIS) regulations for safety. Also, be sure the crate has

Charles Healy Day and his wife, Gladys M. Day, with their Miniature Pinscher, Ericka von Heinzelmennchen. Shown above, in 1931, with their home-built Day Model A Biplane. Photo courtesy of WingNet.

One of Armando Angelbello's dogs swims near his Florida home.

at least a ¾-inch rim around the outside to prevent luggage in the cargo hold from blocking the crate's air vents. Although your dog needs room to stand, lie down, and turn around, his crate should not be so large that he is jostled around during the flight. Ideal size is Vari-Kennel's small: 21"L x 16"W x 15"H. To travel in the cabin, your dog must be able to fit into a crate or soft-sided "Sherpa-style" bag that goes under the seat, usually 21"L x 16"W x 8"H. This is no problem for most Miniature Pinschers.

Provide an empty drip bottle so that airline personnel can give water without opening the crate door, and attach a small bag of your dog's food to the outside of the crate. Mark the carrier "LIVE ANIMAL" and "THIS END UP." Also, label with your name, the complete address and telephone number of your destination, your dog's name and destination (city and airport), and feeding instructions. Encourage your dog to become familiar with his crate before the trip by placing a favorite toy inside and letting him explore. On flight day, don't feed within six hours of departure or give water within two hours. Allow your dog to relieve himself just before putting him in the crate. Make certain he is wearing a well-fitting buckle collar and ID tag (place a label on the back with your name and destination). Don't tranquilize your Min Pin, and never muzzle your dog or use a choke collar for travel.

CAR TRAVEL

To avoid the potential difficulties associated with air travel, many owners prefer to vacation by car, even though it takes longer to reach their destinations. In fact, the ASPCA considers this the most humane way to travel with a pet. Most Miniature Pinschers enjoy car rides, especially when conditioned to outings at an early age. Start with short jaunts, avoiding unpleasant experiences, and reward good behavior with a doggie treat. For safety's sake, train your Min Pin to ride in a crate fastened securely to your car's seat with the seatbelt. Never allow him to jump around loose or ride with his head out the window. Besides distracting the driver, he could injure himself during a sudden stop by falling off the seat into the dashboard or windshield. If your dog is well behaved, he may sit on the seat as long as he wears one of the special canine harnesses on the market. If your car has a passenger's side airbag, consider fastening your dog in the back seat, so that he will not be injured by the airbag's inflation in case of an accident.

To prevent motion sickness, don't feed your dog for several hours before starting on the trip. When he has had a chance to settle down, offer a light meal and water. Stop every few hours for your Min Pin to exercise, but never open the car door until he is securely leashed. And, of course, never leave your dog in a parked car! In warm weather, it takes only minutes for the temperature inside a closed car to reach more than 120°F., even in the shade.

BUS AND TRAIN TRAVEL

Whereas a number of metropolitan bus and rail lines—even San Francisco's historic cable cars—permit small dogs to ride in carriers with their owners, interstate companies, such as Greyhound and Amtrak, don't allow pets on board, either with their owners or as baggage.

RECREATIONAL VEHICLE TRAVEL

Professional handlers have traveled the dog show circuit in customized recreational vehicles for decades as an alternative to flying from site to site, or driving in cramped cars with multiple dogs. Pet owners, too, enjoy the freedom RVs provide to travel with their best friends by their sides, especially with many hotel chains adopting "no pet" policies. In fact, an entire industry is dedicated to making canine travel safe and comfortable for dogs and their owners. Since 1985, Fashion-Craft Products Inc., of Nappanee, Indiana, has offered van conversions, specifically with the "Canine Traveler" in mind. The company also provides larger "Multiple Dog Vans." Features include awnings, dog ramps, crate benches, remote temperature monitors, tie-down rings, and exercise pen carriers, among many others. If you enjoy frequent travel, consider a recreational vehicle to bring the comforts of home—including your Min Pin—along with you on the road.

Customized van from Fashion-Craft Products, Inc.

SHIP TRAVEL

A number of charter boats, ferries, and sightseeing vessels allow well-behaved dogs to accompany their owners. However, the only major cruise line to permit pets is Cunard Line's *Queen Mary 2*. On transatlantic crossings between New York and Southampton, England or Hamburg, Germany, dogs may stay in the ship's kennels, where a trained Kennel Steward provides meals

These hardy outdoor enthusiasts belong to Gerona MacCuaig, of Canada.

> ### PAMPERED PETS, CUNARD STYLE
>
> According to Cunard, the company's pet-friendly policy dates to 1840, when three cats joined passengers on the maiden voyage of the *Britannia*. Other notable pets have included canine film star, Rin Tin Tin, Elizabeth Taylor's dogs, and the Duke and Duchess of Windsor's pets. Today, seafaring canines continue to be treated like royalty with a complimentary gift pack that includes an assortment of toys, fresh-baked treats, a fleece blanket, and doggie coat featuring the *QM2* logo.
>
>
> Twelve kennels are available to pets on transatlantic cruises.
>
>
> A Kennel Steward walks a Bulldog that sports his *QM2*-logoed attire.
>
> Photos courtesy of Cunard Line.

and exercise. Your Min Pin will not be permitted in your stateroom or other public areas, but you may visit him every day and walk him in special indoor or outdoor runs. If your vacation plans include a cruise on the *QM2*, reserve your Min Pin's place early. Remember, too, that if your destination is the United Kingdom, your dog will require a special Pet Passport, or be subject to quarantine. Note that no veterinarian is aboard ship.

HOTEL & MOTEL ACCOMMODATIONS

When irresponsible owners leave behind a trail of destruction—from bathtub drains plugged with dog hair to soiled linens and carpets—hotels become increasingly unwilling to accept pets. Today, conscientious owners, as well as kennel clubs hosting out-of-town exhibitors, find accommodations difficult to obtain after managers have had a few bad experiences.

To ensure that your Min Pin will be a welcome guest, follow these guidelines:

- Never leave your dog uncrated in your hotel room. Wire crates fold flat for easy storage and transport. Not only will a crate prevent destructive chewing or accidental escape if the motel door is opened, it also could save your dog's life from room hazards such as insecticides, poisons, cleaning products, traps, or electric cords.
- Never allow your dog off leash away from home. Make certain he is wearing an ID tag.
- Always clean up after he relieves himself.
- Never bathe or groom your dog in the room.
- Never allow him on furniture. If your Min Pin must sleep with you in bed, bring a blanket from home to place on the sheets.
- Be sure your dog is well trained and doesn't bark if he is left alone.
- Offer to pay for any damage.

Ch. Jothona's Steppin Sabrina, owned by Gerona MacCuaig, surveys the waterfront at her Canadian cottage.

TOURING WITH GROUPS

To assure the comfort and safety of fellow passengers on organized tours, as well as their efficient transfer between planes, trains, and buses, few travel groups allow pets to accompany their owners. However, in the dog world such rules were made to be broken. Fresh Pond Travel, of Marlboro, Massachusetts, specializes in packaged tours for dogs and their owners to major dog show sites around the world. Destinations include Bermuda, the French and Italian Rivieras (where your dog will be welcome in cafés and restaurants), Mexico City, and the Bahamas. Dogs not entered in show competition also are permitted on these tours and may stay with you in your hotel room.

TRAVEL IN THE UNITED STATES

Except Hawaii, which requires a variable-length quarantine (depending on health and vaccination records), destinations within the United States present few travel difficulties for pets and their owners. The most important document to bring with you is your dog's current health certificate signed by the veterinarian, which includes the following information:

- Your name and address.
- Pet's name, species, and breed.
- A statement that your pet is free of and has not been exposed to any infectious or contagious diseases, and that he does not come from a rabies-quarantined area or an area where rabies is known to exist.
- The date when the rabies vaccination was administered, type of vaccine, and, if possible, the serial number of the pet's vaccination tag.

BOARDING YOUR MIN PIN

Although Miniature Pinschers usually enjoy travel, some dogs—puppies under eight weeks, elderly dogs, females in season, nervous pets, or those with health problems—are better left in a boarding kennel or in the care of a responsible dog sitter who will attend to your pet at home. To locate a pet care facility, contact the veterinarian or family and friends for recommendations. You also may check with the American Boarding Kennels Association (ABKA), which provides an online directory of member kennels.

Be sure to visit the facility in person before making reservations for your Min Pin. Make certain the building is clean and well-ventilated, with a comfortable temperature maintained during winter or summer seasons. Find out what types of runs are provided, and whether outdoor runs are secure and protected from the elements. When you have found a boarding kennel that meets your needs, make your reservations as early as possible. Many kennels are booked well in advance for holidays and summer vacations. If your Min Pin never has been away from home, plan a short stay before making extended reservations. Be sure to bring along your dog's favorite bedding and toys, special foods, and any medications he is taking. Finally, enjoy your vacation knowing that your Min Pin is safe and in the care of responsible professionals.

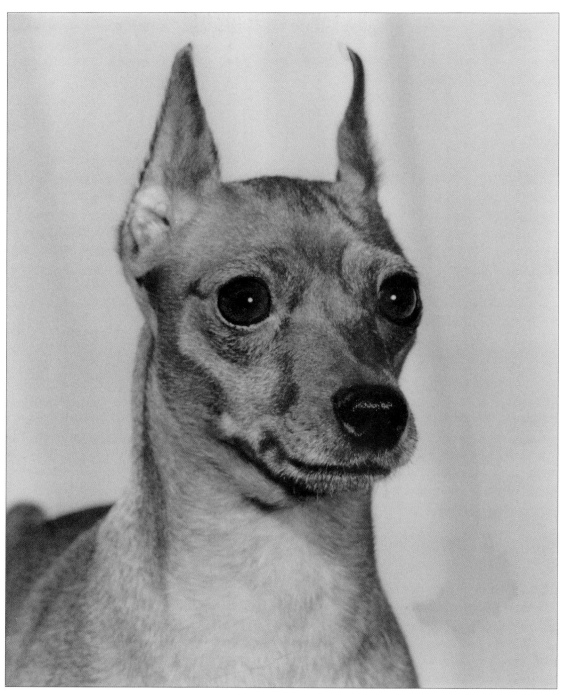

Ch. Jothona's Steppin Sabrina displays the breed's "proud, vigorous, and alert" expression. She is owned by Gerona MacCuaig.

THE OFFICIAL MIN PIN STANDARD
6

Each of the 160-plus breeds currently registered by the American Kennel Club (AKC) has its own official standard, the written description of the physical and mental traits that make a particular breed unique. Although the standard represents the characteristics of the theoretically ideal specimen, no dog conforms perfectly to his standard. Breeding dogs for the show ring is not an exact science, but a combination of scientific principles with artistry, and each breeder interprets the elements of the standard in his own fashion.

Some breeders are known for the emphasis they place on specific aspects of the breed: The dog's beautiful head and ears, level topline and high tail set, distinctive hackney-like gait, or refined, elegant appearance. Exhibitors often acknowledge these subtle differences between bloodlines with references, such as "Sanbrook type," "Rebel Roc type," or "Jay-Mac type." However, breeders know that all parts of the standard, presented in balance and moderation, play a role in creating dogs that look and act like Miniature Pinschers.

DEVELOPMENT OF THE STANDARD

When the Miniature Pinscher Club of America (MPCA) prepared to draft its first standard in the early 1930s, club members sought guidance from Germany's Pinscher-Schnauzer-Klub, dog judge Josef Berta, and breed expert Professor Walther. Exhibitors initially relied on a close translation of the German standard when the

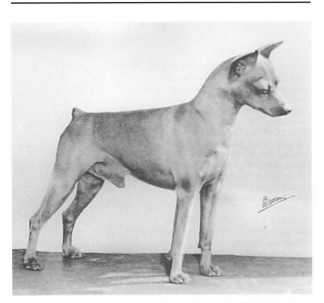

Perhaps the best example of breed type is Ch. Rebel Roc's Casanova v Kurt. Little Daddy, as he was known to his owners, Mr. and Mrs. E. W. Tipton, Jr., won a record 75 all-breed Best in Show awards during his career.

The dog is man's best friend.
He has a tail on one end.
Up in front he has teeth.
And four legs underneath.

Ogden Nash

This German champion from the 1930s shows the "coarse" body type. Note the thick neck and low tail set.

Admonitions against breeding dwarfish Min Pins abounded in the dog press during the 1930s. According to MPCA Secretary K. J. Hedengren, overly small specimens get "a short head, apple head, protruding eyes, weak tiny legs, and generally weak hindquarters."

Miniature Pinscher was shown in the AKC's Miscellaneous Class. However, 1935 marked the introduction of an all-new American standard. (*See Page 265.*)

A particularly controversial feature of this standard, and one that still causes confusion, was the statement that the dog was "a miniature of the large Doberman Pinscher." Many individuals unfamiliar with the dog's background believe that the Min Pin is a relatively new breed, rather than one several centuries old, and that he was created by crossing the Doberman with other toy dogs. Another change from the German standard to the American standard was the addition of minimum weights (5 to 10 pounds), along with a preferred height of 11½ inches. Breeders of the day were quite concerned that judges favored the smallest specimens in the show ring, overlooking their larger, more vigorous, counterparts.

Admonitions against dwarfish dogs flourished in the magazine, *Pure-Bred Dogs/American Kennel Gazette*. In the May 1933 issue, club secretary K. J. Hedengren wrote: "Many fanciers, breeders, and people interested in the breed favor small specimens, disregarding or ignorant of the fact that the breeders in the country of origin have changed from breeding small specimens to type. An elongated head with eyes well fitted into the

Although more heavily boned than some of today's champions, this English Miniature Pinscher from the 1960s illustrates the progression away from the coarser early specimens. Notice the semi-erect ears (permitted in England), arched neck, level topline, depth of brisket, and high tail set. Photo by Thomas Fall.

sockets is very rarely seen on a small specimen of the breed. They get a short head, apple head, protruding eyes, weak tiny legs, and generally weak hindquarters. Very small specimens will lose their teeth very young, in some cases when they are 2 to 3 years old, and will, of course, be subject to disease more than dogs from 8 to 10 pounds, which have more power to fight off a sickness."

The 1950s marked another revision to the standard, adding for the first time the reference to the Min Pin's "precise hackney gait." Until this time, one of the few known descriptions of correct movement was Hedengren's statement in the December 1938 *Gazette*: "The fine show quality of the breed has been pointed out repeatedly; how well they move in the ring, trotting around like a little race horse."

The 1958 standard, which remained in force until 1980, deleted references to the Doberman Pinscher, removed all colors except red, stag red, black and rust, and chocolate and rust, added the height range of 10 to 12½ inches (with disqualifications for oversized and undersized dogs), and deleted the 1935 standard's range of weights.

THE OFFICIAL STANDARD

The current standard, approved in 1980 and reformatted in 1990, appears below in italics. The discussion that follows each section is reprinted, with permission, from the Miniature Pinscher Club of America's *Illustrated Breed Study Guide*, prepared by the Judges Education Committee.

General Appearance

The Miniature Pinscher is structurally a well balanced, sturdy, compact, short-coupled, smooth-coated dog. He naturally is well groomed, proud, vigorous and alert. Characteristic traits are his hackney-like action, fearless animation, complete self-possession, and his spirited presence.

The Miniature Pinscher is nicknamed the "King of Toys" and his self-possession, proud bearing and well-balanced appearance should convince the judge that he deserves that title. He is a natural show dog, not posed or stacked on the floor like many toy breeds, but rather taught to free stack and show himself off.

Miniature Pinschers are judged on the ground, *not* on the table. Use the table *only* to check bite and eye color, for disqualifying faults (thumb marks, white marks over ½ inch, or disqualifying height), and for the presence of both testicles in males. As long as these important points can be determined, do not fault a Min Pin for moving during the examination. Because Min Pins are short coated, physical features and condition can be easily seen; judges do not need to touch every inch of the dog on the table.

Min Pins should be moved around the ring once before tabling. Because they are high spirited, this helps to take the "edge" off. While gaiting, especially the first time around the ring, many Min Pins break gait or stop at least once to shake themselves; this is "breed normal" and should not be penalized. A Min Pin should move with head and tail up; however, ears do not have to be up while moving. After the initial examination, judges who wish to re-check a point on a dog should ask the handler to place him back

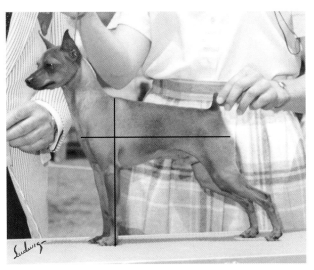

The ideal Min Pin is square in appearance. The dog's body length should equal his height from withers to ground.

on the table. Reaching down on a Min Pin from above can be very disturbing, even though temperament is correct.

Size, Proportion, Substance

Size—10 inches to 12½ inches in height allowed, with desired height 11 inches to 11½ inches measured at highest point of the shoulder blades. Disqualification—Under 10 inches or over 12½ inches in height. Length of males equals height at withers. Females may be slightly longer.

Because the standard permits a 2½-inch spread between the smallest and largest allowed sizes, judges may see a great variation in size in the average class of Min Pins. All dogs within the 10- to 12½-inch range must be judged equally. Proportion and balance are more important than height. A judge should look for the Miniature Pinscher showing proper breed type, balance, soundness, and temperament. This dog should be your choice, regardless of size, as long as he is within the size limit allowed. A typey, well-constructed Min Pin should look the same, regardless of size. Size, in itself, is never a fault as long as it is within the standard.

Finally, if a judge has a question as to whether or not one of his exhibits is "in size," please do yourself, the exhibitor, and the breed a favor by measuring it! You, as the judge, are responsible for upholding the breed standard. Ignoring a dog in your placements because you think he is too big or too small is unfair to the exhibitor and the breed. If in doubt—MEASURE!

Head

In correct proportion to the body. Tapering, narrow with well fitted but not too prominent foreface which balances with the skull. No indication of coarseness. Eyes full, slightly oval, clear, bright and dark even to a true black, including eye rims, with the exception of chocolates, whose eye rims should be self-colored. Ears set high, standing erect from base to tip. May be cropped or uncropped. Skull appears flat, tapering forward toward the muzzle. Muzzle strong rather than fine and delicate, and in proportion to the head as a whole. Head well balanced with only a slight drop to the muzzle, which is parallel to the top of the skull. Nose black only, with the exception of chocolates which should have a self-colored nose.

All-breed Best in Show winner, Ch. Kimro's Space Cowboy V Edgewind, bred by Kimberly Pastella and Robin Greenslade, and owned by his breeders and Howard Schwell.
Photo by Christina Freitag, CMF Photography.

Lips and Cheeks small, taut and closely adherent to each other. Teeth meet in a scissors bite.

A Min Pin's head should not appear too large or too small for his body. From the front, the head appears narrow rather than broad, and tapers slightly to the muzzle. Viewed from the side, the skull appears flat, not rounded or domed. The foreface should be strong, showing definite underjaw, have a slight but definite stop, and be parallel to the top of the skull.

A black nose is required in all colors except chocolates, where the nose is self colored. Lack of underjaw (snipey muzzle), "cheekiness," short muzzles, and broad or round skulls are undesirable.

Teeth should meet in a scissors bite. Occasionally, a judge sees crowded incisors in the bottom jaw giving the impression of a faulty bite. One or two teeth slightly out of line should not be penalized if the bite is otherwise correct. Even bites are a common deviation. It is permissible for Min Pins to have less than six incisors in either the upper or lower jaw as long as the bite is correct, and the jaws line up properly. Undershot or overshot bites are undesirable.

The eyes should be full and oval shaped, not round or bulging. Eye color is as dark as possible in red and black-and-rust Min Pins, even to a true black. This includes the pigmentation around the eye. Chocolate Min Pins, however, have self-colored eyes and eye rims. Common deviations include eyes that are too round. Too-light eyes and yellow eyes are not desirable. Some chiseling under the eyes is desirable. The Min Pin should have a keen and alert expression.

The ears are set high and may be cropped or uncropped, but must stand erect in either instance. Since ear cropping is manmade, an otherwise excellent specimen should not be penalized for a poor ear trim. Ears that are cropped too long may "wing out" slightly. Again, this should not be penalized. Lips and cheeks should be tight; loose flews and drooping lips spoil the clean outline of the head.

Ch. Larcon's Lit'l Wrecking Crew, owned by Norma D. Cacka and Connie Wick. Photo by Candids by Connie.

Neck, Topline, Body

Neck proportioned to head and body, slightly arched, gracefully curved, blending into shoulders, muscular and free from suggestion of dewlap or throatiness. Topline—Back level or slightly sloping toward the rear both when standing and gaiting. Body compact, slightly wedge-shaped, muscular. Forechest well developed. Well-sprung ribs. Depth of brisket, the base line of which is level with points of the elbows. Belly moderately tucked up to denote grace of structural form. Short and strong in loin. Croup level with topline. Tail set high, held erect, docked in proportion to size of dog.

The neck is in proportion to the head and body, of medium length, and nicely arched. The neck should blend smoothly and cleanly into the shoulders. Necks that are too long and thin, "ewe necks," and short, thick necks are all undesirable, as is excess skin or dewlap around the head and throat.

The back is level or slightly sloping to the rear. An extreme slope is not desirable. The topline should remain solid when the dog is gaiting. When viewed from above, the body is compact, wedge shaped, and muscular with well-sprung ribs. The brisket should reach to the elbow. The loin is short and strong. The under-

Ch. Kimro's Space Cowboy V Edgewind.
Photo by Christina Freitag, CMF Photography.

line shows moderate tuck-up. The croup is level with the topline, with a high tail set. Dogs with tails docked too long or too short should *not* be penalized because these are manmade faults. Undesirable traits include rounded croups, low tail sets, "squirrel" tails, and roachy or dippy (sway back) toplines.

Forequarters

Shoulders clean and sloping with moderate angulation coordinated to permit the hackney-like action. Elbows close to the body. Legs—Strong bone development and small clean joints. As viewed from the front, straight and upstanding. Pasterns strong, perpendicular. Dewclaws should be removed. Feet small, catlike, toes strong, well arched and closely knit with deep pads. Nails thick, blunt.

The forechest should be developed enough to be seen when the dog is viewed from the side. The clean, sloping shoulders have moderate angulation. To permit the hackney-like action, the rear is slightly more angulated than the front. Steep shoulders are a common deviation. Loaded shoulders are undesirable. The forelegs should show good bone development, neither too heavy nor spindly and over-refined. The forelegs are straight when viewed from the front, with elbows close to the body. A very *slight* east-west front may be seen in immature puppies, but is not desirable in adults. Narrow fronts and fronts that are too wide and "out at the elbows" are not desirable.

The pasterns are strong and, as viewed from the side, perpendicular. An important point not mentioned in the standard is that the pasterns should be flexible enough to allow the wrist to bend while moving. Weak pasterns are undesirable. Small catlike feet with strong, well-arched toes and deep pads are called for. Long toes, flat feet, and splayed toes are undesirable.

Hindquarters

Well muscled quarters set wide enough apart to fit into a properly balanced body. As viewed from the rear, the legs are straight and parallel. From the side, well angulated. Thighs well muscled. Stifles well defined. Hocks short, set well apart. Dewclaws should be removed. Feet small, catlike, toes strong, well arched and closely knit with deep pads. Nails thick, blunt.

The hindquarters should be well developed, but without bulging or knotted muscles. Viewed from the rear, the legs are straight and parallel. The hocks are well let down. From the side there is a well-defined turn of stifle. Insufficient rear angulation (straight rear) and overangulated rears are common deviations. Cow-hocks, or legs that bow out, are undesirable. The rear feet are the same (small, catlike) as the front. Dewclaws should be removed from both front and rear legs.

Coat

Smooth, hard and short, straight and lustrous, closely adhering to and uniformly covering the body.

Some Min Pins naturally have very thin hair covering the throat and/or underbelly, even though the coat is thicker on other areas. This is very common and should not be penalized. In order to present a smooth, clean appearance for the show ring, Min Pins often have whiskers removed and excess hair trimmed around the ears, tuck-up, and breech areas. Whisker removal is not required.

Color

Solid clear red. Stag red (red with intermingling of black hairs). Black with sharply defined rust-red markings on cheeks, lips, lower jaw, throat, twin spots above eyes and chest, lower half of forelegs, inside of hind legs and vent region, lower portion of hocks and feet. Black pencil stripes on toes. Chocolate with rust-red markings the same as specified for blacks, except brown pencil stripes on toes. In the solid red and stag red a rich vibrant medium to dark shade is preferred.

Disqualifications—Any color other than listed. Thumb mark (patch of black hair surrounded by rust on the front of the foreleg between the foot and the wrist; on chocolates, the patch is chocolate hair). White on any part of dog which exceeds one-half inch in its longest dimension.

It is important to remember that all colors must be judged equally; no one color is to be favored over the others. Note that the broken color pattern of the black-and-rust and chocolate-and-rust Min Pins often presents an optical illusion that makes them appear to be of lesser quality than the solid red dogs, even though this is not really the case. For example, upon cursory examination, the head of a black-and-rust Min Pin may appear to be broader than the identical head on a red dog. Conversely, the black-and-rust Min Pin may appear more refined than his red counterpart. Careful observation is necessary to accurately assess the broken-color dogs.

The markings of the black-and-rust Min Pin, described in the standard, are typical of those of other "black-with-tan-points" breeds. (In chocolate-and-rust Min Pins, substitute "chocolate" where "black" is used in this discussion.) Deviations commonly seen are

Acceptable colors include black and rust (Bluehen's Little Miss Mesty) and solid red (Bluehen's Yellowribbonfortodd). This handsome pair is owned by Sandra J. Mestyanek.

double rosettes on the chest and extensions on the forelegs, black running down the leg, sometimes all the way to the toes. Pencil stripes (line of black hair on top of toes) are desirable, but are seen less often today than in the past. An almost total lack of markings, in which the dog appears to be almost solid black, is undesirable. Thumb marks, a disqualification, may be misunderstood. Quite simply, a thumb mark is a patch, or island, of black hair on the front of the foreleg between the foot and the wrist that is *totally* surrounded by rust-red. If the black hair on the leg is in any way connected to the black on the upper part of the leg, it is an extension as described above and is *not* a disqualification, but a deviation from correct markings.

Judges should be aware that in the solid red Min Pin lighter shading or "brisking" is often seen on the side of the neck, below the base of the ears, over the shoulder blades, and near the vent region. This is completely acceptable, and should not be penalized.

The stag-red Min Pin always has black guard hairs, which create an overlay often over the back like a saddle. The amount of black hairs varies from very few to covering almost the entire dog. The amount and placement of these black hairs are not important.

Although Min Pins are a single-coated breed, the black and rust may have some gray undercoat showing on the side of the neck; this is not to be penalized.

White, which exceeds ½-inch in its longest dimension, is a disqualification, but a scattering of white hairs or "frost" seen on the chest is a deviation, not a disqualification.

Gait

The forelegs and hind legs move parallel, with feet turning neither in nor out. The hackney-like action is a high-stepping, reaching, free and easy gait in which the front leg moves straight forward and in front of the body and the foot bends at the wrist. The dog drives smoothly and strongly from the rear. The head and tail are carried high.

The Min Pin should be sound coming and going, with forelegs and hind legs moving parallel. Coming toward you, the legs should be lifted straight and true. The dog should not single track.

Min Pin movement is often misunderstood. The correct hackney-*like* gait is described fully in the standard. To paraphrase, the dog lifts his front feet up and out with a bend at the wrist while driving from behind. The dog should move forward quickly and smoothly with a minimum amount of effort. Judges must realize that the standard does *not* call for "true" hackney action, which is considered a mincing, inefficient gait with no rear drive.

The front movement must show a definite bend or break at the wrist/pastern joint, while also exhibiting extension and reach, with strong rear drive. The topline should remain solid with the head and tail carried high.

Ch. Altanero Barnstormer in motion with his co-owner/handler Kim Byrd. Ace is a Best in Show winner and qualified for the MPCA Top Twenty competition in 2007. Bred and co-owned by Joanne Wilds and Susan P. Goldman.

While it is important for the front wrist bend to be present, it does *not* have to be high or extreme. In fact, exaggerated front action is often accompanied by a lack of soundness. It should be remembered that the hackney-like action refers to *front* movement only. The smooth and strong rear drive called for in the standard does not permit inefficient lift of rear legs.

The high-stepping front action occurs as a result of the moderately angled front and slightly more angulated rear of a properly built Min Pin. The pasterns must be flexible enough to permit the wrist to bend.

It is important to observe the Miniature Pinscher in side gait, as well as coming and going. Many movement faults may be observed, including loose shoulders, out at the elbows, "mixmaster" (rotary action) fronts, crossing (front or rear), moving too close or too wide, no rear drive, no bend of wrist, or no lift. Some handlers may try to disguise faults or give the appearance of more lift by tightly stringing up their dogs.

Flashy front action is wonderful to see, but the judge must consider the *whole* dog. It also is important for the Min Pin to be sound and have proper breed type.

Temperament

Fearless animation, complete self-possession, and spirited presence.

Temperament is an extremely important part of the Min Pin package. Min Pins are fearless, active, and alert, and should show these traits in the ring. Min Pins tend to be curious and active, so may not stand perfectly still in the show ring. As long as a judge can see the outline and breed type of an exhibit, it shouldn't matter that the dog changes positions, or watches things other than its handler. A Min Pin who cringes or slinks around the ring should *not* be rewarded. The tail should be up whether standing or moving; never clamped down. Although a puppy may be a little unsure of himself, this is obviously not the same as an adult who simply does not have the correct

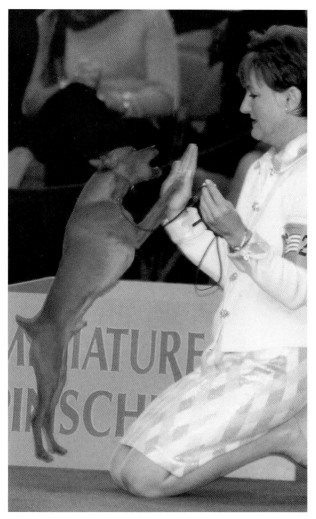

All-breed Best in Show winner, Ch. Kimro's Rocket Man, bred by Kimberly Pastella and Robin Greenslade, shows off his animation and spirit at this dog show. Owned by Howard Schwell.

outgoing, self-assured temperament of the "King of Toys."

DISQUALIFICATIONS

Under 10 inches or over 12½ inches in height. Any color other than listed. Thumb mark (patch of black hair surrounded by rust on the front of the foreleg between the foot and the wrist; on chocolates, the patch is chocolate hair). White on any part of dog which exceeds one-half (½) inch in its longest dimension.

Ch. Mercer's Gold Digger, bred and owned by Janis M. and Frank C. Mercer, shows off the breed's unique hackney-like action.

MIN PIN MOTION
7

What is correct movement in the Miniature Pinscher? In 1938, K. J. Hedengren, secretary of the Miniature Pinscher Club of America, likened it to that of a little race horse. In 1950, when the MPCA revised its earlier standard that merely stated "quick in movement," members added for the first time the term "precise hackney gait." The new standard also prescribed that the dog's forelegs be "coordinated to permit the true action of the Hackney pony." The current standard, reformatted in 1990, calls for a high-stepping, reaching, free and easy "hackney-like action." Because this unique gait is one of the characteristics that distinguishes the breed from others in the Toy Group, what constitutes proper movement in the Min Pin?

A variation of the trot, hackney action occurs when the dog's moderately angulated, sloping shoulder combines with a well-angulated hip joint. This results in a flashy front action, coupled with a strong, driving movement in the rear. In front, the foreleg reaches straight forward with the elbows held close to the body. At the greatest point of extension, the pastern (wrist) "breaks," or bends perpendicular to the ground. In the rear, the Min Pin drives smoothly and powerfully, at the same time maintaining a level topline, proud head carriage, and high tail set. Viewed from the side, the front and rear legs move in parallel planes, with the feet turning neither in nor out. From the front, the legs are lifted straight and true, with tight elbows and shoulders.

VIEWPOINTS ON CORRECT MOTION

As with any trait open to interpretation, proper movement in the Miniature Pinscher has led to considerable debate through the years among breeders, exhibitors, and judges. The following viewpoints—both current and past—illustrate this ongoing controversy and help to further our understanding of both gait and structure.

Armando Angelbello

Founded in 1986, Armando Angelbello's Marlex kennel began with two notable Miniature Pinschers from veteran breeder Ann Dutton's Sanbrook kennel: Ch. Sanbrook Silk Electric, a top winning and top producing Hall of Fame Sire, and Ch. Sanbrook Swept Away, also a top winner in the show ring and Hall of Fame Dam. Mr. Angelbello has held numerous offices in the MPCA and has produced many champions, including several all-breed and specialty Best in Show winners. He discussed the Min Pin's unique gait in his article, "The Min Pin Gait Debate: What's It All About?" This article, reprinted with permission below, originally appeared in *Pinscher Patter*, in 1993, and was updated for this book in January, 2008.

"'We're losing the hackney gait' or 'We're losing soundness.' Depending on which dog is being discussed, these statements have been very common in Min Pin circles for years. I'm certainly no expert on the anatomy or gait of dogs. Therefore, I won't attempt to address shoulder lay-back, *etcetera*. Even the experts can't agree on what kind of shoulders produce the desired Min Pin gait. My views on the subject are mere personal observations and assessments, to date, of the varied and contradictory expert opinions.

"Our breed standard was revised, in 1980, whereby 'precise hackney gait' was replaced with 'hackney-like action' because the definition of hackney gait was lifting the front legs very high and not much rear drive. On the other hand, 'hackney-like action' is defined in our standard very clearly as 'high-stepping, reaching, free and easy gait in which the front leg moves straight forward and in front of the body and the foot bends at the wrist; the dog drives smoothly and strongly from the rear.' This can be clearly noted on profile movement (the go-around).

"'Hackney-like action,' is, in my opinion, very well defined. To add clarity, the standard also dictates 'the forelegs and hind legs move parallel, with feet turning neither in nor out and back level or slightly sloping toward the rear when standing or gaiting.' This speaks to soundness, which can be more clearly assessed on the down and back.

"It puzzles me how some fanciers describe the desired Min Pin gait as 'hackney, like a Hackney pony.' From my observation of the Hackney pony in motion, I would never describe its gait as being 'like a Min Pin' as defined in our breed standard. I definitely would not want a Min Pin with a gait like a Hackney pony, since there's a lot of non-reaching, non-driving, high-stepping movement going on. The Min Pin gait should stand on its own, without comparison to a horse's gait. It is unique, and clearly defined in our standard.

"I agree we need to concentrate and preserve the Min Pin gait, but it's not a 'hackney gait,' and it's not solely measured in profile movement, as the standard also mandates soundness; *i.e.*, sound hackney-like action. And let's not forget that the Min Pin is not a one-dimensional breed—merely identified by his gait. A good specimen first must *look* and *act* like a Min Pin (breed type), the King of Toys. After all, we have seen other breeds move in a similar hackney-like fashion, but they don't look like Min Pins."

Sharon A. Krogh

Sharon Krogh, a respected dog judge and long-time officer of the MPCA, and her husband, David, have bred numerous champions under the K-Roc kennel name, including the Fall 1973 MPCA National Specialty Best of Breed winner, Ch. K-Roc's Black Doubloon. She presented her view on correct gait in a Judges' Study Group guide, held in conjuction with the MPCA National Specialty Show:

Min Pin movement, what is it?
It is misunderstood, maligned, and a mess!
What should it be?
It should be structually sound!
Can it be?
Yes!

"The Miniature Pinscher was bred in Germany as a 'ratter.' The original Standard Pinscher was somewhat larger than the Miniature Pinscher we know today. The Reh Pinscher that was imported to the United States brought with it a standard of breed perfection. When the German standard was interpreted and adopted as the breed standard for the Min Pin in the United States, in 1929, there was no mention of a 'hackney gait.' Note: It is important to bear in mind that the German people only bred dogs that were practical and functional. Without a purpose, dogs had little place in German society.

"Prior to 1950, in the United States, breeders began to exhibit Min Pins that had what was described as 'the gait of a good show horse' or a 'good trotter.' Therefore, the standard that was approved by the parent club, in 1950, included the following two statements: Under General Appearance, 'the natural characteristic traits which identify him from other toy dogs are his precise Hackney gait,' and under Forequarters, 'coordinated to permit the true action of the Hackney pony.'

"Human nature being what it is, movement became even more misunderstood. *If a little hackney is good, then a lot is even better*, and movement suffered.

"Two things happened. The breeder who knew what hackney movement should look like went for the loose shoulder and out-at-the-elbows. The side gait appeared to be a hackney gait. The breeder who did not know came up with a very straight front and rear, and ended up

A UNIQUE HIGH-STEP

These two all-breed Best in Show winners display the high-stepping gait that makes the Miniature Pinscher unique.

Above left/right: Ch. Kimro's Toy Soldier, owned by Robin Greenslade, Kimberly Pastella, and Howard Schwell. Sarge was named Best of Breed at the Westminster Kennel Club and AKC/Eukanuba National Championship dog shows. Photos by Christina Freitag, CMF Photography, and DogAds.

Bottom right: Ch. Marlex Mister Chips, owned by Armando Angelbello, won Best of Breed at the 2007 MPCA National Specialty Show. Photo by Lisa Uhacz.

with a 'German goosestep' or a Smooth Fox Terrier front. Neither promoted a sound, smooth-moving dog! The first flailed about and one wondered just where the next foot would land; the other, if the dog moved too rapidly, probably fell on his nose. There was just no reach or drive, because there were no angles.

"The breed standard of 1980 states, 'Hackney-like action.' The parent club probably felt that the movement of the Miniature Pinscher was in deep trouble, and, hoping to help, toned down the description. The club could not take out this reference entirely, because it supposedly had made our breed unique for some 30 years. The hackney-like action spoken of in today's standard, in my opinion, is pretty basic movement. First, the dog must have angles, both front and rear. He must move forward in a straight line with both drive from the rear and reach and extension in the front. At the outermost point of extension, the pastern breaks downward, prior to the completion of the stride.

"What if the pastern does not break? Well, then we have a nice, sound-moving dog with no hackney-like action. Personally, I like to see a dog that will hold his topline and move smoothly around the ring with reach and drive. If I can see the ever-elusive hackney-like action, I am pleased. If not, I will happily settle for soundness, rather than the messy 'mixmaster,' 'hocky,' or straight specimens.

"It doesn't matter that our 'made in the U.S.A.' version of the German Reh Pinscher doesn't rat. He still needs to move across the room to the food bowl or across the ring to the Best in Show sign!"

Joanne Wilds

Beginning her interest in the sport of dogs through obedience competition with her Labrador Retriever, Joanne Wilds acquired her first Min Pin, in 1992, from Elaine Bingham's Jo-El kennel. Ch. Jo-El's Chances Are not only is an AKC and International champion, but also earned an obedience title and is a registered therapy dog with Therapy Dogs International (TDI). Ms. Wilds also owner-handled Ch. Altanero Mirra Image—the 2006 MPCA Dam of the Year and Hall of Fame Dam—to several prestigious show awards. Bella's son, Ch. Altanero Barnstormer, is an all-breed Best in Show winner. Also, in 2006, Ms. Wilds, along with Susan P. Goldman, were named MPCA Breeders of the Year. A 26-year veteran of the United States Navy, Ms. Wilds shares her home with four Min Pins, including her first—Chaz—now 16 years old. She shares her viewpoint on Min Pin gait in the following discussion:

"The Miniature Pinscher's movement is unique among all breeds, partly because of the use of one specific word—'hackney.' The American standard uses the term 'hackney-like,' which outlines a much different gait from true hackney movement. The true hackney motion involves the lifting up of the front legs with no extension. One example of this movement is the Hackney pony whose front legs not only lift straight up, the rear legs do as well. This gives the appearance of the horse almost moving in place. This movement should not be considered correct for Min Pins.

"The standard describes the hackney-like action as follows: 'a high-stepping, reaching, free and easy gait in which the front leg moves straight forward and in front of the body and the foot bends at the wrist. The dog drives smoothly and strongly from the rear.' Not only is it required that the dog reach forward and extend the front leg in front of the body, it also is required to drive from the rear. No dog that is truly driving from the rear can only lift and bend in front. The extension of the front leg would be a natural consequence when the front and rear assemblies are correct and working in unison.

"I believe that there is a great deal of emphasis placed on the lifting and bending movements. This is detrimental to ensuring that breeders select dogs that have the correct structure to also reach and drive. Dogs that have a great deal of 'hackney,' which can lend itself to 'flashy' side movement, usually fall apart coming at you with elbows flying and no parallel movement because the front shoulder assembly is too straight to allow the extension and there is no rear drive. There is no requirement in the standard for extreme lift or bend.

"The best comparison I have found was given to me by someone that I consider a master breeder, although ironically not of Min Pins. She used the example of another breed of horse to illustrate the movement we should be looking for—the Tennessee Walker. This breed not only extends the front leg but also has exceptional drive from the rear. Although this comparison might be a bit exaggerated, it is the one I keep in mind when I am observing dogs in the ring."

Don and Shirley Meyers

Formerly involved with Toy Poodles, Don and Shirley Meyers chose their first Min Pin puppy because they were looking for a show breed that required a minimum of grooming.

Their Ch. Star-M Trace of Scarlet won Best of Breed at the Spring 1972 MPCA National Specialty. In a September 1975 *Gazette* column, Shirley Meyers is quoted:

"Is every Min Pin born with a hackney gait? No! We see every front fault imaginable in the ring, and breeders tend to regard any fancy or sloppy front action as a hackney gait. We really don't know how this trait originated in the Miniature Pinscher. We do see it in other breeds and it is considered a fault in most. There are some dogs who are built so that it is natural for them to hackney. It all has to do with angulation. In general, the Min Pin shoulder is not well laid back and the withers are high. In other words, there is a steep shoulder. When this is coupled with a well-angulated rear assembly, giving the dog a good thrust forward, the dog must compensate and pick up those front feet to keep from falling on his face. This combination of steep shoulders and good rear angulation produces a tendency to hackney.

"Here, then, is where the puzzle begins. We see Min Pins that are very straight in stifle, but they still hackney. Either they have a lot of thrust from the hip, or the shoulder angulation is still less than the rear angulation. I also have seen dogs that pick up their front feet in a true prancing action, but don't go anywhere; they take 10 steps to travel a foot. We also see 'goosesteppers' that very much resemble little soldiers. They throw the front feet out, but never bend the pastern. A true hackney gait, viewed from the side, should show the front leg bone parallel to the ground, with the pastern bent at a 90-degree angle, and the foot perpendicular to the ground or pointing downward.

"Breeders are trying to preserve the hackney gait but, sad to say, are sacrificing nice straight legs and tight elbows. Should a Min Pin with a good terrier-type front and no hackney gait be put down to one that hackneys very nicely, but is otherwise a poorer dog conformation-wise? I think not, but there are judges who disagree. It all depends on their interpretation of the standard.

"We want to preserve this distinctive feature of the Min Pin, but not at the price of inferior specimens. We want sound fronts with good straight legs. We should worry more about rears—good strong, well-angulated rears which show no signs of cow-hocks or bowed legs. In the process, we will have Min Pins with good strong stifles that will still have the attention-getting feature of the hackney gait."

Gayle Roberson

Now involved with Toy Poodles, Gayle Roberson bred several Miniature Pinscher champions under the Poco a Poco kennel name. She commented on Min Pin gait in an April 1977 column in the *Gazette*:

"How have we lost our hackney gait? And have we lost it—or given it up—because a hackney viewed from the side is a lovely thing, but coming at you is bad news? Our standard (whether you agree with it or not) states: 'The natural characteristic traits which identify the Miniature Pinscher from other toy dogs (*i.e.*, "type") are his precise hackney gait [amended in 1980 to hackney-like action], fearless animation, complete self-possession, and spirited presence.'

"If hackney action exemplifies type, how many typey dogs have you seen? How many puppies with a gorgeous hackney-like action outgrow it, as a puppy would outgrow a loose front, which, in point of fact, usually is the case? It seems that most judges are programmed to look for 'reach and drive' and 'a true moving front' or a 'straight, terrier-like front,' all of which are very nice in their proper place. In my opinion, no Min Pin can come at you with a dead-true front, tight little elbows, no weaving, no crossing over, no 'knitting and purling,' however slight, and still have an honest-to-goodness, heart-stopping, shaking-the-dew-from-her-tiny-little-feet hackney. I personally have seen such hackney action only once, at an Eastern Miniature Pinscher Club Specialty, on an old, gray-faced red lady, and she was truly poetry in motion. What joy was that brief moment!"

U-CD Horizon's Alakazan-D's Shazaam UDT
is owned and trained by Sandra A. Hill, of El Paso, Texas.

ALL ABOUT EARS
8

The Miniature Pinscher's ears, whether cropped or standing naturally erect, consist of four parts: the pinna (earflap), ear canal, middle ear, and inner ear. To aid his keen sense of hearing, the pinna acts as a funnel-like device to channel air vibrations to the ear canal and eardrum. Notice how your dog moves his ears to improve sound reception? Controlled by 19 separate muscles, pinnae are highly sensitive and capable of independent action. The ear canal leads from the opening of the ear to the eardrum, a thin semitransparent membrane between the outer ear and middle ear cavity. Three small bones located in this air-filled chamber transmit sound vibrations to the inner ear, then to the auditory nerve that carries the signals of both hearing and balance to the brain.

COMMON EAR DISORDERS
Problems Affecting the Pinna

Physical Injuries—Wounds to the pinna occur as a result of accidents, vigorous head shaking, or fights with other animals. First, wash the area with a mild antiseptic cleanser. Minor injuries may be treated by applying an antibiotic ointment to the wound. Deep or extensive cuts, though, must be sutured by the veterinarian.

Pressure Necrosis—Bandages that are wrapped too tightly, such as after ear cropping, can impair the blood circulation to the ear and destroy the flap. In fact, one breeder who provided reference material for this book told of a dog whose bandages were left on for a week; when the owner removed the tape, part of the ear was lost too. Follow the veterinarian's directions on ear taping and aftercare, or use the *No Tape Ear Bracing Method* discussed on page 71.

External Ear Problems

Allergies—Vigorous scratching and head shaking, without the discharge or odor that usually accompanies an ear infection, signal a possible allergic reaction. Allergies associated with foods respond to dietary changes. Reactions to environmental allergens, such as pollen, dust mites, grass, shampoos, or other chemicals, may require allergy testing by the veterinarian to identify the source. Allergies that affect the ears are treated like other allergic conditions, usually with corticosteroid medications or antihistamines.

Bacterial Infection—Infections result from water or soap in the ears, mites, excess wax, foreign objects in the ear, or tumors. Symptoms include scratching, head shaking, tenderness, redness, discharge, and odor from the ear canal. The first step in managing external ear infections is to thoroughly clean the ear canal (two to four times daily for two or three days) with a product such as Nolvasan Otic® (Fort Dodge) or Oti-Clens® (Beecham). Use a cotton ball rather than a swab in the ear canal; swabs tend to pack waxy material against the eardrum. After washing, keep the canal dry and apply an antibiotic ointment according to the veterinarian's instructions. The prescription medication Panalog is effective in treating ear infections, and also helps to eliminate ear mites.

Parasites

Ear Mites—Mites that affect the ear canal, *otodectes cynotis*, cause intense itching, scratching, and head shaking, along with a thick, waxy, reddish-brown discharge. Although crusty patches generally are restricted to the ears, mites travel to other parts of the dog's body and are highly contagious to other household pets. Several remedies are effective in killing both the eggs and adult mites. Tresaderm, applied inside the ear, contains an antibiotic as well as an ingredient for inflammation, and requires a 10- to 14-day treatment course. Newer medications include Frontline®, used inside the ear, and ivermectin (Acarexx® or Ivomec®), which is administered in the ear or as an injection. The flea control product, Revolution®, also kills ear mites when applied as a single dose on the skin. Because ear mites spread from animal to animal, all pets should be treated if an infestation is found.

Sarcoptic Mange—Canine scabies, which causes intense itching and raw crusty patches around the tips of the ears, occurs when the tiny female *Sarcoptes scabei* mite burrows into the skin to lay her eggs. After the eggs hatch, adult mites then live on the skin for several weeks. To prevent mites from spreading to other parts of your dog's body, especially the legs, elbows, and face, or to other animals in the household, you must bathe your dog thoroughly in an insecticidal dip. Other treatments include the heartworm preventatives Interceptor® and Sentinel®, given orally, and Revolution, applied topically.

Middle Ear Infections

Most infections of the outer ear clear within 10 to 14 days; untreated, they can cause more serious problems in the middle or inner ear. *Otitis media* also results when infections, such as tonsillitis, spread from the dog's throat to the

DROP-EAR BRITS

Drop-ear dogs are permitted to compete in Great Britain. However, contemporary breeders have achieved attractive, naturally erect ears.

Ch. Schpin Felix.

Fredwell Petite (left) and Ebeoph Red Velvet (right).

Photos by Thomas Fall.

middle ear via the eustachian tube, or through blood-borne microorganisms. Symptoms, often more pronounced than those accompanying external ear infection, include pain, head shaking, and occasionally facial nerve involvement: drooping of the eyelid, twitching of the eye, constriction of the pupil, or drooling. Draining the infected material (often the dog's eardrum has ruptured) and providing air circulation are the first steps in treating the infection, along with systemic and topical antibiotics provided by the veterinarian. In cases where the infection is caused by a foreign body or tumor in the middle ear, surgical correction may be necessary.

Note the different rates at which the ears stand erect. Litter mates owned by Catherine E. Smith.

Inner Ear Disorders

Inflammation—When dogs fail to receive adequate veterinary attention, middle ear infections may spread to the inner ear. This region controls balance, so signs of the disorder include head tilting, circling, shaky gait, stumbling, and falling. Inflammation ultimately may spread to the brain stem, causing additional nerve and motor damage. Treatment is similar to that of otitis media, with the addition of an anti-inflammatory medication and special antibiotics.

Deafness—Congenital deafness is rare among Miniature Pinschers. Most cases involve breeds with a predominantly white or merle coat: Dalmatians, Fox Terriers, Bull Terriers, Collies, and Shetland Sheepdogs. Acquired deafness, affecting one or both ears, usually results from infections, nerve damage, tumors, and old age. Blockages of the ear canal and certain bacterial infections respond to surgical treatment, along with antibiotics. Dogs with congenital deafness, though they adapt well to their household environment, should never be used for breeding.

Some breeders test their adult Min Pins, as well as puppies over five weeks of age, for deafness using the hearing test known as the brainstem auditory evoked response (BAER) test. Several tiny electrodes are placed in the scalp, which measure the neurological response to computer-generated sounds directed into the ear. This test can detect whether a dog has normal hearing in both ears, is deaf in only one ear, or is deaf in both ears. Results are submitted to the database maintained by the Orthopedic Foundation for Animals (OFA).

This natural-ear dog, Ch. Vedhauge Ene, bred and owned by Jytte Pedersen, is from Denmark.

EAR CROPPING

Should you have your Miniature Pinscher's ears cropped? The standard permits both cropped and natural-ear dogs to compete in the show ring, as long as their ears are "set high, standing erect from base to tip." Many exhibitors feel that cropping provides a more graceful appearance than natural ears, and therefore attracts more favorable attention from judges. Breeders frequently sell their show-quality puppies with the ears already cropped. For pet owners, the decision is entirely personal. Cropping offers little, if any, health benefit to offset the surgical risk and lengthy aftercare required. Further, fewer veterinarians today are experienced in cropping—and many disagree with the procedure on ethical grounds, and therefore do not offer cropping surgery in their practices.

Is ear cropping a cruel procedure performed solely for cosmetic reasons? Will ear cropping one day be banned in the United States? These questions have caused much debate among veterinarians, humane organizations, breeders, and owners. Although cropping once was thought to improve hearing and reduce the incidence of ear infections, the procedure is performed mainly to alter the dog's natural appearance and conform to the requirements of the cropped breeds' official standards.

If you decide to have your dog's ears cropped, contact a knowledgeable breeder for recommendations of veterinarians who have experience working with Min Pins. Avoid surgery during the teething period; most experts suggest cropping when the puppy is between 12 and 16 weeks of age. Because the purpose of ear cropping is to enhance the dog's overall appearance, you and the veterinarian must be able to visualize the final result of cropping in relation to the size, shape, and balance of the dog's head. For example, a Miniature Pinscher with a short muzzle and broad skull needs a tapering, slightly longer ear style than does a dog with a small, narrow, or refined head. Show the veterinarian photographs of the ear shape you prefer or mark the cutting lines on the earflap before surgery.

Georgette Curran, of Sunset kennel, provided the following description and photographs of ear cropping surgery.

This method requires no aftercare or suture removal.

Note: Description and photographs of ear cropping surgery are for informational purposes only. Be sure to consult a licensed veterinarian before considering ear cropping and carefully weigh the risks versus the benefits of this cosmetic procedure. The AKC breed standard permits dogs with uncropped ears to compete in the show ring, as long as the ears stand erect.

1. Puppy is under general anesthesia.

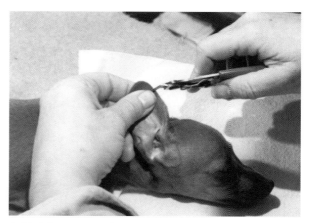

4. Match ears; notch second ear.

7. Newly cropped, before suturing.

All About Ears

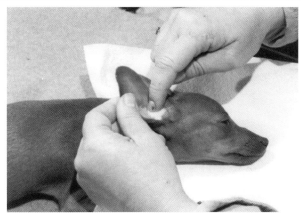

2. Place cotton in each ear to prevent blood from getting into the ear canal.

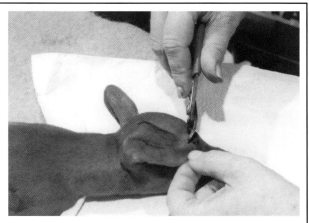

3. Measure the ear for cropping, and notch.

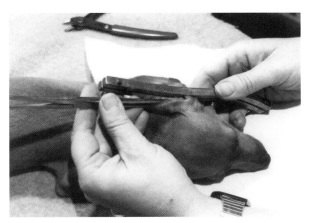

5. Carefully adjust ear clamps.

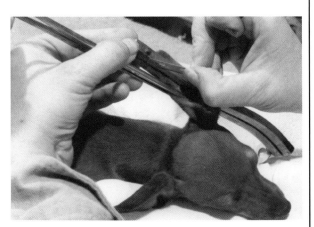

6. Trim excess ear.

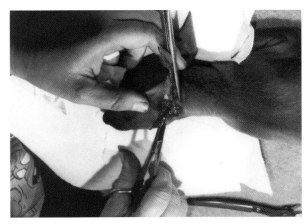

8. Suture with absorbable chromic gut—no sutures to remove.

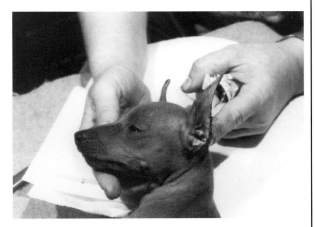

9. Sutured ear.

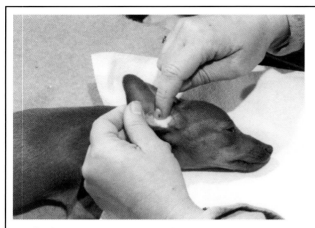

10. Both ears are cropped and sutured.

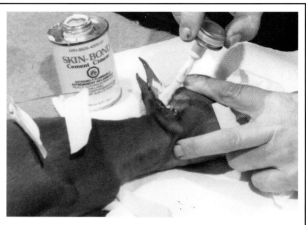

11. Prepare ears for racking; apply Skin-Bond cement to inner earflap.

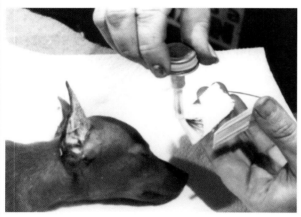

12. Cement ear rack, made from piano wire and cloth tape.

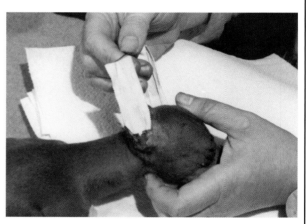

13. Wait one minute; apply ear rack to ear.

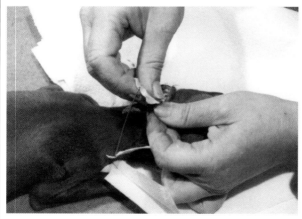

14. Affix second ear to rack.

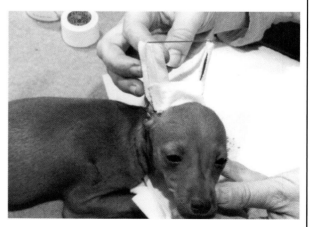

15. Finished ear crop.

EAR BRACING

Ear cropping determines only shape; whether or not the ear stands correctly depends on ear cartilage, muscle control, and bracing techniques. The *No Tape Ear Bracing Method*, recommended by the Doberman Pinscher Club of America, requires no tape, preserves the hair on the back of the ears, causes less discomfort to the dog, and prevents necrosis that can occur from incorrect taping.

How to Brace

Clean the dog's ears well, using hydrogen peroxide for newly cropped ears or alcohol for healed ears. Don't worry about removing the stays. They will fall out by themselves in about 10 days from the oil on the puppy's ear. If your Min Pin's ears refuse to stand after the first bracing, repeat the procedure. You also might want to try breeder Shirley Gillogly's tip of adding 100 mg. to 500 mg. of Vitamin C—an important nutrient in the manufacture and maintenance of collagen and cartilage—to your dog's diet during the period of bracing.

Supplies:

- One puppy (more if you're lucky)
- One square of Dr. Scholl's Molefoam (not moleskin) for two puppies
- Skin-Bond adhesive
- Scissors
- Ruler and pen

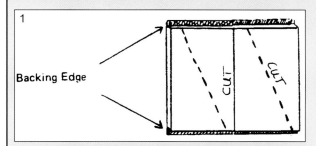

1. Cut Molefoam as shown above. Leave plastic backing on the Molefoam until all cutting is done.

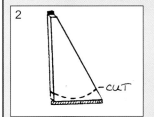
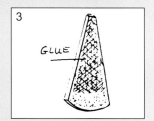

2. Cut off bottom in a slight arc. This removes the "points," rounding the portion to go in the bell.

3. Peel off plastic backing on all stays to be used. There is adhesive on the foam, but it's not sticky enough to stay put. Place an ample amount of Skin-Bond on the white, sticky side, starting about three quarters of an inch from the bottom.

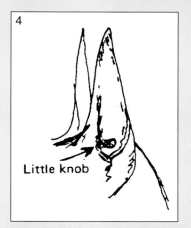
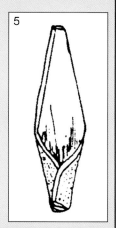

4. Cover inside of dog's ear with Skin-Bond, starting from the little "knob" just above the canal. Wait a minute or so (not the four to five minutes as instructed on the glue). Don't let the puppy shake his head or you'll glue the ear to the side of the head.

5. Roll the base of the stay.

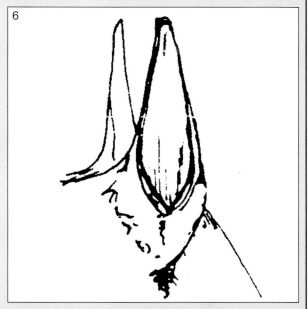

6. Be careful not to let the stay stick to the ear before you have positioned it well into the canal (as far down as you would place any other brace). Hold the ear in the position you want it to stand, attach the stay from the bottom up, straightening edges on healing ears. Rub stay to ear to make certain it's well adhered.

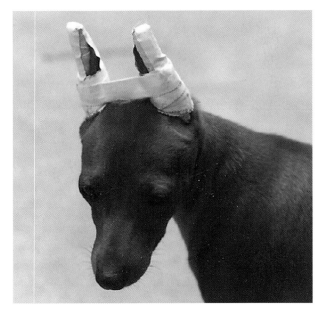
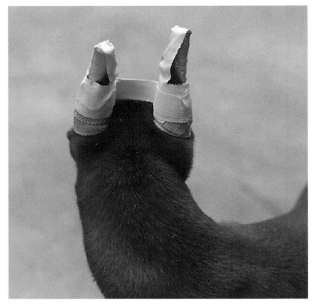

Catherine E. Smith tapes her dogs' ears, as shown, after cropping. She uses ½-inch adhesive tape with tightly rolled cylinder gauze for support inside the ear. The tape remains in place for 10 days, unless irritation occurs.

THE NATURAL UNCROPPED EAR

In 1982, Australian champion Zandor Hey Happy, owned and handled by Lerae Britain Bush, became the first natural-ear Miniature Pinscher to earn an AKC title. Bred by Colin and Judy Weaver, Happy earned 16 points (4 majors) in Hawaii, finishing undefeated with 6 consecutive Best of Breed awards. According to Britain Bush, several judges commented that it was the first time they had seen a Miniature Pinscher with uncropped ears; most admitted that they liked it. Edward and Rose Radel and Georgette Curran also are actively involved in breeding and showing uncropped dogs. Ch. Sunset's Bar-B Rio Grande completed his title in 1984 under Rose Radel's handling, and is the first natural-ear, American-bred male to finish an AKC championship. Radel said, "It's nice to know our breed offers the choice of natural ears. For all who are willing to take on that challenge, we wish you the wonderful success we've experienced and the great joy of knowing it can be done. And, who knows what it may mean to our breed in the future?"

How do uncropped Min Pins fare in the show ring? Although many exhibitors believe that judges favor, consciously or unconsciously, the traditional appearance, most consider the whole dog when making their decisions. Judges interviewed for this book expressed these opinions: "I like the uncropped ear"; "The natural ear is fine if it's on a good head"; "I feel the Miniature Pinscher is attractive with cropped or uncropped ears"; "Uncropped ears are fine. If the breed is to go to uncropped ears, more attention will need to be paid to breeding for correct texture, set, and carriage, but it can be done."

Because a number of countries now prohibit ear cropping—including England, Denmark, Sweden, Australia, South Africa, and Germany—many individuals believe it will one day become obsolete in the United States, as well. However, until club members involved with the large-registration breeds—Doberman Pinschers, Schnauzers, Boxers, Boston Terriers, and Great Danes—amend their standards and policies on cropping, this procedure is likely to continue.

Lerae Britain Bush, who strongly supports the natural look, offered her viewpoint on cropping, condensed from an article in *Dog World* magazine:

"When I visited kennels and attended dog shows in Australia, where ear cropping is illegal, I met several Miniature Pinscher breeders and saw the fine quality of the dogs they were producing and the champions they already had. Their success, of course, is the result of careful breeding to produce ears that will stand erect and to have dogs that most nearly possess all the other requirements of the standard. We, too, must work with genetics—on paper, through proper line breeding, and in the whelping box—so we can be sure that all facets of our finished product represent the best that is humanly possible to achieve. Unless some of us are willing to stop cropping ears, this traditional, rather than required, aspect of breeding and showing dogs will persist and we will continue taking our 3- to 6-month-old puppies to veterinarians for ear surgery.

"Breeders also must try to educate and enlighten the novice to present our breed in ideal condition, while adhering as closely as possible to the total picture most desired to represent the breed. Certainly no judge who is familiar with the standard would deny a dog a ribbon because of ear cropping, and no one can tell us any longer that it's impossible to show dogs with good natural ears. So, the next time you are privileged to witness any usually cropped breed being shown with natural ears, perhaps you might clap a bit louder or take an extra minute to comment to the handler and the judge, who has shown the determination to follow through with courage and adhere to principles of overall quality regardless of ears. We hope breeders, handlers, owners, and judges will find the courage to break this tradition; we have proved that it can be done."

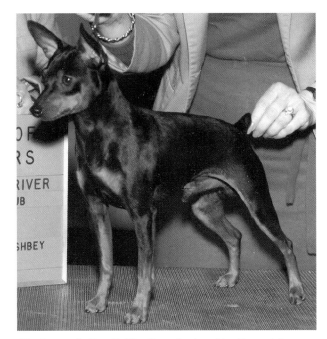

Ch. Sunset's Bar-B Rio Grande, bred by T. and J. Vieira and owned by Georgette Curran and Edward and Rose Radel, was the first American-bred male Miniature Pinscher to finish his championship with natural, uncropped ears.

Ch. Sunset's St. Steven N. B., bred by Georgette Curran and owned by his breeder and Edward and Rose Radel, was sired by Ch. Sunset's Bar-B Rio Grande, and was the second male to finish with natural ears.

NO. 34 IN A SERIES OF VISITS TO HOMES OF FINE DOGS

GEDDESBURG KENNELS

James J. Geddes

This is the famous Geddes Miniature Pinscher, Ch. Mighty Sweet. Now 4 years old, this splendid specimen finished her championship at 6 months and 28 days and is now the dam of 3 champions.

Mr. J. J. Geddes and Mrs. Geddes own and operate Geddesburg Kennels. He is a member of the Professional Handlers Association and a well-known figure on the show circuit. Mr. and Mrs. Geddes specialize in Miniature Pinschers and Italian Greyhounds and sell their fine dogs internationally.

PURINA IS THEIR CHOICE

If you're an average dog owner, your dog's well-being is of more than ordinary importance to you. Yet, you may feel, as some do, that one dog food is just about like another. If you do, we urge you to talk with some of the better professional breeders. Where dog raising is a business, dog food gets its toughest test. It has to deliver the goods—in nutrition, palatability, and economy—or out it goes. So, if you want to do right by that dog of yours, talk to some top-flight dog breeders. You'll be surprised how many are feeding and recommending Purina Dog Chow!

RALSTON PURINA COMPANY
St. Louis 2, Missouri

FOOD FOR THOUGHT
9

Since the first commercially prepared doggie biscuit rolled off the conveyor belt in the late 19th century, breeders and owners, along with their veterinarians, have worked to define the nutritional requirements of dogs and to formulate appropriate foods to meet those needs. From the development of the first "all purpose" diet—advertised as adequate for all stages of a dog's life—to today's highly specialized preparations, the pet food industry has grown to become a multi-billion-dollar-a-year business in the United States alone. In fact, if you stroll down the pet food aisle in your local supermarket, you'll find only a fraction of the 15,000-plus generic, private label, commercial, and premium brands, produced by over 3,000 pet food manufacturers.

THE SIX NUTRIENT CLASSES

With so many products to choose from, how can you determine whether a particular food meets your dog's nutritional needs? First, let's examine the six types of nutrients, or building blocks, found in most dog foods. The term nutrient refers to any component that aids in the body's metabolic processes. This includes regulating body temperature, assisting in the chemical reactions that take place within or outside of cells, acting as structural components of the body, and transporting substances throughout the bloodstream. Three nutrients—protein, carbohydrates, and fat—supply energy that your pet needs to maintain his general health and activity level. Although vitamins, minerals, and water don't provide energy, directly, they play a critical role in regulating many complex internal activities.

Protein

Found in foods such as beef, poultry, fish, eggs, wheat, corn, and soybeans, protein is broken down during digestion into smaller amino acid molecules. Carried throughout the body by

This 5-week-old puppy, owned by Amy Putnam Issleib and Shan Howard, eagerly awaits feeding time.

Shape and color make the breed, vigor and vitality make the dog.
Mrs. D. E. Van Buskirk

the bloodstream, amino acids serve in a variety of roles. Keratin, one type of protein, makes up the basic structure of the dog's hair, nails, and skin. Collagen, another form, constitutes connective tissue such as tendons, ligaments, and muscles. By acting on these structures as enzymes, amino acids help to build, as well as repair, tissue. Amino acids also aid in the production of antibodies, hemoglobin, and certain hormones.

Dogs require 22 amino acids, 12 of which are synthesized within the body. The 10 essential amino acids, which must be supplied in the diet, are listed below:

> **ESSENTIAL AMINO ACIDS**
> - Arginine
> - Histidine
> - Isoleucine
> - Leucine
> - Lysine
> - Methionine
> - Phenylalanine
> - Threonine
> - Tryptophan
> - Valine

The amount of protein your dog requires varies, depending on his stage of life, reproductive status, activity level, overall health, and temperament. During puppyhood, lactation, and periods of stress or convalescence, your Min Pin needs a diet that supplies between 25 and 30 percent protein. However, dogs with advanced kidney disease often manage better on reduced-protein diets. Because protein is not stored in the body—unlike carbohydrates and fat—the part that is not used for energy is converted in the liver to urea, a waste product excreted by the kidneys. When dogs with impaired kidney function consume too much protein, the urea that can't be eliminated begins to accumulate in the bloodstream, causing many of the symptoms of kidney failure. Too little protein rarely is a problem because most pet foods are formulated with adequate levels of this nutrient.

Carbohydrates

Named for the elements carbon, hydrogen, and oxygen, carbohydrates provide your Min Pin's primary source of energy. Sugar and starch, which are broken down in the digestive tract to form simple sugars, are known as soluble carbohydrates. Carried by the bloodstream to the liver, glucose is transformed into glycogen and stored for later use. During periods of activity, as well as between meals, glucose is released and used for energy. Glucose also plays a critical role in nourishing the brain because it's one of the few substances that can cross the membrane known as the blood-brain barrier. If the blood sugar level becomes too low (hypoglycemia), the brain is unable to use oxygen effectively and a dog can go into shock. Hypoglycemia, though rare, sometimes affects toy breed puppies—especially during periods of stress or excitement. (During an attack, feed one to two teaspoons of corn syrup or table sugar.)

Insoluble carbohydrates—cellulose, pectin, guar gum, and mucilage—are known collectively as fiber. Although not considered a nutrient because it can't be digested, fiber affects the digestive process in several ways. Cellulose, by absorbing water, adding bulk, and softening the stools, helps to relieve both diarrhea and constipation. Pectin and guar gum, on the other hand, serve to remove cholesterol and bile acids, and lower the level of cholesterol in the bloodstream. Because fiber decreases the absorption of nutrients, puppies and active dogs should avoid high-fiber diets. If your dog is overweight, though, fiber allows him to feel full while it shortens the time food remains in the intestinal tract.

Fat

Dietary fat contains more than twice the calories per unit of weight as do protein or carbohydrates. It offers a concentrated source of energy that is important during the nutritionally stressful periods of puppyhood, lactation, and active showing or training. Fat also plays a role in the absorption of fat-soluble vitamins—A, D, E, and K, and supplies the essential fatty acids, linoleic acid and linolenic acid. When dogs consume too little fat—from poor quality or stale food—a deficiency in fatty acids may result. Early signs include dry, flaky skin, dull coat, skin lesions, and "hot spots." Over time, consuming too little fat may lead to weight loss, lethargy, reproductive problems, and infertility. Too much fat causes problems, as well, including obesity, steatorrhea (undigested fat, passed in the stool), and pancreatitis (inflammation of the pancreas). Dogs that consume a high-fat diet usually eat less food, overall, so nutritional imbalances also may occur.

Vitamins

Identified in the early 20th century by researchers who determined that laboratory animals could not live solely on purified protein, carbohydrates, and fat, vitamins are organic compounds necessary for healthy growth and development. Vitamins don't supply energy directly, but rather act as coenzymes that help to regulate various processes within the body. Vitamins are classified into two groups—fat soluble and water soluble—according to the means by which they are absorbed, stored, and excreted.

VITAMINS	
Fat-Soluble	Water-Soluble
A	Biotin (B_7)
D	Choline
E	Cyanocobalamin (B_{12})
K	Folic Acid (B_9)
	Niacin (B_3)
	Pantothenic Acid (B_5)
	Pyridoxine (B_6)
	Riboflavin (B_2)
	Thiamin (B_1)
	Vitamin C

Minerals

Although minerals make up less than 1 percent of your dog's weight, they serve a variety of important functions. Minerals help to regulate the blood's acid-base balance, maintain cellular

MINERALS	
Macro Units	Micro Units
Calcium	Iron
Phosphorus	Copper
Sodium	Manganese
Potassium	Zinc
Magnesium	Iodine
	Selenium

water balance, and form the structural components of bones and teeth. Most pet foods supply satisfactory levels of minerals (some even contain excesses). The most important consideration, though, is the balance of minerals—especially calcium and phosphorus. Because these minerals interact with one another, inversely, in building and maintaining the skeletal system, imbalances may lead to lameness, fractures, and abnormal bone development. Supplements—or any diet (such as all meat) that leads to an excess or deficiency in one or more elements—can do more harm than good. Instead of trying to make up for a poor-quality dog food by adding vitamins and minerals, choose a balanced preparation formulated for your dog's stage of life.

Water

Your Min Pin needs water more than any other nutrient. Whereas dogs can go many days without food, the loss of 10 to 15 percent of body water can cause serious illness and even death. Because the thirst mechanism responds to physical exertion, environment, and health status, your dog always needs access to fresh drinking water. Dogs also obtain water from the metabolic processes that take place within the body, as well as from the water content of food itself. If your dog eats canned food (which contains about 70 percent water), for example, he will drink less from his bowl than a dog fed a dry diet (10 percent water). Your dog normally regulates his water intake according to outflow (from urination, respiration,

The first dry biscuit for dogs was developed by James Spratt. This photo, circa 1901, shows an automatic hoist delivering Spratt's Dog Cakes from ovens to the steel floor of the drying room.
Photo courtesy of the American Kennel Club.

lactation, vomiting, or diarrhea), so always consult the veterinarian if you notice an increase or decrease in water consumption.

HOW MUCH TO FEED

The amount of food your dog needs depends on several factors: age, activity level, health, stage of life, and season (warm or cold weather). Surprisingly, small dogs require more calories per pound of body weight than do large breeds. This is because most of the energy a dog uses is given off as heat, radiated from the surface of his skin. Small breeds have a greater proportion of skin surface, relative to their weight, so more heat is carried away from their bodies. In fact, a 5-pound dog has six times more body surface, per pound, than does a 100-pound dog.

DAILY MAINTENANCE REQUIREMENT (MER)	
Body Weight (pounds)	Energy (calories)
6 pounds	50/pound of body weight
9 pounds	45/pound of body weight
12 pounds	40/pound of body weight

The first step in determining how much to feed is to figure your dog's Maintenance Energy Requirement using the chart below. If your Min Pin is young, pregnant, or nursing, she needs more food than one that is not. Inactive or overweight dogs need less. Keep in mind that your dog's physical condition is the ultimate test in deciding how much to feed. Ideally, you should be able to feel the ribs but not see them. By observing your dog's physique, along with periodic weight checks, you can make certain your Min Pin remains in peak form.

Multiply the Maintenance Energy Requirement by the MER Factor, next page, to estimate your dog's daily caloric intake.

TYPES OF DOG FOOD
Dry Food

The dry biscuit was the earliest commercial food product for dogs. Introduced in England, in the 1860s, James Spratt's Patent Meat Fibrine Dog Cake had the market to itself until the dawn of the 20th century when Clarence Gaines, Ralston Purina, and others joined the competition. Although these rations consisted mainly of cereal grains—dog food actually was an offshoot of the breakfast food industry—by adding fresh meat to the kibble, owners could feed their dogs the most nutritionally complete product available.

Today, dry food claims more than 80 percent of the market. Its advantages include convenience, ease of preparation and storage, and moderate cost. Because dry food contains about 10 percent water, buyers pay only for the nutrients, themselves, instead of water and expensive packaging. Cereal grains and soybeans make up most of the protein, carbohydrates, and vegetable fat in dry foods. Meat, poultry, fish, and liver, in the form of dried meal, also contribute protein and animal fat. Additional fat often is sprayed on the nuggets after the mixture has been baked to ensure adequate levels of essential fatty acids.

Feeding a dry food is the most popular method, but you need to be aware of certain disadvantages. First, some brands are less digestible and palatable than soft-moist or canned dinners, especially when fed dry. If you choose a dry food, consider adding warm water to soften and expand the nuggets. Then mash with a fork to form a soft consistency. This counteracts the abrasiveness of dry dinner for tooth-cleaning purposes, but even hard biscuits don't completely eliminate tartar buildup. And, because dry meal contains less water than your dog needs each day, always see that he has free access to his water bowl.

Another problem with dry pet food is that fresh meat can't be added at the factory because its water content is too high. To be sure that the animal protein in the dinner comes from top-quality sources, look for a brand that features meat or poultry meal, instead of "by-products." Finally, examine the package carefully before purchasing. Avoid bags in which the fat has soaked through. These are more likely to be contaminated or rancid.

Soft-Moist Food

Shaped like hamburger patties or meat chunks, soft-moist foods combine fresh meat with soybeans or grains, animal fat, vitamins, minerals, and water to form a flavorful, highly digestible diet. These products offer convenience, as well.

FACTORS AFFECTING MAINTENANCE ENERGY REQUIREMENT	
Activity	MER Factor
Growth	
Birth to 3 months	2 times MER
3 to 6 months	1.6 times MER
6 to 12 months	1.2 times MER
Work (1 hour exercise)	1.1 times MER
Gestation	
First 6 weeks	1 times MER
Last 3 weeks	1.1 to 1.3 times MER
Peak Lactation	
3 to 6 weeks	2 times MER (4-puppy litter)
	4 times MER (8-puppy litter)
Inactivity	0.8 times MER

Single-serving packages need no refrigeration and have a fairly long shelf life. However, to guarantee freshness and prevent the food from drying out, preservatives and humectants may be added. Some formulations also include food coloring

Michele L. Basye's puppies eye their bowl of puppy food.

to create the effect of fat-striated beef chunks or hamburger. If you choose a soft-moist preparation, make certain the cellophane wrapping is intact. Contact with air can cause the food to deteriorate or become rancid. Keep in mind, too, that the sugar added to some soft-moist foods may lead to digestive upsets in sensitive dogs.

Canned Food

Two varieties of canned foods are available: meat and ration. Meat products consist mainly of meat and/or meat by-products, along with expanded nuggets of soy flour known as "textured vegetable protein." Colored brown or red, these pieces are easy to mistake for meat chunks if you're unfamiliar with canned pet food. Most meat dinners also contain vitamins and minerals because the all-meat preparations of the past often led to serious nutritional imbalances. In fact, because it contains more protein and fat than other products, canned meat should be given chiefly when your dog's energy needs are high—during growth, stress, pregnancy, or lactation. Canned rations, on the other hand, offer a balance of meat, carbohydrates, animal fat, vitamins, and minerals, and are suitable for all stages of life. A number of premium canned foods are prepared to look and taste like a human-grade stew, with a mixture of meat and vegetables.

RAW FOOD DIET

Since the mid-1990s, a growing number of owners have adopted a diet based on raw foods for their pets. There are several variations of the raw food plan. However, one of the more popular goes by the acronym, BARF, which stands for "Bones and Raw Food" or "Biologically Appropriate Raw Food." Developed by Dr. Ian Billinghurst, an Australian veterinarian, the premise behind BARF is that an "evolutionary" diet provides greater health benefits than do commercially prepared cooked foods. By feeding the type of diet consumed by the dog's wild ancestors throughout the centuries—based on raw meaty bones, and raw muscle meat, organs, vegetables, and fruit—today's pets can enjoy fresher breath with fewer dental problems, better coats and less odor, and improved immune function with fewer allergies. According to Dr. Billinghurst's Web site, his raw diet will "maximize the health, longevity, and reproductive capacity" of pets, and "minimize the need for veterinary intervention." Raw diet proponents believe that by cooking food, vital nutrients and enzymes are destroyed in the process.

If you decide to try a raw food diet for your Min Pin, three feeding methods are available:

- Homemade diets, including the BARF plan, Ultimate Diet, and Volhard Diet. These are the most time-consuming and labor-intensive programs for pet owners, and it's important to properly balance ingredients to avoid nutritional deficiencies and excesses.
- Combination plans based on commercially available grain products to which raw meat then is added.
- Pre-packaged frozen foods, which are complete and balanced, without the need for further supplementation. These include patties and minces.

Note that these programs have not yet been endorsed by the American Veterinary Medical Association (AVMA), or most practicing veterinarians. They point out pitfalls in feeding a raw diet—the most serious of which is the potential for food-borne illnesses. Studies have shown that raw meat often contains the bacteria *E. coli* and salmonella, and possibly various parasites. In addition, a diet based on raw bones may lead to fractured teeth, blockages, and perforations that could require emergency surgery. Few scientific studies have been performed, to date, to verify the health claims of raw food advocates.

SPECIAL NUTRITIONAL NEEDS
Growth (Weaning to 12 Months)

When you pick up your puppy from the breeder, one of the supplies you should receive is a small portion of the food he is accustomed to eating, along with detailed instructions on how and

FEEDING GUIDE	
Optimal Body Weight	Approximate Daily Feeding
5 lb.	¼ lb.
10 lb.	½ lb.

when to feed. Your Min Pin will grow rapidly in the next year, from a bouncing pup to an elegant adult. To make certain he receives the proper level of nutrients during this critical stage, choose a food that is specially formulated for growth. It should be easy for your puppy to digest, energy dense, and at least 29 percent protein. Because nutritional deficiencies, as well as excesses—especially vitamins and minerals—affect puppies more seriously than adults, be sure the diet you provide is guaranteed to be complete and balanced.

To determine how much to feed, follow your breeder's suggestions. He has many years of experience in evaluating his puppies and should be able to estimate your pet's food intake at 3, 6, and 12 months. Your puppy will need less food, overall, if you feed a high-quality brand. In fact, your biggest problem will be to avoid overfeeding. Because fat cells increase in both size and number during puppyhood, too much food during this critical stage can predispose your Min Pin to obesity. Watch your puppy's condition carefully, and increase or decrease his food intake as needed.

Maintenance (Adulthood)

As your puppy approaches his first birthday, you'll notice that he has begun to reduce his

FEEDINGS PER DAY	
Age	# Meals per Day
Weaning to 3 months	4
3 to 6 months	3
6 to 12 months	2
Adult Maintenance	1 or 2
Sedentary, Overweight, Senior	2+ (smaller)

Active Min Pins such as Ch. Shadowmist's Sable Scheme CD RN OA OAJ may require special "performance" diets to support their high energy levels. Owned by Doralyn Wheatley.

food intake along with his activity level. This is the time to change his diet to one designed for maintenance. Whenever you change your dog's diet, always introduce the new food gradually to avoid causing a digestive upset. Start by mixing one quarter of the new food with three quarters of his regular meal. Over about a week's time, continue to add more of the new dinner until he is eating it exclusively.

Should you add table scraps to your pet's food? Because most owners find it hard to resist their dog's pleading eyes, adding a tiny bit (less than a tablespoon) of lean meat or chicken, potato, rice, or cooked vegetables usually won't upset the nutritional balance of the dinner. Cut back on the treats, though, if he starts to gain weight. And be sure to have a bowl of fresh water available, especially if you serve a dry or soft-moist food.

vide both a nutritionally dense, easy-to-digest formula, and one flavorful enough to interest him in eating.

Canned foods or dry "performance" diets, with their higher fat contents, work well for dogs under emotional and physical stress. You also can add a tablespoon of vegetable oil per cup of regular dry food to increase its energy density. Divide your dog's dinner into two portions: feed the first at least four hours before the competition and the second, one to four hours afterward.

Remember, the most important nutrient your dog needs when under stress is water. Dogs don't perspire, but they can lose considerable fluid from their respiratory tracts when they pant to cool off. Give your dog a drink of water between show classes or during travel—especially in warm weather.

Feeding During Stress

Although toy breeds don't work for their livings—herding sheep, pulling sleds, or tracking lost children, like many larger dogs—they often expend as much energy competing on the show circuit, performing in obedience trials, or simply romping around the house. In fact, because the mental stress involved in a heavy show schedule can actually depress your dog's appetite, it's important to pro-

Obesity

Known for his lean, wedge-shaped physique, your Min Pin should never be allowed to become plump. Many factors contribute to obesity: consuming too much food or a high-fat diet, lack of exercise, spaying or neutering, old age, and genetics. Excess weight can contribute to heart, liver, and kidney disease, cancer, skin problems, arthritis, and reproductive difficulties. Overweight dogs face greater risks during surgery, both from the procedure, itself, and the anesthesia. In short, obesity not only affects the quality of your dog's life, but his lifespan, as well.

If you suspect your Miniature Pinscher needs to lose weight, have the veterinarian perform a thorough physical examination. The doctor should check for fluid retention, internal parasites, and pregnancy, which sometimes are mistaken for excess weight. Other problems that contribute to obesity include hormonal imbalances, thyroid disease, diabetes mellitus, and heart or kidney disease. The veterinarian also can help you develop a weight loss plan for your dog, involving both diet and exercise, and a schedule for achieving his goal weight.

The best way for your dog to lose weight is by combining a high-fiber, reduced calorie food, with exercise. Unless the veterinarian has uncovered a condition that could be worsened by activity, your Min Pin should take one or two 10- to 15-minute walks each day. Naturally, if your dog has been sedentary, you'll need to begin such a program slowly. However, the benefits of exercise are well worth the effort. First, activity helps to burn calories directly. More importantly, it continues to raise your dog's metabolic rate even when he is resting. Exercise improves heart function and

prevents the loss of muscle that often accompanies dieting, as well. Finally, regular exercise provides a time when you and your dog can be together, away from the distractions of a busy household, sharing the pleasure of one another's company.

Chart information adapted, with permission, from Small Animal Clinical Nutrition III.

Ch. Kimro's Maid In Manhattan, bred and owned by
Kimberly Pastella, Robin Greenslade, Howard Schwell, and Monique Westover.
She was a 2005 Westminster Kennel Club Award of Merit winner
and a 2006 MPCA Top Twenty finalist.

IN SICKNESS AND HEALTH
10

Is your Miniature Pinscher active, alert, and interested in his family and surroundings? Is he sleek and well-muscled, neither too fat nor too thin? Are his eyes dark and bright, his coat thick and glossy? When a dog isn't feeling well, he can't describe his symptoms to his owner. It's important, therefore, to watch your Min Pin's condition and be alert to any subtle changes. Notice whether your dog is eating or drinking more or less than usual. Does he seem overly tired or have difficulty getting up or lying down? Does he have skin problems, such as itching, crusty patches, flaking, or sores? Many illnesses are fully curable when treated early, whereas others are preventable through a program of vaccinations and checkups. Providing regular care and attention will enable your Min Pin to maintain his good health throughout his lifetime.

BASIC CARE
Checking the Pulse Rate

To count your dog's heartbeat, place your fingers or palm directly over his heart, on the left side of his chest behind the elbow. You also can take his pulse at the femoral artery, located at the inner part of the thigh. In a healthy dog, the pulse is strong and steady. It ranges from 80 to 140 beats per minute, though puppies and small dogs have faster rates than large dogs. Because a rapid or slow pulse can signal a variety of ailments, always bring such changes to the attention of the veterinarian.

Collecting Fecal and Urine Samples

Various illnesses require the collection of fecal or urine samples to detect the presence of parasites or determine the cause of infection. Examined under a microscope, these samples enable the doctor to prescribe the best medication, as well as monitor the treatment process. A fecal specimen should be checked within three hours of obtaining it, especially if the technician must inspect for parasite eggs. When eggs mature and burst, they become more difficult to identify. To obtain a urine sample, place a disposable container such as a small foil pan under your dog when he urinates, then transfer the urine to a clean bottle. Always collect your dog's urine in the morning when it's more concentrated.

Giving Medication

To give your dog a pill, grasp the top of his muzzle behind the canine teeth and gently press his lips inward. With your other hand, place the tablet as far back in his throat as possible. Close his mouth, tilt back the head, and stroke his throat until he swallows. If your dog has difficulty taking pills, coat the tablet with butter or place it in a small piece of cheese or hamburger. Keep in mind that some medications are specially coated time-release formulas, so never crush a pill or break open a capsule without first checking with the veterinarian.

The beginning of health is to know the disease.
Cervantes

To give a liquid medicine, use a plastic eyedropper marked with a measuring scale. Form a pocket between your dog's teeth and lips by gently pulling the skin outward. Tilt his head back and slowly release a small amount of liquid into the pocket. Stroke his throat until he swallows. Never pour a liquid directly down your dog's throat; this could cause him to choke or inhale the medication into his lungs.

Taking Temperature

Lubricate a rectal thermometer with petroleum jelly and insert the bulb end about an inch into your dog's rectum. Hold the thermometer in place for two to three minutes. (If you have difficulty using a rectal thermometer, try one of the in-the-ear devices.) Normal temperature is between 100.5°F. and 102.5°F. Slight variations may be due to excitement or exercise, but a reading above 102.5°F. usually indicates a fever.

INFECTIOUS DISEASES

Dogs are susceptible to a variety of infectious diseases. Some are caused by viruses; others result from exposure to bacteria, fungi, or protozoa. Newborns acquire immunity to certain diseases from the colostrum, the dam's first milk, but this protection is only temporary. To guard against common infectious diseases, have your puppy, as well as adult dog, vaccinated according to the veterinarian's recommended schedule. (For current vaccination guidelines, visit the American Animal Hospital Association's Web site at www.aahanet.org.)

Canine Influenza

First identified in racing Greyhounds in 2004 at a track in Florida, canine influenza made headlines a year later when veterinarians discovered cases occurring in pets throughout the United States. This is a highly contagious viral respiratory illness that causes coughing, low-grade fever, and nasal discharge. However, the mild form may progress to a more severe variety, with high fever (104°F. to 106°F.) and pneumonia-like symptoms. Because canine influenza is a new disease, believed to have mutated from an equine influenza strain, dogs have no naturally acquired immunity. Antibiotics are needed to treat secondary bacterial infections, but coughing may last up to three weeks.

Canine influenza is an airborne virus, which also is transmitted through dog-to-dog contact, such as sharing toys and water bowls. Currently, there is no vaccine against the disease. The best way to prevent your Min Pin from contracting canine influenza is to limit his exposure to other dogs—especially those showing signs of respiratory illness. Because the virus easily is killed by disinfectants, be sure any boarding kennels or other pet care facilities that your dog frequents employ good infection-control practices. (Canine influenza has not been shown to affect humans.)

Corona Virus

Corona virus primarily attacks the gastrointestinal tract, causing vomiting, severe diarrhea, and fatigue. No specific cure exists. However, adult dogs are better able to fight the disease than are young puppies. Because corona virus spreads quickly among dogs, be sure to keep your facilities clean by using a disinfectant solution of household bleach and water (1:30 dilution). Corona can be prevented with a vaccine, such as Duramune® CV-K.

Distemper

This highly contagious disease is transmitted through direct or indirect contact with an infected dog. Urine and fecal material, as well as secretions from the dog's eyes or nose, harbor the virus. Distemper also is spread by air currents and contaminated objects, including crates, kennel runs, and food dishes. Canine distemper is so widespread that it's almost impossible to prevent exposure. In fact, most adult dogs will come into contact with the virus at some point in their lives.

Signs of distemper include nasal discharge, watery eyes, vomiting, coughing, weight loss, diarrhea, and fever. In some cases, the virus causes rapid growth of the tough keratin cells on the dog's foot pad, resulting in a hardened pad. As the disease progresses, it may attack the nervous system, leading to twitching, convulsions, and partial or complete paralysis. Even if a dog recovers, this damage often is permanent. Distemper is the greatest single disease threat to the world's dog population, according to veterinarians. More than half of all adult dogs that contract the disease die of it. In puppies, as few as one in five survives. There is no cure for distemper. The only way to prevent the disease is through annual inoculation.

Infectious Canine Hepatitis

Spread by contact with feces, urine, or the saliva of infected animals, hepatitis affects the dog's liver and kidneys, and the lining of blood vessels. Puppies are susceptible to a fatal form of the disease, characterized by the sudden onset of bloody diarrhea, fever, and vomiting. Occasionally, a puppy dies even without visible symptoms. Adults generally develop acute hepatitis, which causes jaundice, enlarged tonsils, bleeding gums, and pain or swelling of the liver. The cornea of the eye may become blue or cloudy. Canine hepatitis—not the same variety as human hepatitis—is diagnosed by a blood test. Treatment involves controlling vomiting and diarrhea, along with therapeutic doses of B-complex and B_{12} vitamins. Your dog can be protected against ICH by annual vaccination.

Kennel Cough

Infectious tracheobronchitis (kennel cough) affects the upper respiratory tract and its primary symptom is a harsh, dry, persistent cough. Spread by airborne viruses or bacteria, the disease often occurs in boarding kennels, animal hospitals, dog shows, and shelters. Toy breeds and puppies require special attention because their

Check with the veterinarian for the recommended vaccination protocol for your Miniature Pinscher. Photo courtesy of Durvet, Inc. Animal Health Products.

smaller nasal passages may become obstructed. A home vaporizer often helps to relieve congestion. To treat kennel cough, you'll need to isolate the sick dog from other animals in the household, provide antibiotics, and, in some cases, cough medicine. *Bordetella bronchiseptica*, a bacterial infection, and parainfluenza are both controlled by a painless intranasal vaccine, such as Intra-Trac® II. Also, most distemper/hepatitis vaccines protect against parainfluenza and adenovirus.

Leptospirosis

A bacterial disease caused by spirochetes, leptospirosis is transmitted through contact with the urine of infected animals. Rodents, the primary carriers of one form of the disease, contaminate the dog's food or water supply. Dogs also contract leptospirosis through the mucous membranes of the nose or mouth, cuts in the skin, or less frequently during breeding. Symptoms include vomiting and diarrhea, listlessness, and fever. Your dog may develop sores in his mouth or a brown coating on the tongue. If his liver and kidneys become involved, the whites of his eyes may turn yellow, or he may drink and urinate more than usual. The spirochetes that cause leptospirosis in dogs also cause Weil's disease in humans, so be sure to take rigorous precautions when handling an infected dog. (Bacteria can be shed in the urine for several months—even up to a year.) Antibiotics help a dog fight the disease, but some animals require hospitalization. In high-risk areas, consider having your dog vaccinated every six months.

Parvovirus

Parvovirus first appeared in the United States in 1978, and has spread rapidly throughout Great Britain, Australia, South Africa, and Europe. Highly contagious, this viral disease is transmitted through contact with fecal material of infected dogs. Parvo, which can survive for long periods in the environment, has been diagnosed wherever dogs are found—in parks, boarding kennels, animal shelters, and dog shows. It's carried on the dog's hair and feet, or by contaminated cages, shoes, or other objects. The disease attacks cells that reproduce rapidly, such as those in the lining of the gastrointestinal tract, bone marrow, lymph nodes, and heart. It can take two forms: diarrhea (enteritis) and heart inflammation (myocarditis). The first causes tiredness and depression, loss of appetite, vomiting, and severe diarrhea. The feces may be light gray or yellowish, possibly streaked with blood. Treatment involves replacing lost electrolytes and fluids, controlling vomiting and diarrhea, and fighting the infection with antibiotics. Myocarditis, seen most often in puppies less than three months old, occurs without gastrointestinal symptoms. The youngster may act depressed, and stop nursing or eating. Death may occur in just a few days. Puppies that survive often have permanently damaged hearts and may die of heart failure weeks or months later. There is no specific medication to kill the virus in infected dogs. Never allow your Min Pin to come in contact with fecal material, and keep your kennel area clean. The best prevention is yearly inoculation.

Rabies

Veterinarians diagnose more than 7,000 cases of rabies each year in the United States. Skunks, raccoons, foxes, and bats, along with dogs and cats, are the most common carriers. Rabies virus, found in the saliva, is transmitted by a bite from an infected animal. Symptoms usually develop from two weeks to three months after exposure. Severe bites—especially near the head or face—may cause signs sooner. An infected dog often undergoes personality changes. He may become withdrawn or irritable. Bright light hurts his eyes. Rabies ultimately leads to paralysis and death, but some dogs first go through a phase of aggressive behavior and roaming. Most states require vaccination at one- to three-year intervals in order to obtain a dog license. However, in 2005, The Rabies Challenge Fund Charitable Trust was formed to conduct research into extending the time between vaccinations. Researchers hope to prove—by measuring serum antibody titers—that immunity lasts at least five years after inoculation. By reducing the number of vaccinations a pet receives over his lifetime, the potential for a variety of adverse reactions can be minimized.

The American Veterinary Medical Association (AVMA) recommends the following:

- Have your dog routinely vaccinated against rabies. To ensure continued maximum protection, follow the veterinarian's advice and observe local rabies-control regulations.
- Obey your town's leash and licensing laws.
- Report stray animals to the local animal control authority.
- Don't keep wild animals as pets.
- Teach children to avoid strange animals, especially wild animals.

NEUTERING

The most important step you can take to ensure your Miniature Pinscher's health—next to obtaining regularly scheduled inoculations—is to neuter your puppy before he reaches sexual maturity. The surgical procedure in which the sex organs are removed is called spaying in females and castrating in males. Neutering not only avoids the possibility that a dog accidentally will become pregnant or sire an unwanted litter, but also offers numerous benefits to her or his physical and emotional well-being. For example, spaying before six months of age nearly eliminates the chances that a female will contract mammary, uterine, or ovarian cancers. It also avoids the problems associated with twice-yearly heat cycles. The hormonal changes that take place during these seasons may be one of the risk factors for developing reproductive cancers.

Males, too, benefit from castration before they reach full maturity. They are less likely to show undesirable behaviors, such as marking, mounting, aggression, or roaming. Castration also helps to reduce the possibility of developing testicular cancer, prostate disease, hormonal dysfunction, and perianal adenoma (a growth around the anus). Although neutering is major surgery, it's considered safe—especially for young dogs with immature reproductive organs. (Neutered dogs can't compete in the show ring, but may participate in all obedience and performance events.)

NONSURGICAL STERILIZATION

In 2003, the U.S. Food and Drug Administration (FDA) approved the world's first nonsurgical product for sterilizing male puppies between three and ten months of age. Neutersol® (Abbott Laboratories) is given by the veterinarian as an injection into each testicle using a fine needle. No general anesthesia is required but some puppies may need mild sedation. The procedure takes only a few minutes and your Min Pin is able to go home. Neutersol provided permanent sterilization in 99.6 percent of cases during the first field trial. A larger study of 10,000 dogs in Mexico showed that the product is both safe and effective. Complications from the injection are relatively minor, and include temporary swelling of the testicles, local pain and inflammation, and vomiting and diarrhea. Neutersol works by shrinking the testes and prostate. However, because the testicles are not removed, some testosterone still may be produced. This form of sterilization neither prevents behavioral problems nor the various physical diseases associated with the presence of male hormones.

A category of drugs, called Gonadotropin-Releasing Hormone (GnRH) agonists, takes a different approach to nonsurgical sterilization. Delivered by an implant (similar to an identification microchip) placed between the dog's shoulder blades, these products produce antibodies that prevent the pituitary gland from releasing luteinizing hormone (LH) and follicle-stimulating hormone (FSH). Without these two key hormones, dogs are unable to reproduce. Although the effects of the implant are temporary, lasting up to a year, suppressing the sex hormones—estrogen and progesterone in females, and tes-

GnRH AGONISTS

Name	Method	Application	Duration	Approved?
Suprelorin® Suprelorin12® Peptech Animal Health	Implant (deslorelin)	Male dogs (ongoing studies on female dogs)	6 months 12 months	Australia 2004 New Zealand 2005
Gonazon® Intervet International BV	Implant (azagly-nafarelin)	Female dogs and cats	12 months	European Union 2006
GonaCon™ National Wildlife Research Center	Vaccine	Deer, wildlife	Multiple years	Not yet approved by the FDA

You'll need to use a wormer if your Min Pin shows signs of worms.
Photo courtesy of Durvet, Inc. Animal Health Products.

tosterone in males—provides a number of health benefits akin to surgical neutering. (The implant must be repeated annually to provide permanent sterilization.) To date, GnRH agonists have not been approved for use in dogs in the United States.

For additional information on preventing unwanted pregnancy, see pages 179-180.

TREATING COMMON AILMENTS
Constipation

Constipation occurs when your Miniature Pinscher's diet is low in fiber or fluid, or when he overeats. It also results from lack of exercise, eating foreign matter (grass, bones, paper, cloth), tumors, spinal injury, or an enlarged prostate gland in males. Most dogs improve when they consume a diet high in fiber, and exercise daily. For occasional bouts of constipation, give Milk of Magnesia or add one teaspoon of mineral oil to your dog's food.

Coughing

This can be caused by an allergy, sore throat or tonsillitis, infection, worms, lung disease, or heart failure. Try to identify whether the cough is dry, moist, gagging, or wheezing. Over-the-counter cough medicine may relieve mild cases, but veterinary treatment is needed when coughing is accompanied by a fever, nasal or eye discharge, vomiting, or difficulty breathing.

Dehydration

The loss of water and electrolytes (sodium, potassium, and chloride) often follows prolonged diarrhea, vomiting, fever, or heat exhaustion. Signs of dehydration include dryness of the mouth, sunken eyes, loss of skin elasticity, muscle twitching, and shock. Serious cases require prompt veterinary attention. In its early stages, dehydration responds to electrolyte replacement formulas such as Pediatric STAT.

The following mixture also is effective:
   ¼ teaspoon potassium chloride
   ½ teaspoon salt
   ½ teaspoon baking soda
   1½ tablespoons sugar
   1 quart water

Mix all ingredients and keep refrigerated. Use in place of your dog's regular drinking water.

Diarrhea

Changes in your dog's diet, infection, worms, allergies, and stress can cause diarrhea. Withhold solid food for 12 to 24 hours and give ½ to 1 teaspoon of Pepto-Bismol® or Kaopectate® every 4 to 6 hours. Follow with a bland diet of cottage cheese, rice, cooked egg, or lean hamburger. If other symptoms are present or diarrhea lasts longer than 36 hours, consult the veterinarian.

Insect Stings

These can cause pain and swelling at the site of the sting. Clean the area with rubbing alcohol and remove the stinger, if you can see it, with

INTERNAL PARASITES

Type	Contact	Symptoms	Treatment
Hookworms	Contaminated soil or feces, from the dam at birth or during nursing.	Anemia, diarrhea, dark bloody stools, eggs in the feces.	pyrantel pamoate, fenbendazole, mebendazole
Roundworms	Contaminated soil or feces, from the dam at birth or during nursing.	Coughing, vomiting, pot-bellied appearance, worms passed in stool.	pyrantel pamoate, fenbendazole, piperazine
Tapeworms	Raw meat or fish, fleas are intermediate hosts.	Poor coat, diarrhea, weight loss, segments in the feces.	praziquantel, epsiprantel, fenbendazole
Threadworms	Feces, penetration of the skin.	Diarrhea, lung infection.	fenbendazole, ivermectin, thiabendazole
Whipworms	Eggs in contaminated soil.	Weight loss, mucoid-like diarrhea, bloody diarrhea.	pyrantel pamoate, fenbendazole, praziquantel, milbemycin oxime

tweezers. Try not to squeeze the stinger or it will release more toxin. Apply a cold compress to reduce swelling. Some dogs are particularly sensitive to insect stings and may experience an allergic reaction. Labored breathing, swelling of the tongue, or loss of consciousness require immediate veterinary attention.

Skunk Odor

If your dog has come into contact with a skunk, check his eyes to determine whether they have been irritated by the spray. If so, hold his eyelids open and wash his eyes under a gentle stream of lukewarm tap water. Follow with eye ointment. To remove skunk odor, bathe your dog in tomato juice, then rinse with soap and water. If skunks inhabit your area, you may want to keep a special shampoo, such as Skunk Off, on hand.

Vomiting

Many illnesses cause vomiting, including distemper, hepatitis, pancreatitis, and ulcers. Dogs also vomit as a result of excitement or nervousness, motion sickness, worms, or eating spoiled food. To treat occasional bouts, withhold food for 12 to 24 hours. Give an antacid, such as Pepto-Bismol, and allow your dog plenty of rest. Feed a bland diet for a day or two. Vomiting usually is not serious. However, if your dog has a fever, diarrhea, vomits blood, or is ill for more than 24 hours contact the veterinarian.

Worms

Worms that affect dogs include roundworms, tapeworms, hookworms, and whipworms. Dogs can acquire worms in the uterus or through nursing from an infected mother, or from contact with contaminated soil or feces. Worms also may enter the body as a result of eating raw meat or fish. Fleas play a role in the spread of tapeworms, serving as the intermediate hosts. Pets usually get worms by sniffing or licking infected material. However, the larval stage of hookworms can penetrate the skin.

Because puppies may be born with worms, they should be wormed at two to three weeks of age and again at five to six weeks. Be sure to bring a fresh stool sample to the first veterinary appointment. To prescribe the best medication, if it's needed, the veterinarian must examine the specimen under a microscope to identify the kind of worm involved. He then can choose the safest product to use. When your pet is rid of worms, you can help to prevent reinfestation by keeping your yard clean and free of feces. Also, avoid places where strange dogs come together. Worms are less of a problem in adult dogs, which seem to acquire some natural immunity that helps them fight off the parasites.

FIRST AID FOR SERIOUS CONDITIONS

First aid is an emergency treatment, administered to save your dog's life and prevent additional injury. It should never take the place of professional attention. In case of serious accident or illness, remain calm. Be sure to give priority to life-threatening conditions. Give artificial respiration or heart massage, if needed. Control severe bleeding before you attend to minor injuries.

Artificial Respiration

Your dog can stop breathing for many reasons. His air passages may be blocked by a piece of toy or bone, food, or fluids. Shock, injury, heart disease, and asphyxiation also can cause difficulty breathing. This is always a life-threatening emergency—a dog can die within three to five minutes after his oxygen supply is cut off. Make certain your dog's air passages are clear and he is breathing without difficulty before you treat other, less-serious, injuries.

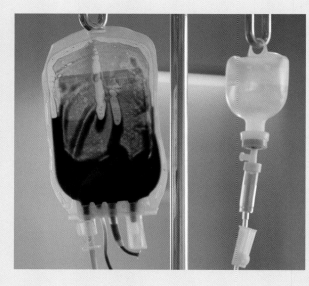

To perform artificial respiration:
- Lay your dog on his side, extending his head and neck to straighten the airway.
- Open his mouth and pull the tongue forward. Wipe off any foreign matter inside the mouth.
- Place both hands on his chest between the shoulder blades and the last rib.
- Press firmly for two to three seconds.
- Release the pressure for two to three seconds.

Repeat this pressing and releasing procedure until your dog breathes on his own.
If your Min Pin's chest has been injured, or if the previous method has been unsuccessful, use mouth-to-nose artificial respiration:

- Pull his tongue forward and close the mouth.
- Blow into your dog's nostrils until the lungs expand (use small breaths for a toy breed).
- Remove your mouth so that air is expelled.

Repeat the procedure until he is breathing on his own.
Seek veterinary help as soon as possible. If necessary, have someone drive you to the animal hospital while you continue to give artificial respiration.

Bleeding

Severe bleeding is a life-threatening emergency that requires immediate action. Always control bleeding before treating lesser injuries. Keep your dog quiet, and apply a sterile gauze pad or clean cloth over the wound. Press firmly until the bleeding stops. If a second gauze pad is needed, place it directly over the original dressing without removing the first bandage. If bleeding cannot be controlled, make a tourniquet from strips of gauze or cloth. Wrap around the injured limb above the wound, and tie a half-knot. Place a pencil on top of the loop and knot. Tighten carefully to stop bleeding. Tourniquets always must be used with caution to avoid cutting off the circulation to the affected area. Be sure to seek immediate veterinary assistance. Many animal hospitals have canine blood products on hand and can provide a transfusion in case of extreme blood loss.

Choking

Symptoms of choking include gasping for breath or gagging, pawing at the mouth or throat, and profuse salivation. If your dog is deprived of oxygen, he can lose consciousness and die within just a few minutes. A procedure similar to the Heimlich maneuver, in humans, often is successful in dislodging a foreign object blocking your dog's esophagus:

- Open his mouth and pull the tongue forward. See whether you can reach the obstruction with your fingers or forceps.

- Place your dog on his side.
- Using both hands, press the abdomen below the rib cage with a firm upward thrust.

Repeat until he expels the foreign object or it can be extracted with forceps.

Fractures
Signs of a fracture include crying out in pain, swelling, limping, or exposed bone. First, treat for bleeding or shock. Then, pad the site of the break with a temporary splint. Wrap the leg with gauze or cloth strips. Place splints on the top and bottom of the fracture and tie in place. Carefully transport your dog to the veterinary clinic.

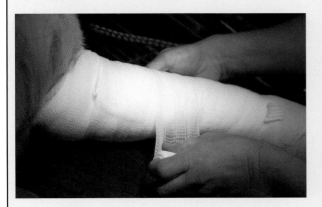

Heart Massage
Your dog's heart may stop beating as a result of injury, poisoning, electrical shock (chewing an electric cord), or serious illness. If you can't detect a heartbeat, begin heart massage immediately. You also may need to provide artificial respiration.

- Loosen your dog's collar and check the airway for obstruction.
- Lay your dog on his right side.
- Place your palms on both sides of the chest. (For very small dogs or puppies, place the thumb on one side of the chest and the fingers on the other.)
- Push downward with the hand on top, using the bottom hand for support.

Repeat compression six times, then wait five seconds. (With artificial respiration, give two to three breaths.)
Continue heart massage until his heart begins to beat or until no pulse can be detected. (A dog can live only three to four minutes after his heart stops beating.)

Heat Exhaustion and Heat Stroke
Dogs don't perspire through their pores the way people do. Because they release body heat primarily through panting, they are unable to tolerate prolonged exposure to heat. The most frequent causes of heat stroke are leaving a dog in a closed car, kenneling outdoors without enough shade or water, and exercising during hot weather. Puppies, older or overweight dogs, and those with chronic health problems are most susceptible. Symptoms of this serious condition include elevated body temperature, rapid heartbeat, staggering, dilated pupils, and pale gums. Cool your dog immediately with cold compresses, or soak him in cool water. Monitor his body temperature to make certain it does not fall below normal. Seek veterinary attention as soon as possible.

Shock
Shock—when a dog's circulatory system is unable to supply enough oxygen to vital organs—may result from poisoning, injury, heat stroke, or severe illness. Watch for a weak, rapid heartbeat, labored breathing, pale gums, cool skin, and low body temperature. Keep your dog warm and quiet, be sure his air passage is clear, and attend to serious injuries and bleeding. Shock is a life-threatening emergency that can lead to coma and death without prompt veterinary attention.

Music City's Scarlet Twiggy, owned by Betty Remington.

SENIOR CARE
11

As with many of the smaller breeds, the Miniature Pinscher is a hardy, long-lived dog. In fact, a lifespan of 15 to 17 years is not uncommon. Although a dog's hereditary background plays a role in the aging process, proper care and attention by his owner also contribute to good health in his advancing years. Before discussing specific strategies for maintaining your dog's health, it's important to understand what the aging process is—and isn't. Your Min Pin's body is made up of millions of cells: bones, muscles, organs, skin, and hair. Throughout his lifetime, these cells are nourished by oxygen and nutrients carried by the bloodstream. When the cells die, new ones are formed to take their place. During the aging process, these cells die off faster than they can be replaced. Old age is not a disease, nor must it be accompanied by disease. Most dogs enter their senior years with little or no visible decline in health. The most common signs of aging are lessening of activity, slowing of metabolism, and reduction in the efficiency of organs and glands.

PREVENTIVE CARE
Diet

Weight gain is a common problem when dogs grow older. The Miniature Pinscher tends to retain a good appetite, even during illness. However, as he slows down, he may begin to add pounds. This, in turn, puts a strain on his internal organs and may result in a shortened lifespan. To maintain his most healthful weight or to lose weight, if necessary, your dog's caloric intake must be adjusted. This is determined on an individual basis, considering his ideal weight, temperament, and activity level. The veterinarian can provide specific information on proper diet. However, older Min Pins should consume about 40 calories per pound of body weight each day. Feeding two smaller meals usually works well.

Healthy seniors need adequate levels of protein, but too much can create an excess nitrogen load that must be handled by the liver and kidneys. A dog diagnosed with advanced kidney disease could develop kidney failure by consuming more protein than he can handle. Carbohydrates, such as grains and vegetables, help your dog maintain his energy and are more easily digested than are fatty foods. Several pet food manufacturers have formulated prescription diets (available through the veterinarian) for dogs with heart, gastrointestinal, or kidney disease. There also are many diets that are specially balanced with the optimum levels of protein, carbohydrates, fat, vitamins, and minerals

---

Make me content
With fading light;
Give me a glorious sunset
And a peaceful night.
Norman B. Hall

When it's chilly outside, Midnite's For Pete's Sake, owned by Mark and Karen Fiorentino, wears this handsome sweatsuit.

for the aging dog. Table scraps and between-meal treats are the most common culprits in weight gain.

Exercise

Most dogs tend to slow down as they age, but they still can benefit from regular exercise. A daily walk (when your dog is healthy and does not have heart or kidney disease) offers many benefits. Aerobic exercise burns calories, tones muscles, and improves the efficiency of his heart and lungs. It helps the bloodstream to carry oxygen and nutrients to every cell in his body. A walk around the neighborhood provides a psychological boost, as well. Your mighty Min Pin can explore his kingdom, while meeting both new and familiar human and canine friends. Try to walk your dog on a soft surface, such as grass or soil. In inclement weather, you'll need to provide this short-haired dog with a coat or sweater. Conversely, in hot weather, walk your dog during the early morning or evening hours. If he has been sedentary for a while, approach this new regimen gradually. Walks should be very short and easy until your dog builds stamina. If he enjoys it, swimming is an excellent activity that puts little stress on his joints. Several Min Pin owners report that they buy "kiddie pools" in the summer for their dogs to play in. (Always monitor your dog when he is swimming.)

Safety

The number one killer of dogs is the automobile. However, the responsibility lies not with drivers, but with owners who allow their dogs to run free. No dog should roam unsupervised. For older dogs whose hearing and eyesight have diminished, this practice is particularly dangerous. All dogs—especially toy breeds—need a safe and secure environment with a fenced-in yard or enclosed kennel run. Safety is important indoors, too. Never permit your elderly Min Pin to jump on or off furniture, as this may cause a sprain or broken bone. Also, avoid rearranging the furniture if your dog has vision difficulties. A few common-sense precautions can help your Min Pin remain mobile and pain-free throughout his senior years.

Veterinary Attention

Regular visits to the veterinarian are important in both the prevention and early diagnosis of illness. By the time your Min Pin is seven or eight years old, he should be examined every six months. Veterinarians recommend that certain tests be performed before the onset of disease in order to have baseline measurements for comparison purposes. The most common screening procedures are urinalysis, stool exam, complete blood count, electrocardiogram or cardiac ultrasound, and chest x-ray. Occasionally, liver and kidney function tests also are performed. A thorough physical exam is useful, too, in diagnosing tooth and gum disease, tumors, problems in vision or hearing, nutritional deficiencies, and coat and skin conditions. As in human medicine, early detection is the key to successful treatment.

PROBLEMS AFFECTING OLDER DOGS
Arthritis

The most common form of arthritis to affect dogs is osteoarthritis, a progressive disease that causes pain, swelling, and inflammation of the joints. Nearly a quarter of all senior dogs experience symptoms: difficulty lying down or getting up; reluctance to walk, run, or climb stairs; stiffness or limping; crying or even growling when touched in a particularly sensitive area. Large breeds face the greatest risk of developing arthritis. However, small dogs also are susceptible—especially those that are overweight. Losing weight and participating in moderate exercise not only reduce pain, but also strengthen the muscles that support the joints and increase mobility. Other predisposing factors include hip or elbow dysplasia, earlier injuries to the joint, or simply repeated wear and tear that come with advancing age.

If your Miniature Pinscher shows signs of arthritis, have the veterinarian perform a complete examination. X-rays can pinpoint joint narrowing and destruction, as well as new bone formation around the joint. The veterinarian may recommend nonsteroidal anti-inflammatory drugs. NSAIDs work by inhibiting prostaglandin, a form of fatty acid that induces inflammation. Although newer NSAIDs are safer than previous drugs, they still carry a risk of side effects. If you notice vomiting, diarrhea, or fatigue, contact the veterinarian

At 14 years of age, Ch. Jay-Mac's Scarlet Ribbon, owned by Colleen Flight, maintains the distinguished appearance that made her one of South Africa's top show dogs.

immediately. More serious problems include gastrointestinal bleeding, and kidney or liver damage. (Never double up on NSAIDs, or give along with aspirin or cortisone.) Although NSAIDs work quickly to relieve pain and inflammation, they don't halt the progression of osteoarthritis.

Cartilage, which covers the joints to provide a cushion during movement, continues to degrade until the friction of bone-on-bone contact causes pain that limits the joint's range of motion. The nutritional supplements, glucosamine and chondroitin, help to repair cartilage. Glucosamine, which comes from shellfish, is a natural component of cartilage, whereas chondroitin, derived from animal cartilage, improves elasticity and inhibits its breakdown. Researchers also have seen improvement from adding omega-3 fatty acids to the diet. All three of these "nutraceuticals" are found in prescription diets, such as Hill's® Prescription Diet® j/d™ Canine and Purina Veterinary Diets® JM®, that are specifically formulated for dogs with arthritis. With a multifaceted approach to treatment that may include medication to relieve pain and inflammation, supplements to rebuild cartilage, acupuncture, chiropractic care, and—in severe cases—surgery on the joints, dogs with osteoarthritis can enjoy an improved quality of life well into their senior years.

Coat and Skin Problems

Skin is the body's largest organ. The outer layer, or epidermis, is thickest over the nose and foot pads. The most delicate areas are the groin and underarm. Beneath this layer, the dermis supplies nourishment to the epidermis. It also gives rise to the skin appendages—hair follicles, sebaceous glands, eccrine glands, and toenails. When your Min Pin ages, his skin may become dry and scaly. This occurs because his oil-producing glands are slowing down. Regular brushing and rubbing with a grooming cloth improve the coat's health by distributing these oils to the entire hair shaft. Massaging your dog's skin aids

NSAIDS APPROVED FOR TREATING OSTEOARTHRITIS IN DOGS

- DERAMAXX® (deracoxib)
  Novartis Animal Health
- EtoGesic® (etodolac)
  Fort Dodge Animal Health
- Metacam® (meloxicam)
  Boehringer Ingelheim Vetmedica
- Previcox™ (firocoxib)
  Merial Limited
- Rimadyl® (carprofen)
  Pfizer Animal Health
- Zubrin® (tepoxalin)
  Schering-Plough Animal Health

blood circulation and stimulates new growth. It helps to remove dirt and dead hair, as well, because older dogs tend to require less frequent bathing. Many Min Pins gray as they age, and the rate of graying is hereditary. Evidence also suggests that a deficiency of PABA (para-aminobenzoic acid, one of the B-complex vitamins), may result in early graying. Other important nutrients are biotin, another B-complex vitamin, and omega-3 fatty acids. Because thinning hair or bald patches can signal a variety of ailments, contact the veterinarian if you notice changes in your Min Pin's coat.

Cognitive Dysfunction Syndrome

Shifts in activity level. Forgets commands. Restless at night. Housebreaking accidents. These and other behavioral changes may signal the onset of Cognitive Dysfunction Syndrome (CDS) in elderly dogs. According to a study by U.C. Davis School of Veterinary Medicine, nearly two-thirds of dogs ages 11 to 16 show at least one sign of the disorder. CDS is a progressive condition that results from a series of complex physical and chemical changes that take place within the brain. These include:

- Reduction in brain mass.
- Vascular changes that impair blood flow.
- Increased levels of the enzyme monoamine oxidase (MAO-B), which is known to

deplete the neurotransmitter (chemical messenger) dopamine. In humans, a deficiency of dopamine is a key factor in Parkinson's disease, as well as Alzheimer's disease. It plays a role in a number of critical functions within the brain.
- Increased levels of free radicals, leading to DNA damage within cells. This damage eventually may result in cellular mutation and death, and even cancerous conditions.
- Buildup of amyloid plaques. Beta amyloid is a harmful protein substance that impairs the function of neurons and neurotransmitters, and leads to cell death. This accumulation of plaques, in dogs, is similar to that seen in human Alzheimer's patients, except dogs don't develop the characteristic late-stage "tangles." Young dogs have very little amyloid, whereas seniors have much greater amounts. The level of buildup is strongly associated with the degree of cognitive dysfunction.

Managing CDS—Owners often are the first to notice changes in their pets' behavior. It's important to bring such signs to the veterinarian's attention, as soon as possible, so that blood tests and other screenings may be performed to rule out various medical problems. Only when conditions, such as vision and hearing loss, pain, heart and neurological disorders, or hormonal abnormalities, are ruled out is the diagnosis of CDS appropriate. Although the disease is progressive and currently no cure is available, early intervention is vital in improving symptoms and delaying development of the disease, along with maintaining a positive quality of life. Successful management typically involves three elements: medication, nutritional supplementation, and behavioral training and enrichment activities.

Currently, ANIPRYL® (Pfizer Animal Health) is the only FDA-approved drug for treating the clinical signs of CDS. Anipryl (selegiline hydrochloride) works by inhibiting the action of MAO-B, thereby enhancing the action of dopamine. It also offers a protective effect to cells and helps to reduce the production of free radicals. Other medications, including nicergoline and propentofylline, which are not yet approved by the FDA, may benefit dogs by increasing blood flow in the brain, along with guarding against further cell damage.

BEHAVIORAL CHANGES ASSOCIATED WITH CDS	
Confusion / disorientation • Becomes lost in house or yard • Gets "stuck" in corners • Stares into space • Wanders / paces • Forgets previously learned commands • Increased anxiety	Rule out vision and hearing problems.
Social / environmental interaction • Changes in activity level • Doesn't greet owners • Doesn't respond to petting • Doesn't want to play	Rule out vision and hearing problems, pain, heart and neurological disorders.
Sleep / wake cycle • Sleeps more during the day • Awake or restless at night	Rule out vision and hearing problems, pain, heart and neurological disorders.
Housetraining • Goes to the bathroom indoors • Doesn't signal to go out • Can't find the door	Rule out GI and urinary tract problems, and hormonal conditions, such as diabetes.

A variety of clinical trials suggest that supplementing the diet with antioxidants—especially vitamins C and E, and beta carotene—slows the progression of CDS by neutralizing the harmful effects of free radicals. Ginkgo biloba, phosphatidylserine, and other essential fatty acids also are being studied to determine their role in combating the signs of CDS. According to Hill's Pet Nutrition, dogs that consume its specially formulated Hill's® Prescription Diet® b/d® Canine—which contains antioxidants and fatty acids—show improvement in performing tasks as early as two to eight weeks after starting on the diet. Another antioxidant supplement, Aktivait® (Vet-Plus), is given daily in capsule form.

Because elderly dogs with Cognitive Dysfunction Syndrome may forget their commands, make housetraining mistakes, or even get "lost" in their own home, perhaps the most important component in improving daily life for both owners and their pets is a consistent program of mild exercise, simple training routines, and mental stimulation. As discussed previously in this chapter, exercise not only improves overall circulation but also provides much needed opportunities for socializing, exploring, and stimulation. Walk at an easy pace and keep treks short if your dog is out of shape. For added interest, spend part of the excursion in areas your dog is not familiar with. This offers a variety of new "smells" even if his vision or hearing has diminished.

You *can* teach an old dog new tricks—or retrain old tricks. One of the most common signs of CDS is forgetting previously learned commands or housetraining rules. Significant progress is possible when you spend a few minutes each day practicing simple training exercises. Be sure to approach training with patience and kindness, remembering your Min Pin's limitations, and follow all successful attempts with a positive reward, such as a treat, favorite toy, or play period. Games play a key role in mental stimulation, as well. Try fetch, hide-and-seek, find-the-treat, and others to give your dog the opportunity to solve puzzles.

By taking action at the first signs of CDS—with medication, an antioxidant-rich diet, and enrichment activities—owners can help their Min Pins enjoy their senior years despite whatever disabilities may occur.

Heart Disease

When dogs grow older, they may cough or become short of breath after relatively light activity. The pulse may be rapid or weak, and their muscles may lose their tone and firmness. These symptoms sometimes indicate the early stages of heart failure. Aside from birth defects, heartworms, and infections, old age is the most common factor predisposing the Min Pin to heart disease. Unlike humans, dogs rarely develop hardening of the arteries. Canine heart disease usually involves the valves or heart muscle. When the valves become diseased, blood leaks back into the heart chambers. A weakened heart muscle has difficulty pumping blood throughout the dog's body. Treating heart disease is complex. Often, the liver, lungs, and kidneys also are involved. Management consists of a low-calorie diet, if your dog is overweight; reduced sodium intake, with diuretics to control fluid retention; and some restriction of activity. Depending on the particular problem, the veterinarian also may suggest medication to strengthen heart contractions and regulate the heartbeat.

Kidney Disease

Is your Min Pin drinking and urinating more than usual? Combined with vomiting or diarrhea, weight loss or dehydration, or fatigue or muscle weakness, these symptoms may point to a problem with the kidneys. Kidney failure may be sudden and acute—in cases of infection, such as leptospirosis or distemper, exposure to antifreeze or rat poison, excessive amounts of grapes or raisins, or even as a side effect of certain medications. Pet food contaminated with harmful additives led to a number of kidney failure cases, in 2007, and a widespread recall of many popular brands. However, the most common ailment to affect dogs is the slowly progressive chronic renal failure (CRF). Nearly 25 out of every 1,000 dogs above 10 years of age show signs of CRF. Kidney failure often accompanies congestive heart failure in elderly dogs.

The main purpose of the kidneys is to remove toxins from the blood and safely excrete them in the urine. The kidneys then return water to the body to prevent dehydration. Other functions include regulating the balance of minerals, calcium and phosphorus, and electrolytes, potassium, sodium, and chloride; controlling blood pressure; and producing the hormone, erythropoietin, which stimulates the bone marrow to make red blood cells. When the filtering units, called nephrons, become damaged, the kidneys no longer function properly. This causes waste products—blood urea nitrogen (BUN), creatinine, and phosphorus—to build up in the blood. Urine becomes more dilute when nephrons can no longer reabsorb water, and may contain bacteria or protein. Blood and urine tests are used to diagnose kidney disease. However, signs may not be apparent until at least three-quarters of the supply of nephrons no longer function properly.

Conservative treatment aims to control symptoms of CRF while minimizing further damage to the kidneys. Diet plays a key role in this process. Because urea is a byproduct formed when the body metabolizes protein, veterinarians traditionally have recommended low-protein diets for their patients with kidney failure—and even for healthy senior dogs. However, recent studies show that adequate levels of protein are critical in preventing malnutrition, weight loss, and muscle weakness for dogs of all ages. Today, veterinarians suggest matching the protein level to the severity of kidney failure. Dogs with early stage CRF need a diet that contains a moderate level of high-quality protein, whereas those with advanced disease benefit from protein restriction. Reducing protein helps dogs feel better because fewer waste products, which may cause nausea or vomiting, enter the bloodstream. It helps to lower the amount of phosphorus, as well. Elevated levels lead to hyperphosphatemia, which affects not only the kidneys but also the skeleton and heart. Phosphate binders, such as Renagel® (GelTex Pharmaceuticals, Inc.) and Epakitin™ (Vétoquinol), may be given if dietary restriction fails to lower phosphates in the blood.

Another component involves the addition of fermentable fiber, such as beet pulp, to the diet. This enables beneficial bacteria in the intestinal tract to metabolize nitrogen-based wastes and eliminate them in feces rather than urine. The recently developed supplement, Azodyl™ (Vétoquinol), contains a specially formulated combination of these bacteria that target BUN and creatinine. By safely excreting toxins from the bowel, through a process the company calls Enteric Dialysis®, Azodyl helps to prevent further damage to the kidneys.

Because dogs with CRF have difficulty concentrating their urine, water-soluble vitamins—B-complex and C—along with vitamin D, calcium, and potassium may be needed. Omega-3 fatty acids, combined with vitamin E, have shown promise in reducing inflammation and slowing the progression of kidney failure. Prescription diets formulated for CRF, including Eukanuba Veterinary Diets Early Stage or Advanced Stage and Hill's® Prescription Diet® k/d® Canine, contain these added nutrients. Make certain that fresh drinking water always is available.

Medications used to treat the effects of kidney failure include the ACE inhibitor, enalapril, to reduce protein loss in urine; calcitriol, to regulate calcium and phosphorus levels; H2 blockers, to improve nausea and vomiting that may accompany advanced kidney failure; and the hormone, erythropoietin, to treat anemia.

Dialysis and Kidney Transplantation—Fluids may be given—intravenously or under the skin—to boost the kidneys' ability to filter wastes. Adding fluid increases the blood volume that flows through the kidneys. This gives the remaining functioning nephrons more opportunities, with each "pass" of the blood supply, to remove urea, creatinine, and phosphorus. However, fluid therapy still relies on the kidneys.

Hemodialysis, in contrast, uses a machine—an artificial kidney—to clean the blood. Dr. Larry Cowgill established the first dialysis center for pets, in 1990, at U.C. Davis School of Veterinary Medicine. Using human devices modified to accommodate small pets, blood is removed, circulated through a special filter, and then returned to the body. Dialysis may be provided on a short-term basis, for acute kidney failure resulting from antifreeze ingestion or various infections, or permanently, in cases of chronic renal failure. Each treatment takes at least five hours and must be scheduled three times a week. Recovering dogs may need several weeks of dialysis before their kidneys function on their own. The Animal Medical Center, in New York City, estimates the cost of the first three to four weeks of hemodialysis at $10,000 to $15,000. Services also are available at the following Schools of Veterinary Medicine: University of California, University of Pennsylvania, Tufts Cummings, and Louisiana State University.

The newest—and most aggressive—treatment is transplantation. Pioneered at U.C. Davis more than 20 years ago, the surgery's early success was limited by dogs' rejection of their new kidneys. However, improved drugs to suppress the immune system have enabled the college to renew its transplant program. Patients and donors must undergo a strict battery of tests and be healthy—except for their kidneys. Postsurgical complications still occur. U.C. Davis lists on its Web site a 40 percent survival rate, with the longest transplant recipient living 8 years. Auburn University's College of Veterinary Medicine is working to develop a surgical procedure that might eliminate the need for lifelong medication. By performing a bone marrow transplant along with the kidney transplant, dogs may be less likely to reject their new organs. Costs for screening, surgery, and hospitalization are $11,000 to $13,000 at U.C. Davis, with medications at $100 or more a month. The University of Florida also performs kidney transplant surgery in dogs.

Joanne Wilds' first Min Pin, International Champion Jo-El's Chances Are CD CGC TDI, turned 15 in May 2007. Chaz was shown in western Europe and completed championship requirements in Spain, Portugal, and Gibraltar, as well as being an AKC champion, obedience title holder, and registered therapy dog.
Chaz was bred by Elaine Bingham of Jo-El Kennels. Owned and loved by Joanne Wilds.

Urinary Incontinence

Characterized by dribbling or the loss of urine during sleep, incontinence affects up to two million elderly female dogs in the United States alone. Although incontinence can occur in young dogs, as well as males, spayed females are at the greatest risk due to their reduced levels of estrogen. To properly control urination, the bladder's sphincter muscle—controlled by the nervous system—remains closed until the dog needs to urinate. Estrogen is a key hormone in providing tone to the sphincter. When the muscle relaxes too much, the dog involuntarily leaks urine.

One method of treatment is to supplement this lack of estrogen with replacement hormones. Short-acting natural estrogens, such as Incurin (Intervet International B.V.), are preferred over the older synthetic hormone, diethylstilbestrol (DES). However, the current treatment of choice for urinary incontinence is phenylpropanolamine (PPA)—a nonhormonal drug that acts directly on the sympathetic nervous system. By stimulating receptors in the urethra, PPA increases the sphincter's tone to alleviate urine leakage. Improvement may be seen in as little as a week. Side effects are rare, but may include loss of appetite, restlessness, and increased blood pressure. PPA medications—Propalin™ (Vétoquinol), Cystolamine® (Veterinary Products Laboratories), or Proin® PPA (PRN Pharmacal)—may be combined with estrogen supplementation, if needed, and must be continued for life.

Elderly males also may suffer symptoms of dribbling, frequent urination, and loss of control when the prostate gland becomes enlarged. The prostate is located at the base of the bladder, partly surrounding the urethra. When it enlarges, it presses on the outlet of the bladder. The two most common methods of treating an enlarged prostate are castration (preferred) and the administration of estrogen.

Tumors

A tumor is any kind of lump, growth, or swelling that occurs on the skin or inside the body. Malignant, or cancerous, tumors invade and destroy. When cancer cells multiply, they replace healthy tissue and spread to other parts of the body. Benign tumors usually are contained, and can be removed surgically. Lipomas, warts, and papillomas are the most common noncancerous growths in older dogs. Elderly females often develop a smooth, round tumor, called a lipoma, around the breast area. This slow-growing capsule of fat cells is set apart from surrounding body fat. The veterinarian may surgically remove the lipoma for cosmetic reasons, or to rule out cancer. Warts and papillomas are small skin growths that may be removed if they become irritated or start to bleed.

About half of all canine cancers are visible as growths or sores on or beneath the skin, in the perianal area, mouth, or breast tissue. Be sure to have the veterinarian check any lump or sore that does not heal. Internal cancers most often occur in the gastrointestinal or reproductive tracts. Symptoms include difficulty eating or digesting food, bowel disturbance, or vaginal discharge or bleeding. One of the most common—and preventable—cancers in older females is mammary cancer. Occurring in dogs over six years of age, signs include enlargement of the breast and occasionally skin ulceration. If cancer is confirmed, the tumor must be surgically removed. Early detection is essential in treating this cancer before it spreads. Spaying females before the first heat cycle greatly reduces the likelihood of developing mammary cancer in later years.

Vision Problems

Watch your Min Pin's eyes as he grows older; many illnesses reveal themselves in changes in the eyes. Jaundice, a disease of the liver, often causes the whites of the eyes to yellow. Kidney disease may show up in the retina as hemorrhage. Excessive brightness in the whites of the eyes may signal anemia, whereas twitching could indicate an ear infection, concussion, or stroke. Often, dogs acquire a bluish-gray haze over their eyes, due to the normal aging of the lens. Called nuclear sclerosis, this condition rarely causes significant vision loss and treatment is not necessary. Nuclear sclerosis may be confused with cataracts, a condition in which the lens becomes partially or fully opaque. Hereditary factors are involved in cataract development—especially juvenile cataracts—and certain breeds seem to be more susceptible than others. They also may be a complication of diabetes. (Cataracts form in 75 percent of dogs diagnosed with diabetes.) Dogs may retain some degree of vision even when the lens becomes opaque. Cataracts—if left untreated—frequently cause inflammation within the eye that requires regular lifetime use of medicated eye drops. This lens-induced uveitis eventually can lead to glaucoma or detached retina. Surgical removal of the lens and implantation of an artificial lens restores functional vision when your dog is completely blind. The procedure performed on dogs is very similar to human cataract surgery.

Ch. Kelly-Radel's Music Man is the most titled Miniature Pinscher in the breed's history. Owned by Edward T. and Rose J. Radel, and bred and co-owned by Sharon Kelly, Skippy is a World, International, American, Bermudian, Costa Rican, Dominican, Canadian, South American, Peruvian, Bi-Peruvian, and Puerto Rican champion, and Champion of the Americas.

READY, SET, SHOW
12

One of the earliest dog shows reported in the United States took place in Chicago on June 4, 1874. Sponsored by the Illinois State Sportsmen's Association and featuring an entry of 21 dogs, the event was described in *Field and Stream* as "an exhibition of dogs without any attempt at testing their hunting ability." Three years later, the prestigious Westminster Kennel Club held its first show in New York City's Hippodrome. Today, more than 2,600 all-breed and specialty clubs host over 1,300,000 entries each year. According to recent statistics, Miniature Pinscher championships accounted for nearly 200 of the 16,000-plus titles awarded annually by the American Kennel Club.

Why have dog shows enjoyed such popularity during the past 100 years? For many exhibitors, showing is an activity in which the entire family can participate. Children and adults have the opportunity to make friends and travel, as well as to learn new skills and test their abilities in competition with other dog enthusiasts. Most individuals begin showing dogs as a hobby. As their knowledge increases and they develop a critical eye for their chosen breed, some persevere to become serious breeders. These dedicated enthusiasts show their dogs for a variety of reasons: to spotlight their kennels' accomplishments, to compare the results of their breeding programs with those of other kennels, and to let others see those dogs that could improve their own lines.

Ch. Donnelly's Midnight Lace, owned by Don and Mary Donnelly, finished her championship at the Westminster Kennel Club Dog Show. According to the Donnellys, Lacy loved the show ring. When the audience applauded, she would prance and lift her front feet as high as her chest. Lacy is a powerful, beautifully marked Miniature Pinscher with a natural hackney gait and a graceful, arched neck.

Let us, then, be up and doing,
With a heart for any fate;
Still achieving, still pursuing,
Learn to labor and to wait.
Henry Wadsworth Longfellow

Ch. Merrywoods Wild Irish Rose and Ch. Merrywoods Call Me Karlee are two sisters owned by Hal and Patsy Pawley. Photo by Tim Golden.

CLUBS AND CLASSES

Dogs earn the title, "champion," by competing for points against others of the same breed at member, licensed, and specialty shows. Member shows are held by clubs that are members of the American Kennel Club. Licensed shows are given by nonmember clubs that have been granted permission to hold a particular show. Specialty shows, both regional and national, bring together Miniature Pinscher fanciers for a variety of educational programs, as well as show and obedience competition. Sanctioned matches—called fun matches—don't award points, but provide an excellent training arena for inexperienced dogs and handlers.

In breed competition, Min Pins may enter one of seven regular classes: Puppy, Twelve-to-Eighteen Month, Novice, Amateur-Owner-Handler, Bred-by-Exhibitor, American-Bred, or Open. Each class further is divided into sections for dogs and bitches. Because your Min Pin may be eligible to enter more than one class—Bred-by-Exhibitor and Open, for example—always select the category in which he stands the best chance of finishing undefeated. (The seven class winners are the only dogs that go on to compete for show points.)

Puppy Class

Puppies that are between 6 and 12 months of age, and not yet champions, compete in this class. Shows with a large number of entries, such as national or local specialties, may further divide the field into Six-to-Nine Month and Nine-to-Twelve Month Classes. The Puppy Class is ideal for youngsters that are not fully developed or are inexperienced in showing. Min Pins often win points from this class and some even earn their championships. For example, Starluck's This One Is Mine, owned, handled, and bred by Betty Radcliffe, took Best of Breed and Group 1 from the Puppy Class. Armando Angelbello's Ch. Marlex Mercedes won Best Puppy in Sweepstakes in her first show at the 1995 MPCA National Specialty and went on to finish her championship from the Six-to-Nine Month Class with a Best of Breed and Group 2. However, the greatest accomplishment by a puppy took place at the Idaho Capital City Kennel Club's show, in 1982, when Ch. Zellmat's Whiff of Kloeber, owned and handled by Nancy Mathieu and bred by Irene Kloeber and Linda Talbot, went Best in Show from the Puppy Class. At six months and eight days old, she is believed to be the youngest bitch (all breeds) to win Best in Show.

Twelve-to-Eighteen Month Class

This division, a stepping stone from Puppy to the more advanced classes, is open to all non-champions between 12 and 18 months of age. Often, handlers choose this class when others are expected to have a large number of entries.

Novice Class

This class is for beginners that have not yet won three first prizes in Novice, a first place in Bred-by-Exhibitor, American-Bred, or Open, or one or more championship points. At large shows, Novice often has fewer entries than the more popular Puppy and Open Classes and it allows less-experienced handlers to compete with others at the same level.

Amateur-Owner-Handler Class

This class, beginning in 2009, is for non-champion dogs that are handled by their amateur owners. No professional handlers or their assistants, or dog judges, are permitted.

Bred-by-Exhibitor Class

Dogs entered in this class must be owned, or co-owned, and handled by the breeder or a member of his immediate family: spouse, parent, brother, sister, or child. The Bred-by-Exhibitor Class is an excellent choice for Min Pin breeders interested in highlighting their kennels' accomplishments.

American-Bred Class

When dog shows began in the United States, many top winners came from established British and European kennels. To stimulate interest in domestic breeding programs, the AKC initiated a special class for American-bred dogs. Any dog (excluding champions) over six months, bred and whelped in the United States, is eligible to compete in this category. Many handlers use American-Bred as a transition between Puppy or Novice and Open for less-mature or inexperienced dogs.

Open Class

Miniature Pinschers over six months, including foreign dogs, compete in the Open Class. (Foreign puppies also may compete in the Puppy Class.) Professional handlers show in this category and all dogs must be mature, well trained, properly presented, and in top condition. Although Min Pins develop fairly early, compared with other breeds, they should be at least a year old before you embark on an extensive showing schedule.

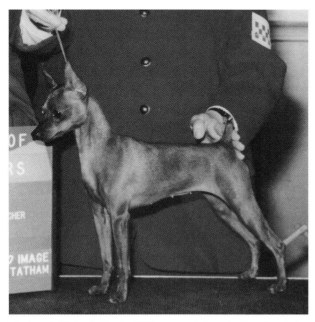 

Karlee (left) took Best of Winners at the Yankee Miniature Pinscher Club and Rose (right) won Best of Breed at the Warrenton Kennel Club dog shows. Both Min Pins are handled by the Pawleys.

Ch. Bentwater Peppermint Twist, owned by Sherry Bernard, placed first in Group competition.

Winners Class

After the judge has finished evaluating all male Miniature Pinschers in the seven classes (assuming each class had entrants), the first-place winners then compete in the Winners Class to determine the Winners Dog. This is the only male that receives championship points. The second-place finisher in this event takes Reserve Winners. Judging of female Min Pins follows the same pattern. The class winners meet to vie for Winners Bitch and the second-place Reserve Winners.

Best of Breed

When all regular classes have been judged, the Winners Dog and Winners Bitch, Champions of Record, and dogs that have completed the requirements for a championship, compete for Best of Breed. If the Winners Dog or Winners Bitch wins, he or she automatically receives the award Best of Winners. If another dog wins BOB, the Winners Dog and Winners Bitch compete together after the judging for Best of Winners.

To select the Best of Opposite Sex to Best of Breed, all entries of the opposite sex, including the Winners Dog or Winners Bitch, compete. For example, if the BOB choice is male, all females in the class, and the Winners Bitch, compete for the title Best of Opposite Sex. At an all-breed show, the Best of Breed winner goes on to Group judging and, if he or she wins first place, then to Best in Show.

CHAMPIONSHIP POINTS

The Winners Dog and Winners Bitch are the only two Miniature Pinschers that receive championship points. To become a Champion of Record, a dog must earn 15 points. He must win six or more points at two shows—three or more points (called a major) at each show—under two different judges. An additional judge (or judges) awards the remaining points. An excellent dog, therefore, can finish his championship in three shows, by winning three 5-point majors.

The number of points a dog can win varies from zero to five, depending on the number of

(Ch.) Shellamar's The Dream Catcher, owned by Cheryl M. O'Brien and handled by L. Mae Evans, took major points at this dog show as Best of Winners and Best of Opposite Sex.

dogs defeated. If the Winners Dog or Winners Bitch wins Best of Breed, all BOB competitors are added to the number of defeated dogs in regular classes to determine the points. If the dog wins the Toy Group or Best in Show, he takes the highest number of points (often five) earned in Group or Best in Show competition.

NONREGULAR CLASSES

Specialty shows often feature a variety of nonregular classes, which do not carry championship points. Except for the Veterans Class, these take place after Best of Breed competition.

Veterans Class

Open to both champions and nonchampions, the Veterans Class is held before Best of Breed judging and is the only nonregular class in which the winner also competes for Best of Breed. Dogs must be over a certain age, usually seven years. Since gaining the AKC's approval in 1992, spayed bitches and neutered dogs are eligible to compete at independent specialties and shows that don't offer additional prizes beyond Best of Breed.

This class is an excellent choice for the young-at-heart show veteran. He may even surpass the current favorites. Six-time MPCA National Specialty Best of Breed winner Ch. Mercer's Desert Dust Devil won two of his national titles from the Veterans Class—at 7 and 10 years of age. Ch. Pine Hollow's Peter Pan and Ch. Roadshow Steppin on the Edge also won their National Specialty Bests of Breed from this class, in 1986 and 1999, respectively. With proper care, Miniature Pinschers hold their age well. Competition in the Veterans Class is an excellent choice for older dogs that miss the excitement of the show ring.

Brace Class

A brace—two dogs owned by the same exhibitor—is judged on the matching of size, color and markings, general appearance, and type. Males and females compete together, and the winning brace goes on to represent the breed in Brace Group competition and (if eligible) Best Brace in Show.

Team Class

This class is similar to the Brace Class, except the judge evaluates the merits of four dogs, competing as a team.

Stud Dog Class

The stud enters with two or more of his offspring, which may be from different litters or dams or have different owners. Only the characteristics of the offspring are judged. However, the winner of the class is the stud dog, although he, himself, was not judged.

Brood Bitch Class

This is similar to the Stud Dog Class, with the bitch and two or more of her offspring entered. Judged on their overall quality, the offspring may be from different litters and have different sires. Like Veterans, the Stud Dog and Brood Bitch Classes are open to neutered dogs and spayed bitches.

Ch. Lulin Banana Smoothie, owned by Carole Anne Mohr-Rio and bred by Luis M. Colarte and Linda J. Colarte, is shown taking first place in the 12-18 Month Class.

A Miniature Pinscher is the object of
these children's delight in this shoe advertisement from 1943.

Futurity Stakes

This event is open only to dogs between the ages of 6 and 18 months, from litters that were nominated before birth. In addition, the individual puppy must be nominated before he reaches four months. Judged in separate classes according to age, males and females may compete together, depending on the number of entries. In a Futurity Stake, owners and breeders of the winning dogs receive a portion of the entry fees. Puppies must enter one of the show's regular classes to qualify for the Futurity.

Sweepstakes

Specialty shows also offer Sweepstakes prizes for puppies and veterans. Each entrant pays a fee that is divided among the Best Puppy in Sweepstakes, Best of Opposite Sex to Best Puppy, Best Veteran in Sweepstakes, and Best of Opposite Sex to Best Veteran. The first four winners in each class divide the prize money. Separate classes are held for dogs and bitches, which further are divided according to age: 6 to 9 months, 9 to 12 months, and 12 to 18 months. As with Futurity Stakes, Sweepstakes puppies must be entered in one of the regular classes. In the Veteran's Sweepstakes, dogs over a certain age (usually seven years) compete for prize money. Veterans don't have to be entered in regular competition, and may be neutered. Since its initiation at the MPCA National Specialty Show, the Veteran's Sweeps has proved immensely popular with owners, dogs, and spectators.

JUNIOR SHOWMANSHIP

Junior Showmanship provides young enthusiasts with the opportunity to learn the correct method of handling their chosen breed, practice and improve their skills, gain experience before showing dogs in regular classes, and develop good sportsmanship—win or lose. Unlike other show competition, Juniors are judged solely on their handling ability and skill. The show qualities of the dog are not considered.

Classes include Junior and Senior sections—depending on the handler's age, and Novice and Open—according to the number of first prizes won. Junior handlers are judged on proper breed presentation, skill in handling the individual dog, knowledge of ring procedures, and appearance and conduct. The junior must know how to move his dog correctly, be familiar with common gaiting patterns, and be able to stack the dog and/or use the examining table. The Miniature Pinscher makes an excellent choice for Juniors, because of the dog's small, easy-to-handle size, as well as his simple grooming requirements. Juniors will need to devote extra time to table training, though, because Min Pins don't like to stand still for examination.

Ch. Mahan's Tasmanian Devil was bred, owned, and handled by Barbara Mahan. He was one of dog judge Sharon Krogh's favorite dogs. "He was 12¼ inches tall and moved like a dream," she said.

Ch. Ampins Lit'l Rascal O Larcon, owned by Amy Putnam Issleib.

THE SHOW PUPPY
13

What is a show-quality Miniature Pinscher? Is he a dog free of disqualifying traits, such as white spots or thumb marks? A dog with a minimum of faults? Or is he something more—a special competitor whose bold and fearless outlook proclaims him the King of Toys? For most exhibitors, the term "show quality" comprises those elusive characteristics of type, balance, soundness, and personality that, when combined, distinguish an average Min Pin from a great one. Ch. King Eric v Konigsbach and Ch. Rebel Roc's Casanova von Kurt had it, and they were able to pass on those qualities to their many champion offspring. Breeders have worked hard over the past several decades to define and set type in their lines, and today's show ring boasts many fine competitors.

EVALUATING PUPPIES FOR SHOW POTENTIAL

Determining show potential involves a good deal of knowledge and a lot of luck, according to the late Dr. Buris R. Boshell of Bo-Mar kennel. "One of the features that always has an effect on our selection is the disposition of the puppy. If we have a puppy in the litter that is constantly coming to us and always getting out of the box and trying to socialize, we take a special look at that one," Dr. Boshell wrote. On several occasions, Mrs. Boshell has selected a show prospect based on the puppy's outstanding personality; often the dog has turned out to be a big winner. This was true with Ch. Bo-Mar's Road Runner and, more recently, Bo-Mar's Satellite. Road Runner and Satellite "never see a stranger" and truly act like the King of Toys: a big dog in a little package.

At 3½ months of age, (Ch.) Ampins Lit'l Rascal O Larcon, owned by Amy Putnam Issleib, exhibits the traits that made him a champion: characteristic Min Pin expression, gracefully arched neck, straight back and level topline, small round feet, and high tail set. Photos by Candids by Connie.

Every thing that grows
Holds in perfection but a little moment.

William Shakespeare

Frontenac's Zipedde Zita, bred by Armand and Jacline Gratton, is owned by Edris Matulock.

Another consideration is good parentage. "The litter must be in good physical condition, so you can tell whether faults found in the pups are caused by the breeding," said George Byron, during a lecture to Australia's 4 P's All-Toy Club. (During the 1950s, Mr. Byron imported the first pair of Min Pins in Australia.) Watch all the puppies in a litter romp together, Byron suggested, then set apart the most alert, active, and healthy puppy or puppies for further consideration. Because gait is a key feature of the breed, Byron also advised watching for cow-hocks, flat feet, pigeon toes, and loose shoulders. Although a young puppy's movement is not well developed, he should move straight, turning neither in nor out.

The breed standard provides specific height requirements, so size is an important consideration when evaluating puppies. "If a dog is obviously much bigger than the rest in the litter, chances are quite good he will go oversize," said Dr. Boshell. "On the other hand, if the puppy is a runt, the chances are fairly good that he will never improve. We are, therefore, more likely to take something from the middle." Breeders who keep meticulous records on their puppies often are able to predict approximate adult size. "I can make an educated guess within ¼-inch on my own bloodlines," said the late Marie Munson of Tay-Mar kennel. "However, this changed when I brought in new blood and I had to start over again."

Puppies should have a nice wedge-shaped muzzle, flat head (not domed like a Chihuahua's), high close-set ears, dark eyes, and a gracefully arched neck. According to Dr. Boshell, "If the eyes are small, they are probably never going to get larger and, as a result, you'll get the very undesirable 'pig eye.' On the other hand, if the eyes look like those of a Chihuahua, they probably also will never improve." Show puppies should have a well-balanced, relatively short body, with a deep but not overly broad chest. Look for a straight, level topline (not rounded or humped), and a good high tail set. "Add to these traits a thick, healthy coat, vigor, intelligence, and that 'indefinable something' that even at a young age promises class in the show ring," said George Byron, "and you'll have a Miniature Pinscher with true show potential."

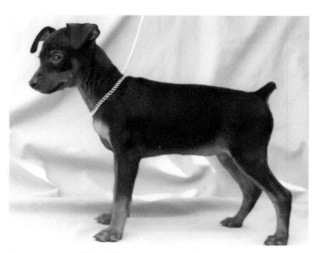

Pawznplay's Wee Weiler, from the Frontenac kennel, is owned by Lorraine Lyons.

LOCATING YOUR SHOW PUPPY

One of the best ways to find a prospective show puppy is to attend a variety of dog shows, especially the MPCA National Specialty or regional specialties. By observing dogs from different lines, you can begin to notice subtle distinctions in the types of dogs that breeders are producing. Be sure to purchase the show catalog, so that you can identify the dogs by their handlers' arm band numbers. The catalog also is a valuable resource for the names and addresses of breeders. Take notes in your catalog about the features you like and dislike about the dogs.

Also, consider subscribing to the MPCA's quarterly publication, *Pinscher Patter*, which features photographs, and pedigree information, of current show dogs. When you begin to narrow your list of potential kennels, you can start to contact breeders. Take your time in selecting your show puppy. Visit as many kennels as possible to see both the puppies and adults first

Photos, courtesy of Mauriene Pierce.

These handlers know the importance of early show training. Above: Armando Angelbello works on table training a puppy whose ears recently have been cropped.

Right: Amy Putnam Issleib practices correct show stance with Bluehen's Katydid of Ampns.

hand. Don't overlook distant breeders; many are willing to provide videos and photographs of their dogs. If you're a novice, you might consider having the puppy evaluated by a knowledgeable handler or judge. Be patient; most kennels breed no more than one or two litters each year and usually have waiting lists for the most promising puppies.

What is the best age to purchase your show puppy? Between four and six weeks, puppies are just getting up on their feet. Although breeders can discern disqualifying faults, such as white spots, most of the features are not yet formed. By six to eight weeks, though, puppies often mirror their adult structure. "I can get a brief glimpse of what each puppy will be," reported Marie Munson. "Head, ears, topline, and tail set are either good or bad. The brisket is where it will stay, the rear is strong or weak, and the hocks are either straight or cow-hocked. Leg and elbow structure does not change much after this period." Puppies often go into one or more growth stages before they reach maturity at 1 to 1½ years of age. Depending on the characteristics of the bloodline, puppies can develop cow-hocks, high rump, soft back (the back appears to bounce up and down), or loose elbows. In Marie Munson's line, these growth stages occurred at about 8½ weeks and 5 months of age. During this time,

Marie had the puppies' ears cropped and began training for the show ring. "Their little minds are starting to fill and if you don't put what you want in there, they'll fill with a lot of things you don't want," she explained.

Many owners prefer a young puppy in order to have the pleasure of watching him mature or because they believe a puppy will better bond with his family. However, faults and imperfections can develop between puppyhood and adulthood. The benefits of purchasing an older puppy or adult—if you're serious about showing—are many. Most traits will be apparent, including correct bite. In addition, the ears will be cropped and some degree of early training will have begun. The puppy might have competed at match or point shows, making your training easier. Of course, older puppies often cost more than youngsters. The breeder has put more effort and expense into training, feeding, and veterinary care. Only you can decide whether you're willing to risk choosing a young puppy that might never reach his potential as a show dog.

GROOMING FOR THE SHOW RING

About a week before the show, bathe your Min Pin with a gentle protein or baby shampoo. Rinse completely, then pour a mixture of ½-cup

Listerine® in one cup of water over the dog, from head to tail. Rub down with a coarse towel, washed without fabric softener, until your dog is dry. Trim the whiskers (optional) and any hair that extends beyond the edges of the ears. With thinning shears, tidy any stray hairs on the chest, legs, neck, or rump. Trim underneath his belly with scissors or electric clippers (using a #10 blade) to give a neat, clean outline. Just before entering the ring, brush with a bristle brush or rub the coat with the cloth side of a grooming glove. Several handlers apply a light spritz of coat polish or mink oil to add a glossy sheen. Clip the toenails and apply an anti-slip product to your dog's feet for better traction on grass or indoor matting.

EARLY SHOW TRAINING

Your Min Pin must be attentive to you in the show ring, and one way to accomplish this is with the judicious use of bait. "Start early to develop hand-eye coordination with your puppy," advised professional all-breed handler, Sue Lackey. "Every day before meals, call your puppy to you with a treat in hand. When he uses his ears correctly, praise him lavishly and reward him. Gradually withhold the treat until he is doing exactly what you want—stacking himself and looking alertly at you. The transition to the show ring will then be an instinctive, natural one."

One mistake handlers sometimes make, according to Lackey, is to concentrate so much on baiting that they fail to notice that the dog is standing incorrectly. "Many people stand right over the dog to bait him. This causes the little dog to rock back in order to see the handler, thereby giving the appearance of a 'ewe neck' and straight front. Practice baiting your dog in front of a floor mirror so you can observe what the judge sees. Get some distance between you and your dog when you bait so he uses his neck and front."

Another aspect of show preparation is lead training. "If you properly lead-train your Min Pin and keep him under control at all times, you

To be successful, a handler must learn how to present his Miniature Pinscher to the dog's best advantage, advises Sue A. Lackey. Shown here with (Ch.) Onlyone Rockin' L, owned by Thomas W. Baldwin. Note the dog's natural, uncropped ears.

should have no trouble showing him," explained Marie Munson. "Don't allow your dog to pull on the lead. This makes him look choked and it will lift his front legs off the floor. From the moment you enter the ring with your dog, don't touch him until you put him on the table for the judge's examination." Armando Angelbello, who has handled many top champions, described the Min Pin as great fun to show, but often unpredictable. "The dog's animated, inquisitive, and daring nature in the ring can make a handler look good, yet those same traits also can make him look bad and out of control." According to the late Bill Kleinmanns, owner of Ch. Bo-Mar's Road Runner, you should practice "road work" regularly with your Min Pin. "Walk the dog on-leash at a controlled pace," he suggested. "Continuous exercise at show-gait speed is better than allowing the dog to run loose in the backyard. When your Min Pin enters the ring, he will gait naturally at the correct pace."

You'll need to work on training your dog to stack, or stand properly for the judge's evaluation, as well. "The most distinctive feature of the Miniature Pinscher is his ability to present himself in the show ring, rather than being constantly posed by the handler," stated Sue Lackey. "The rule when showing Min Pins is hands off! He should be trained to stack himself 'four-square,' without assistance, and to always be alert and attentive to his handler."

Along with stacking on the ground, your Min Pin also must become accustomed to table examination. Patti Proctor, an experienced Min Pin handler, recommended that new puppy owners introduce their Min Pins to the table at an early age. "Set the puppy up and make him feel comfortable. Have strangers touch the dog while he's on the table and give lots of praise." Be patient, however. "Min Pins are not the greatest on table examination and it's sometimes difficult to get them on

Above: (Ch.) Sanbrook Savanna took Best of Winners from the Six-to-Nine Month Puppy Class for owner Ann Dutton and handler Armando Angelbello.

Right: Wil-B's Trissie and Tracie won Best Brace in Show the first time they competed as a brace. Their owner, Wilma Griffith, believes this is the first all-breed Brace BIS for red Miniature Pinschers.

Above: Ch. Dazl Reh Bold Elegance v Marlex, bred by Rex and Lonnie Phillips and owned by Chris Smith, Barbara Stamm, and Armando Angelbello. Shown with his breeders, judge Gloria Knapp, and handler Armando Angelbello. Rusty is a Top Ten Min Pin at just nine months of age.

Right: Ch. Sunbrook Indian Love Chant, owned by Sherry Bernard, is a Group-placing bitch and Honor Roll Dam.

all-fours and to stand still," noted Armando Angelbello. "Most judges, however, don't penalize them for it. Min Pins look their best when they hit the end of the lead, out in front of the line, with head and tail held high and proud."

Concentrate on perfecting your dog's performance at fun matches, said Lackey, where winning is not all-important and where you'll be relaxed. "Most owner-handlers are unaware of the mistakes they make in the ring and are quick to blame their defeat on 'politics.' Don't fall into this trap. Be objective about yourself and your dog. Be realistic about your dog's quality. If you're a novice, seek the advice of a qualified, experienced professional who is familiar with the breed. Handlers and judges are always willing to help someone who *wants* to learn. They also are a bit more objective than your competitors.

"Don't show your dog (and expect him to win) until he's ready," she advised. "You may know he's a great one, but if the dog is underweight, immature, or poorly trained, you'll lose—and deservedly so. Prepare yourself and your dog. Make certain you're trained as a team so those show-day nerves won't upset your performance. Be aware of handling mistakes you may make. Successful owner-handlers—and there are many—know their dogs' limitations and have learned how to present their dogs to their best advantage. There is no substitute for training and conditioning."

"It takes many, many years of exhibiting to understand and master the art of showing," added Patti Proctor. "If you can learn one thing at every show you attend, whether about Miniature Pinschers or another breed, learn it and keep an open mind."

Ch. Whitehouse's Oh Danny Boy followed in his father's (BISA BISS Ch. Elan's Shiloh V Whitehouse) footsteps, being shown by his breeder/owner Judith A. White. He was shown a couple of times as a puppy by his new owner, Sandee White, but was sent to Judith for his show career. He finished in two weekends earning a Best in Specialty Show at the Miniature Pinscher Club of Greater Houston and then a Group 3 coming from the classes at the huge Astrodome show. Danny went on to be a top Special, earning several more Best in Specialty Show awards and an all-breed Best in Show award. He also was a top producer—the sire of two MPCA National Specialty winners, along with Best of Breed winners at Westminster Kennel Club and AKC/Eukanuba National Championship dog shows. He lived with his owner, Sandee White, until his death, in 2007.

THE JUDGE'S VIEW
14

The cornerstone of judging the Miniature Pinscher is a thorough knowledge of the breed and its standard. To qualify as a judge, an individual must have at least 10 years' experience with a particular breed. He must have raised at least four litters, finishing two champions. Prospective judges are tested by the American Kennel Club on their specific knowledge of the breed, and on ring rules and judging procedures. After becoming licensed, many judges study related dogs—others in the same group, for example—and continue to add new breeds to their repertoire. Although the primary duty of a judge is to select the best specimen at a particular show, and to award points to the top-placing dog and bitch from the classes, his influence goes much deeper. Because breeders enter shows to evaluate the success of their breeding programs and to compare their results with those of other kennels, judges also play a key role in the development of the breed and in defining correct type. When a particular breeder's line conforms to the standard but fails in the show ring, that breeder may alter or abandon his own vision of type for that of the prevailing favorite. As with dog judge Josef Berta, whose description of the ideal Min Pin resulted in Germany's attractive, vigorous, and healthy specimens, today's judges must never abandon their responsibility to the future of this noble breed.

JUDGING BASICS

Judges develop various methods of evaluating and examining dogs through their experience with specific breeds. Although their techniques may vary from show to show, depending on the breed being examined, ring size and condition, or weather, judges follow the same pattern with each dog in a particular class. If you're a novice, a good way to prepare for your turn in the ring is to watch how the judge directs handlers in earlier classes.

First Impressions

Before examining the dogs individually, the judge attempts to gain an overall impression of the entries, either by observing the dogs from a distance or by having the entire class gait around the ring. This allows the judge to form an opinion of their type and balance. Those with the potential for placing may be apparent at this point. However, the judge does not separate the class until he has examined each dog.

Individual Examination

Min Pins, like other small breeds, are examined on the table. The judge may begin with your dog's head and mouth, then proceed down his neck, front, shoulders, body, and hindquarters. To inspect the bite, either you or the judge must open your dog's mouth. When examining

---

He was my friend, faithful and just to me.
William Shakespeare

EVALUATING THE MINIATURE PINSCHER

By Madeline K. Miller
Judges' Education Committee, Miniature Pinscher Club of America

When the average dog person thinks of Miniature Pinschers, the first thing likely to come to mind is "Hackney" or Hackney-like action. As a successful breeder-judge of this great breed, I DON'T agree with this assessment. In my opinion, the most defining measure of the breed is the *overall package*. Breed type, which includes outline, balance, hackney-like action, soundness, and correct temperament, makes the Min Pin the unique and wonderful breed that it is. While hackney-like gait is *ONE* characteristic of the breed, it is not the *ONLY* important trait. After all, I have seen breeds as diverse as Chihuahuas and Salukis exhibit (incorrectly) hackney gait. This surely does not make them Min Pins!

When a Min Pin enters the ring, the judge should see an aristocrat. They are called the "King of Toys" and must look and act the part. The Min Pin is a square dog with a smart, sleek, well-balanced, alert appearance. All the parts should gracefully flow together; the well-proportioned head, nicely arched neck blending smoothly into the shoulders, the level or slightly sloping topline, with level croup and high tail set in a muscular, wedge-shaped body combine to form one beautiful package. The Min Pin is known for his alertness, spirited presence, self-possession, and fearless animation.

Please don't be annoyed by the very temperament traits that define the Min Pin. Don't expect these little dynamos to stand like statues on the table or the ground. Min Pins are NOT judged on the table. The dogs are judged on the ground, with the table used only for a quick examination to check bite, testicles on males, eye color, and for disqualifications. This is a short-haired, single-coated breed whose physical features and condition are easy to see and evaluate without a lot of touching and fussing. Both dogs and handlers will be grateful if time on the table is kept to a minimum! Remember that Min Pins should not be faulted for moving or shifting impatiently on the table. Whether or not a dog stands on the table is a criterion that must NOT be used in the judging process; it has absolutely nothing to do with the quality of an exhibit.

On the ground Min Pins may become easily distracted and not stand still for very long. When I judge, I really don't care if they all stand in a perfect row like wooden toy soldiers, but I do want to see them "show off." They may do this by baiting for the handler, focusing on a dog in the next ring, watching a bird or butterfly at an outdoor show, or who knows what?!! They are active and curious, but have a short attention span. Not knowing what they will do next is part of their charm, and judges should learn to enjoy their antics. Please remember that Min Pins are not hand stacked on the ground, they should be taught to show themselves.

Min Pins often stop and shake at least once when they are moving. The Min Pin should gait with head and tail up. Ears may or may not be up while moving. Some handlers will tightly string up the dog trying to hide a poor front or in the mistaken belief that the dog will have better front action. Don't hesitate to ask for a loose lead. I like to see a Min Pin move out smartly ahead of the handler, but this is "icing on the cake" and not all of them can or will do this. A Min Pin who "slinks" around the ring or moves with tail down should NOT be rewarded, as this is incorrect breed temperament. A puppy may be a little unsure of himself, but an adult MUST have that great attitude that says, "Look at Me."

The correct hackney-like action is often misunderstood. The standard calls for a "high stepping, reaching, free and easy gait in which the front leg moves straight forward and in front of the body and the foot bends at the wrist. The dog drives smoothly and strongly from the rear." Note that the standard does NOT indicate that the higher the leg lifts the better. In fact, many dogs with extreme front action, when seen straight-on are out at the elbow, cross over, or have "mix-masters," all unacceptable. The side gait is correct if the dog moves in a straight line with good rear drive, front reach and extension with the pastern bending before the foot comes down. The amount of lift and bend may vary from dog to dog.

> While flashy front movement is marvelous to see, it's NOT ENOUGH. Min Pins also must have breed type, be sound coming and going, and exhibit rear drive.
>
> The Min Pin must be between 10 and 12½ inches at the highest point of the shoulder, with disqualification at both ends. All dogs within this height range should be judged equally. If there is any question about height, the judge should measure the dog. The exhibitors will respect you for this far more than putting a dog at the end of the line because you "think" it looks too big or too small.
>
> A word about color: all colors are to be judged equally. Min Pins may be solid clear red, ranging from dark mahogany to light red. Stag red is a red base coat with an intermingling of black hairs, called sable in some other breeds. In both cases, the medium to dark shades of red are preferred. The black with rust-red markings and chocolate with rust-red markings often are at a disadvantage because the broken colors create an optical illusion and may make the dogs APPEAR to be built differently than their red counterparts. Judges must be careful to assess these colors fairly.
>
> I must mention "man-made" faults. Min Pins may be shown with natural or cropped ears, as long as the ears are erect. Both types should be given equal consideration. Among the cropped dogs, there are many that have less-than-attractive ear crops; *i.e.*, short and wide, uneven lengths, missing tips. Obviously, this is man-made and should not be used to fault the dog. The same is true for tails docked too short or too long. Tail set and carriage are the important points, not length.
>
> To sum up, judge the WHOLE dog, reward the virtues, penalize faults to the extent of the deviation from ideal, and don't make Min Pins one-dimensional by only looking at their side gait!
>
> *Reprinted, with permission, of Madeline K. Miller.*

a male dog, the judge also checks to make certain the testicles are properly descended in the scrotum. Remember, your dog is judged solely on his condition at a particular show, not according to past wins or future potential.

Gaiting

After the table examination, the judge usually directs you to move your dog down and back in a straight line—going from and coming back to the judge. When your dog returns, he should free stack. Remember, hands off! "This breed is self stacking, and shows stance and temperament much better that way," explained dog judge, Thelma R. Brown. The judge then directs you to take your dog around the ring to the end of the line of competitors, to properly evaluate his profile and side movement. Occasionally, a judge may request that you and another handler gait your dogs at the same time to compare the two dogs' movement. Finally, the whole class is sent around again so the judge can confirm his placements.

Measurements

If your dog appears to be under 10 inches or over 12½ inches in height, the judge may measure him with a device called a wicket. To deter-

BIS BISS Ch. Sunsprite's Absolutely Sable, shown with owner Kimberly Pastella in the Group ring at Westminster in 1998 after winning the breed.
Photo by Gay Glazbrook.

mine whether he meets the minimum height requirement, the judge places a 10-inch wicket over the highest point of the dog's shoulders. If the legs of the wicket just touch the floor, or do not touch the floor, your dog meets the minimum height. To measure maximum allowable height, the judge uses a wicket set at 12½ inches. Unless both legs of the wicket touch the floor, your dog is measured out. Measuring helps the judge assess his own accuracy if a particular dog looks larger or smaller than other entries. Never be embarrassed if the judge wants to measure your dog.

Excusals and Disqualifications

Under certain circumstances, a judge may excuse or disqualify a dog. Dogs are excused for shyness or viciousness, illness, lameness, or having a grooming or coloring product applied to their coats. Excused dogs may not compete further at that show, but remain eligible to participate in future shows. Disqualifications include faults mentioned in the standard, along with dogs that are blind or deaf, neutered, or surgically altered (excluding tail docking, ear cropping, or dewclaw removal). Disqualified dogs may not compete again without being reinstated by the American Kennel Club.

Placing the Dogs

During examination and gaiting, the judge mentally sorts the entries and begins to decide the final placements. He often rearranges the order of the dogs in the class, and may dismiss those not under consideration. In a large class, the judge may reduce the number of potential placements in two or three eliminations.

JUDGES' OPINIONS

The process of dog judging is confusing to many newcomers—and even to veterans. Why does a judge choose a certain dog? How can novices better prepare their dogs? What is the judge looking for in a winning dog? To help clarify these

Left and above: Am. Can. Ch. Patapin Yogi Bear, Number 1 Miniature Pinscher in Canada in 2004. Yogi has been invited two years in a row to the prestigious Eukanuba Dog Show. Bred and owned by Patricia Gauthier of Patapin Miniature Pinschers.

BISS Ch. Trotwood Flyin Tiger (left), a Specialty Show winner and multiple Group winner, was bred and owned by Kathy A. Helming. All-breed Best in Show winner Ch. Carovels Jacobs Ladder (right) was the Number 1 Min Pin in 1995 and 1996, a Pedigree Award Winner, and a 2-time Best of Breed winner at Westminster Kennel Club. Owned by Philip and Jeffrey Helming, and handled by Kathy A. Helming.

questions, David and Sharon Krogh and Madeline K. Miller—who have extensive experience judging Miniature Pinschers—have offered their opinions:

What mistakes do handlers (novice or experienced) make most frequently?

Krogh: Either getting down with their dogs, or baiting their dogs into them. Getting down is a big NO-NO with a Min Pin. They should be self assured, and bait off of anything but the handler—the crowd, the other dogs in the ring—but never the handler. When the handler baits the dog into them, it spoils the neck and topline. All dogs should be trained to stand for examination!

Miller: Stringing up the dogs and going too fast.

What common faults do you see in Min Pins being shown today?

Krogh: Today's Min Pins are too refined, they are slab-sided and have bad feet. Oh, yes, and we see a lot of light eyes.

Miller: Flat feet with long toes, croupy, low tail sets, soft toplines. Over-exaggerated front lift, which causes problems coming and going.

What qualities of the Min Pin are most important to you?

Krogh: Soundness, balance, and proportion. With attitude, he should say, "I am the King of Toys."

Miller: The overall dog; *i.e.,* balance, outline, movement. Proper temperament—"fearless animation."

Do you see the correct hackney-like gait today?

Krogh: Yes and no, but that doesn't bother us. The "hackney-like action" is the hallmark of the breed in the United States and Canada, and we must live with that. But, this breed was bred in Germany, and they didn't breed dogs that could not do a job. Min Pins were bred to rat! What good would the hackney-like action do on a ratter? Soundness should be first and foremost.

Miller: Yes, sometimes.

IT'S ABOUT ATTITUDE!

By Joanne Wilds
Pinscher Patter, June 2005

There have been many articles written in *Pinscher Patter* and other publications discussing those aspects of the standard that breeders consider critical to defining the Miniature Pinscher. Movement, type, and size are just a few of those specific items that have been addressed.

After 13 years in the breed, and some experience in both the conformation and obedience rings, I feel that there is one section of our standard that is starting to lose importance with judges, to the detriment of our breed as show dogs and pets.

Our standard describes the Miniature Pinscher as having "fearless animation, complete self-possession, and spirited presence." And, for me, dogs must display this temperament, especially in the show ring.

As dog shows have progressed into our modern times, we all have begun to realize that a good deal of emphasis, for better or worse, is now placed on the "show" part of that phrase. I certainly appreciate seeing a dog displaying that "spirited presence" in the ring. And I know that dogs can overcome other tangible faults when they are "showing" themselves. That is why it is especially difficult for me to watch a class of dogs being judged in which there is one that is not displaying this attitude. I feel bad for the exhibitor because I know that, while we would all love to have these mighty "kings" keep four on the floor and follow our instructions in the ring, we would rather they made fools of us with their sometimes-outrageous "spirited presence" than have to coax an obviously nervous dog around the ring.

We all know which faults of structure we will accept, given an overall quality dog, and those we cannot accept regardless. I have, as I am sure you all have, had a dog place at the end of a class, or not at all, because of a certain fault that the judge would not accept: a wide skull, long toes, *etcetera*.

Ch. Altanero Barnstormer is a top show dog for his breeders, Joanne Wilds and Susan P. Goldman. He is co-owned by his breeders and Kim Byrd.

If you could give one piece of advice to new breeders or novice handlers to help them produce and show better dogs, what would it be?

Krogh: Find a mentor in your breed. Someone who has a record for breeding good dogs. Listen to that person when they speak! Learn your bloodlines, learn how to put a pedigree together. If your PLANNED breeding program doesn't work, find good pet homes for the puppies. Then start over. Don't show a bad dog just because you don't have a better one, breed a BETTER dog.

Miller: Study the standard and try to breed only the best. Get a mentor who can guide you in breeding and showing. HAVE FUN!

While I believe that, most of the time, I can understand a judge placing my dog, given a fault that he/she might not like, I have a hard time being placed behind (or not at all) a dog that is not showing proper temperament. Of course, anyone would naturally not appreciate being given a low placement, but what is really beginning to disturb me is that I am seeing improper temperament being rewarded more often at shows.

If a dog being shown has his tail and ears down as he is being gaited or standing/stacking, I feel that not only is this dog not exhibiting proper temperament, but that it is not possible for anyone to accurately judge other aspects of the standard—tail set, topline, gait—of such a dog. How can you tell if the dog's movement is "a high-stepping, reaching, free and easy gait," or the tail set is "high, held erect, docked in proportion to size of dog," or the topline is "level or slightly sloping toward the rear both when standing and gaiting," if the dog's tail is clamped to the rear? In the same vein, how can you tell if the ears are "set high, standing erect from base to tip" if they are held down and the head is also being held in a lowered position?

For each class, the judge has to determine the best dog based on each dog's faults and strengths and what they will or will not accept. I have observed that many times a dog that is not "showing"—head, tail, ears down—has many strengths when you see him again displaying proper breed temperament. But when I see such dogs in the ring missing this critical element of the standard, it is pretty much impossible for me to evaluate the other elements. I would not even attempt to judge the dog's overall quality as I feel it would be unfair to the dog, as well. And to see a dog being rewarded by placing in, or even winning (and, yes, I have seen that), a class when he is not displaying proper temperament causes me great concern. Given those other faults that do not directly affect each other—wide skulls do not interfere with evaluating movement or toplines—it is difficult for me to understand how a dog not showing proper temperament can ever effectively be judged on his overall quality.

Certainly, it is possible, and I have experienced it myself, that a dog has a bad day and simply won't "get up" to show. This does not mean the dog has a bad temperament or that it is not a good quality animal. But, if the dog is not displaying proper temperament, how can you really evaluate the dog's overall quality?

While the "show" in dog show is important, we must also remember the basic reason that dog shows were started—to evaluate and choose the best dogs for breeding. To place dogs displaying improper temperament over dogs that are showing proper temperament, regardless of other tangible faults does a disservice to our breed. If these dogs win classes, and possibly even win points, they are, in essence, being promoted as good breeding stock. They also are being promoted to the public, potential pet owners, watching the show as good examples of our breed.

The intangible strength—proper temperament—of this breed, the "big dog" in a little package, the "spirited presence," is the center from which all tangible strengths are supported. Without that attitude, they cannot be great show dogs.

When it comes to showing and living with our great breed, for me—**It's about attitude!**

Reprinted, with permission, of Joanne Wilds.

Ch. Pevenseys Wild N Bold, bred by Pamella Ruggie and owned and handled by Armando Angelbello, is a Top Ten Miniature Pinscher, with multiple Best in Specialty Show and Group wins. Wild N Bold also is an Honor Roll sire with 15 champion offspring, to date.

UNDERSTANDING GENETICS
15

How can we breed better dogs? Minimize conformation faults? Eliminate hereditary disorders? For centuries, fanciers have sought to improve the quality of domestic animals by mating those specimens that possessed the characteristics desired in the offspring. Thick-wooled sheep were bred to others with thick coats, top-producing beef and dairy cattle to fellow producers, fleet-footed horses to those with speed and stamina. Early dog enthusiasts, many of whom began their trade as stockmen, applied similar principles to develop the keen hunters, gentle retrievers, and feisty terriers we know today.

Surprisingly, the scientific principles behind these early breeding programs have been uncovered only within the last century. Gregor Mendel, the father of modern genetics, published his landmark work, *Experiments in Plant Hybridization*, in 1866. However, the treatise remained virtually unknown until it was rediscovered by scientists in 1900. What made Mendel's study of the simple garden pea so significant?

Many researchers before Mendel had crossed plants to form hybrid varieties, and most believed that the characteristics of the parents somehow came together and "blended" in the offspring. Mendel's conclusions, which form the basis of our present understanding of inheritance patterns, differed. Based on eight years of experiments crossing pea plants of contrasting traits (white or purple flowers, tall or dwarf vines, green or yellow seed pods), Mendel observed that in each pair one member seemed to mask the expression of the other. He identified this member, or allele, as dominant over the other.

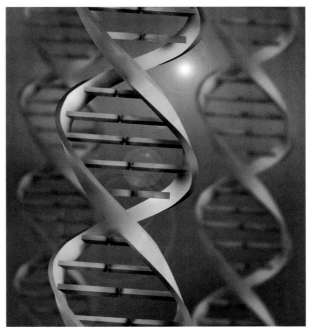

The double helix structure of DNA first was described, in 1953, by James Watson and Francis Crick.
In 1962, they shared the Nobel Prize in Physiology or Medicine with fellow DNA researcher Maurice Wilkins.
© Photographer: Lorelyn Medina
Agency: Dreamstime.com

Nothing in the world can take the place of persistence.
Calvin Coolidge

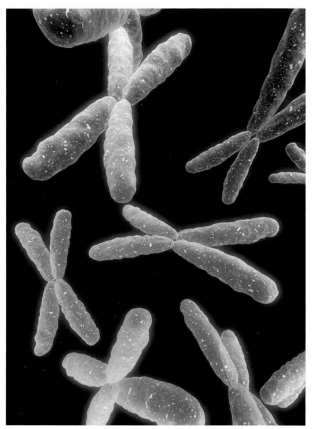

Dogs have 78 chromosomes, arranged as 39 pairs. The narrowed central area is called the centromere.
© Photographer: Sebastian Kaulitzki
Agency: Dreamstime.com

Mendel also discovered that for any single pair of traits, the offspring showing the dominant characteristic occurred in a three-to-one ratio over those with the recessive trait. Perhaps Mendel's greatest contribution to animal breeders was his observation that when he crossed plants that differed in two or more characteristics, all combinations occurred randomly in the new generation.

CHROMOSOMES AND GENES

Within the nucleus of nearly every cell exist molecules of deoxyribonucleic acid, which provide the instruction set for every part and process of an animal. DNA takes the form of a ladder, shaped as a double helix. The rungs consist of four chemical bases: adenine, cytosine, guanine, and thymine. These are abbreviated A, C, G, and T. Adenine always pairs with thymine, and cytosine with guanine, to form base pairs. Dogs have approximately 2.4 billion base pairs. It is this specific pairing that allows a cell to divide into two identical copies. During cell division, the DNA molecule "unzips" down the center, creating two half-segments. Their adjacent halves then are recreated by a special enzyme to form two segments identical to the original forms. The ladder's backbone is made up of sugar and phosphate molecules.

Each strand of DNA is organized into chromosomes. Dogs have 78 chromosomes, arranged as 39 pairs. One member of each pair comes from the sire and the other from the dam. This complete set of chromosomes is called the genome. Along the length of each chromosome lie thousands of genes. The sequence of chemical bases identifies each gene—about 19,300, in all. Surprisingly, only about 1 percent of all base pairs represent coding DNA. The purpose of the other 99 percent is not clearly understood. However, these pairs may provide spacing for the genes or stabilize the chromosome.

Genes that influence specific traits, such as pigment in a dog's coat, always occur at the same location (locus) on the same chromosome. In addition, the alleles (alternative forms) of different genes behave independently of one another (some exceptions apply). Dog breeders who identify desirable traits in both sire and dam can attempt through a long-range breeding plan to combine and maintain those characteristics. Let's apply Mendel's principle to the following *fictitious* example (in fact, the traits likely result from the actions of multiple genes). As shown in the chart on the next page, the first generation cross between a dog with *erect ears/long tail* and one with *drop ears/short tail* produces only puppies with erect ears and a long tail (EeLl). However, when the offspring are mated in the second generation, four possible phenotypes and nine genotypes occur.

> **EAR AND TAIL GENETICS**
>
> E = erect ears (desirable)
> L = long tail
> e = drop ears
> l = short tail (desirable)
>
> **FIRST GENERATION CROSS:**
> EELL (erect ears, long tail) x eell (drop ears, short tail)
>
> | | el | el |
> |----|------|------|
> | EL | EeLl | EeLl |
> | EL | EeLl | EeLl |
>
> Offspring are all EeLl (erect ears, long tail)
>
> **SECOND GENERATION CROSS:**
> EeLl x EeLl
>
> | | EL | El | eL | el |
> |----|------|------|------|------|
> | EL | EELL | EELl | EeLL | EeLl |
> | El | EELl | **EEll** | EeLl | **Eell** |
> | eL | EeLL | EeLl | eeLL | eeLl |
> | el | EeLl | **Eell** | eeLl | eell |

Phenotypes (Visible Traits)

Erect ears-long tail (E*L*)
Drop ears-long tail (eeL*)
Erect ears-short tail (E*ll)
Drop ears-short tail (eell)

Genotypes (Genetic Traits)

Erect ears-long tail: EELL, EELl, EeLL, EeLl
Drop ears-long tail: eeLL, eeLl
Erect ears-short tail: EEll, Eell
Drop ears-short tail: eell

Thus, puppies with the desirable erect ears and short tail (shown in bold in the chart) occur in only 3 of 16 possible combinations, or roughly 19 percent of the offspring. How, then, can a breeder preserve these characteristics? Mating two dogs that are "pure," or homozygous, for the traits (EE and ll), will produce offspring that exhibit and carry only the desirable characteristics. Dogs heterozygous for erect ears (Ee) also carry the recessive gene for drop ears, and could produce puppies with drop ears if mated with another drop-ear carrier. The difficulty, of course, is knowing which dog is pure and which carries the undesirable trait. The main guideline has been a test mating between the dog in question and another dog known to carry (or show) the same recessive gene. If any puppies from such a cross have drop ears (in this example), both dogs are carriers.

Another complication is that chromosomes that form a pair, homologous chromosomes, are not always transmitted intact to offspring. Sometimes, during the division of reproductive cells (meiosis), a section of one chromosome breaks off and transposes with a piece from the other. In this type of exchange, called crossing over, the genes from the transposed section, which might have come from the sire, join those genes inherited from the dam. Genes that are located near one another on the same chromosome are less likely to become separated. Such linked genes play a crucial role in a variety of genetic studies.

INCOMPLETE DOMINANCE

Mendel's plant experiments showed that the dominant allele in a contrasting pair of traits masked the expression of the other member. Certain characteristics, though, show incomplete or partial dominance. In Miniature Pinschers, for example, solid red coat color is dominant over tan markings (black or chocolate background). A dog that inherited one red allele and one tan-points allele should appear as solid red. In fact, this combination often produces the color known as stag red, or red with a sprinkling of black hairs. When genes are fully dominant, breeders can identify the genotype mainly by test matings or knowing the traits of a particular dog's ancestors. With incomplete dominance, the genotype often can be determined by the visible phenotype.

POLYGENIC INHERITANCE

Most characteristics that are important to dog breeders—height, weight, angulation—are under the control of many genes, each of which plays a relatively minor role but in combination produces significant differences. Working with a large number of genes adds to the difficulty of identifying which dominant and recessive genes are carried by prospective mates. Further, environmental factors, such as fetal nutrition, disease, and hormone levels, also affect the expression of many polygenic traits. Only by observing what given sires and dams produce, through detailed records on each puppy, can breeders achieve any degree of predictability in their lines.

CELL DIVISION (MITOSIS)

The dog's body is composed of millions of cells, each of which contains within its nucleus all the genetic information needed to regulate the activities of every other cell. During mitosis, the cell divides to form two cells exactly like itself. These new cells continue to divide throughout the dog's lifetime to form other new cells that are genetically identical.

REPRODUCTIVE CELL DIVISION (MEIOSIS)

The sex cells, or gametes, unlike other cells within the dog's body, contain only 39 chromosomes, half the full complement. During meio-

---

GENETICS TERMINOLOGY

Allele—Alternative forms of a gene that occupy the same site (locus) on a chromosome.

Autosomal—Refers to any chromosome other than the pair of sex (X or Y) chromosomes.

Chromosome—Within the nucleus of each cell, these strands of DNA contain the basic units of inheritance, the genes. Dogs have 39 pairs of chromosomes.

DNA—Molecules of deoxyribonucleic acid, which provide the blueprint for every part and process of an animal.

Dominant—The member of a specific pair of genes that is capable of masking the presence of the other member.

Gene—Occurring in pairs (one from the sire and one from the dam), like the chromosomes on which they are situated, these complex chemical structures carry the blueprint of heredity to the offspring.

Genotype—The genes that a dog carries, which may or may not be apparent by his appearance.

Heterozygous—A gene pair that consists of different alleles, such as B/b (B, black pigment; b, brown pigment).

Homologous—Chromosomes that form a pair, one from each parent.

Homozygous—A gene pair that consists of the same alleles. (B/B or b/b)

Locus—The location of a gene on the chromosome; genes that influence specific traits always occur at the same locus.

Phenotype—The observable characteristics of the dog.

Recessive—A gene that is masked by the dominant member of the pair; must be present in duplicate to be expressed.

X-Linked—Females have two X chromosomes (XX), whereas males have one X and one Y (XY). When a recessive disease gene is located on an X chromosome, males develop the disease because they then have no normal X chromosome. Females are carriers.

Zygote—The fertilized egg, containing one set of chromosomes from the sire and one from the dam.

sis, called reduction division, the chromosomes replicate and arrange themselves in pairs, with one member of the pair going to each of two new cells. This sorting of chromosomes to the new cells occurs in a purely random manner. In the formation of sperm or ova, one gamete could contain a large portion of its genetic matter from the dog's sire; another from the dam (the puppy's grandfather or grandmother). Understanding what happens during meiosis helps explain why puppies within the same litter often differ from one another. It also underscores the importance of choosing prospective mates that are prepotent for desirable traits. That is, the same allele is carried on each of the two chromosomes and is automatically passed to the offspring.

PUPPIES: MALE OR FEMALE?

A dog inherits one sex chromosome from each parent. Females possess two X chromosomes (XX), whereas males have one X and one Y (XY). When one of the dam's eggs is fertilized by a sperm bearing the X chromosome, the resulting puppy is female (the dam passes one X chromosome to each puppy, male or female). When the sperm carries the Y chromosome, the offspring is male. Although males transmit X and Y chromosomes in roughly equal numbers, more male puppies tend to be conceived because the Y-bearing sperm reaches the egg more quickly. Balancing the equation, several studies suggest that a greater percentage of female embryos result in live births.

In 2007, a company called XY Inc., based in Fort Collins, Colorado, produced the first litter of puppies resulting from specialized cell-sorting technology that identifies X- and Y-bearing sperm. Consisting of three females and two males, this Labrador Retriever litter was 60 percent accurate in delivering the desired outcome of female puppies. XY Inc.—in partnership with Colorado State University and DakoCytomation, the company that makes the cell-sorting equipment—produced the first sex-selected calf, in 1999, using frozen sexed semen and artificial insemination. (In 1992, Mastercalf Ltd., in England, produced the first sex-selected calf using *in-vitro* fertilization. Mastercalf later was acquired by XY Inc.) It also has produced the first sex-selected foals, piglets, lambs, dolphins, and kittens. Although the commercial potential for sex-selected puppies is far more limited than that of dairy cattle (its major endeavor), specific organizations, such as service dog trainers, may prefer litters of predominantly one sex.

GENETIC DISORDERS

The Min Pin is a remarkably healthy and vigorous dog, with few of the hereditary disorders associated with the more popular (and less carefully bred) dogs. In a survey for this book, most breeders who responded found few genetic disorders in their lines. Those who had experienced problems mentioned cleft palate, uterine inertia at whelping, demodectic mange, overshot or undershot bites, and retained puppy teeth. The following conditions also have been identified in the breed:

Legg-Calvé-Perthes Disease

The hip joint is a ball-and-socket arrangement in which the muscles and ligaments, as well as the shape and fit of the ball within the socket, help to maintain stability while providing a wide range of motion. A variety of hip problems affect dogs, some inherited and others due to injury or trauma. Legg-Calvé-Perthes disease (LCPD), named for the three doctors who identified the disorder in children, in 1910, occurs mainly in small breeds and results from an interruption in the blood supply to the head of the femur. When nutrients are unable to reach the area, cell death occurs and the ball becomes distorted and flattened.

Symptoms include sudden or progressive pain and lameness—usually in puppies between five and eight months of age—followed by muscle atrophy, shortening of the affected leg, and limited movement. LCPD may involve

> **THE FUTURE: GENETIC TESTING FOR LEGG-CALVÉ-PERTHES DISEASE**
>
> With donations from the Miniature Pinscher Club of America and Min Pin breeder Helen Chrysler Greene, along with the Westie Foundation of America, the American Kennel Club Canine Health Foundation is funding research at the University of Pennsylvania School of Veterinary Medicine into mucopolysaccharidosis type VI (MPS VI) and its possible association with Legg-Calvé-Perthes disease.
>
> MPS VI results from an enzyme deficiency that interferes with the breakdown of large sugar molecules in the body. This buildup leads to skeletal abnormalities similar to those seen in LCPD. By studying MPS VI in Miniature Pinschers—the first dog breed in which it was identified—researchers have discovered a mutation in the arylsulfatase gene. A DNA test can identify normal and affected dogs, as well as those who carry this mutated recessive gene. Knowing which animals are carriers is important for breeders because those dogs show no signs of the disease itself.
>
> Currently, Dr. Urs Giger and his team at Penn are working to determine whether MPS VI is related to LCPD. Because both disorders cause similar bone changes, the researchers speculate that some Min Pins diagnosed with LCPD also have MPS VI. The team is collecting DNA samples from dogs with LCPD or MPS VI. They plan to investigate whether dogs with LCPD test as normal, affected, or carrier in the MPS VI test. The ultimate goal is to develop a screening test specifically for Legg-Calvé-Perthes disease, which will allow breeders to choose only normal, noncarriers for their breeding programs.

one or both hips. Management of the disease before flattening of the bone has occurred includes rest, restricted exercise, proper diet, and pain relievers. About 25 percent of dogs recover without further treatment, although healing may take up to six months. When the ball has become distorted, surgical removal of the femoral head and neck (a procedure called excision arthroplasty) usually relieves the dog's pain and lameness. Improvement takes place gradually—up to a year after surgery—as the muscles develop to take the place of the ball-and-socket joint.

A variety of factors may predispose dogs to LCPD: infection, injury, hormonal imbalances, and abnormalities of the blood vessels in the hip. Because the disease tends to run in families, studies are underway to determine whether genetic factors are involved. Recently, the Orthopedic Foundation for Animals (OFA)—an organization dedicated to controlling the incidence of orthopedic and genetic diseases in dogs—created a database specific to LCPD. Breeders submit x-rays of their dogs' hips, which are reviewed by a board certified radiologist for any abnormalities. The results are placed in a database accessible to individuals considering dogs for their breeding programs. By carefully selecting dogs with sound hips, LCPD may one day become a disease of the past.

Patellar Luxation

Characterized by limping, pain, and difficulty straightening the knee, patellar luxation—dislocation of the kneecap—is a common orthopedic disorder in dogs. Although many breeds are affected, small dogs are up to 12 times more likely to experience dislocations than are large dogs. One or both knees may be affected. Several factors predispose dogs to knee problems, including weak ligaments and misalignment of the tendons and muscles that straighten the joint. Frequently, the "groove" in the femur is too shallow, which allows the kneecap to slip temporarily or permanently out of position.

Luxating patellas (LP) are graded from 1 to 4, depending on the severity of the dislocation. Dogs with Grade 1 patellas, the mildest form, have kneecaps that slip out of position only when the knee is manipulated during examination. It then returns to the proper position. At Stage 4, though, dogs have patellas that are constantly out of position and fail to return

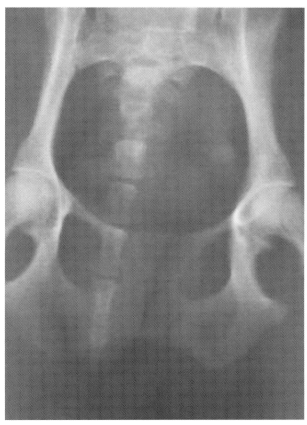

This dog has "normal" ratings for LCPD and patellas, and an "excellent" rating for hips, according to the Orthopedic Foundation for Animals' database. Photo courtesy of Cindy McNeal.

even with the hind leg fully extended. Dogs with Grade 1 or 2 patellas often have a normal gait and experience pain only when the slippage occurs. These dogs may benefit from complete cage rest along with pain medication to allow the knee to stabilize.

Surgical treatment—stabilizing procedures or bone reconstruction—helps patients with joint discomfort that affects their daily lives. A rest period is required following surgery but most dogs show considerable improvement. Because heredity is believed to play a strong role in the development of LP—the OFA tracks cases in its orthopedic database—breeders should avoid using affected dogs in their breeding programs.

Progressive Retinal Atrophy

First identified in the Gordon Setter, in 1909, progressive retinal atrophy (PRA) refers to a group of hereditary eye disorders that affects more than 100 breeds worldwide. It corresponds to retinitis pigmentosa, in humans. As its name suggests, PRA is a progressive disease that causes degeneration of the retina. In healthy dogs, the retina is the area at the back of the eye that takes in light. Specialized photoreceptors, called rods and cones, line the retina and convert the incoming light into electrical impulses that travel along the optic nerve to the brain. There, the signals are interpreted as images. Rods are responsible for black-and-white and night vision, whereas cones enable color and day vision.

The most common form of PRA is late-onset progressive rod-cone degeneration (prcd). Miniature Pinschers usually develop signs between five and seven years of age. Dogs first lose the function of rods, leading to night blindness. As the disease progresses, cones deteriorate and dogs become blind even in daylight. Secondary cataracts may form in the late stages. There are no outward signs that a dog has PRA, such as watery or red eyes. However, owners may notice dilated pupils and greater reflectivity of the retina. PRA usually affects both eyes. Currently, no treatment is available. However, some veterinarians believe that adding antioxidants to the diet might slow the degeneration of the retina, allowing a longer period of functional vision. Vitamin A is being tried experimentally in human retinitis pigmentosa. (Always check with the veterinarian before giving supplements.) Keep in mind that dogs affected with PRA rarely experience pain or discomfort. With a little extra consideration, such dogs can live a normal lifespan as family pets.

Why has PRA—one of the most studied genetic diseases in dogs—been so hard to eliminate? The greatest difficulty, until recently, has been in distinguishing dogs that have normal vision but carry the mutated gene, from non-carriers. Breeders were forced to study pedigree information or perform test matings to identify carriers. For example, when a noncarrier is bred to a dog known to be affected with PRA, all puppies will have normal vision. If any offspring of these normal dogs develop the disease, it will show that both parents carry at least one recessive PRA gene. Now, as a result of decades of research by Dr. Gustavo Aguirre, currently at the University of Pennsylvania School of Veterinary Medicine, and his team of investigators, breeders finally can rely on DNA tests to determine whether their dogs are normal/clear, carriers, or affected. Progressive rod-cone degeneration has been found to be inherited recessively, with the gene mutation mapped to canine chromosome 9. However, dominant and X-linked forms also exist in certain breeds. In 1998, OptiGen®, with Drs. Aguirre and Gregory M. Acland, offered the first prcd marker test for Portuguese Water Dogs. Marker tests look for changes in genetic sequences located near—and usually inherited with—the mutated gene, when the disease gene, itself, has not been found. Since the prcd gene was identified, in 2005, OptiGen now tests for the mutation directly. (A test is not yet available for Miniature Pinschers.)

Owners interested in up-to-date information on PRA should contact the Canine Eye Registration Foundation (CERF). Founded in 1974, by Mrs. Dolly Trauner of San Francisco, CERF functions as a national database for dogs that have been tested and certified free of hereditary eye diseases by board certified veterinary ophthalmologists. Dogs that are free of any hereditary eye abnormalities at the time of examination receive a CERF certificate, good for one year. The results also are sent to the AKC and appear on registration certificates and pedigrees. As more breeders test their dogs for PRA, and register the results with CERF, this devastating disease may eventually be eradicated from the canine population.

THE CANINE GENOME: DNA CODE OF THE DOG

For nearly 20 years, dogs and their genes—the canine genome—have been the subject of intense interest. Since the early 1990s, when the Morris Animal Foundation, American Kennel Club, and Orthopedic Foundation for Animals funded studies at the University of Michigan and Michigan State University, the goal has been to identify the genes responsible for more than 450 hereditary diseases in dogs. Before the mutant genes, themselves, had been found, early research focused on locating markers—gene variations close to the disease-causing genes on the same chromosome. Because markers usually are inherited along with the problem gene, tests could be developed that screen not only for affected dogs but also for carriers. To date, approximately 30 single-gene mutations have been identified, and tests now are available for eye problems, bleeding disorders, enzyme deficiencies, narcolepsy, and others.

In 2003, Ewen F. Kirkness, Ph.D. and his team at The Institute for Genome Research (now the J. Craig Venter Institute), produced the first sequence of the canine genome. This private data set—from Dr. Venter's Standard Poodle, Shadow—represented a partial sequence covering about 80 percent of the genome. A year later, the National Human Genome Research Institute (NHGRI) provided $30 million in funding to develop a complete genome of the dog. A Boxer, named Tasha, was chosen from among 60 breeds. The Boxer was more inbred, with less variation between the paired chromosomes, making her genetic background easier to sequence. Tasha's genome, developed by Kerstin Lindblad-Toh, Ph.D. and her associates at the Broad Institute of MIT and Harvard, and Agencourt Bioscience Corporation, covers more than 99 percent of the genome and is publicly available to scientists worldwide.

Not only will this complete map of the dog's genes enable breeders to screen for hereditary disorders in their bloodlines, ultimately leading to healthier pets, but also increase our understanding of many human illnesses. For example, of the genetic diseases known to affect dogs, nearly three quarters also occur in people—heart disease, cancer, epilepsy, hip dysplasia, and vision and hearing disorders. When the dog genome is compared to the completed human and mouse genomes, abnormal strings of base pairs are more easily located. In fact, dogs provide many advantages to researchers. Through centuries of selective breeding, often tracing back to a few key ancestors, dogs show a greater difference between breeds than do most species. This isolated gene pool predisposes certain breeds to specific illnesses, and suggests that only a small number of loci are involved—making the disease genes easier to find. In addition, purebred dogs have detailed pedigree records that go back many generations, enabling affected dogs and carriers to be more readily identified.

Breed clubs and breeders also have played key roles in the search for hereditary diseases by providing blood samples of normal and affected animals for screening purposes. Currently, the Miniature Pinscher Club of America, along with the AKC Canine Health Foundation, is funding studies of thyroid disorders and Legg-Calvé-Perthes disease in Min Pins. Other groups support research into progressive retinal atrophy, von Willebrand's disease, copper toxicosis, and many others.

"The advances of the past three years in canine genetics have been enormous," wrote Elaine A. Ostrander, Ph.D., Chief and Senior Investigator at NHGRI, in a 2007 article in *American Scientist* magazine. "The dog genome has been mapped and sequenced. A host of disease loci have been mapped, and, in many cases, the underlying mutations identified. Certainly, the next few years will bring an explosion of disease-gene mapping. The genetics of canine cancer, heart disease, hip dysplasia, and vision and hearing anomalies have all been areas of intense study, and investigators working on these problems are poised to take advantage of recent advances. What will the companion animal and scientific communities do with this new information? It is certainly hoped that the disease-gene mapping will lead to the production of genetic tests and more thoughtful breeding programs associated with healthier, more long-lived dogs."

The field of genetics is one of the most rapidly developing of all the sciences. Progress is made nearly every day in unveiling the secrets of the DNA code. Ultimately, our current understanding of the canine genome—when combined with tomorrow's advances—will continue to benefit not only dogs but also their human best friends.

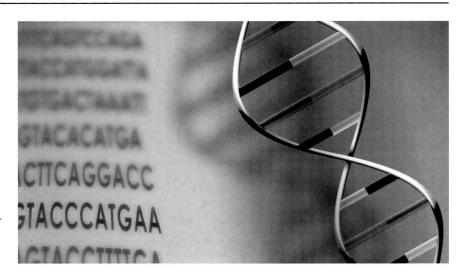

The canine genome comprises 2.4 billion base pairs carrying approximately 19,300 genes.
© Photographer: Rolffimages
Agency: Dreamstime.com

This group of alert Miniature Pinschers, owned by Sandra J. Mestyanek, depicts four coat colors: red, black and rust, chocolate and rust, and blue and rust.

IN LIVING COLOR
16

What accounts for the differences in coat color among dogs, from the snowy white Maltese to the ebony Labrador, the auburn-red Irish Setter to the silvery Weimaraner? All shades, surprisingly, result from the extension, restriction, or dilution of two forms of melanin. Eumelanin produces the black and dark brown colors; pheomelanin gives the yellow or reddish ones. To understand these color variations, it's necessary to visualize the structure of the dog's hair. Each hair shaft is composed of a central core, or medulla, which contains rows of cells alternating with air spaces. Encircling the medulla is a solid cortex, and around that a thin cuticle. The type of coat is influenced by the relative size of the cortex and medulla, whereas its apparent color depends on the distribution, size, and structure of the pigment granules. Researchers have pinpointed genes at 12 loci, to date, that influence the coloration and markings of dogs. The following gene variations affect Miniature Pinschers.

GENES THAT CONTROL COLOR IN THE MINIATURE PINSCHER
Locus A / The Agouti Series

Named for the South American rodent that clearly shows the banded hair pattern of this locus, the agouti series influences both the amount and distribution of pigment in individual hairs and throughout the coat. Two alleles (versions of a gene) affect the Miniature Pinscher: a^y (fawn or sable) and a^t (tan points). The dominant a^y allele restricts dark pigment to produce a red coat, with an intermingling of few to many darker hairs. However, the dominance of a^y over a^t is not complete. Min Pins that are $a^y a^y$ in genotype tend to have a sable coat, whereas those that are $a^y a^t$ have distinct black hairs throughout the coat, called stag red. The recessive a^t, depending on the action of genes at other loci, is responsible for tan points against a black, chocolate, blue, or fawn base coat. The gene involved in the agouti series is *agouti signal peptide* (ASIP).

Three braces of Miniature Pinschers that competed at the 1992 Miniature Pinscher Club of Greater Los Angeles Specialty Show represent the red, blue-and-rust, and black-and-rust coat colors. Photo by Candids by Connie.

Locus B / The Black-Brown Pair

The dominant **B** gene (**BB** or **Bb**) allows the formation of black pigment in the coat, nose, eye rims, and foot pads. The recessive **b** gene (**bb**) lightens eumelanin to produce brown, chocolate, or liver pigmentation. (It has no effect on red). Researchers have proposed three variations of **b**: **b^s**, **b^d**, and **b^c**. Although chocolate dogs range from rich brown to light tan, no consistent differences have been attributed to the six possible combinations of these new alleles. Because a dog that carries the recessive **bb** pair can't produce black pigment, standards that allow a chocolate-colored coat also must permit "self-colored" noses, eye rims, and foot pads. The gene involved in determining black or brown coloration is *tyrosinase related protein 1* (TYRP1).

Locus D / The Dilution Pair

Unlike other color genes, the dilution pair (**D/d**) acts upon genes at other loci to influence the expression of color, rather than to create color itself. Min Pins with the density **D** gene (**DD** or **Dd**), required by the standard, have deep rich pigmentation. Those with the dilution **d** gene (**dd**) are blue (**B*dd**) or fawn (**bb/dd**) in coloration, with gray or fawn noses, eye rims, and foot pads. [* *Refers to any other hypostatic, or concealed, allele of a gene.*] Only one recessive dilution gene has been identified, to date. However, the possibility of others is under investigation. The gene involved in dilution is *melanophilin* (MLPH).

Locus E / The Extension Pair

The extension **E** gene (**EE** or **Ee**), which refers to the extension of dark pigment rather than tan, allows black pigment to appear evenly over the entire coat. Complicating the expression of the extension alleles are their interaction with those of the agouti series. In Min Pins that are **a^{y}a^y**, for example, the **E** gene has little dark pigment on which to work. Sable dogs, therefore, represent a conflict between **E**, which extends eumelanin, and **a^y**, which attempts to inhibit its formation. (Dogs need at least one

Ch. Devileen's Aqua Sambuci UD (black and rust) and Ch. Fillpin's Foxfire CDX (red), are owned and trained by Bedford and Mary Bates.

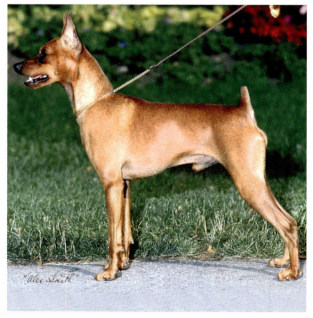

Am. Can. Ch. Dynasty's Jackie's Surprise, bred and owned by Helen Chrysler Greene, is a top-winning red Min Pin for Dynasty kennel.

Ch. Larcon's Lit'l Wrecking Crew, owned by Norma D. Cacka and Connie Wick, shows the typical "tan points" markings.
Photo by Candids by Connie.

dominant **E** gene in order to be influenced by the agouti series.) The **e** gene (**ee**) restricts the formation of dark pigment and creates a uniform cream, yellow, or red coat without any black hairs or shadings on the hair shaft. The color of the nose, eye rims, and foot pads depends on the genes present at Loci B and D.

The gene involved in the extension of eumelanin is *melanocortin 1 receptor* (MC1R).

Note: Miniature Pinschers carry genes for normal pigmentation at other loci, including those involved in graying, spotting, ticking, and merle colors and patterns.

STANDARD MIN PIN COLORS
Red

This solid-colored coat includes shades from light blond to deep mahogany, although most owners and dog show judges prefer medium to deep tones of red (like the Irish Setter). When choosing a Miniature Pinscher, keep in mind that both the red coat and rust-red markings on the black-and-rust coat may deepen as the puppy matures.

Stag Red

Named for a species of russet-red deer found in European forests, this color shows a distinct intermingling of black guard hairs against a red base coat—usually over the back and on the sides of the neck. Like the solid-red coat, the background ranges from light to dark, with deeper shades of red preferred.

Black and Rust

Glossy jet black, with sharply defined rust-red markings on the cheeks, lips, lower jaw, throat, above each eye, chest, vent region, and lower portion of hocks and feet. Lack of "pencil marks" (a line of black hair on the top of each toe) or the presence of double rosettes on the chest are minor faults.

GENES INVOLVED IN COAT COLOR

STANDARD COLORS

Sable Red: $a^y a^y$ B* D* E*

Stag Red: $a^y a^t$ B* D* E*

Black and Rust: $a^t a^t$ B* D* E*

Chocolate and Rust: $a^t a^t$ bb D* E*

OTHER COLORS

Clear Red: B* (or bb) D* ee

Tan: B* (or bb) dd ee

Fawn: $a^y a^y$ (or $a^y a^t$) bb dd E*

Fawn and Rust: $a^t a^t$ bb dd E*

Blue and Rust: $a^t a^t$ B* dd E*

* Refers to any other hypostatic, or concealed, allele of a gene.

Chocolate and Rust

Rich "fudgey" chocolate, with the same rust-red markings as the black and rust. Nose, eye rims, toenails, and pencil marks on toes are brown (self colored).

OTHER COLORS
Clear Red

Three variants of red coat color occur in Min Pins: sable red and stag red, influenced by the agouti series, and the less common clear red, determined by the extension pair's recessive **e** gene (**ee**). The **ee** pair masks all of agouti's alleles to form a red coat completely devoid of any black hairs. Because nose pigment, along with eye rims and foot pads, relies on Locus B, clear red Min Pins may have either black or brown features. Understanding the genotype of these dogs helps to explain the puzzle of how two black and rusts sometimes produce red puppies. (The tan-points allele is recessive to sable, so a black-and-rust sire and dam can't carry hidden genes for the sable coat. However, they *can* possess recessive **ee** in the extension pair to produce clear red puppies.)

Tan

When a dog with the clear red genotype carries the dilution factor **dd** instead of the usual **D***, he is considered a dilute red—more commonly called a tan. The red coat lightens to a cream-red, whereas the black nose, eye rims, and foot pads appear gray. (Dogs that carry the brown **bb** pair have fawn-colored features.) As with the clear red, the extension pair's **ee** overrides the agouti series to produce a solid tan coloration.

In Living Color

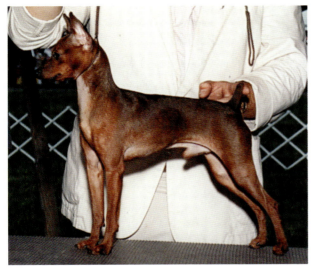

Previous page: Bluehen's Ltl Blue Valentine CD (blue and rust) and Bluehen's Mini Chocolatechip (chocolate and rust), owned by Sandra J. Mestyanek.

Top left: Red Ch. K-Roc's Piece Of The Roc, bred, owned, and handled by Sharon Krogh. According to his owner, "Butch was so special. He had it all, and his movement was just right, too."
Top right: Black-and-Rust Bluehen's Li'l Reggie Greene, bred and owned by Frank and Norma D. Cacka.

Center left: Stag Red Ch. Midnite's Man In Motion, a multiple Group placer, owned by Mark and Karen Fiorentino.
Center right: Blue-and-Rust Rio's Blueberry Muffin, also is owned by the Cackas who have been enthusiastic supporters of blue Min Pins.

Bottom right: Chocolate-and-Rust Ch. Onlyone Chocolate Fudge, bred and handled by Norma D. Cacka.

Top left: Ch. Dynasty's Jackie's Surprise, owned by Helen Chrysler Greene, won multiple Groups for his owner.

Top right: This chocolate-and-rust Min Pin, named Forest, shares his home with Dale Householder.

Center right: A pair of fawn puppies from Robyn Thomason's Prancealots kennel.

Left: UKC Ch. Phelan's Mystic Magic became the first blue champion, in February 2008, at the United Kennel Club's Capitol Terrier Association Show. Molly was bred by John Presswood and is owned by Martha C. Wojtaszek.

Fawn

Resulting from a combination of two recessive pairs, **bb** and **dd**, fawn Min Pins are a dilute chocolate that appears pale tan with an almost silvery tone. Because fawns carry the dominant extension **E** gene (**E***), the agouti series determines whether dogs have an intermingling of stag hairs or rust/tan points with a fawn base coat. Fawn Min Pins have fawn-colored noses, eye rims, and foot pads, as well.

Blue and Rust

A dilution of black and rust, blue and rust was removed from the AKC standard, along with harlequin and yellow, primarily because of their persistent coat and skin problems and lack of consistent quality. (*See section on Color Dilution Alopecia that follows.*) However, blue has long been supported by a number of breeders in the United States, as well as overseas, who are working to have the color reinstated. Blue dogs always have been permitted in all forms of obedience competition, and quite a few have achieved titles. In May 2007, the United Kennel Club (UKC) added blue as an approved color, giving these dogs the opportunity to compete in the conformation ring for UKC championship titles. (The first blue UKC champion is shown on the previous page.) In May 2008, fawn-and-rust Min Pins also became eligible for UKC championships.

Right: Robyn Thomason's puppies, shown clockwise from bottom center, include chocolate, fawn, red, black, and blue coat colors.

Bottom right: This pair of young, blue-coated puppies are from Robyn Thomason's Prancealots kennel.

Below: Shea (front dog) is tan with a blue nose. Rusty (dog in back) is red with a black nose. Both dogs were bred by Robyn Thomason and are owned by Becky O'Leary.

THE HARLEQUIN COAT PATTERN

Hertha von der Kammer-Brugger popularized the coat color pattern known as harlequin. According to an article written by Mrs. van der Kammer-Brugger, her mother was given a white Miniature Pinscher with black spots and ticking and rusty red markings in 1888. In 1929, the pair imported two harlequins from Hanover, Germany to found their Cinderella kennel in New York City. The last known harlequin Min Pins were bred in the early 1960s.

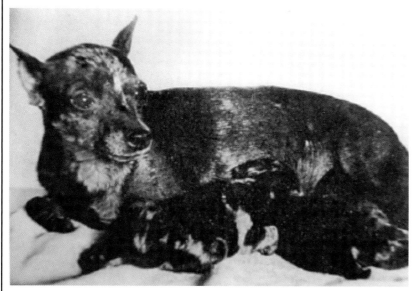

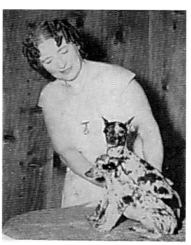

Above: The 1958 book, *Pet Miniature Pinscher*, included this photograph of a harlequin dam and her puppies.

Above right: Cinderella's Solveigh von der Kammer.

Right: Cinderella's Vicky von der Kammer and Cinderella's Fritzi von der Kammer.

Harlequin

This coat pattern—gray, tan, chocolate, or white background with black, tan, or chocolate patches—originated in Germany and attracted considerable interest in the United States through the efforts of Hertha von der Kammer-Brugger, one of the founding members of the MPCA. Although the 1929 standard permitted harlequin, dogs entered in a 1932 show at Madison Square Garden were denied ribbons by the judge, who felt they were an "objectionable and improper" color. By 1935, club members succeeded in removing the color from the revised standard. However, Mrs. von der Kammer-Brugger continued to breed her harlequins (which commanded high prices from enthusiastic pet owners) through the 1960s. A few years later, the last of her harlequin litters were bred and the pattern since has become extinct. (Because the harlequin and merle genes involved are dominant, it's likely impossible to authentically restore this color.)

COLOR DILUTION ALOPECIA

A variety of breeds with the dilute color gene, including both the Doberman Pinscher and Miniature Pinscher, may experience problems with their hair and skin. This hereditary condition, called color dilution alopecia (CDA), causes patchy hair loss, mainly over the blue (dilute black) or fawn (dilute chocolate) portions of the coat. The hair is dry and brittle, and breaks easily during bathing and brushing. The skin, too, becomes red, scaly, and thickened. Secondary bacterial infections may invade the hair follicles. Dilute puppies are born with normal-looking hair coats. The age at which CDA appears varies not only between breeds, but also among members of the same breed. Min Pins usually show signs between four months and three years of age. *It's important to note that not all dilute dogs will develop color dilution alopecia.*

Diagnosis is made by examining pulled-out hairs under a microscope and/or performing a skin biopsy. There is no cure for CDA, and hair loss often is permanent. (However, dogs otherwise are healthy.) Medicated shampoos and lotions help to reduce flakiness and soothe inflamed skin. Antibiotics are given if the skin becomes infected. Because of the serious nature of this disease, potential puppy buyers who are considering blue or fawn Min Pins should seek out only reputable breeders who have their dogs examined for CDA, along with other inherited disorders that affect the breed's health and well-being. Research currently is underway—with the help of blue fanciers—to locate a DNA marker for color dilution alopecia. This would identify affected dogs, as well as carriers, by means of a simple blood test. Dogs with CDA should not be used for breeding.

Coat color genetics is a complex and rapidly growing field of study. Differences in terminology regarding coat color, and the genes involved, further complicate our understanding of inheritance patterns. For links to source information—both general and breed specific—see References at the end of this book.

OPERATION BLUE PRINTS

Blue-coated Miniature Pinschers date to the founding kennels of Germany—where they were highly prized by fanciers—and were part of the first official breed standard when the Miniature Pinscher Club of America was founded in the United States. In 1950, the standard was revised and blue now was considered a fault. By 1980, the color was deemed a disqualification, and blue dogs no longer were permitted to compete in the show ring. According to MPCA records, this action was taken due to coat problems and lack of quality. However, the ban never was meant to be permanent. The secretary of the MPCA, in 1980, wrote in private correspondence, "It is not the intention of the Miniature Pinscher Club of America to ban the blues forever. With selective breeding with sincere breeders and an improvement of the breed of blues over several years, they may be reinstated in the standard." In 1995, a group of enthusiasts petitioned the club for reinstatement of the blues, but on the advice of veterinarians who expressed concern about color dilution alopecia the MPCA rejected the proposal.

Blue-coated Min Pins continue to enjoy a strong following. In 2005, Cindy McNeal founded the Web site and eGroup, Operation Blue Prints (www.operationblueprints.com). The group currently boasts more than 170 members. She outlines her goals for OBP as follows:
- Provide an understanding, as well as the history, of the blue Miniature Pinscher.
- Bring blue fanciers together so the color can be studied and improved upon.
- Provide a forum in which breeders can work through the challenges of developing proper "type" in a color that is disqualified from conformation competitions.
- Discuss coat and skin issues caused by color mutant alopecia, which affects only *some* blue Min Pins.
- Assist in research to find the DNA marker for CDA.
- Educate prospective buyers to prevent their purchase of poorly or irresponsibly bred puppies.
- Prevent the extinction of the blue Miniature Pinscher.

OBP has succeeded in two major accomplishments:
- Participating in research to find a DNA marker for color dilution alopecia. Owners of both normal and affected blue dogs are encouraged submit blood samples to Dr. Tosso Leeb's laboratory in Bern, Switzerland for investigation into genetic mutations involved in CDA. The goal is to develop a test that will detect both affected dogs and carriers of CDA.
- Petitioned the United Kennel Club to include blue in its official standard. As a result of OBP's efforts, since May 2007, blue Min Pins have been eligible to compete at UKC shows for championship titles.

MIN PINS ARE A COLORFUL BREED

Above: Ch. Dynasty's Spirit Of The West was bred by his owner, Helen Chrysler Greene. Roy won an all-breed Best in Show award in 2007.

Right: AKC Ch. UKC GRCH Tri-Del Mega Dittos is a chocolate-and-rust Miniature Pinscher, bred and owned by Cindy McNeal. Rush finished his AKC championship with three majors and was shown exclusively in the Bred-by-Exhibitor Class.

Above: Ch. Jothona's Steppin Sabrina, owned by Gerona MacCuaig, overlooks the waterfront at her Canadian cottage.

Left: Ch. Zwergpin Limited Edition, owned by Mike and Helen Towell, surveys his home in Australia.

In Living Color

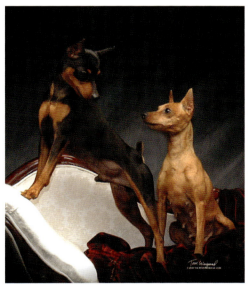

Above: Ch. Altanero Barnstormer is the 2008 MPCA National Specialty Best of Breed winner, and has won an all-breed Best in Show and multiple Group placements in his distinguished show career. He was bred by Susan P. Goldman and Joanne Wilds, and is owned by his breeders and handler Kim Byrd.

Top left: Ch. Devileen's Aqua Sambuci UD (black and rust) and Ch. Fillpin's Foxfire CDX (red) are owned and trained by their Canadian owners, Bedford and Mary Bates. Photo by Vavra.

Center left: Ch. Sultans Suspect is shown with his dam, Ch. Sultans Sultry Temptress. Martin was the 2001 MPCA Futurity winner, multiple Group winner, and Specialty Show winner. Sylvia shares her son's accomplishments as the first MPCA Futurity winner, in 1995, and multiple Group and Specialty winner. She also is a Hall of Fame Dam with 12 champion offspring. Martin and Sylvia are owned by Gretchen Hofheins-Wackerfuss.
Photo by Tom Weigand, Inc.

Bottom left: Music City's Scarlet Twiggy, owned by Betty Remington.

MIN PINS ARE AN ACTIVE BREED

Ch. Keystone Mi Vida Loca MX MXJ OF, owned by Gina Day, is a champion in the conformation ring who is now competing for her Master Agility Championship. She holds the Master Agility Excellent (MX), Master Excellent Jumpers With Weaves (MXJ), and Open FAST titles. At eight years of age, Vida still is in top form for competition.

Ch. Whypin Little Bitaluck CDX AD is encouraged by his owner Rae Galea, of Australia, on the dog walk.

Above: MACH Jocks Nemesis Tiny A UDX, owned by Donald Roback, is one of the top obedience and agility champions. He was the first Miniature Pinscher to earn both Master Agility Champion (MACH) and Utility Dog Excellent (UDX) titles.

Center right: Karen Egbert's Min Pin, Bubba, easily masters the tire jump.

Right: Ch. Harper's Kopper Baron CDX, owned and trained by Dee Stutts of Tucson, Arizona, breezes over the broad jump in this practice session.

In Living Color

This lovely stained glass artwork was crafted by Lerae Britain Bush.

Post card and first day cover are from the author's collection.

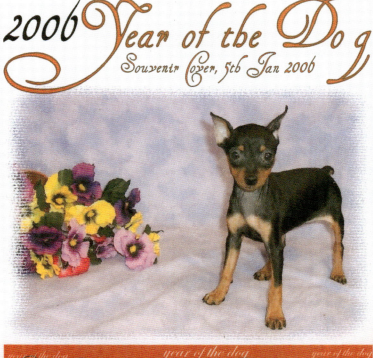

Christmas Island Year of the Dog cachet 5th Jan 2006

\multicolumn{4}{c}{**SUMMARY OF COAT COLOR GENES**}			
Allele	**Description**	**Gene**	**Chromosome**
Locus A a^y	Fawn, red, or sable. May have intermingling of black hairs.	Agouti signal peptide (ASIP)	24
a^w	Wild (wolf) type with banded hairs. Hairs are cream/gray.		
a^t	Tan points.		
a	Recessive black with no pheomelanin (yellow/red) in the coat.		
Locus B B	Black pigment.	Tyrosinase related protein 1 (TYRP1)	11
b	Brown pigment.		
Locus C C	Permits dark pigmentation.	Tyrosinase	21
c^{ch}	Chinchilla. Black and silver hairs.		
c^e	Extreme dilution. White hair with black pigmentation of nose and eyes.		
c^b	Albino, with blue eyes.		
c	True albino, with pink eyes.		
Locus D D	Dark pigmentation. Not diluted.	Melanophilin (MLPH)	25
d	Diluted, black to blue (gray) or red to tan.		
Locus E E	Black or brown pigmentation is allowed (eumelanin is produced).	Melanocortin receptor 1 (MC1R)	5
e	Red or yellow pigmentation (only pheomelanin is produced). A recessive clear red coat.		

SUMMARY OF COAT COLOR GENES

Allele	Description	Gene	Chromosome
Locus G G	Puppies are born with a black coat that turns silver.	Unknown	Unknown
g	Normal pigmentation.		
Locus H H	Harlequin pattern.	Unknown	Unknown
h	Non-harlequin pattern.		
Locus K K	Dominant black.	Beta-defensin 103 (CBD103)	16
k^{br}	Brindle.		
k	Normal pigmentation.		
Locus M M	Merle (patchy) pattern.	SILV	10
m	Normal pigmentation.		
Locus S S	Solid (non-spotted) pattern.	Microphthalmia associated transcription factor (MITF)	20
s	White dog with various spotted patterns.		
Locus Se Se	Black mask.	Unknown	Unknown
se	No mask.		
Locus T T	Ticking in a white coat.	Unknown	Unknown
t	No ticking.		

Four generations of Miniature Pinschers, ranging in age from 8 months to 13 years, display the stamp of Gerona MacCuaig's breeding program.

BREEDING BASICS
17

Why breed? As with any creative endeavor, the reasons why people breed dogs are as varied as the individuals themselves. Perhaps you have shown another kennel's Miniature Pinschers and would like to try your hand at raising your own champions. Maybe you've found a male that you believe would complement your bitch's strong points, while overcoming a particular fault, and want to test the results of such a mating. Perhaps, through your understanding of the Min Pin's background—from research into the dog's history or travel to his country of origin—you have set as your goal the development of a bloodline that emphasizes certain aspects of the standard that you consider most significant.

Although the progression from owner to breeder comes naturally to those who love dogs and appreciate the special camaraderie they provide, raising Min Pins involves far more than simply producing puppies. There already are too many dogs without homes—even purebreds—to breed simply on a whim or as an experiment. Are you willing to accept the obligations, as well as the rewards, that come with being a responsible breeder? For example, would you breed only those dogs that, to the best of your knowledge, are physically and mentally sound? Eliminate from your program any dog that produces a serious fault in his or her offspring—even if your favorite stud or bitch were involved? Will you assume responsibility for every puppy you sell, by screening prospective owners to determine whether they can care for a puppy? Would you take back a dog that didn't work out and find him a new home?

Unfortunately, some individuals base their decision to breed on a variety of ill-conceived plans: to create a puppy "just like" the beloved family pet, to teach children about "the birds and bees," or to satisfy the bitch's "maternal instinct" before having her spayed. Often, the motive is profit. Min Pin puppies—from pet shops as well as the top kennels—sell for hundreds of dollars. However, reputable breeders *invest in* rather than *gain from* their enterprise.

THE FOUNDATION BITCH

Assuming that you have decided to take on the responsibilities involved in dog breeding, where do you begin? Should you obtain a female or male Min Pin? Or, as some suggest, one of each? Because you can utilize the services of any of the top males standing at stud simply by paying a fee, the most efficient way to embark upon your breeding program is to acquire the best female you can afford. The first consideration,

---

Quality is never an accident; it is always the result of high intention, sincere effort, intelligent direction and skillful execution; it represents the wise choice of many alternatives.
Willa A. Foster

then, before you rush into making a purchase, is to know what you want. What is your vision of the ideal Miniature Pinscher? You must not only read the standard, but also understand how it translates into a flesh-and-blood animal. For example, what is your interpretation of a "not too prominent foreface," "slightly arched neck," or "clean, sloping shoulders, with moderate angulation"? Can you pick out the various strengths and weaknesses in a group of show dogs? Do your choices agree, for the most part, with the judge's? Only after you have formulated a clear mental picture of the type of dog you hope to produce can you start the search for the female destined to become the cornerstone of your kennel.

Making the Selection

The basis of choosing a top quality foundation bitch is to determine what genes—desirable and undesirable—she carries, and is likely to transmit to her offspring. This is an educated guess, at best. However, you can begin by learning what she already has produced, especially when mated with males from different bloodlines. Are the majority of her puppies good representatives of breed type, or is she known for only one or two "flyers"? A matron that produces consistent quality is by far the better choice if you're able to acquire one. Unfortunately, knowledgeable breeders rarely part with their top bitches. If you're a novice, you may have to settle for a young, unproven bitch, possibly a daughter or granddaughter of the favored matron.

In this case, the characteristics of the female herself—combined with a study of her pedigree—offer an indication of her value in breeding. Is she healthy and sound, for example, with regular estrous cycles, and no abnormalities that could hinder her ability to whelp or raise a litter? Is she a good breed representative: strong front and rear, level topline, high tail set, long elegant neck, height between 11 and 11½ inches? Does she have a solid, stable temperament—outgoing, happy, and fearless?

Above: Ch. Shajawn Fame, bred by Linda Talbot, and owned by Matt Debelock and Dan Flanery.

Below: Ch. Sunbrook Buckskin Gal, bred by Ruth H. Norwood and Linda Stevens, and owned by Ruth H. Norwood.

SANBROOK KENNEL

Careful breeding, attention to detail, and a vision of the ideal Miniature Pinscher has given Ann Dutton's Sanbrook kennel its reputation for quality. Her dogs form the foundation of many of today's top kennels.

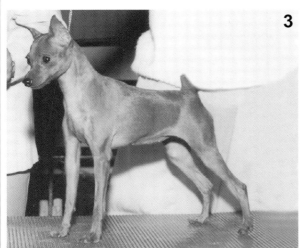

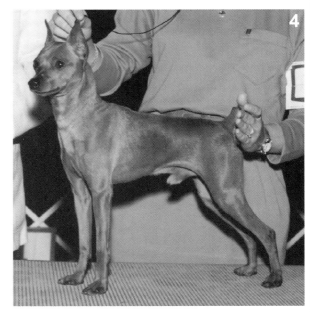

1. Ch. Sanbrook Swept Away, owned by Armando Angelbello.

2. Ch. Sanbrook Silk Sarong, owned by Ruth H. Norwood.

3. Ch. Sanbrook Little Sister, owned by Nancy Gwynne.

4. Ch. Sanbrook Secret Scheme, owned by Catherine Smith.

5. Ch. Sanbrook Racing Silks, owned by Sara McCutchen and Ann Walker.

Kimro's foundation bitch, BIS BISS Ch. Sunsprite's Absolutely Sable, is shown with her breeder, Marcia Tucker. In addition to being an all-breed Best in Show winner, herself, she is the foundation behind three generations of all-breed BIS winners for Kimberly Pastella and Robin Greenslade: Ch. Kimro's Rocket Man (son), Ch. Kimro's Space Cowboy V Edgewind (grandson), and Ch. Kimro's Toy Soldier (great-grandson). According to Abby's owners, "If you start with a great bitch and a great mentor you can accomplish so much."

Take your time in selecting your all-important foundation bitch. Visit as many kennels as possible to see what type of Min Pin each is producing. Don't overlook distant breeders; many are willing to provide interested buyers with videos and photographs of their most promising dogs. Before you make your final decision, though, it's best to observe each prospect in person. Also, be prepared to pay a substantial price for a mature matron (especially if one or more of her puppies have become champions). If cost is a determining factor, you may be able to obtain an older female from a breeder who is retiring or reducing the size of his kennel, or a young, untried bitch.

What About Faults?

No Miniature Pinscher meets all the criteria of the perfect breed specimen. Often, the successful brood bitch is not even a show dog or champion, herself. Possibly, a minor flaw has kept her out of competition, or an accident such as a broken leg or lost teeth, or certain types of corrective surgery. A single weakness should not rule out a promising female. However, those with several faults—particularly involving structure and overall soundness—should be avoided. The fewer problems you bring into your line at the beginning, the less will have to be bred out later.

UNDERSTANDING PEDIGREES

Does your Miniature Pinscher have "papers"? For many buyers, a puppy's AKC registration and accompanying pedigree—especially one with impressive-sounding ancestors—suggest a high standard of quality. But what is a pedigree, and what can it tell us? Named for the French term, *pied de gris*, or "crane's foot," from its pattern of lines that resemble the spreading toes of a crane, a pedigree is simply a written chart of a dog's ancestors. Pedigrees are indispensable to modern breeders, but the formal recording of a dog's background is a relatively recent practice. Major Topham and Colonel Thornton, noted 19th-century Greyhound breeders and coursing enthusiasts in Great Britain, became the first to publicize their breeding records, although several hound kennels had maintained their own private registries. When The Kennel Club, in Great Britain, and the American Kennel Club were formed, and owners began to show their dogs in formal competition, recording pedigrees in "stud books" became standard practice.

Today, all pedigrees follow the same format. The sire and dam of a particular dog make up the first column on the left side of the chart; grandparents, great-grandparents, and earlier generations appear progressively further to the right. In each parental pair, the sire's name comes above the dam's, thus by connecting the top line of the pedigree you can delineate the so-called "tail male" line of descent (through the sire's family). Pedigrees also include champion and obedience titles, and may offer registration numbers, stud book dates, birth dates, coat colors, and Top Producer (TP), Hall of Fame (HOF), or Register of Merit (ROM) status.

The most significant aspect of the pedigree for breeding purposes, though, is the dogs themselves. Before deciding on a potential stud, and especially when adding a new female, it's of the utmost importance to know firsthand the virtues and faults carried by a majority of ancestors. Photographs are a good place to start. Dr. Buris R. Boshell's and Viva Leone Ricketts' books provide excellent sources for reviewing prominent Min Pins of the 1950s, 1960s, and 1970s. *Pinscher Patter*, published quarterly by the MPCA, also includes photos of current stud dogs, show and obedience winners, and champions of record. An interesting online source of both early and current photographs and pedigrees is PawVillage.com, which traces Min Pins back to their earliest known AKC-registered ancestors. After you have identified the significant contributors within the pedigree, you can use the available photos, and information from owners about their dogs' strengths and weaknesses, to create a visual family tree. (Before considering a particular mate, always check the pedigree's accuracy with the stud dog owner.)

Pedigrees can show us a great deal—from highlighting the "great producers" to uncovering the sources of hidden faults, but they should be used only as a general guide in making breeding decisions. A star-studded pedigree is no guarantee of equally stellar offspring. By far, the most important factors are the individual dog and the assortment of genes he has available to pass on, and his recognized ability to produce quality puppies. For experienced breeders who understand the historical background of the Min Pin and how it relates to their own and others' bloodlines, pedigrees then become increasingly meaningful.

CHOOSING THE STUD

Before discussing specific breeding systems—inbreeding, line breeding, and outcrossing—some general principles apply in selecting the best stud to mate with a particular bitch. First, in order to know what you require in the stud, you must know what you already have in your bitch. What are her strengths and weaknesses? What features do you hope to enhance or correct by the breeding? What *must* the stud provide? Only by being able to visualize what you want from a particular mating can you attempt to achieve it.

The next step is to narrow your array of candidates by studying photographs of prospective studs (and, if possible, their close relatives—sire and dam, brothers and sisters), along with their pedigrees to see how each bloodline meshes with that of your female. Try to visit several kennels to examine the dogs in person, and pay close attention to the Stud Dog Class (where the quality of the offspring, rather than the stud, himself, is judged) at MPCA Specialty Shows. Your female's breeder, knowing the faults and virtues of the line, also can offer suggestions on worthy males.

The most important consideration in selecting a stud—as it was in your choice of foundation bitch—is the dog's power to stamp his excellence consistently upon the puppies he produces. Breeders call this ability "prepotency," which technically refers to the homozygosity, or purity, of the gene pairs that influence desirable characteristics. If the dog carries a pair of dominant genes for a particular attribute, B/B for example, he will pass on that feature to all of his offspring regardless of the contribution of the female.

The task, then, is to choose the male that offers the greatest promise of preserving the purity of your bitch's strengths, while introducing the needed genetic factors to overcome her faults. Of course, knowing which dogs to bring together challenges even the most experienced breeders, and requires both acumen and insight, combined with some degree of intuition and luck.

The Stud Service Contract

As soon as you have decided on the male you want to use, be sure to contact his owner well in advance of your bitch's heat cycle to make the arrangements. At this time, you can find out the stud fee and whether he will be available when you anticipate needing the service. To eliminate any confusion about breeding terms, most stud dog owners provide written contracts that must be signed by both parties before the service is given. Points usually covered in the contract include: the stud fee and when it's due; whether the owner will accept a puppy in place of the fee; who chooses the puppy and at what age; what happens if the bitch fails to conceive or produces only one puppy; and whether any veterinary tests—for brucellosis or other infectious diseases, for example—are required before the mating. If you're a newcomer to dog breeding, don't hesitate to ask the stud's owner—or another experienced breeder—to explain the various terms before you sign the contract.

BREEDING PROGRAMS
Inbreeding

The system known as inbreeding involves the mating of closely related individuals—father and daughter, mother and son, or brother and sister—in order to concentrate in the offspring the virtues of the family line. Many varieties of livestock, as well as domestic dogs, have been developed as a result of inbreeding. In fact, the most effective way to create and maintain a prepotent, or true-breeding, strain is by bringing together dogs with similar genetic backgrounds. Whenever you see a string of nearly identical Miniature Pinschers, you can generally assume that the breeder has used some form of close breeding—inbreeding, line breeding, or a combination of the two systems—to stabilize and perpetuate the quality of the foundation animals.

Mary Silfies' Ch. Reh-Pin's Walk This Way is an example of line breeding, with Ch. Sanbrook's Twist & Shout appearing in both the sire's and dam's line. His bloodline also includes Ch. Elan's Shiloh v Whitehouse, BISS Ch. Redwings On The Cutting Edge, Ch. Sanbrook Smooth Operator, and Ch. Sanbrook Swept Away further back in his pedigree.

The problems with inbreeding, and the reason breeders approach it with caution, are twofold. First, such a program not only concentrates the favorable attributes that are present in the bloodline, but also it sets any underlying problems. And when such defects appear, they are usually difficult to eliminate. Most significant, though, minor conformation faults, as well as serious genetic defects, show up more frequently in strains that are highly inbred. Many believe inbreeding *causes* such weaknesses, but in reality the system merely illuminates what already exists in the dogs' backgrounds. Because recessive genes can lurk hidden for generations, covered by the more favorable dominants, their appearance through inbreeding confirms for the breeder that a particular trait is carried by the sire and the dam. Obviously, no one wants to produce puppies with problems—especially those affecting health or overall soundness. Yet, only by acknowledging defects when they occur, and identifying the animals involved, can you hope to eradicate flaws and further the improvement of the breed.

Line Breeding

To achieve the benefits of inbreeding, with fewer problems, the majority of breeders utilize the program called line breeding. The meaning of this term—depending on the context in which it's used and the specific goals of the breeder—usually signifies matings between more distant relatives: grandparent and grandchild, uncle and niece, aunt and nephew, half-brother and half-sister, and cousins. Line breeding also refers to the practice of repeatedly breeding back to specific foundation animals, with the same favored ancestor appearing on both the sire's and dam's branch of the family tree.

The theory behind line breeding is that by mating individuals from similar bloodlines, the virtues held by these dogs will be preserved much like they are with inbreeding. At the same time, any faults that might occur will develop slowly enough that they can be dealt with one at a time. Keep in mind that regardless of which breeding system you use, it's the genes, themselves, that carry the ingredients of inheritance. When a pair of dogs with a similar pool of genes is brought together, the outcome—and the reason the system works—is that, genetically, such a mating functions as inbreeding. According to Philip Onstott, in *The New Art of Breeding Better Dogs*, line breeding, when it succeeds in its purpose of intensifying and purifying the attributes of the strain, is in fact inbreeding [at the genetic level]. When it fails (and thereby avoids the hazards of inbreeding) it not only is not inbreeding, but also in a genetic sense is not even line breeding.

Outcrossing

After several generations of mating related animals, you'll probably discover that your bloodline lacks one or more qualities necessary for the continued growth and development of your breeding program. In this situation, you may decide to go outside your own strain to bring in the necessary attribute. Unfortunately, outcross matings also introduce a variety of new genes—not all of them favorable. To minimize the risk of adding unknown faults to your line, first try to locate the virtue you require within your dog's own family tree. Because you're familiar with the traits carried within the line, you'll have a better chance of overcoming a single weakness, while holding onto positive characteristics.

If you must bring in a dog from outside your line, try to select a top-quality, all-around specimen. Look for the desired feature in a balanced, rather than exaggerated, form. For example, instead of choosing a tiny stud to compensate for a large bitch, you'll achieve

Kathy A. Helming's BISS Ch. Trotwood's Hot Lead proves his merits as a stud dog as he stamps his signature quality on four of his champion sons shown at right.

1. BISS Ch. Trotwood's Frankly Speaking.

2. Ch. Trotwood's Hot Topic.

3. BISS Ch. Trotwood's Top Flight V. Danzig.

4. Ch. Trotwood's Lickety Split.

more consistent results by using a correctly sized 11- to 11½-inch male. When you have successfully added the quality, you then will need to breed the offspring resulting from the outcross mating back to your original line (through line breeding or inbreeding) in order to preserve it.

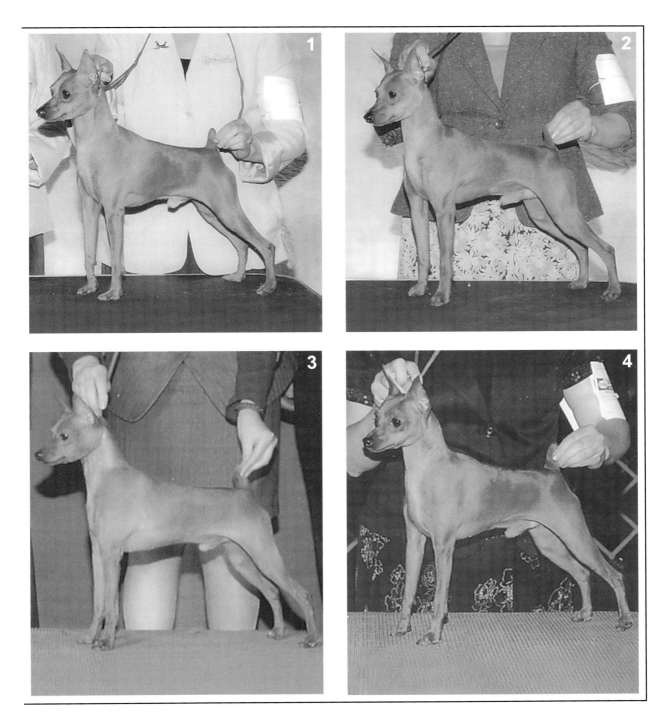

It's said that the politician looks to the next election, whereas the statesman looks to the next generation. Likewise, in dog breeding, the "backyard breeder" makes his decisions based upon his next litter of puppies. The breeder who truly understands the Miniature Pinscher, in general—and his own dogs, in particular—knows what he wants to achieve (and how he proposes to go about it) 10 generations from now. Be patient; success in dog breeding rarely comes overnight. Only by studying your dogs and their background, acknowledging their strengths and weaknesses, and applying scientific principles to your breeding program, can you journey toward the fulfillment of your goals.

Ch. Sanbrook Silk Electric, a multiple MPCA National Specialty Best of Breed and Stud Dog Class winner, sired 74 champions to become the Number 2 Hall of Fame Sire. Bred by Ann Dutton, and owned and handled by Armando Angelbello.

THE STUD DOG
18

The reproductive system of the male consists of the testes and epididymis, located within the scrotum, and the prostate gland, spermatic cord, urethra, and penis. Under the influence of the pituitary gland's output of follicle-stimulating hormone (FSH) and luteinizing hormone (LH), the paired testes produce both the male sex hormone, testosterone, and the gametes from which the bitch's eggs are fertilized. Because heat affects the viability of sperm cells, the testes are located outside the dog's body in a pouch called the scrotum. This twin sac, covered by a network of sweat glands and hair follicles, allows the testicles to remain several degrees cooler than body temperature. By contracting the scrotum's cremaster muscle, dogs are able to retract the testes to regulate their warmth during cold weather.

The scrotum also contains the long, tightly coiled structure called the epididymis. Spermatozoa produced in the testes pass through this tube, where they develop and become motile. Mature sperm remain in the base of the epididymis until ejaculation, when contractions force the cells along the *vas deferens* to the urethral tract of the penis. In dogs, seminal fluid is discharged in three distinct fractions. The first portion is relatively clear, with few sperm cells. The second, milky or gray in appearance, contains the sperm. Both occur within the first few minutes of ejaculation. The final fraction, which makes up nearly 70 percent of semen volume, is composed primarily of fluid from the prostate gland.

Situated just below the bladder, partly surrounding the urethra, the prostate produces an alkaline liquid that neutralizes the acidity of both the male's urethral tract and the bitch's vagina. Prostatic fluid helps to propel the sperm and provides a source of nutritive energy on their journey to the uterus and oviducts. Because dogs lack two of the accessory sex organs found in other animals—seminal vesicles, which act as a holding area for sperm, and Cowper's glands, which provide additional fluid at ejaculation—semen is discharged in a slow trickle rather than a burst. This requires a lengthy union, or "tie," that normally lasts from 10 to 30 minutes. To keep the dogs in position, a special gland—called the *bulbus glandis*—located at the base of the penis, swells under constriction of the bitch's vaginal muscles to maintain the tie. When the male deposits the last fraction of semen, relaxation of these muscles allows the two dogs to separate.

Ch. Marlex Mariachi, bred by Armando and Xio Angelbello and owned by Chris Smith. Ritchie is a Hall of Fame Sire with 32 champion offspring.

CRYPTORCHIDISM

From *cryptos*, meaning hidden, and *orchis*, for testis, cryptorchidism describes the condition in which one or both testes are retained within the abdomen. Although dogs with one retained testicle often are called monorchid, this term actually refers to those with only one testicle present (either descended or retained) within the body. The correct term for a dog with two testicles, one of which has not descended into the scrotum, is unilateral cryptorchid; two undescended, bilateral cryptorchid.

Because the testes begin to pass through the inguinal ring (the passage that connects the abdomen with the scrotum) by the 50th to 60th day of gestation, most puppies' testicles are fully descended at birth or soon afterwards. Males with one or both testes retained at six months of age are considered cryptorchid and are ineligible to compete in AKC shows. (Judges check each dog for two properly descended testicles, even when the dog has competed at previous shows.)

Cryptorchidism is believed to have a hereditary basis in dogs, and those affected should not be bred. Because sperm are unable to develop properly at the higher temperature present in the abdomen, males with two retained testicles are sterile. Those with one normal testicle may be able to produce sperm, but usually have lower fertility rates than dogs with two normal testicles. Most veterinarians recommend castration, both to eliminate cryptorchid males from breeding programs and because the condition seems to be associated with several types of (sometimes malignant) testicular tumors.

RESPONSIBILITIES OF THE STUD DOG OWNER

Your Miniature Pinscher quickly finished his championship and now shows promise as a "special." Perhaps he's already won a Group award, gaining recognition from judges and breeders alike. If his pedigree backs up his accomplishments, including one or more significant sires or dams, you may consider promoting his merits as

a stud dog. What is involved in raising a male to become a good stud? What are the responsibilities of the stud's owner?

Health Requirements

Males used for breeding, like their female counterparts, must be in excellent health and overall condition. Because certain vitamin deficiencies can affect fertility, as well as the stamina needed for frequent matings, proper diet and regular exercise are important in maintaining a stud's virility. Young males (under three to four years), dogs involved in an active schedule of showing, or dogs that are used regularly at stud often need a high-protein performance diet to maintain optimum condition. Should you

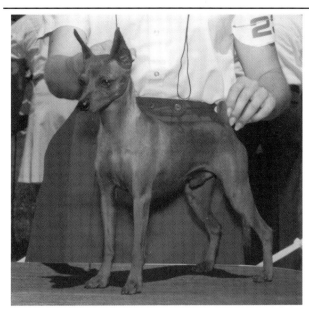

Above: Ch. Bluehen's Solidgoldgntleman, sired by Ch. Bluehen's Scarlet All Over, is a Hall of Fame Sire, with 22 champions. Bred and owned by Norma D. Cacka.

Right: Ch. Bluehen's Scarlet All Over, sired by Ch. Gil-Pin's Southern Gentleman, is from an all-champion litter of four.

Previous page, top: From the same litter is Ch. Bluehen's Thornbird Fiona.

Previous page, bottom: Ch. Gil-Pin's Southern Gentleman, owned by Norma D. Cacka, is on the MPCA Honor Roll of Sires, with 18 champion offspring.

add extra vitamins or minerals to your dog's diet? Although low levels of vitamins A and E can affect the development of the testes during puppyhood, as well as the quality of sperm produced, most premium dog foods contain sufficient vitamin levels for active dogs. Often, adding only one element to an otherwise balanced diet results in imbalances or deficiencies in other nutrients. When your Min Pin ages or his schedule slows down, obesity may become a problem. Excess body fat can lead to reduced fertility and lack of interest in females. Fat located around the scrotum also affects the quality of sperm by insulating the testes against normal heat loss. In addition, fat joins chemically with the fat-soluble steroid hormones, preventing their normal functioning in the body. If your Min Pin is gaining weight, switch to a high-fiber diet, with reduced levels of protein and fat, until he regains his trim body form.

The Pre-Breeding Veterinary Examination

Before you plan the first mating, have the veterinarian perform a complete checkup. This should include an examination of your dog's genitals for any signs of discharge or swelling, or any abnormality that could interfere with breeding. You also will want to have a fecal test for parasites, as well as blood tests for heartworms and the bacterial infection *Brucella canis*. (See *page 178*.) Before, or soon after, his first mating, a complete semen evaluation—measuring the volume, motility, and sperm count—is advisable. This should be done yearly, in addition to the brucellosis test, or any time two or more consecutive bitches fail to conceive.

Promoting Your Stud

For novices who believe setting up a stud kennel is an easy way to earn money for a function that "comes naturally" to dogs, consider the following questions before you begin: Have you studied the breed standard and your dog's pedigree to better understand his strengths and weaknesses? Would you refuse a mating with a bitch of inferior quality, or a poor match for your particular stud? Are you willing to study the genetics of the breed, as well as the physical aspects of mating? Is a reliable person available to travel to and from the airport to pick up and deliver bitches that have been shipped? Are you willing to assume responsibility for the safety and welfare of bitches in your care? Can you determine the right time to breed, based on visual and behavioral cues, or by hormonal testing?

Although much of the responsibility in dog breeding rests on the owner of the dam, stud owners invest considerable effort in learning about the breed, studying books and articles on mating and its related difficulties, maintaining secure kennel facilities, obtaining veterinary help (and knowing when it's needed), and even placing puppies. Consider, as well, the financial costs involved in raising a stud: travel expenses to local and national shows, entry and handler fees, advertising in club or trade magazines, building or buying kennel runs or crates to house visiting bitches, and hiring extra help to assist during matings. Unless your male is an exceptional representative of the standard, known for his whelping box accomplishments, be prepared to rely on your own resources—not occasional stud fees—to promote his merits.

PLANNING THE FIRST MATING

Min Pins can be used for breeding for the first time at about 12 to 18 months. Because the first mating sets the stage for later experiences,

(Ch.) Dogwood's Ginseng, at two months of age.

breeders generally suggest using a mature, easy-going bitch that can be counted on to accept his advances without creating a fuss or snapping. If the match is a desirable one, genetically, a female from his own kennel is a good choice. If you use an outside bitch, plan her arrival for one or two days before her fertile period so that she can settle down before the actual mating. You can help the pair become acquainted by placing the dogs in adjoining crates or kennel runs. When you have selected a partner for your male, make certain the bitch is receptive (in estrus) before you make the introductions.

Avoid feeding for several hours prior to breeding. Just before the actual mating, take both dogs outside (separately) to urinate. If you prefer to wash the dogs' genitals before breeding, use plain water or mild soap and rinse well. Strong disinfectants are spermicidal, which you don't want at mating time. Actually, courtship behavior between dogs is stimulated by the scent of pheromones from the bitch's vagina and anal glands. Sight and sound are of minor importance; dogs that are blind or deaf are equally able to mate.

ASSISTING WITH THE MATING

Min Pins are small and lightweight, so one person usually can handle the mating. Choose a quiet place, such as a spare room, without the

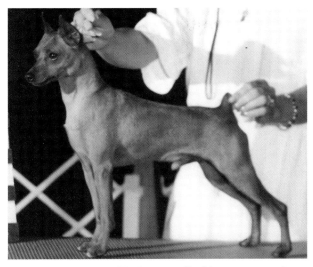

Above: As an adult, Ch. Dogwood's Ginseng earned Best of Winners at the 1990 MPCA National Specialty Show. A multiple Group winner, he was bred and owned by Sue E. Shore.

Right: Ch. Desert Flower of Dogwood, a black-and-rust dog owned by Sue E. Shore, was sired by Ch. Dogwood's Ginseng.

distraction of television, loud music, or visitors. Make certain the dogs have secure footing—a rubber mat or piece of old carpet works well. When you first bring the dogs together, keep both on leash. Typically, the male will sniff or lick the region around the bitch's vulva. If you have calculated the time correctly, she should encourage his advances by playing, flirting, or turning her hindquarters toward him. If she moves away or growls, wait about 24 hours before trying again.

From the start, train your male to accept handling and assistance during mating. Dogs left to their own devices in the beginning often refuse help even with uncooperative bitches. To steady the bitch, hold her by the collar or chest. If she tries to sit or move away, place one hand under her stomach and raise her hindquarters (try not to interfere with the male). If he misses the vaginal opening, turn her so she is properly lined up. Always be patient—especially with youngsters—offering plenty of praise and encouragement. When the male first penetrates, his penis is only partially erect. After he grasps the female around her sides with his forelegs, he begins thrusting, treading up and down with his hind legs.

When complete penetration occurs, the contractions of the bitch's vagina and sphincter muscles cause the penis to become fully erect. The bulb located at the base of the penis swells, joining the dogs in a "tie," which lasts up to 30 minutes. Dogs can sire puppies with a tie of only a few minutes or none at all. After the tie is accomplished, the male usually moves off the bitch to a more comfortable position. He unclasps his forelegs and places his front feet on the floor to the side of the bitch, then lifts one of his hind legs over her back (you can help him, if needed) and the two stand rump to rump. Continue to steady both dogs so neither attempts to pull apart.

After he deposits the final fraction of semen, the bitch's muscles relax and the pair can separate. Occasionally, the gland remains swollen and he is unable to release. Never attempt to break a prolonged tie forcibly; this could cause serious

Ch. Shajawn's Free Hand (above) sired 68 champion offspring and Ch. Shajawn Semi Tough (top right) sired 45 champions to become Hall of Fame Sires. Both dogs were bred by Linda Talbot.

Right: Ch. K-Roc's Kopper Kidd, owned by David and Sharon Krogh, was a Group and Best in Show winner. A very sound Min Pin with a great head, his pedigree was almost exclusively Bel-Roc breeding. Although he only was used about a half-dozen times as a stud, he sired 18 champion offspring and is an MPCA Honor Roll Sire.

damage to the penis (which contains a bone that could be broken) or the vaginal tract. To relieve pressure on the bulb from the grip of the bitch's sphincter muscles, turn the male around to his original mounting position. Then, carefully push his rear toward the bitch to increase the depth of penetration. If the two are still unable to separate, try placing an ice pack on the scrotum to cool the blood flowing to the penis.

After mating, allow the bitch to rest in her crate for several hours (preferably without first urinating). This helps to prevent the semen from draining from her vagina and improves the odds of conception. If she has experienced difficulty in becoming pregnant, hold her on your lap with her hindquarters slightly elevated (her rear on your lap and her chest resting on the chair) for 30 minutes or so. Also, check the male to be sure his penis has retracted fully in its sheath. You may want to rinse his genitals in tepid water to soothe any irritation. After the last mating— two or three days following the first day of ovulation—let the bitch's owner know that she is ready to return home. If long-distance travel is necessary, allow an extra night of rest before shipping.

Hall of Fame Sires
(20 Champions to Qualify)

Ch. Carlee Nubby Silk (116)	Ch. March-On Charkara Make A Deal (26)
Ch. Sanbrook Silk Electric (74)	Ch. Sanbrook Twist And Shout (26)
Ch. Bo-Mar's Road Runner (73)	Ch. Pevensey Stray Cat Strut (25)
Ch. Shajawn's Free Hand (68)	Ch. Sanbrook Smooth Operator (25)
Ch. Redwings On The Cutting Edge (58)	Ch. Pevensey Gold Prospector (24)
Ch. Carlee Southern Prancer (47)	Ch. Sunsprite Luth'r Of Pevensey (24)
Ch. Rebel Roc's Casanova von Kurt (47)	Ch. Bandbox Cut The Bull (23)
Ch. Shajawn Semi Tough (45)	Bel-Roc's Snicklefritz v Enztal (23)
Ch. Sunbrook Red Cloud (38)	Ch. Jay-Macs Pippin (23)
Ch. Von Dorf's Dominator (37)	Ch. Parker's Guardian Angel (23)
Ch. King Eric v Konigsbach (36)	Ch. Bluehen's Solidgoldgntleman (22)
Ch. Bo-Mar's Drummer Boy (35)	Ch. Rei Mar Chip Off The Ol'Bloc (22)
Ch. Sunsprite Eli V Chateau Acres (35)	Ch. Sunsprite Night Games (22)
Ch. Elan's Shiloh V Whitehouse (34)	Ch. Ariston's Knight Rider (21)
Ch. Ruffians Starbuck (33)	Ch. Jay-Mac's Pat Hand (21)
Ch. Marlex Mariachi (32)	Ch. Accent's Justaminpin (20)
Ch. Delcrest Gold Nugget (31)	Ch. King Allah V Siegenburg (20)
Ch. Shieldcrest Cinnamon Toast (29)	Ch. Mercer's Desert Dust Devil (20)
Ch. Halrok Headliner (28)	Reh-Mont's Artistry In Rhythm (20)
Ch. Rebel Roc's Jackpot (28)	Ch. Risingstar Claim To Fame (20)
Ch. Sanbrook Impossible Scheme (28)	Ch. Roadshow Cut The Mustard (20)
Ch. Jay-Mac's Moon Eagle (27)	Ch. Sunsprite Silk Dandy (20)
Ch. Sunbrook Masked Warrior (27)	Ch. Whitehouses Te N Te (20)
Ch. Fillpin's Madric Lucas (26)	Ch. Whitnel Thunderhead (20)

ARTIFICIAL INSEMINATION

Would you like to breed your bitch to a distant stud, yet avoid the stress and hazards of travel? Prevent the spread of sexually transmitted diseases? Preserve your top stud's semen for use after his death? For those interested in trying a mating by artificial insemination (AI), several methods have been approved by the AKC (and other registry groups). Fresh semen, collected just before insemination, is used when both dogs are on hand but can't mate naturally. This may be due to an uncooperative bitch, perhaps with a structural problem such as a narrow vagina or scar tissue, or to a stud with stiffness or weakness in his hindquarters. By chilling semen and adding a special buffer to protect the cells, sperm remain viable long enough to permit overnight shipping. Fresh chilled semen has been shipped as far as Europe and Australia, resulting in live puppy births. Although AI has allowed farmers to improve the production capabilities of livestock—especially in the dairy industry—by efficiently selecting sires with desirable traits, dog breeders in the United States have accepted it cautiously. Few Min Pin breeders use AI, possibly because quality studs are found throughout the country and the breed is small and relatively easy to ship.

Ch. Keystone Alley Gator (left), owned by Amy Fields,
won Best Brood Bitch at the 2006 MPCA National Specialty Show.
She is shown with her offspring, Ch. San Spur's First Class Ticket (middle)
and Ch. San Spur's Standing Ovation v Mau-D (right).

THE BROOD BITCH
19

The reproductive system of the bitch consists of the paired ovaries, oviducts, and uterine horns, and the vagina, cervix, and vulva. The ovaries are small bean-shaped organs, located in the back of the abdomen near the kidneys. As with the testes in the male, the ovaries serve the dual role of producing both the gametes (sex cells) and the specialized hormones needed for reproduction. Newborns' ovaries contain nearly 700,000 eggs, about half of which survive to 1 year. By 5 years of age, the number is about 33,000, and at 10 years, a few hundred. In puppies, the eggs are not fully mature and can't be fertilized by sperm. At puberty, fluid-filled follicles begin to form around several of the eggs. These sacs enlarge and protrude—the ovaries resemble a cluster of grapes—and finally rupture at ovulation.

The eggs then enter the narrow, twisting tube, known as the oviduct, or fallopian tube, where fertilization takes place. The fertilized eggs, called zygotes, continue to travel through the oviducts to one of the uterine horns. Before implantation occurs, zygotes can travel from one horn, through the body of the uterus, to the opposite horn. (Dogs with only one ovary have shown an even spacing of puppies in the two uterine horns.) These Y-shaped tubes, with their rich blood supply during pregnancy, provide a warm, protective incubator in which the puppies develop. The uterus also secretes a special "uterine milk" to nourish the growing puppies before the complex structure of the placenta has formed.

The two horns of the uterus connect at the uterine body, through which the puppies pass at birth. Located between this chamber and the vagina is the cervix, a kind of doorway that separates the internal tract from the outside environment. Near ovulation, the release of estrogen causes the cervix to open to permit the entry of sperm. During pregnancy, the production of progesterone allows a thick mucous seal to form over the cervix that prevents vaginal bacteria from entering the uterus. Penetrating this seal during pregnancy can lead to infection and possibly death of the fetuses.

Ch. Altanero Mirra Image, bred by Susan P. Goldman and co-owned by Joanne Wilds. Bella earned multiple Group placements and won Best of Opposite Sex at both the 2001 inaugural AKC Dog Classic and the 2002 Westminster Kennel Club Dog Show. She is a Hall of Fame Dam, with eight champion offspring in two litters.

PARAMETERS OF THE ESTROUS CYCLE IN THE BITCH				
	Proestrus	Estrus	Metestrus	Anestrus
Duration Average: Range:	9 days. 3 to 16 days.	9 days. 4 to 12 days.	75 days. 60 to 90 days.	125 days. 15 to 265 days.
Vulva	Swollen.	Swollen.	Folded.	Folded.
Vaginal Discharge	Blood-tinged.	Yellow-tinted.	None.	None.
Male Dog	Attracted, nonacceptance.	Attracted, acceptance.	Not attracted.	Not attracted.
Vaginal Smear nucleated: nucleus absent or pyknotic: cornified:	Decreasing number. Absent. Increasing number.	Disappeared. Pyknotic. Numerous.	Increasing number. Absent. Disappear rapidly.	Present. Few. None.
Hormones Estrogen LH Progesterone	Concentration increases, with maximum 1-2 days prior to LH maximum. Increases, with maximum the day before or the day of standing estrus. Very low concentration.	Decreasing. Ovulation at maximum concentration, or 1-2 days later, and then decreasing. Abrupt increase.	Not measurable. Low concentration. Maximum 10 days after LH peak, then decreasing concentration.	Slow increase toward the end of the cycle.
From *Reproduction in the Dog and Cat*, by Ib J. Christiansen.				

The vagina extends from the cervix to the hymen—a membrane that may be partly or completely closed before puberty, and beyond to the vulva. Sometimes called the birth canal, the vagina accommodates the dog's penis at copulation and allows the passage of puppies during whelping. The outermost part of the reproductive tract is the vulva, which responds to the changing levels of estrogen. Before and during estrus, the vulva becomes swollen. This change in appearance, along with behavioral cues, provides a useful signal to determine the best time for mating.

THE ESTROUS CYCLE

The rising and falling levels of four hormones—estrogen and progesterone produced in the ovaries, and follicle-stimulating hormone (FSH) and luteinizing hormone (LH) from the pituitary gland—cause the complex physical and behavioral changes that occur during the estrous cycle. Unlike many animals that have several fertile periods during their estrous cycles, the bitch is considered seasonally monestrus, having only one estrus during the breeding season, regardless of whether or not pregnancy results. Bitches may or may not have two breeding seasons per year.

The interval between heat periods averages 8 months, but it varies from 100 to 400 days.

Following is a description of the four stages of the bitch's cycle—proestrus, estrus, metestrus, and anestrus. Keep in mind that some veterinary authors use slightly different criteria in identifying the characteristics and length of each phase.

Proestrus

This stage lasts about nine days, extending from the first sign of blood-tinged discharge and vulval swelling to the acceptance of the male. Behavior changes often occur just before or during proestrus, such as restlessness, excitability, and increased thirst and urination. Pheromones—hormone-like substances undetectable to humans—are secreted in the urine and from the vagina that attract males. However, at this point, the bitch is uninterested in their advances. She may discourage mounting by growling, snapping, or moving away. Proestrus and estrus are both considered the "follicular" phase of the cycle. Follicle-stimulating hormone levels begin to rise and interact with the ovaries, leading to an increased output of estrogen. Estrogen, in turn, stimulates the visual signs of heat and assists in the release of luteinizing hormone at ovulation.

Estrus

True estrus also averages nine days, and covers the time from the bitch's first acceptance of the male until she refuses further breeding. Estrogen levels decline and progesterone rises. However, the main hormone involved is luteinizing hormone, which brings about ovulation. This surge of LH causes the mature follicles in the ovaries to rupture, usually about two days after the onset of estrus. The bitch's vulva still is somewhat swollen, but the discharge has changed from red to clear or straw colored. The primary means of identifying estrus is behavioral. Normally, the female begins to flirt with the male and tries to attract him. She may turn her hindquarters toward him, lower her back, and raise her pelvis.

Metestrus

This phase begins when the bitch refuses the male, and males are no longer attracted by the release of pheromones. Both the vulval swelling and discharge have diminished, and her behavior is calmer. Dogs enter metestrus, the "luteal" part of the cycle, about six days after ovulation. After the follicles in the ovaries have released their eggs, temporary endocrine glands known as *corpora lutea* (singular: *corpus luteum*) develop, which produce progesterone.

Veterinary authors differ in their definitions of this stage. L. E. McDonald, D.V.M., Ph.D. (*Veterinary Endocrinology and Reproduction*, Lea & Febiger) limits metestrus to the time when the corpus luteum is forming and becoming functional (about 2 days) and views the latter part of the cycle (50 to 80 days) as diestrus or pseudopregnancy. Ib J. Christiansen (*Reproduction in the Dog and Cat*, Baillière Tindall/W.B. Saunders), on the other hand, defines metestrus

	Optimal Breeding Dates	
	DAY	
	1	First day of bloody discharge
	2	
	3	
	4	Estrogen levels declining
	5	Progesterone levels rising
	6	
	7	
	8	
	9	
	10	LH Surge
Breeding	11	
	12	Ovulation
Breeding	13	
	14	Optimal breeding time
Breeding	15	

These two Min Pins from Vera Halpin Bistrim's Halrok kennel became important foundation bitches for David and Sharon Krogh's K-Roc breeding program. Halrok Heat Wave Of K-Roc (left) and Ch. Halrok Happy Talk (right) both produced Best in Show winners for the Kroghs.

as the 60- to 90-day period from the first refusal of the male until the corpus luteum diminishes. Regardless of the terminology used, this stage is characterized by the influence of progesterone in both pregnant and nonpregnant bitches.

Anestrus

The resting phase between estrous cycles averages 125 days, but varies from 4 to 9 months. During anestrus, the ovaries remain inactive with low hormonal output.

THE RIGHT AGE TO BREED

Puberty begins around six months of age, in puppies, when the pituitary gland starts to release higher levels of the gonadotropic hormones, follicle-stimulating hormone and luteinizing hormone. This causes the ovaries and the follicles containing the eggs to develop. Miniature Pinschers reach puberty—the start of the first estrous cycle—between eight and nine months of age, on average. However, a number of factors influence the onset of puberty. Bitches that freely interact with males tend to mature earlier than isolated or kenneled dogs. Optimum nutrition—without overfeeding—and regular exercise also play a key role. Climate, season, and light, which affect development in some species, have shown only a minor influence in dogs.

Bitches are capable of becoming pregnant during the first estrus, but most breeders suggest waiting until the second or third heat.

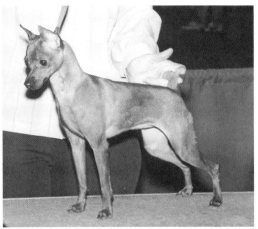

Ch. K-Roc's Kopper Hellzapoppin (above), owned by Ellen Michel and Barbara Stamm, became a foundation bitch for March-On kennel. Other important bitches for Ellen Michel and Barbara Stamm are March-On Merely Elegant (above left) Ch. March-On Strike My Hart (above right), Ch. March-On Dinah Mite (right).

By 18 to 24 months of age, a bitch is ready, physically and emotionally, for the rigors and responsibilities of pregnancy and motherhood. Waiting also allows time for certain breed faults (improper dentition or oversize or undersize, for example) or genetic diseases to appear. Although three years is considered the latest for a first pregnancy, Min Pins often remain fertile and capable of producing healthy puppies into their seventh or eighth year.

THE PRE-BREEDING EXAMINATION

Several months before breeding, have the veterinarian perform a thorough physical examination. The doctor should check the vulva, vagina, and mammary glands for any problems that could interfere with mating, achieving the "tie," or nursing the puppies. If a vaginal stricture (an obstruction due to inflammation, injury, or an internal growth) is found, it can be corrected surgically before breeding. Other considerations to discuss with the veterinarian are past episodes of infertility or whelping complications, irregular estrous cycles, abortion or stillbirth in past litters, the occurrence of genetic problems in the breed, and the overall condition of the bitch.

The pre-breeding exam also should include a fecal test for parasites and blood tests for heartworms and canine brucellosis. Deworming, if necessary, should begin early enough that parasites are eliminated without having to give medicine during pregnancy. (Heartworm preventives are considered safe during pregnancy.) In addition, when booster shots are due, give all inoculations at least 30 days before breeding, so the dam can pass maximum immunity to her puppies.

CANINE BRUCELLOSIS

Brucella canis, a form of the bacteria known to cause abortion in livestock, was identified among kenneled dogs in the late 1960s. Although abortion, usually between the 41st and 55th day, is the main symptom, brucellosis also causes conception failure, stillbirth, and occasionally the delivery of weak puppies that have little chance of survival. In males, exposure often leads to inflamed testes, abnormal sperm, and infertility. Brucellosis spreads rapidly among dogs, usually from contact with the vaginal discharge, milk, or urine of infected dogs. The disease is transmitted sexually, and also may be passed from a dam to her puppies. Rarely, dogs can contract other strains of brucellosis from infected livestock. All dogs used for breeding, and all new dogs that join a kennel, should be tested at 6-month to 1-year intervals for Brucella canis. Antibiotics, such as tetracycline or streptomycin, sometimes are given. However, dogs that test positive should not be used for breeding. Keep in mind that people are susceptible to brucellosis—not only from drinking unpasteurized milk from a contaminated animal (the most common method of transmission), but also through contact with infected dogs, stillborn puppies, or aborted fetuses in a kennel.

REPRODUCTIVE HORMONES	
Estrogen	Estrogen is produced in the ovaries. Secreted by the follicles that surround the eggs, estrogen causes the visual signs of heat: swelling of the vulva, blood-tinged discharge, and attraction of males. Estrogen levels rise for 10-14 days in proestrus, peak 2-3 days before estrus, then abruptly fall, causing the LH surge and onset of ovulation.
Follicle-Stimulating Hormone (FSH)	Follicle-stimulating hormone is produced by the pituitary gland. FSH stimulates the ovarian follicles to develop, as well as the release of estrogen, which helps to prepare the uterine lining for pregnancy.
Progesterone	Progesterone is produced by *corpora lutea*, temporary endocrine glands that form in the ovaries. Levels remain low during anestrus and proestrus, then begin to rise early in estrus. Progesterone, which is an important hormone in maintaining a pregnancy, remains elevated for 2-3 months, whether or not the bitch becomes pregnant. Tests that measure progesterone in the blood help to pinpoint ovulation.
Luteinizing Hormone (LH)	Luteinizing hormone is produced by the pituitary gland. The LH surge, during estrus, occurs rapidly over a 24-hour period, triggering ovulation two days later. Tests that measure LH levels in the blood are the most accurate means of identifying when ovulation will take place.

THE BEST TIME TO BREED

Most bitches conceive when bred 10 to 12 days after the first visible signs of proestrus (bloody discharge), or 2 to 3 days following the onset of estrus (when the discharge becomes pale and the bitch allows mounting). Occasionally, bitches have irregular cycles with few cues for the breeder. Age can affect when ovulation occurs; young bitches tend to ovulate early in estrus, whereas older females may ovulate near the end of the cycle. Uterine infections, obesity, and certain medications—especially hormones given to delay heat or prevent pregnancy—also influence ovulation. Because incorrect timing is the main factor in infertility, you may want to use one of the following tests, in addition to visual signs, to more accurately determine the best time to breed.

Hormonal Tests

The hormones that play the greatest role in the timing of ovulation are progesterone and luteinizing hormone. Progesterone increases gradually during proestrus—rising just before the LH surge—and remains high during estrus and metestrus. Blood tests that detect these rising levels help to pinpoint ovulation by predicting the LH surge, which triggers the ovaries to release eggs. Although progesterone tests, such as OVUCHECK® Premate (Synbiotics Corporation), allow breeders to estimate ovulation, the most accurate blood test measures luteinizing hormone directly. Because the LH surge lasts only 24 hours, tests need to be performed daily, starting about three days into proestrus. Once the surge occurs, ovulation takes place about two days later. The eggs need another two days to mature before fertilization is possible, so the optimal breeding date is four days after detection of the LH surge.

CANINE BIRTH CONTROL

If you want to delay or prevent the onset of estrus in a bitch that will not be bred during a particular cycle, consider the use of canine birth control. Ovaban® (megestrol acetate), a prescription medication from Schering-Plough Animal Health, is the only birth control pill approved for use in dogs in the United States. It works by suppressing the pituitary gland's output of follicle-stimulating hormone. To postpone estrus for a show or vacation, start the pill 1 week before

Ch. Sanbrook Swept Away, sired by Ch. Sanbrook Silk Electric, is a Hall of Fame Dam, with eight champion offspring.

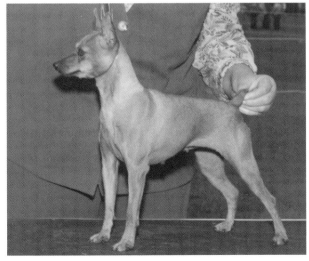

Ch. Bluehen's Touch of Class, owned by Frank and Norma D. Cacka, is a Hall of Fame Dam, also with eight champion offspring to her credit.

the event (at least 1 week before proestrus) and continue for up to 30 days. This schedule temporarily suppresses estrus, and increases the interval until the next normal cycle. To prevent estrus for one cycle, begin the pill as soon as your bitch shows signs of proestrus and continue for eight days. This will delay estrus for two to nine months.

A liquid contraceptive also has been approved for use in dogs. Mibolerone (an androgenic steroid), given orally or in a dog's food, works by blocking the effects of luteinizing hormone. Start mibolerone at least 30 days before proestrus to prevent pregnancy, and continue for up to 24 months. Both products may cause side effects: weight gain, uterine infection, breast development, and loss of fertility. If you plan to breed your bitch at a later date, or if she is a valuable part of your breeding program, consider carefully before using any hormonal products.

PSEUDOPREGNANCY

False pregnancy usually occurs about 60 days after the onset of estrus. Dogs may experience such minor symptoms that their owners are unaware of any physical or behavioral changes. Common signs include breast development—even to the point of producing milk, vomiting, diarrhea, weight gain, and uterine cramps. Bitches also may exhibit maternal habits of nest building and "mothering" small toys or other puppies or kittens in the household.

The exact cause of pseudopregnancy is unknown. Hormone levels show little difference between affected and unaffected bitches at the same point in their cycles. Diagnosis is based on a physical exam to rule out true pregnancy or uterine infection. Symptoms usually start to disappear within two to four weeks. However, the condition tends to recur. The medications Ovaban and mibolerone reduce the outward signs of false pregnancy, but the only preventive is to have your female spayed. This surgery should be performed during anestrus, after the symptoms have abated.

Ch. Sultans Sultry Temptress, owned by Gretchen Hofheins-Wackerfuss and bred by her owner and Ann Dutton. She was the first MPCA Futurity winner, in 1995, and won Best of Opposite Sex at the 1996 and 1998 National Specialty. She is a Hall of Fame Dam with 12 champion offspring. According to her owner, "Sylvia still rules the roost at the Sultans kennel at 13 years of age. She is a beauty as a show dog, mother, and retiree."

MISALLIANCE

The best way to prevent accidental pregnancy is to keep your bitch indoors or securely confined in her crate during her fertile period. Neighborhood males are remarkably adept at climbing over or crawling under fences—even negotiating outdoor kennel runs. Until recently, a "mismate" shot, containing the synthetic estrogen, diethylstilbestrol, was given to prevent the fertilized eggs from implanting in the uterus. However, this has been associated with serious side effects, such as uterine infection and bone marrow suppression, and is no longer recommended. A variety of new drugs—most of them experimental and off label—are being used in the United States and Europe to terminate unwanted pregnancy. These drugs include prostaglandin-F2alpha (dinoprost tromethamine), dopamine agonists (bromocriptine and cabergoline), corticosteroids (dexamethasone), antiprogestins (mifepristone), and others. Although they work by different means, the

Hall of Fame Dams
(8 Champions to Qualify)

Ch. Jay-Mac's Silk Stockings (25)	Rika's Rolling Pin V Jecamo (9)
Ch. Jay-Mac's Ramblin Rose (22)	Ch. Sanbrook Stage Struck (9)
Ch. Redwing's Above Suspicion (20)	Ch. Sanbrook Wrapped In Silk (9)
Ch. Gypsey Of Alema (19)	Ch. Shajawn American Dream (9)
Rolling Greens Sparkle (17)	Sunsprite Sasparilla (9)
Ch. Carlee Classie Chassie (16)	Ch. Whitehouse's One Tough Cookie (9)
Ch. Parker's Second Hand Rose (16)	Ch. Altanero Mirra Image (8)
Goldmedal Girl Of Shamrock (15)	Ch. Bluehen's Touch Of Class (8)
Ch. Reh-Mont's Dinah Lee (14)	Ch. Blythewood I'll Lite Your Fire (8)
Ch. Rocky Point Penny Ante (13)	Ch. Bud-Lee's Spittin Image (8)
Ch. Jay-Mac's Miss Michigan (12)	Ch. Carlee Cover Me In Silk (8)
Sanbrook Silk All Over (12)	Ch. Carlee Love Unlimited (8)
Ch. Sultans Sultry Temptress (12)	Ch. Carlee Satin Sachet (8)
Ch. Sunbrook Indian Amber (12)	Chateau Acres Almond Joy (8)
Ch. Blythewood Me Jane (11)	Cox's Miss Dynamite (8)
Ch. Gaela Run For The Roses (11)	Ch. Driftwinds Mighty Foxfire (8)
Ch. Granbar's Glamour Girl (11)	Jo-Len's Born To Be A Star (8)
Onlyone Perpetual Motion (11)	Ch. Keystone Alley Gator (8)
Ch. Seville's Rhapsody In Red (11)	Ch. Mercer's Desert Storm (8)
Bergeron's Miss Heidi (10)	Ch. Mercer's Ida Redbird (8)
Ch. Blythewood I'll Turn You On (10)	Ch. Merrywood's Once Upon A Time (8)
Ch. Marlex Electra Madness (10)	Ch. Ms T'Seas Mi (8)
Mile-Bet's Dancing Doll (10)	Ch. Parker's Ruby Red Dress (8)
Ch. Carlee Careless Love (9)	Ch. Reh-Mont's Sweet Georgia Brown (8)
Ch. Carlee Southern Exposure (9)	Roadshow's Will Of The Wind (8)
Del Rey's Keepsake (9)	Ch. Rollin Rock's Queen Royale (8)
Ch. Edgewind's Hakuna Matata (9)	Ch. Sanbrook Fantasy In Silk (8)
Ch. Halrok Halla Luya (9)	Ch. Sanbrook Swept Away (8)
Ch. Kloeber's Cookie Cutter T'Seas (9)	Sanbrook Sultana (8)
Ch. Mara's Pinot Chardonnay (9)	Ch. Sunbrook Feathered Headress (8)
Ch. Pevensey's Ciara (9)	

result is to suppress the output of progesterone, which supports successful pregnancies. Many breeders prefer not to give hormones and allow the pregnancy to proceed. (The quality of future litters is not affected by puppies produced from an accidental mating.) When no future litters are desired, or your bitch no longer will be shown in the conformation ring, you may choose to spay her after a mismatch. This operation is considered safe when performed within the first two weeks, but should not be attempted during the later stages of pregnancy.

Ch. T'seas Mi Promise March-On, winner of the 2005 MPCA National Specialty Brood Bitch Class, is shown with two of her sons: Ch. Windwalker Over The Top and Ch. Windwalker Cool Hand Luke. Luke won Best of Breed at the 2005 National Specialty. Promise has produced six champions, to date, and is an Honor Roll Dam. She shares her home with owner Roberta (Bobbie) Mills-Bowhay.

THE EXPECTANT MIN PIN
20

Pregnancy averages 9 weeks in dogs, ranging from 57 to 69 days after a successful mating. For the first 8 to 12 days, the newly fertilized eggs remain in the oviducts where early cell division takes place. These blastocysts, as they are called, then travel to the uterine horns, moving to arrange themselves evenly within the tubes. By the third week, the developing placental system allows the fetuses to implant in the uterine wall where they remain for the duration of the pregnancy. By the 28th day, the fetuses have formed definite round swellings within the uterine horns. Often, you can feel the puppies by gently palpating the abdomen. As the pregnancy progresses, the horns continue to increase in size, both from amniotic fluid and the puppies' growth, until the swellings no longer are distinct to the touch. By day 40, the bitch's nipples start to develop and become pink and her stomach begins to enlarge. During the last two to three weeks, you may notice the puppies' kicks or feel their heads and rumps through the abdominal wall.

METHODS TO DETECT PREGNANCY

You may be able to rely solely on changes in behavior, appetite, and appearance to determine whether your bitch is pregnant. "One month after breeding, she starts to expand," said breeder, Laurie Chism. When a bitch has a history of false pregnancy, missed heats, or is too nervous or overweight to allow palpation of the abdomen, confirming pregnancy is more difficult. Young females, and those bred for the first time, may be slower to "show" because their muscles are firmer and the puppies may be carried higher under the rib cage. The mammary glands also develop later, producing milk just before or during delivery. If you believe your bitch was bred at the correct time but doesn't appear to be pregnant, take her to the veterinarian for one of the following tests:

Ultrasound

Very high frequency sound waves, directed in a controlled beam into a dog's body, create echoes that enable the technician to detect internal movements, such as a puppy's motion in the uterus or the beating of his heart. A method called B-scanning allows the counting of pups and also shows the presence of dead fetuses. From the 29th to the 35th day, ultrasound is 85 percent accurate in diagnosing pregnancy; after 36 days, and in cases of non-pregnancy, 100 percent.

Radiography

X-rays indicate swellings within the uterine horns from the 30th to 35th days. About 10 days to 2 weeks later, the puppies' skeletons have calcified to the point that they show enough contrast

---

Before beginning, prepare carefully.
Cicero

on x-ray film to be able to count them and locate their positions. Performed during the later stages of pregnancy, radiography is considered safe for both the dam and her developing puppies.

Blood Testing

The placenta produces a special hormone, known as relaxin, that helps to relax the dam's pelvis before she delivers her puppies. Relaxin levels start to increase by the fourth week, peak by the seventh week, and fall just before birth. Because relaxin is produced only when an embryo implants in the uterine wall, it is considered a specific marker for canine pregnancy. Several test kits, including FASTest® RELAXIN (MegaCor Diagnostik GmbH) and Witness® Relaxin (Synbiotics Corporation), are available that measure relaxin levels in the blood. These tests can detect pregnancy as early as 20 days following the LH surge. They also can distinguish false pregnancy and identify cases of retained placentas or fetal resorption.

FEEDING AND EXERCISE

Because the first changes to occur involve the development of the fetal membranes and accumulation of amniotic fluid, rather than the rapid fetal growth that takes place later, your Min Pin's energy requirements remain fairly stable for the first half of pregnancy. Unless she is underweight, she can continue to consume her regular maintenance diet. Avoid vitamin and mineral supplements, unless the veterinarian recommends them. These extras can cause a variety of nutritional disorders that may be harmful to the developing puppies. In particular, don't give additional calcium or vitamin D. By suppressing the production of parathyroid hormone, excess calcium during pregnancy may lead to imbalances that actually increase the risk of eclampsia during lactation.

Occasionally, a bitch will show signs of "morning sickness," with nausea and loss of appetite, around the fourth week. You can alleviate this by changing her food to an easy-to-digest formula and feeding two smaller meals per day. By the last three to four weeks, the dam's nutritional needs increase considerably, depending on temperament, activity level, and the number of puppies she is carrying. If you have not already done so, switch to a high-quality growth/lactation diet. Gradually increase the amount of food until she is receiving about 25 percent to 30 percent more than maintenance. Remember, too, that Miniature Pinschers need more calories per pound of body weight than do larger dogs. By the last 10 days, your dog's abdomen may have enlarged so much that she can't eat all the food she needs in two meals. Change to three or four meals, or offer free choice. Always have fresh water available, especially if the food is a dry kibble.

Exercise is important; good muscle tone not only aids in weight control, but also helps to prevent uterine inertia during whelping. Early in pregnancy, your Min Pin can remain as active

Ch. Zwergpin Famen Glory, owned by Mike and Helen Towell, of Australia, awaits the birth of her puppies.

The Expectant Min Pin

> **WHELPING SUPPLIES**
>
> Assemble the following supplies and place within easy reach of the whelping box:
>
> - Clean newspapers.
> - Disposable baby diapers.
> - Clean towels.
> - Hot water bottle or heating pad.
> - Cuticle scissors.
> - Hemostat for clamping umbilical cords.
> - Dental floss or heavy thread for tying cords.
> - Iodine for disinfecting navels.
> - Antiseptic.
> - Disposable gloves.
> - Lubricating jelly.
> - Scale for weighing puppies.
> - Replacement bitch's milk and nursing bottles.

as she was before becoming pregnant. After she begins to show, though, she should avoid vigorous exercise and jumping—limiting her workout to a daily walk.

PREPARING FOR THE PUPPIES' ARRIVAL

About two weeks before the anticipated due date, start to accumulate the necessary supplies and prepare the whelping box. Min Pins generally prefer a quiet, warm, draft-free area apart from general traffic within the home. A secluded corner of the dining room, utility room, or spare bedroom is ideal. Several well-made whelping boxes are available from dog supply companies, but many of these are too large for Min Pins. You can make a suitable box from wood or use the bottom half of a fiberglass shipping crate. The best size is about 2 by 3 feet, with 6- to 8-inch sides. This allows her to step over the sides of the box, while keeping the youngsters from crawling out. Place a ledge around the inside walls a few inches from the bottom. Puppies often snuggle into corners and the dam could injure them if she lies down and presses against the side of the box.

If the box is wood, coat with a washable non-toxic paint for easy cleanup. A few days ahead of time, thoroughly disinfect all supplies, as well as the floor and walls of the whelping area. Add several layers of clean newspapers to the bottom of the whelping box. Because puppies need good traction to nurse and move around, place a piece of indoor-outdoor carpet or a heavy bath mat on top of the newspapers. Prepare a smaller cardboard box, too, with a heating pad or hot water bottle, to hold the newborns while the mother is busy delivering the rest of her litter.

THE NORMAL DELIVERY

How can you tell when parturition—delivery of the puppies—is near? During the last day or two, your Min Pin will become restless and begin to prepare her nest. She often changes from one position to another and can't seem to get comfortable. She may avoid family activities, preferring the peace and quiet of her whelping box. If your dog has a close relationship with a certain family member, she may choose to remain nearby rather than seeking seclusion.

Take your bitch's temperature daily, starting about the 57th day. A fairly reliable sign of impending delivery is the drop in temperature, from an average of 101.5°F. to 99°F. or below,

Stages of Fetal Development	
DAY	
0	LH Peak
2	Ovulation
10-12	Blastocysts enter uterus
21	Embryos implant in uterine wall
23-28	Relaxin hormone levels rise
24-28	Fetal heartbeat detectable by ultrasound
28-30	Prolactin hormone levels rise
28-32	Uterine swellings palpable
44-48	Fetal skull detectable by x-ray
62-63	Progesterone hormone falls
64-66	Parturition (puppies born)

Above: Ch. Delcrest Southern Belle Royal Vista, owned by Michele L. Basye, won this Best of Breed prize when she was pregnant with a litter of three puppies. She was a Top 20 contender and competed at Westminster Kennel Club Dog Show, in 2002.

Right: Ch. Haycoss Hynote Kaaba and her puppies enjoy a sunny day on their lawn in Australia.

which occurs 12 to 24 hours before whelping. Because this drop is caused by a decline in circulating progesterone, test kits also can help to pinpoint delivery time.

Contact the veterinarian when the due date approaches and find out who will be on duty for a night emergency or home visit. Keep your telephone and the number of the clinic handy near the whelping box. You'll also want to have on hand one or more reference books on pregnancy and puppy care, which include detailed information on whelping and complications that are beyond the scope of this book. (*See Bibliography.*)

Pre-Labor

During this stage, which normally lasts 4 to 12 hours, the cervix starts to dilate and the first uterine contractions begin. Because these contractions are weak and intermittent, concentrated near the cervical opening, they are easy to miss. Your bitch's behavior offers the best clue that labor has begun. Typical signs include loss of appetite, possibly accompanied by vomiting; trembling or shivering; and panting. Some bitches seek a quiet place to deliver their young; others prefer their owner's presence. Reassure your dog if she seems nervous by speaking in a soft, comforting voice and, though difficult, remain calm yourself. As pre-labor progresses, the puppy nearest the end of the uterine horn (usually from the side containing the most puppies) enters the body of the uterus and begins to press against the cervix. This pressure helps to expand the opening with each contraction until the cervix can accommodate the head and forefeet. After the cervix is completely dilated, the first puppy is ready to enter the birth canal.

Active Labor

When active labor begins, the contractions become more intense and frequent, with visible straining or abdominal pressure. Some bitches take a sitting position, arching or bracing themselves against the side of the whelping box. Others lie on one side to deliver their puppies. After several hard contractions, the water bag begins to protrude like a bubble at the opening of the vulva. This signals that the puppy is entering the vagina. The bag then ruptures, either spontaneously during a contraction or by the bitch licking it, to provide additional lubrication. As soon as the head and shoulders pass through the cervix, the puppy emerges with relative ease.

Usually, the newborn is partially or fully encased in the amniotic sac, which must be broken quickly so that he can breathe. An experienced dam breaks this membrane herself, then licks her puppy to stimulate his breathing and circulation, and to dry him off. If this is your bitch's first litter, she may need your help in removing the sac. Hold the puppy with a small dry towel and gently pull the membrane away from his head. Then, use the cloth or a bulb syringe to remove any remaining fluid from his mouth and nostrils. Let the mother take over and continue to clean and admire her youngster.

After each delivery, the dam passes a placenta, or afterbirth. Opinion is divided about whether or not she should consume the placenta. Some bitches do this naturally, whereas others are not interested. Although the placenta contains hormones that help the uterus to contract after giving birth and aid in letting down the bitch's milk, eating more than one or two may cause vomiting or diarrhea. In any case, a retained placenta can lead to a serious infection, so count the placentas and make certain one is expelled with each puppy. (*See Postwhelping Care of the Dam, page 190.*)

If the placenta remains in the uterus after delivery but the umbilical cord is visible, grasp the cord and slowly pull downward to free the afterbirth. You also will need to sever the cord from the puppy if the dam has neglected to do so. Clamp the hemostat on the cord about one inch from the puppy's body. Tear or cut the cord

> **DANGER SIGNS**
> - Failure to deliver the first puppy 24 hours after the rectal temperature drops.
> - Active straining four to five hours before the first puppy, or one to two hours between puppies.
> - Resting period of four to six hours between puppies, or when the bitch stops labor after delivery of some but not all of her puppies.
> - Signs of obvious pain or systemic illness (rapid pulse, vomiting, trembling, collapse).
> - Abnormal discharge (black, green, bloody) for 12 hours with no delivery of puppies.
> - Pregnancy that lasts beyond 63 days, with no signs of going into labor.

This puppy from Doralyn Wheatley's kennel is only a few hours old.

A 2-week-old youngster, bred by Canada's Lorraine Lyons.

on the side of the clamp away from the puppy. Leave the hemostat in place until the bleeding stops. If the cord continues to bleed, tie the end about ½-inch from the body with dental floss dipped in alcohol. Trim the ends of the floss so the dam can't pull on them and injure the puppy's navel, then dab the end of the umbilical cord with iodine. The cord will shrink and fall off in a few days.

Before the next set of contractions starts, allow the first newborn to nurse. Most find the "food supply" naturally, attracted by the dam's warmth and nudging. If a puppy has difficulty, set him near a nipple and place a drop of the dam's milk on his tongue. Hold him in place for a few moments until he gets the idea. When the contractions for the second arrival start, remove the first puppy to a small cardboard box. Use a heating pad set on low, or a hot water bottle covered with towels, to keep the youngster warm.

When all the puppies have been delivered, take the dam outside to urinate. Sponge off the area around her abdomen and hindquarters with a wet washcloth, but don't use soap or antiseptic. Clean the whelping box and replace the newspapers with fresh ones. Cover this layer with towels or baby diapers. Usually, the dam is ready for a light meal, either her regular food or broth. When she has settled down, return her puppies to her and be sure all are able to nurse.

DIFFICULT DELIVERIES

Min Pins that are in good physical condition, at optimal body weight and adequately exercised, usually deliver their puppies with few complications. Difficulties can and do arise, even in the healthiest dams, so you'll need to know the warning signs and how such problems can be corrected before one or more puppies is lost.

Uterine Inertia

A common cause of difficult birth is uterine inertia, or the failure of the uterine muscles to expel the puppies. Contractions are weak, infrequent, and unproductive. Often, the bitch shows

Ch. Keystone Alley Gator, owned by Amy Fields, has won the the Miniature Pinscher Club of America's Dam of the Year, Hall of Fame Dam, Best Brood Bitch, and Best Veteran Bitch awards.

no signs of labor; in some cases delivery is slower than normal. Primary inertia occurs when the release of oxytocin, a pituitary hormone that stimulates contractions and the release of milk, is inhibited. When a bitch is nervous, she voluntarily stops her labor contractions (this was a protective mechanism for dogs in the wild) and fails to resume them. Another form, called secondary inertia, results when the muscular wall of the uterus is stretched from a single large puppy or large litter. Normal contractions weaken as labor progresses and the bitch tires. This condition tends to occur more often in older, overweight, out-of-shape bitches. Hereditary factors may be involved, along with low levels of calcium in the bloodstream or a hormonal imbalance. Both types of inertia may respond to mild exercise, such as a short walk in the backyard. Oxytocin, administered by injection, usually is effective in starting or strengthening contractions, but it only can be given when the cervix is fully dilated and when the difficulty is not due to an obstruction.

Large Puppies

Single-pup and some multi-pup litters may contain a puppy that is too large to pass through the pelvis. If the head is through the opening but the shoulders are stuck, you may be able to assist the delivery. Wash your hands thoroughly with disinfectant soap or use surgical gloves. Clean the bitch's vulval region with plain water and insert a small amount of sterile lubricant into the vagina. If the head is visible, use a clean terry washcloth to grasp the puppy (still in the sac) and pull gently downward. Synchronize your efforts with the bitch's contractions if she hasn't tired. Pull slowly and steadily so the vagina can accommodate itself to the puppy's size. As soon as the pup is free, remove the sac and clear his mouth and nose of fluid.

Breech Position

About 60 percent of puppies arrive in the normal position, head first. Breech, or rear-first, births also occur in dogs, usually without complications. If the shoulders seem to be stuck, but the rear legs are out, grasp the legs carefully with terry cloth and pull downward. Try to avoid breaking the sac or the puppy could try to breathe and suck fluid into his lungs. Apply firm, steady traction, rotating the puppy's shoulders from side to side until he is free. Remove the sac quickly and clear away all fluid.

When to Seek Veterinary Assistance

Occasionally, complications arise that are beyond the expertise of even the most experienced breeder. A puppy may arrive with the crown of his head first instead of nose first, or with a front or rear leg first. One may be too large to pass through the pelvic opening, even with assistance, or the bitch herself may have an abnormality that prevents delivery. Always seek veterinary help—without delay—if something seems to be wrong, before your bitch becomes exhausted and gives up. Many times, the puppies and dam can be saved by early care: giving hormones to help the uterus contract, forceps delivery (this should never be attempted at home), or Caesarean section.

Caesarean Section

Difficulties such as too-large puppies, malpresentations that can't be corrected vaginally, inertia that fails to respond to hormones, premature separation of the placenta, and structural abnormalities of the bitch require an operation, known as a Caesarean section, in order to save as many puppies as possible. Timing is important. Experimentally, when surgery is performed within the first 24 hours after the start of labor, more than 80 percent of the puppies survived. When delayed from 28 to 50 hours after contractions begin, only 30 percent survived.

Puppies from Kathy Helming's (left) and Amy Putnam Issleib's (right) kennels.

Usually, a Caesarean is performed under complete anesthesia, although some veterinarians may give an epidural injection. An incision is made in the middle of the abdomen between the row of milk glands, or on the flank. A flank incision does not interfere with nursing and may heal more quickly. A second incision is made in the body of the uterus and each fetus is removed in its amniotic sac, along with each placenta. After both incisions are closed and the dam regains consciousness, she and her puppies can go home.

Make certain your dam rests and stays warm following a Caesarean section. She must avoid vigorous exercise and jumping. If she is too groggy to allow her puppies to nurse, you may have to feed them by hand. Watch for signs of infection, especially within the first 24 to 48 hours; this requires immediate treatment. Most bitches can become pregnant after a Caesarean and, depending on the reason for the procedure, may be able to whelp future litters normally.

POSTWHELPING CARE OF THE DAM

When the last puppy has been delivered, take your Min Pin to the veterinarian for a thorough examination. Bring along her puppies for their first checkup, too. When infections or other complications are detected early, treatment can begin before the health of the puppies suffers. Common problems after whelping include the following:

Acute Metritis

Uterine infection, caused by the bacterium *Escherichia coli*, results when a placenta or dead fetus is retained in the uterus, or when a breeder fails to maintain stringent cleanliness when attending the bitch. Symptoms may include fever, loss of appetite, and abnormal vaginal discharge. A thick yellowish or greenish discharge indicates infection, whereas reddish-brown is normal after whelping. If your bitch shows signs of metritis, she needs immediate medical attention. In addition to antibiotics to fight infection, treatment usually includes an injection of prostaglandin or oxytocin to expel the retained placenta or fetus. Puppies that have acquired an infection from the dam also may need medication.

Mastitis

A dam may develop one or more inflamed mammary glands that cause discomfort when her puppies try to nurse. The most common symptom is sore breasts, often warm to the touch, with hard nodules within the tissue. The milk from affected glands may be thicker than normal, with traces of blood or pus. Mastitis results when bacteria enter the nipples and travel upward to the glands. However, dogs also develop inflammation without systemic infection. If you suspect mastitis, have your dog's milk tested for *Staphylococcus* or *Streptococcus* bacteria. Antibiotics are given in case of infection, and baby aspirin eases the soreness and burning. Warm compresses applied to the affected glands several times a day encourage drainage. Puppies may continue to nurse in cases without infection, or the glands may be covered. Youngsters that are old enough should be weaned.

Eclampsia

More common in small breeds than in large ones, eclampsia results when the mechanism that regulates the level of calcium in the dam's blood is unable to compensate for the loss of calcium in her milk. Giving calcium supplements during pregnancy increases the risk that eclampsia will develop. Watch your bitch closely during the early stages of nursing, when the puppies are one to three weeks old. Eclampsia progresses rapidly—often in less than 12 hours—from restlessness, nervousness, and panting to shaky, unsteady gait, muscle spasms, and convulsions.

Calcium, administered intravenously, usually reduces the symptoms within 15 to 30 minutes. Removing the puppies for 24 hours also relieves the drain of calcium from the mother's body. Temporarily feed a milk substitute to puppies that are too young to wean. Bitches with a history of eclampsia need a diet, while nursing, that provides a minimum of 1.4 percent calcium and a calcium-phosphorus ratio of at least one-to-one. Also plan to wean puppies as early as possible.

FEEDING THE NEWBORN
Colostrum

Nature provides a unique mechanism for transferring immunity from a dam to her puppies. When adults are inoculated, complex protein molecules, known as immunoglobulins, develop. Because these molecules are too large to pass to puppies through the placenta, newborns receive only about 10 percent of their immunity via the bloodstream. Ninety percent of maternal antibodies pass to the offspring in a special milk, called colostrum.

During the first 24 to 72 hours after giving birth, the dam produces a thick, yellowish, milk-like fluid that contains antibodies, as well as growth hormones. Although the digestive system of an adult normally breaks down proteins into smaller amino acids, during the first 24 to 36 hours the newborn's intestinal tissue is able to absorb the large molecules of immunoglobulin. By three to five days of age, the lining of the puppy's intestines has developed so that only smaller components are absorbed.

To provide puppies with maximum immunity, inoculate the dam about one month before breeding (if she is due for vaccination) to ensure that her antibody level is high, and make certain all the puppies receive a good measure of colostrum. This early fluid intake also serves an important function in the cardiovascular system by increasing the newborn's blood volume. If colostrum is not available—if the dam dies and a substitute mother is not at hand—isolate the puppies and keep all supplies scrupulously clean to minimize the risk of infection.

Lactation

Min Pins double their birth weight in the first week and continue to gain steadily until about three to four months of age. To assist your dam in producing enough milk to satisfy her pups' demands, as well as her own needs, continue to

---

REARING ORPHANED PUPPIES

Keys to Success

- Don't overfeed, especially during the first few days, to allow for adaptation to the milk replacer.
- Use a milk replacer with a similar composition to bitch's milk, such as Esbilac.
- Maintain proper cleanliness of all feeding utensils.
- Weigh the puppies regularly to monitor their growth and to establish correct feeding levels.
- Maintain a warm, draft-free environment with adequate humidity.
- Keep the puppies clean and aid their bowel movements and urination, if necessary.
- Don't feed too often; feeding frequency should allow the stomach to empty before feeding again.
- Control diarrhea quickly (seek veterinary help when needed).
- Change formula composition slowly.
- Start the puppies on solid food as early as possible. By three to five weeks introduce Esbilac Puppy Weaning Formula or a gruel mixture of puppy food and warm water.

From "Feeding of Orphan Puppies,"
Nutrition and Management of Dogs and Cats.

How Much To Feed	
Age in weeks	Daily calories/pound of body weight*
1	60
2	70
3	80 - 90
4	90+
*Divide into four equal feedings.	

Environmental Temperature Guidelines	
Age	Temperature
Birth to 7 days	85°F. to 90°F.
8 to 14 days	80°F. to 85°F.
15 to 28 days	80°F.
29 to 35 days	70°F. to 75°F.
35+ days	70°F.

feed the same nutrient-dense growth/lactation diet given during pregnancy. Dogs that tend to be nervous or hyperactive do well on a growth *cat* food because this formula is richer than most dog foods. Dams that consume diets too low in nutrients, or that are difficult to digest, may experience chronic diarrhea while nursing.

Most Min Pins need 1½ times their normal caloric intake during the first week of lactation, twice as much during the second week, and up to three times normal intake during the third week. To calculate the added demands during peak lactation—from the third to the sixth week—allow an extra 100 calories per pound of puppy-weight, in addition to the dam's maintenance. For example: If a dam has four 1½-pound puppies (6 pounds total), she needs an extra 600 calories, plus 300 to 350 calories to satisfy her own needs (for a 7-pound bitch). To supply this extra energy, feed a calorie-dense food in several meals or offer free choice.

During lactation, before solid foods are introduced, the dam's milk alone supplies her puppies with all the nutrients and energy required for their rapidly developing bodies. To be sure each litter mate receives his share, weigh the puppies daily and encourage any "laggers" to nurse often. Place smaller puppies at the nipple, while temporarily removing the others. Any puppies that cry often or fail to gain weight are not receiving enough milk, and their diets should be supplemented with a milk replacement formula.

Supplemental Feeding

When Min Pin dams are healthy and well nourished, they can handle the feeding duties of a 4- to 6-puppy litter without difficulty. Supplemental feedings, in addition to—or instead of —the dam's milk, may be necessary in cases where the litter size is unusually large (more than six puppies), she can't produce enough milk even for a small litter, or an infection, such as mastitis, is present and the puppies are unable to nurse. Because cow's milk is lower in protein and fat and higher in lactose than bitch's milk, you'll need to feed a commercial milk replacement formula such as Esbilac® (PetAg). Ideally, feedings should be six hours apart. However, if you want to avoid night duty you can arrange them at 8:00 A.M., 11:30 A.M., 3:30 P.M., and 9:00 P.M. If the puppies cry between feedings, increase the frequency to every four hours.

Bottle Feeding—To feed by this method, you'll need small bottles appropriate for Min Pin puppies, such as the PetAg Pet Nurser Kit (2-ounce size) or Foster & Smith's specially angled feeding bottles. Using one for each pup, sterilize the bottles and nipples by boiling, or wash them thoroughly in hot, soapy water. (Remember, puppies orphaned at birth have not received immunity to disease organisms from the dam's colostrum.) If you're using a powder formula, mix enough for 24 hours and store the leftover portion in the refrigerator. At feeding time, place one serving of milk in each bottle and warm to body temperature, about 100°F. Hold the puppy upright in the palm of your hand, with his head tilted up and outstretched slightly. Don't feed a puppy on his back as you would a baby. Place a drop of milk on the tip of the nipple and insert the nipple in the pup's mouth.

Lucia F. Winkler's Min Pin puppy enjoys a nap with her larger Doberman pal.

These baskets of puppies are from Ray and Judy Bohnert's Equinox kennel (above) and Mauriene Pierce's kennel (right).

To ensure that everyone is getting his full share of formula, use a separate bottle for each puppy. If one tires or stops drinking, he can return to the same bottle to finish. Using individual bottles also helps to reduce the spread of germs from puppy to puppy through unclean nipples. When all the pups have finished, you must burp them like a baby to expel any swallowed air. With orphans or puppies that have been removed from the dam, you also will need to stimulate their urge to urinate and have a bowel movement. This can be accomplished by wiping the abdomen and anal area with a cotton ball soaked in warm water.

If a puppy strangles while nursing, take the bottle away immediately. To remove milk from the pup's nose and windpipe, brace the puppy (on his back) between your palms. Holding his head and spine in a straight line, raise your hands over your head and swing down in an arc. Repeat several times, if necessary, until all the fluid comes out.

Tube Feeding—To avoid the possibility of strangulation, which can lead to pneumonia or even death in young puppies, experienced breeders prefer to feed by stomach tube. This is not as difficult as it seems because newborns have not yet developed a gagging reflex. You'll need a 3- or 6-c.c. syringe, a No. 5 feeding tube, and the same bitch's formula used for bottle feeding. Some syringes and tubes are disposable; reusable equipment must be thoroughly cleaned after each feeding.

To determine the correct length of tube, extend the puppy's head, then place one end of the tube at his mouth and measure the distance to the point just behind the elbow or before the last rib. If the tube is too long, it can double over in the pup's stomach and injure the esophagus when it's removed. Mark the correct distance with a permanent marking pen. Prepare the formula and warm to about 100°F. Place the amount for one feeding in the syringe and depress the plunger to expel any air.

Hold the puppy in the palm of your hand or rest his body on padded towels. Moisten the tube with milk and insert in the puppy's mouth. Gently pass the tube down the throat to the length of the mark. If the tube will not go that far, it may be in the trachea instead of the esophagus. Remove the tube and begin again. (You also can tell if the tube is in the lungs by placing the end in a cup of water and checking for bubbles.) When the tube is in place, slowly depress the plunger and inject about one third of the formula. Wait a few moments and give another third. Don't feed too quickly or the milk will come back up the puppy's mouth or nose. When the stomach looks plump or you feel any resistance, stop feeding. With tube feeding, like bottle feeding, you must burp the puppy and assist with his urination and bowel movements.

Weaning

When the puppies' eyes open and they start to move around the pen on their own, usually by about three to four weeks, most start to notice their dam's food dish. You can encourage pups to begin eating solid food by mixing the dam's food—a high protein, easy-to-digest formula—with warm water to form a thick gruel. Avoid homemade preparations, such as cereal, milk, or baby food. This type of diet does not contain adequate nutrients and encourages "picky habits" in adulthood. If you choose a balanced

HOW MUCH TO FEED GROWING PUPPIES	
Age	Amount
Birth to 3 months	2 times maintenance
3 to 6 months	1.6 times maintenance
6 to 12 months	1.2 times maintenance
Maintenance: 35 to 50 calories per pound, depending on activity level, age, and environment.	

puppy food, supplementation will be unnecessary. Bolder puppies often discover the new food on their own. However, you can spread a dab of the mixture on their lips or even place them in it. When one or two begin to eat from the dish, the others tend to follow. Clean up any uneaten gruel after an hour to prevent spoiling. Early in weaning, allow the puppies to continue to nurse for two or three meals a day. However, by five to six weeks, youngsters should be on puppy food (with less water added to the mixture) exclusively. To help reduce the dam's heavy milk production when the puppies stop nursing, avoid feeding her on the first day, but provide plenty of fresh drinking water. Feed one quarter of the normal pre-pregnancy diet on the second day, half on the third day, three quarters on the fourth day, and resume her full ration on the fifth day.

Growth and Development

Growing puppies have a much greater need for protein and other nutrients than adults, so continue to feed the growth diet until about one year of age. Puppies younger than three months can begin with four meals per day; from three to six months, three meals; six months onwards, one or two meals. Allow each puppy to consume all he wants in a 20-minute period. By controlling your pup's food intake—limiting the feeding time and avoiding extra treats—you can encourage normal growth and development, yet reduce his risk of obesity or skeletal problems.

Always feed youngsters a soft, easy-to-digest formula. Dry food is acceptable (some brands contain less sugar, salt, and additives than canned or semi-

Puppies from Robyn Thomason's Prancealots kennel–clockwise from far right: blue and rust, dilute red, clear red, fawn and rust, dilute red, and black and rust.

Above: A promising litter from Gerona MacCuaig's Jothona kennel, in Canada.

Right: This sleepy puppy from Cindy McNeal's Tri-Del kennel enjoys a warm, sunny day.

moist food), but you must soften the food with warm water for young or teething puppies. After the permanent teeth come in, pups should consume their food with only a little added water to help keep their teeth and gums clean and healthy.

DEWCLAW REMOVAL AND TAIL DOCKING

Min Pins are born with extra fifth toes, called dewclaws, on the pasterns of the front and sometimes the back legs, which usually are removed. The veterinarian can perform this procedure, as well as dock the puppies' tails. However, pups tend to go through less stress when the removal is done at home. Make certain the newborns are nursing well and in good physical health. By the third or fourth day, most puppies are able to tolerate these procedures with few complications. The following supplies are needed:

- 6-inch mosquito forceps, sterilized in boiling water.
- 8-inch Kelly forceps, sterilized in boiling water.
- Absorbable suture.
- Alcohol.
- Clotting powder.

To remove the dewclaws, have someone hold the puppy gently on his back. First, wipe the area around the toe with a cotton ball soaked in alcohol. With the mosquito forceps, clamp the dewclaw as close as possible to the leg. If closing the forceps does not cut the toe, twist the forceps or cut the dewclaw with sharp cuticle scissors. Apply clotting powder and gauze, if needed.

Tail docking generally is performed at the same time the dewclaws are done. Determine the correct length, based on the anticipated size and overall balance of the adult dog. "We find half an inch [two vertebrae] to be the best length," advised Juanita Kean, of Janeff Miniature Pinschers. "Anything shorter appears too short at maturity." To dock the tail, swab the tail with alcohol, then clamp at the correct distance with the Kelly forceps. Twist the forceps to remove the end of the tail, and apply clotting powder. Use one or two absorbable sutures to close the skin. If an infection or other problem develops, contact the veterinarian immediately.

Ch. Whypin Lawson Lad CDX AD, owned and trained by Rae Galea, of Australia, shows off his jumping ability.

THE OBEDIENT MIN PIN
21

Have you ever watched a Miniature Pinscher perform in the obedience ring? Although a relatively uncommon breed in formal competition, many of these stylish dogs have developed a regular following, both for their lively presentation as well as their unexpected antics. "Min Pins move quickly, and either do a terrific job or flunk badly," reported veteran trainer John Yarwood. The Yarwoods' dog, Duchess Patti von Tanenbaum CDX, was especially popular with spectators. When someone in the audience would exclaim, "Isn't she cute," Patti took it as her cue to become a "little ham," walking around the ring on her hind legs and forgetting the exercises. With patience and persistence—along with a sense of humor—you'll find obedience training an enjoyable, yet challenging, hobby. Perhaps the greatest reward is the unique bond it creates between you and your dog.

THE ORIGIN OF OBEDIENCE COMPETITION

The sport of obedience began in the United States, in the 1930s, primarily through the efforts of Helene Whitehouse Walker, a well-known breeder of Standard Poodles. Until this time, most dog training involved sporting and working dogs. Using England's field trials as a guideline, Mrs. Walker sought to create a competitive test, consisting of a series of obedience exercises, to prove the intelligence and trainability of her Poodles. In October 1933, she hosted the first all-breed obedience test at Mount Kisco, New York. The exercises included heeling off leash, retrieving a dumbbell, sit-stay and down-stay, recall, and broad jump. In 1936, the American Kennel Club published its first official *Regulations and Standards for Obedience Test Field Trials*, which further encouraged owners to train and compete with their dogs.

Currently, more than 500 Miniature Pinschers have earned AKC obedience titles. Many supporters are first-time trainers, interested in pursuing a rewarding activity with their pets. Several young handlers have worked with Min Pins in 4-H projects. Breeders and professional trainers also participate in obedience to showcase their dogs' versatility. According to Gail Freisinger, the intelligence of the breed is remarkable. "It's almost like having a gifted child in the house," she explained.

OBEDIENCE ACHIEVEMENTS

The first Miniature Pinscher to win the Companion Dog (CD) title, and reportedly the first of any toy breed, was Ch. Fred v Philippsberg, in 1937. He was owned by Caroline Clark Roe, an avid obedience enthusiast and dog judge, who wrote of her dog's success: "I find the little pinschers very easy to train for obedience work and they give as good a performance in the trials as the big dogs... I sincerely urge the owners of Miniature Pinschers to devote a bit of time in preparing their dogs for the obedience tests. The results and the pleasure of achievement will doubly repay for the time and effort exercised."

Five years later, in 1942, Little Prince, owned by Rollin W. Gilmore, became the breed's first Companion Dog Excellent (CDX). In 1948, Dorothy M. Britton's dog, Nikki v Radar, earned the first Utility Dog (UD) degree. Min Pins have succeeded in the demanding sport of tracking, as well, with the first Tracking Dog (TD) title awarded in 1958 to Adina E. Rossiter's dog,

Above and right: Midnight Magni v Haymount UD, shown with owner Catherine E. Smith. Gypsy won the 1965 Blanche Saunders Memorial Trophy. She also won Highest Scoring Dog in Trial her first time in the ring for her first Novice leg. She received this honor from Milo Pearsall, a noted authority on obedience.

Kipmik's Barefoot Contessa UD. In 1983, Joyce A. Capoccia's dog, Parker's Lil' Flash CDX, became the first, and to date only, Tracking Dog Excellent (TDX). At publication, only three Min Pins—Wee D's Weeble Minute UD, owned by Judie Clark, and Der Stutz Tigger UD and Der Stutz Cinnamon Twig UD, owned by Velma Janek—have earned the prestigious title, Obedience Trial Champion (OTCh.).

Suzanne Harvey promoted training and competition during the 1960s with her two Utility Dogs, Wiltrakis' Sparkplug and Lexington's Sea Biscuit. "These little dogs can do just about anything a big one can and often a great deal better," she commented. "Min Pins are such great and showy little workers, it's a real shame more of the fancy doesn't give obedience a go!"

Credit for promoting the sport also goes to Kathryn J. Marshall, whose Wee Midget Von Blitzen CDX is one of only a handful of dogs to earn two perfect scores of 200 points. Another dog trained by Mrs. Marshall, Urray Golden Penny II, is believed to be the first Min Pin to earn Utility Dog titles in both the United States and Canada. In May 1974, six years after earning her U.S. title and three months before her 11th birthday, Penny took the Canadian title with 197 points and her 11th High in Trial. "It continues to amaze me the number of obedience judges who tell me they are surprised to see a good working Min Pin," stated Mrs. Marshall. "Maybe it's because they don't see many; it certainly isn't because the dogs can't make a good showing."

CONFORMATION VERSUS OBEDIENCE TRAINING

Should show dogs also train for obedience competition? Although owners often finish their dog's championships before starting obedience work, the two forms of training are not necessarily incompatible, depending on the individual dog and handler. Ch. King's Hi Fashion Image of Mira UD, owned by Mrs. C. D. Bourke, is an example of a dog that always knew which ring she was in. After she finished her U.S. championship, Mrs. Bourke retired her from the show ring for three years to compete in obedience. Just two weeks after winning High in Trial, she went out with a new handler and won three Bests of Breed and her Canadian championship. According to Mrs. Bourke, "There are no hard and fast rules as to which avenues should be followed first, or if both should be pursued simultaneously. If you have a new champion or a prospect, do not think that obedience competition is out for you. The two are most compatible. By the same token, if you have already begun your obedience work, or even completed it, and feel that you have a nice breed specimen, don't hesitate to set out to conquer that field also. Our breed is so easy to travel with and to show—what with the small size, hardiness, and smooth coat—there is no excuse to miss out on any of the exciting facets of the fancy!"

GETTING STARTED
Choosing a Dog to Train

There are quite a few things that should be taken into consideration before deciding which dog to train for obedience competition, advised Dee Stutts of Tucson, Arizona, who is considered the foremost authority on Min Pin obedience training. "Number one for us is the personality of the dog. We prefer the friendly, outgoing, eager type." Merlin Van De Kinder, a Canadian Kennel Club conformation and obedience judge who has been involved in dog training for many years, agreed: "I think that someone who wants to go into obedience training should be very careful in picking out a puppy. You want a very active, devoted type that is eager to please."

Another factor to consider in choosing a dog for obedience training is gender. "Although each dog is an individual, we have noticed that males are more independent and can be easily distracted," added Dee Stutts. "Females tend to give you their attention—which is all-important when trying for high scores." Remember, though, females can't compete or attend classes when in season, and breeders who also compete in obedience may need to plan litters around show or training schedules.

Training Classes

It's possible to train your dog at home for competition; however, you'll find it much easier to work with a knowledgeable trainer. By attending group classes, including the popular puppy kindergarten, your Min Pin will develop important social skills necessary for the hectic atmosphere of dog shows and obedience trials. The most important consideration in choosing a training class is the quality of instruction. Ask to observe one of the classes (without your dog). "Talk to the instructors and students and observe their techniques to see if this is for you and your dog," advised Mary Silfies, who has earned High Scoring Miniature Pinscher and High Scoring Toy awards with her dog, Ch. De-Min Diamond Danger CDX. "With these little guys, you can't yell out commands and corrections. This is much too intimidating to this breed. A much softer approach is needed."

Dee Stutts, shown with Der Stutz Twinkle Little Star UD.

Above: Ch. Der Stutz Gypsy Sweetheart UD was Dee Stutts' first Utility Dog.

Below: Ch. Joy's Lady Ginger CD, an MPCA National Specialty Best of Breed winner, also excels in obedience. Here, she is shown winning High in Trial with her owner, Dee Stutts.

Try to find an instructor with experience training a variety of breeds, including small dogs. "I found quickly in my early training of Shazaam [Horizon's Alakazan-D's Shazaam UDT] that the same methods of training do not apply to Min Pins—or toys, for that matter," stated Sandra Hill, who has trained several different breeds to their Utility Dog titles. "He is very willing and obedient, but at the same time is very stubborn—terrier-like—and willful to do things his own way. He also is very vocal and demands things his way with a variety of whines, barks, and screams. Although Shazaam is a small Min Pin (10 inches), he is not a nervous, shaky dog, but thinks he is a big dog and is quite calm and not afraid of any dog or person."

"Min Pins are too smart and feisty for the average obedience handler," added Velma Janek, who has trained two Min Pins to the title Obedience Trial Champion. "If I try something and it doesn't work, I try something else. My students tell me that I must stay awake nights thinking up new training methods, but I don't... I just try to pinpoint the problem and think it out."

After you begin taking a class, be sure to practice the exercises at home. Be consistent in training, but work no longer than 15 minutes at a time. Never work with your dog when you're tired or upset. With Min Pins, especially, it's important to be "enthusiastic, upbeat, happy, and smiling. You must make training fun," advised Karen Egbert, who trains her dogs in agility and obedience. "When I get their collars out, they get so excited," she said.

When your dog does an exercise correctly, give plenty of praise and petting. A number of trainers also use treats as a reward. Be careful, though, advised Martha Fair, who trained Fairhaven's Impulsive Mia to her Utility Dog degree. "They focus too much on the food and forget to work. Food is given when I teach the exercise; after it's learned, the food is then a reward for doing it right."

Rewards Of Training

Why train your Miniature Pinscher? Whether you're considering a competitive career with your dog or just want a well-trained companion, the effort put into training will more than repay itself. "Our greatest satisfaction comes from working with our Min Pins," said Dee Stutts. "We are so proud of our little ones as they learn different exercises on their way to obtaining a degree. Each new event learned brings about another way to please his master and audience. Our dogs are very enthusiastic when they sense we are on our way to another outing of training or showing."

"Miniature Pinschers are so regal looking while performing," added John Yarwood, who has earned 17 obedience titles with his Min Pins. "With patience, understanding, and firmness, you can train this breed to outscore the competition. To have these little dogs finish High in Trial is worth every minute spent on them. Remember, it's just you and your dog in the ring. When you end up in the ribbons, you and your little Min Pin have done so much for this terrific breed."

RULES & REGULATIONS

Formal obedience competition is structured into three progressive levels: Novice, Open, and Utility. All registered dogs over six months of age are eligible to compete in AKC events, including neutered dogs and those with certain faults that would disqualify them in the show ring. Dogs that are not registered with the AKC, but have a Purebred Alternative Listing (PAL) number, also qualify for competition. Other registry organizations, such as the United Kennel Club, sponsor obedience trials, as well.

Obedience is judged on a point scale. Basically, the judge has a mental picture of an ideal performance and subtracts points for each deviation from it, such as a crooked sit or excessively slow recall. To earn an obedience title, your dog must achieve qualifying scores of at least 170 out of 200 points, under three different judges. Each qualifying score is known as a "leg" toward a title. He also must earn at least half of the available points in each exercise.

In Novice competition, dogs receive the title Companion Dog; in Open, Companion Dog Excellent; in Utility, Utility Dog. These award designations—CD, CDX, or UD—follow the dog's registered name.

Unlike conformation competition, there is no limit to the number of dogs that may qualify for a title at a given show. For example, if all of the dogs in the Novice Class correctly perform the required exercises, all will receive green qualifying ribbons and earn legs toward their CDs. In addition, dogs with the four highest scores in each of the three classes receive ribbons and any special prizes offered by the show-giving club. When judging is complete, the dog receiving the highest qualifying score in any regular class, and the dog with the highest combined score in Open and Utility, win ribbons and any additional prizes donated by club members. If two dogs earn the same score, they are individually tested by performing the entire Novice "heel free" exercise.

Bluehen's Blueprint For Valdon, owned by Valerie Edwards and Joan Krumm, is shown winning first place in the Novice Class at the 1992 MPCA National Specialty Show.

Above: Bluehen's Ltl Blue Valentine CD is the first blue-and-rust Miniature Pinscher to earn the Companion Dog degree. Also, note her natural, uncropped ears. Owned and handled by Sandra J. Mestyanek.

Below: Handlers and dogs at the Miniature Pinscher Club of Greater Tucson prepare for the "long sit" exercise.

REGULAR CLASSES
Novice

The Companion Dog degree consists of those commands that all dogs should know to be good companions: heeling on and off leash, coming when called, standing for examination, and remaining in the sit or down position until released.

The "heel" and "heel free" exercises consist of slow, normal, and fast heeling, right and left turns, about turns, and halts. Your dog must maintain correct heel position—close to your left side and in line with your hip—without additional commands. During the halts, he must sit at your left side.

The "figure eight" exercise, performed on leash, involves the dog and handler making two figure-eight loops around two ring stewards who are standing eight feet apart. Your dog must

NOVICE EXERCISES	
1. Heel on Leash and Figure Eight	40 points
2. Stand for Examination	30 points
3. Heel Free	40 points
4. Recall	30 points
5. Long Sit	30 points
6. Long Down	30 points
Maximum Total Score	**200 points**

maintain correct heel position and sit whenever you're told to halt. One problem competitors face with Min Pins is that some judges consider correct heel position to be at the handler's ankle, rather than the hip. Points then are deducted because the dog appears to be lagging or forging.

In the "stand for examination," performed off leash, your dog must remain standing while the judge approaches and touches his head, body, and hindquarters. He will lose points or fail if he moves his feet, sits, lies down, or displays shy or aggressive behavior. Although some Min Pins don't like this exercise, those that have been shown in the conformation ring do well because they are more accustomed to being handled by strangers. "We find that our champions do very well in obedience after conformation training," stated Dee Stutts, whose Ch. Harper's Kopper Baron CDX began obedience work at 4½ years old. "The stand for examination is no problem because they are pretty well settled down and are not afraid of strangers."

The "recall" demonstrates that your dog will come reliably when called. From the sit position, on the command to come, your dog must come quickly and sit directly in front of you. On the finish command, he must go to heel position and sit. One problem is that Min Pins are so smart, they begin to anticipate the commands, reported Stutts. "They are eager to please and will often do an exercise before you tell them to. One of the greatest temptations is moving to the heel position after the recall. We have made this two separate exercises in practice sessions, and don't finish from the recall very often."

Ch. Der Stutz Kermit CDX finishes the figure-eight exercise.

Ch. Der Stutz Rock of Gibraltor CDX takes the high jump.

The "long sit" and "long down" are group exercises, which means your Min Pin must compete with a variety of other dogs in the ring. After giving the stay command, you must go to the far end of the ring with the other handlers and turn to face your dog. When the judge instructs the handlers to return—after one minute—walk back to your dog, around behind him, to heel position. Your dog must not move until the judge declares, "Exercise finished." The long down is performed like the long sit, except your dog must remain lying down for three minutes before you're told to return. Min Pins often have trouble with these exercises, perhaps because they prefer more active skills such as heeling or jumping, or because they tend to have short attention spans and easily get bored. Don't give up! Many Min Pins have passed the Companion Dog test with flashy performances.

Open

In Open competition, your dog must perform both the "heel free" and "figure eight" off leash. These two exercises are scored according to the guidelines given in Novice.

The "drop on recall" is similar to the recall performed in Novice, except your dog must drop to the down position on command. When told to come (after dropping), he must move briskly and sit directly in front of you. Some Min Pins don't like to go to the down position. "The drop on recall was our downfall," stated Sandra Hill. "Shazaam would stop and go halfway down. We flunked several Open classes by just half an inch—his elbows were off the floor."

For the "retrieve on the flat" your dog must remain in the stay position while you throw the dumbbell about 20 feet away. On command, your dog must go directly to the dumbbell, pick it up, and bring it back to you. When your dog is sitting directly in front of you, the judge orders, "Take it." You must then signal your dog and take the

JUMP HEIGHTS FOR MINIATURE PINSCHERS

Dog's Height at Withers	Jump Height
9" to less than 10½"	12"
10½" to less than 12"	14"
12" to less than 13½"	16"

dumbbell. This is a difficult exercise, according to Velma Janek. "Retrieves are hard to teach because Min Pins just don't want anything in their mouths that they can't eat." You'll need practice—and a lot of patience—when covering this exercise.

In the "retrieve over the high jump," your dog must leap the high jump, both going and coming, to retrieve the dumbbell. Although the retrieve command may require extra work, Min Pins love to jump and usually do well in all the jumping exercises. "Without a doubt, the most successful exercises are those that require jumping," noted Martha Fair. "My dogs have been known to take some of the jumps between exercises just because they are there."

To complete the "broad jump," your dog must remain in the sit position until he is given the command to jump. He must clear the jump, without touching it, and return to sit directly in front of you. Min Pins usually have no difficulty clearing the broad jump. According to Velma Janek, "They are all born with 'springs' in their legs, so the jumping exercises are fun for them."

The group exercises consist of the "long sit" and "long down." In Open competition, handlers must leave the ring and remain out of sight of their dogs. For the long sit, the time period is three minutes; the long down is five minutes. Unfortunately, Min Pins have short attention spans and don't like to sit still. You'll need to devote extra time to these two exercises so that your dog will perform reliably.

Broad Jump hurdles are arranged so the dog covers a distance equal to twice the height of the High Jump, as set for the particular dog. Three hurdles are used for jumps of 28 to 44 inches; two hurdles for jumps of 16 to 24 inches.

OPEN A EXERCISES

1. Heel Free and Figure Eight	40 points
2. Drop on Recall	30 points
3. Retrieve on Flat	20 points
4. Retrieve over High Jump	30 points
5. Broad Jump	20 points
6. Long Sit	30 points
7. Long Down	30 points
Maximum Total Score	**200 points**

Kimdora's Be-Boppin' Karrie UD OA OAJ
Owned by Doralyn Wheatley

Karrie's titles include UD (Utility Dog), OA (Open Agility) and OAJ (Open Agility Jumpers).

Right: Flying over the bar jump.

Bottom left: Karrie is shown intently working the scent articles in Utility.

Bottom right: Karrie successfully returned the correct scent article.

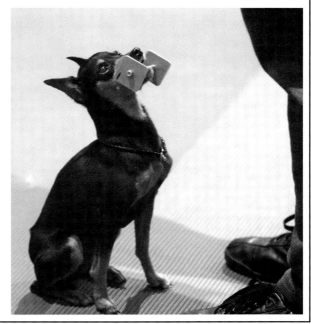

Utility

The "signal exercise" consists of off-leash heeling, along with signals to stand at heel position, stay, drop, sit, come, and finish. Only hand signals are allowed and you may not give any verbal commands during this exercise.

For the two "scent discrimination" exercises, you'll need to provide one set of metal and another set of leather scent objects, consisting of five numbered articles per set (available from training supply catalogs). To pass these exercises, your dog must be able to locate, by scent, each of the two articles marked with your scent, pick up the correct article, and return it to you.

In the "directed retrieve," your dog must retrieve the correct glove from among three placed in the ring, using as a guide the direction indicated by your hand/arm signal. Velma Janek

UTILITY A EXERCISES	
1. Signal Exercise	40 points
2. Scent Discrimination Article No. 1	30 points
3. Scent Discrimination Article No. 2	30 points
4. Directed Retrieve	30 points
5. Moving Stand and Examination	30 points
6. Directed Jumping	40 points
Maximum Total Score	**200 points**

suggested purchasing a set of small gloves, so your dog won't trip over a large, hanging glove during the retrieve.

The "moving stand" is similar to the stand in Novice, except your dog is heeling when the stand command is given. He must remain in position while you walk about 10 feet in front of him. The judge then approaches and goes over your dog, as he did in Novice. When he has finished, your dog must return, on command, to correct heel position.

During the "directed jumping" exercise, your dog must follow your command to execute either the bar jump or the high jump, which have been set up on either side of the ring. The judge decides which jump is to be taken first, and your dog must complete both to pass the exercise.

Utility Dog Excellent

After your dog has earned his Utility title, he may continue to compete for the Utility Dog Excellent (UDX) award. To earn this designation, dogs must achieve qualifying scores in both the Open B and Utility B classes at 10 obedience trials. For the score to count toward the UDX, there must have been six or more dogs entered in Open and three or more in Utility.

OBEDIENCE TRIAL CHAMPION

Dogs that have earned their Utility Dog titles receive points when they place first or second in Open B or Utility (Utility B, if class is divided). To qualify as Obedience Trial Champion (OTCh.), dogs must win three first place prizes (one first place in Open and one in Utility) under three different judges, at all-breed obedience events. Dogs also must accumulate 100 points, awarded based on the number of dogs competing. Unlike other obedience titles, the OTCh. designation precedes the dog's name: OTCh. Der Stutz Tigger UD, for example.

NONREGULAR CLASSES

Specialty shows and training clubs often feature a variety of nonregular obedience classes. These include Graduate Novice, in which dogs perform a selection of Novice and Open exercises; Brace and Team, where two or four dogs compete together; Veterans, for dogs over seven or eight years of age; and Versatility, in which handlers draw a combination of six exercises—two each from Novice, Open, and Utility.

AGILITY

Based on the popular spectator sport of horse jumping, Agility made its debut at the Crufts Dog Show, in England, in 1978. John Varley, a member of the entertainment committee, worked with trainer Peter Meanwell to develop an exciting demonstration to be held between Group judging. When they outlined the specific elements of the Agility test and built the necessary pieces of equipment, Mr. Meanwell began training the dogs. He then asked a friend from another dog club to form and train a team so that they could hold a competition. This generated such interest that, in 1980, The Kennel Club granted Agility official status and created the *Regulations for Agility Tests*.

Agility first appeared in the United States in the mid-1980s, due largely to the efforts of enthusiasts, such as Charles (Bud) Kramer, author of *Agility Dog Training For All Breeds*, and the newly formed United States Dog Agility Association (USDAA). In addition to drafting the *Official Rules and Regulations* of the sport, holding seminars for local dog clubs, and developing construction plans for the various

Karen Egbert's dogs, Big Dan (red) and Bubba (black and rust), love to compete in Agility.

obstacles, the association also coordinates the Pedigree Grand Prix of Dog Agility, a major national tournament supported by Pedigree Dog Food. The American Kennel Club also holds competitive Agility trials and awards the titles, Novice Agility (NA), Open Agility (OA), Agility Excellent (AX), and Master Agility Excellent (MX). Each category offers a Jumpers With Weaves title, as well. (*See page 215 for a complete list of titles.*) The top AKC award is Master Agility Champion (MACH). The first Miniature Pinscher to earn the MACH designation is MACH Windy Acres Coffee Allis-Good CGC AD, owned by Victoria Ford. Coffee started agility lessons in 1997 and gained his MACH title in 2002 at five years and seven months of age.

In Agility, dogs are timed as they run through an obstacle course. The handler runs with his dog (off leash), directing him through the course with verbal commands and hand signals. Time penalties are given for dogs that exceed the course time. Penalties also are given for a variety of errors in negotiating the jumps (tire, wall, broad, and bar) and obstacles (tunnels, weave poles, seesaw, A-frame, dog walk, and pause table). To allow all breeds the opportunity to perform well, dogs are measured before the test, and the heights of the obstacles are adjusted according to the dog's size.

Because Min Pins naturally are energetic and excellent jumpers, they do quite well in Agility. Karen Egbert of Harrison, Idaho has been training and competing with her dogs since 1989. Ch. Egberts Rowdy Rascal CD is believed to be the first Miniature Pinscher with the USDAA titles Agility Dog and Advanced Agility Dog, and Agility Dog of Canada. Rowdy qualified

Ch. Shadowmist's Sable Scheme CD RN OA OAJ
Owned by Doralyn Wheatley

Reba has her breed championship, CD (Companion Dog), RN (Rally Novice), OA (Open Agility) and OAJ (Open Agility Jumpers) titles.

twice for the national Grand Prix in Houston, Texas, and competed with Egberts Danny Boy in the USDAA Masters class. Rowdy and Big Dan also performed in Brace competition and were the only brace at the 1992 Spokane Dog Training Club show to finish with no faults and under course time. "Agility demands perfection, speed, coordination, and all-around teamwork in a physical test for the dog and trainer," said Karen Egbert. "Min Pins are a great breed. They are intelligent, loving, and willing to please. They will work their hearts out for you. They have the speed, coordination, and drive to be excellent in Agility."

According to Egbert and trainers at the Spokane Dog Training Club, you should avoid jumping your dogs at full height until they are at least one year of age. If your Min Pin is a "couch potato," begin Agility training slowly. Older Min Pins, or those with health problems, should be examined by the veterinarian before starting a vigorous exercise program.

Above: Ch. Whypin Tommison CD flies through the tire jump.

Below: Ch. Whypin Little Bitaluck CDX AD successfully negotiates the dog walk.
Both dogs are owned and trained by Rae Galea.

MIN PINS LOVE TO RUN ...

Ch. Kimro's Rocket Man AX AXJ quickly exits the tunnel. Rocket was bred by Robin Greenslade and Kimberly Pastella and is owned by Howard Schwell.

Ch. Shadowmist's Sable Scheme CD RN OA OAJ, owned by Doralyn Wheatley, also runs through the tunnel obstacle.

Am. Can. UKC Ch. Goldmedal The Look of Eagles CD OA OAJ AXJ NJP TT CGC makes a quick exit from the chute. Owned by Barbara Zagrodnick.

Am. Can. Ch. Goldmedal St Nick CD VCD1 OA OAJ NJP TD CGC NACV NGCV RAV-N JAV-N GAV-N excels at the weave poles.

Am. Can. UKC Ch. Goldmedal Larrimie Of Victor CD RA CGC runs through the agility course. Larry won High in Trial when competing for his Companion Dog title. Nick and Larry also are owned by Barbara Zagrodnick and hold obedience titles both in the United States and Canada.

... AND JUMP

Ch. Averson Keystone Connection CDX MX MXJ is owned by Susan Souza.
Photo courtesy of Averson Miniature Pinschers.

Nick, shown on the previous page performing the weave poles, also jumps with ease. Nick is the breed's only Versatile Companion Dog (dogs must complete CD, NA, NAJ, TD titles) and the second Min Pin to hold breed, obedience, tracking, and agility titles.

Ch. Goldmedal Honey Dijon NA NAJ CGC, owned by Barbara Zagrodnick, loves to jump. Here, Dijon easily clears the bar.

Ch. Goldmedal Honey Dijon NA NAJ CGC effortlessly masters the tire jump.

Four Obedience Competitors
Trained by Gretchen Hofheins-Wackerfuss

Left: Ch. Sultans Shameless CDX, who excelled in both the conformation and obedience rings. She was Winners Bitch at the 1996 MPCA National Specialty Show and was the Number 2 MPCA obedience dog in 1998.

Right: Der Stutz Zelda Zing UD was the top-ranked obedience toy breed in the early 1990s, and won High in Trial at MPCA National Specialty Shows in 1989 and 1993. Her breeder was well-known obedience trainer, Dee J. Stutts.

Left: Sultans Lovin' Siren UDX CGC was the first female Miniature Pinscher to earn the Utility Dog Excellent title. She holds numerous records in competition, including High in Trial at three MPCA National Specialty Shows, top-ranked obedience toy, and Number 1 MPCA obedience dog in 1996, 1997, 2000, and 2001. According to her owner, "Ethyl is still the Queen and the love of my life at 15 years young."

Right: Ch. Pevenseys Lovin' It Up CD, a chocolate-and-rust Min Pin, bred by Pamella Ruggie, was High in Trial from the Novice B Class at the 2007 MPCA National Specialty.

Left: Ch. Whypin Lawson Lad CDX AD, owned and trained by Rae Galea, effortlessly negotiates the A-frame. He became the second dog in Australia to hold the Agility Dog title.

Above: He receives some gentle guidance through the weave poles.

TRACKING

Tracking is a sport in which all breeds may compete successfully, using their natural ability to recognize and follow the scent of a track layer. In fact, when the American Kennel Club published its first official set of obedience regulations, in 1936, tracking was a required element of the Utility Dog test. As interest in obedience competition increased, the AKC formed a separate Tracking Dog (TD) test in 1947. It later added Tracking Dog Excellent (TDX) and Variable Surface Tracking (VST) tests. Dogs earn the highest title, Champion Tracker (CT), after completing all three tests.

In the Tracking Dog test, dogs cover a 440- to 500-yard course, consisting of 3, 4, or 5 turns (at least 2 right-angle turns). The scent on the track is between 30 minutes and 2 hours old, and the terrain may not change abruptly or cross a paved road or body of water. The Tracking Dog Excellent test is considerably more difficult, and so far only one Min Pin has earned the TDX degree. Dogs are required to cover an 800- to 1,000-yard course, aged 3 to 5 hours, with 2 cross tracks. In this test, the track covers a variety of ground conditions and obstacles, such as woods, vegetation, gullies, streams, fences, roads, or bridges. Dogs competing in the Variable Surface Tracking test must be able to follow a scent, despite changing track conditions. Over a 600- to 800-yard course, aged 3 to 5 hours, dogs cover at least 3 different surfaces, including 2 areas devoid of vegetation, such as concrete, sand, gravel, or asphalt. According to the AKC, the training required to pass the VST "must be designed to develop the inner drive, motivation, and determination necessary for the dog to work with intensity and perseverance."

The object of a tracking test is for your dog to locate an article, or articles, dropped by the track layer. Dogs work in a tracking harness on a 20- to 40-foot leash. You may encourage your dog with verbal commands, but may not physically guide or direct him. (In TDX competition, you may assist your dog when obstacles, barriers, or terrain require, according to the AKC.) There is no time limit to find the article(s), but your dog must appear to be actively searching.

Sandra Hill, who trained Shazaam, said her Min Pin is an excellent tracker. "He's my second tracking dog (along with a Belgian Tervuren) and is one of the best I've seen. Shazaam absolutely loves to track and he pulls so hard in his harness that his front feet come off the ground. We track in sand, cacti, stickers, thorns, heat, and wind in El Paso, Texas, and these do not seem to bother Shazaam at all.

"Training a Min Pin requires a lot of patience and a sense of humor," added Sandy. "They are unpredictable, headstrong, and love to play games with their owners. However, I would not trade Shazaam for anything. He is a doll to live with and I love training him. He excels at any exercise that involves rewards and praise: retrieving, jumping, scent discrimination, and tracking. Shazaam is a unique dog and a lovely companion."

U-CD Horizon's Alakazan-D's Shazaam UDT, owned and trained by Sandra A. Hill, of El Paso, Texas.

AKC Agility Abbreviations

AJP Excellent Agility Jumpers With Weaves "A" Preferred: For a title, dog must earn 3 qualifying scores in Excellent A Jumpers With Weaves Preferred class under at least 2 different judges.

AX Agility Excellent: For a title, dog must earn 3 qualifying scores in Excellent A Agility class under at least 2 different judges.

AXJ Excellent Agility Jumper: For a title, dog must earn 3 qualifying scores in Excellent A Jumpers With Weaves class under at least 2 different judges.

AXP Agility Excellent "A" Preferred: For a title, dog must earn 3 qualifying scores in Agility Excellent "A" Preferred Class under at least 2 different judges.

FTC FAST Century: Requires the MXF title plus one hundred Excellent B FAST agility class qualifying scores of 60 points or greater. The FTC title initials will be followed by a numeric designation indicating the quantity of times the dog has met the requirements of the FTC title.

FTCP FAST Century Preferred: Requires the MFP title plus one hundred Excellent B FAST agility class qualifying scores of 60 points or greater. The FTCP title initials will be followed by a numeric designation indicating the quantity of times the dog has met the requirements of the FTCP title.

MACH Master Agility Champion: In order to acquire the title, a dog must achieve a minimum of 750 championship points and 20 double qualifying scores obtained from the Excellent B Standard Agility class and the Excellent B Jumpers With Weaves class.

MFP Master Excellent FAST Preferred: For a title, dog must earn 10 qualifying scores in Excellent B FAST Preferred agility class under at least 2 different judges. Trial at which XFP was earned does not count toward the 10.

MJP Master Excellent Jumpers With Weaves "B" Preferred: For a title, dog must earn 10 qualifying scores in Excellent B Jumpers With Weaves Preferred Agility class under at least 2 different judges. Trial at which AX was earned does not count toward the 10.

MX Master Agility Excellent: For a title, dog must earn 10 qualifying scores in Excellent B Agility class under at least 2 different judges. Trial at which AX was earned does not count toward the 10.

MXF Master Excellent FAST: For a title, dog must earn 10 qualifying scores in Excellent B FAST agility class under at least 2 different judges. Trial at which XF was earned does not count toward the 10.

MXJ Master Excellent Jumpers With Weaves: For a title, dog must earn 10 qualifying scores in Excellent B Jumpers With Weaves Agility class under at least 2 different judges. Trial at which AX was earned does not count toward the 10.

MXP Master Agility Excellent "B" Preferred: For a title, dog must earn 10 qualifying scores in Excellent Agility Preferred "B" class under at least 2 different judges. Trial at which AXP was earned does not count toward the 10.

NA Novice Agility: For a title, dog must earn 3 qualifying scores in Novice A and/or B Agility class under at least 2 different judges.

NAC National Agility Champion: The winner of the annual National Agility Championship shall be entitled to be designated National Agility Champion of _____(year).

NAJ Novice Agility Jumper: For a title, dog must earn 3 qualifying scores in Novice A and/or B Jumpers With Weaves class under at least 2 different judges.

NAP Novice Agility Preferred: For a title, dog must earn 3 qualifying scores in the Novice Agility Preferred class under at least 2 different judges.

NF Novice FAST: For a title, dog must earn 3 qualifying scores in Novice A and/or B FAST agility class under at least 2 different judges.

NFP Novice FAST Preferred: For a title, dog must earn 3 qualifying scores in Novice A and/or B FAST Preferred agility class under at least 2 different judges.

NJP Novice Jumpers With Weaves Preferred: For a title, dog must earn 3 qualifying scores in the Novice Jumpers With Weaves Preferred class under at least 2 different judges.

OA Open Agility: For a title, dog must earn 3 qualifying scores in Open Agility class under at least 2 different judges.

OAJ Open Agility Jumper: For a title, dog must earn 3 qualifying scores in Open Jumpers With Weaves class under at least 2 different judges.

OAP Open Agility Preferred: For a title, dog must earn 3 qualifying scores in Open Agility Preferred class under at least 2 different judges.

OF Open FAST: For a title, dog must earn 3 qualifying scores in Open FAST agility class under at least 2 different judges.

OFP Open FAST Preferred: For a title, dog must earn 3 qualifying scores in Open FAST Preferred agility class under at least 2 different judges.

OJP Open Jumpers With Weaves Preferred: For a title, dog must earn 3 qualifying scores in Open Jumpers With Weaves Preferred class under at least 2 different judges.

PAX Preferred Agility Excellent: For a title, a dog must achieve 20 double qualifying scores obtained from the Preferred Excellent B Standard agility class and the Preferred Excellent B Jumpers With Weaves class. Qualifying in both the Preferred Excellent B Standard agility class and the Preferred Excellent B Jumpers With Weaves class on the same day equals one (1) double qualifying score.

XF Excellent FAST: For a title, dog must earn 3 qualifying scores in Excellent A FAST agility class under at least 2 different judges.

XFP Excellent FAST Preferred: For a title, dog must earn 3 qualifying scores in Excellent A FAST Preferred agility class under at least 2 different judges.

Used with permission from The American Kennel Club, Inc. All rights reserved.

Obedience Titles

UTILITY DOG TITLES

Baron von Stolzenkamp
Owner: David B. Van Houten

Baum's Little Elmer
Owner: Mrs. Barbara W. Finley

Bracy's Mindy Sue
Owner: A. Bracy

Burgundy Bit of Sugar and Spice
Owner: Unknown

Captain Kim of Dascom
Owners: George and Fiona Mullen

Crimson Magic Southern Belle
Owner: Shirley Mason

Ch. Dae Lings Allspice
Owners: Dave and Lee Epling

Der Kavalier of Pine Hollow
Owners: N. Leon Duffer and W. R. Ptomey, M.D.

OTCH Der Stutz Cinnamon Twig
Owner: Velma Janek

Ch. Der Stutz Gypsy Sweetheart
Owners: Dee Harper and Stewart M. Nordensson

OTCH Der Stutz Tigger
Owner: Velma Janek

Der Stutz Twinkle Little Star
Owner: Dee J. Stutts

Der Stutz Zelda Zing
Owner: Gretchen S. Hofheins-Wackerfuss

Ch. Ericson Miller Der Stutz
Owner: Phillip D. Miller

Fairhaven's Impulsive Mia
Owner: Martha E. Fair

Gingiber of Beland
Owner: Mrs. Elsa Beland

Goldmedal Lucky Ole Sun
Owners: Patrice Delehanty and Barbara Zagrodnick

Goldmedal Marty JusJazzy
Owners: Patrice Delehanty and Barbara Zagrodnick

Ch. Hans Von Tejas
Owner: Mrs. Leo J. Murphy

Horizon's Alakazan-D's Shazaam
Owner: Sandra Hill

Huskerland's Missina Snoople
Owner: Beverly Lammert

Joy's Baron Von Frederick
Owners: John O. and Helen S. Yarwood

Joy's Jolly Jack
Owner: John O. Yarwood

Katrina von Scheuring
Owner: Dorothy E. Wilkinson

Keen's Zsa-Zsa Von Rex
Owner: Camille Degen Robertson

Kimdora's Be-Boppin' Karrie
Owner: Doralyn Wheatley

Kimdora's Mega Flashfire
Owner: Doralyn Wheatley

Ch. King's Hi Fashion Image of Mira
Owners: Dr. and Mrs. C. D. Bourke, Jr.

Kipmik's Barefoot Contessa
Owner: Adina E. Rossiter

Layla's Double Trouble
Owner: Unknown

Lexington's Sea Biscuit
Owners: Scott and Suzanne A. Harvey

Ch. Meret's Ton Of Trouble
Owner: Ethel L. Mercer

Midnight Magni von Haymount
Owner: Catherine E. Smith

Millie D's Prince Albert
Owner: Fiona Mullen

Nikki von Radar
Owner: Mrs. Dorothy M. Britton

Nor-Li's Darling Wendy
Owner: Anna S. Naumann

Pow Wow Oak's Artful Dodger
Owner: Patrice Delehanty

Ch. Rollin Rocs Bugsie Bandit
Owner: Jean Henry

Obedience Titles

Ruff 'N Rowdy Jason Von Duffer
Owner: Charles Philip Carter

Sanbrook Scarlet For Karitom
Owner: Elizabeth Growick

Scheuring's Wee Red Ricrac
Owner: Dorothy E. Wilkinson

Shadowmist's Over the Rainbow
Owner: Gerald Crosby

Thunderstone's Lucky Tiger
Owner: J. A. Edwards

Tora Dancer Brannen
Owner: Masako Brannen

Urray Golden Penny II
Owner: Mrs. Kathryn J. Marshall

OTCH Wee D's Weeble Minute
Owner: Judie Clark

Whisper Valley's Too Tall Boy
Owner: Karen Carnahan

Wiltrakis' Sparkplug
Owners: Scott and Suzanne Harvey

UTILITY DOG EXCELLENT TITLES
Hot to Trot Don't Call Me Tiny
Owner: Gerald Crosby

Jock's Nemesis Tiny A
Owner: Don Roback

Shansu
Owner: Michael F. Widhalm

Sultans Lovin' Siren
Owner: Gretchen S. Hofheins-Wackerfuss

Tazz's Message From A Star UDX2
Owner: Gerald Crosby

Timline Shansu Bro to Battle UDX4
Owner: Michael F. Widhalm

TRACKING DOG TITLES
Easy Does It Drum'n Up CDX
Owner: Bobbie Crissey

Ch. Goldmedal Olympia CD NA TDI CGC
Owner: Barbara Zagrodnick

Ch. Goldmedal St Nick CD VCD1 OA OAJ NJP CGC
Owner: Barbara Zagrodnick

Hi-Spirit Spiderman CDX
Owner: Velda Pearson

Horizon's Alakazan-D's Shazaam UD
Owner: Sandra Hill

Kipmik's Barefoot Contessa UD
Owner: Adina E. Rossiter

Parker's Lil' Flash CDX
Owner: Joyce A. Capoccia

Thunderstone's Lucky Tiger UD
Owner: J. A. Edwards

Timline Ain't Misbehavin' CD NA NAJ
Owner: Jan Plagenz

Waylyn's Thimble of Bahia CDX
Owner: Annabel Allen

TRACKING DOG EXCELLENT TITLES
Parker's Lil' Flash CDX
Owner: Joyce A. Capoccia

OBEDIENCE TRIAL CHAMPIONS
OTCH Der Stutz Cinnamon Twig UD
Owner: Velma Janek

OTCH Der Stutz Tigger UD
Owner: Velma Janek

OTCH Wee D's Weeble Minute UD
Owner: Judie Clark

MASTER AGILITY CHAMPIONS
MACH Jocks Nemesis Tiny A UDX
Owner: Donald Roback

MACH4 Pinehurst Penny Lane CD MXP NJP OF
Owner: Debra Shigmatsu

MACH7 Pinehurst Tiger Woodson CDX OAP OJP OF
Owner: Debra Shigematsu

MACH Valdon's Jest Clownin Around CD
Owner: Joan Krumm

MACH Windy Acres Coffee Allisgood CGC
Owner: Victoria Ford

Can. Ch. Dobiranch's Zipper of Paulee, owned by Edris Matulock, shows off the collection of ribbons that made him Canada's Number 2 Miniature Pinscher, in 1985.

THE MINIATURE PINSCHER IN CANADA
22

The Miniature Pinscher is a relatively uncommon breed in Canada, with about 300 dogs registered annually by the Canadian Kennel Club (CKC). Some of the earliest dogs, like those in the United States, arrived with families settling in Canada from Europe—especially Germany, England, and Scandinavia. Although it's difficult to pinpoint Canada's first involvement with the lively little pinscher, by the 1950s and 1960s a number of kennels were actively involved in breeding and showing: Airlane (Mrs. Winnifred Wartnow), D'Arcis (Garry and D'Arcis Herald), Golden Circle (Mrs. Alice Barton), Harlow (Mr. and Mrs. James F. Proctor), Hillrise (Mrs. Ethel Sipes), Lo-Bob (Mr. and Mrs. Robert Waters), Sonna (Mrs. E. J. Anson), and Wild Rock (Mrs. R. A. Hewitt). The quality of today's Min Pin—his attractive appearance, vigor, and outgoing personality—is a direct result of these early breeders' commitment to excellence.

FOUNDING KENNELS
Airlane

Mrs. Winnifred Wartnow introduced the breed in British Columbia, starting in 1945 with a pet Miniature Pinscher. She and her husband fell in love with their dog, and later acquired Ch. Dollymount's Hobo de Jareaux and Dollymount's Taffie, their pet's sire and dam. Producing more than 50 champions since 1955, Mrs. Wartnow discussed her Airlane kennel and the breed's early history:

Can. Ch. Airlane's Sunrise, owned by Winnifred Wartnow.

One cannot say just what a Min Pin is.
To me, he is part clown, part acrobat,
part human, part dog, part lion,
very much a moocher, and quite lovable.

Winnifred Wartnow

Above: Winnifred Wartnow's first litter produced Can. Ch. Airlane's Thunderbolt, a top stud dog in Canada.

Below: Can. Ch. Airlane's Lucky Lady was an MPCA Specialty Show winner in 1968.

"I first saw Hobo when he was 10 months old—what a dream! Nearly two years later, Mrs. Lucky of Washington's Dollymount kennel told me I could buy him, along with Taffie, if Taffie liked me. I fed her candy all the way home—she loved me! Taffie was an older dog, so we could only breed her once. Airlane, named because the kennel was under the 'airlane,' began in 1955 when she had four puppies. Among them was our first home-bred champion, Ch. Airlane's Thunderbolt."

Thunderbolt became one of Canada's top sires, with 15 champion offspring to his credit. He sired the first Canadian-bred Miniature Pinscher to win Best in Show, in Canada (Ch. Airlane's Meteor of Wild Rock), as well as the second Min Pin to win this honor (Ch. Lo-Bob's Amber Dust). "Through the years, I've learned a lot about animal breeding from the 'Indian People' of Canada," explained Mrs. Wartnow. "They say that in the spring all things are new and coming to life, so I have always tried to breed my females in February or March, if possible. I believe the reason I've been successful with my Miniature Pinschers is that they are my heart and soul," she added. "As a licensed judge in Canada, the United States, Brazil, and Australia, I've always judged honestly. I remember the times my dogs have lost in the ring and how much it hurt. My advice to a newcomer is to be honest with your kennel and you will never go wrong."

Lo-Bob

Another prominent early kennel was Lo-Bob, founded in 1956 by Mr. and Mrs. Robert Waters of Surrey, British Columbia. Mr. Waters, an all-breed dog judge, acquired his first Min Pin from Miss Michael Carmichael's Of the Hill kennel, located in Tyler, Texas. Ch. Lo-Bob's Amber Dust, a Best in Show winner, played an important role in his kennel's breeding program. However, the best-known Min Pin owned by the Waters may be Int. Ch. Mystery Gal of Lo-Bob. A beautiful dog with a long, graceful neck, square body, high tail set, and correct small feet, she finished her U.S. championship with three 5-point majors and was the second-ranking Min Pin, in Canada, in 1965.

CURRENT KENNELS

Today, Canadian breeders continue the tradition established by early pioneers. Their active schedule of showing, often traveling hundreds of miles to attend events, and the formation of the Canadian Miniature Pinscher Club foster much interest in this spirited little dog. Many newcomers have joined the ranks of Min Pin exhibitors and breeders. A partial list of kennels follows:

In eastern Canada, Jacline and Armand Gratton's Frontenac kennel, Inga Paquin's Premina kennel, Jean Verner's Winatout kennel, and Emile Vroye's Mogador's kennel, all in Quebec; Judith Wellwood's Juddawood kennel, in New Brunswick; and Helen Cox's Suebon kennel, Patricia Gauthier's Patapin kennel, Gerona MacCuaig's Jothona kennel, Paul Nice's Rway kennel, Jean Sparks' Min Springs kennel, Robert and Glenys Johnson's Hafenstadt kennel, James and Louise Procter's Harlow kennel, Ed and Darlene Riley's

Airlane's Can-Do is pictured winning Best Canadian-bred Puppy at his first show.

Can. Ch. Airlane's Meteor of Wild Rock, bred by Winnifred Wartnow and owned by Mrs. Hewitt, was the first Canadian-bred Miniature Pinscher to win Best in Show.

Kaybrooke kennel, and Shirley William's Shirwill kennel, all in Ontario. Western Canada includes Edris Matulock's Zipedde kennel, in Saskatchewan; Wendy Beck's Dawnaquinn kennel, Kathy Davies' Summit kennel, Bonnie Foster's Mightymite kennel, Twyla Taylor's Taylor Ranch kennel, Lorna Radkie's WW kennel, Marleen Whiskin's Silkwood kennel, all in Alberta; and Dianne Bailey's Harr kennel, Sandra Dunham's Bezee kennel, Ray and Judy Bohnert's Equinox kennel, Myrna Keyser's Teralea kennel, Marguerette and Allan Mosher's Crittendale kennel, Melissa Dostalek's Pocketmouse kennel, Carol and Les Snaith's Sancardou kennel, and Lorraine Lyons' Pawznplay kennel, all in British Columbia.

For more information on breeders, puppies, or stud dogs, contact the Canadian Kennel Club or obtain a copy of *Dogs in Canada* magazine.

SHOWING YOUR DOG
The Entry Form

All dog shows held under the authority of the Canadian Kennel Club provide premium lists for prospective exhibitors. To enter a show, you must submit the entry form with the following information:
- Name of breed
- Name of dog
- Event Registration Number
- Sex
- Color
- Name of breeder
- Place and date of birth
- Name of sire and dam
- Class in which the dog is entered
- Name and complete address of owner
- Signature of the owner or authorized agent
- Name of handler (if not shown by owner or family)

Classes

Junior Puppy is for dogs between 6 months and under 9 months of age.

Senior Puppy is for dogs between 9 months and under 12 months of age.

Int. Ch. Mystery Gal of Lo-Bob, bred and owned by Robert Waters.

12–18 Month Class is for dogs 12 months of age and under 18 months of age on the day of the show.

Canadian-Bred is for dogs born in Canada. Champions of any other country are excluded.

Bred-by-Exhibitor is for dogs bred by the exhibitor. The handler must be the owner/co-owner and the breeder/co-breeder of the dog. The owner/breeder must handle the dog at the class level, but need not handle the dog for further awards.

Open is for all dogs.

Specials Only—Dogs who have already obtained their Canadian championships are called Specials and are entered in the Specials Only class. Entrants must be registered with the CKC or have an Event Registration Number.

Exhibition Only is for dogs who will be at the show, but will not be entering the show ring or competing. Dogs entered in this class shall be listed in the catalogue with the same information as dogs entered in regular competition. Dogs in this class may not compete in any Regular Class, but may be entered and compete in any Non-Regular Classes and/or Parades Only.

Veterans Class (Specialty shows) is for dogs 7 years of age and over on the day of the show. Dogs entered in this class may be spayed or neutered.

Ring Procedure

Dog shows proceed in a similar fashion to AKC shows held in the United States. The judge begins with the Junior Puppy Male and awards first through fourth place ribbons. He continues with Senior Puppy Male, Canadian-Bred Male, Bred-by-Exhibitor Male, and Open Male. When all the male classes have been judged, the dogs placing first in each class enter the ring to compete for Winners Male. The dog that placed second to Winners Male in a regular class then is brought into the ring to compete for Reserve Winners Male. The procedure is repeated for all female dogs.

Best of Breed entrants consist of the Winners Male, Winners Female, and Specials Only (champions). After the judge selects Best of Breed, he chooses Best of Opposite Sex to Best of Breed. From the Winners Male and Winners Female, he selects the Best of Winners. If the Winners Male or Winners Female wins Best of Breed, the dog automatically is named Best of Winners.

At all-breed shows, the Best of Breed winner competes in the Toy Group and that winner then competes for Best in Show. Puppies also compete for Best Puppy in Breed and go on to Best Puppy in Group and Best Puppy in Show.

Canadian Championship

In order for your Min Pin to earn a Canadian championship, he must earn a minimum of 10 points under at least 3 different judges, at least one 2-point win, and be registered with the CKC. The only dogs that earn champion-

Above: Can. Ch. Bee Jay's Stingray is a Best in Show winner for owner, Beth Bujea.

Left: Am. Can. Ch. Bee Jay's Photo Finish, bred by Billie Jean Shuler and owned by Beth Bujea, is a Best in Show winner that also won Best of Breed at the 1986 MPCA National Specialty Show.

ship points are the Winners Male and Winners Female. The point schedule varies from zero to five per show, depending on the number of dogs the Winner defeated. In addition to championship points allocated at the breed level, a dog awarded Winners that also places in Group or wins Best in Show earns additional points (not to exceed five points total).

BREED STANDARD
General Appearance

The Miniature Pinscher originated in Germany and is named the Reh Pinscher due to his resemblance in structure and animation to a very small species of deer found in the forests. This breed is structurally a well-balanced, sturdy, compact, short-coupled, smooth-coated toy dog. He is naturally well groomed, proud, vigorous, and alert. The natural characteristic traits which identify him from other toy dogs are his precise hackney gait, his fearless animation, complete self-possession, and his spirited presence.

Faults: Structurally lacking in balance, too long or short-coupled, too coarse or too refined (lacking in bone development causing poor feet and legs), too large or too small, lethargic, timid or dull, shy or vicious, low in tail placement and poor in action (action not typical of the breed requirements). Knotty overdeveloped muscles.

Size

Desired height 11 to 11½ inches (28 to 29 cm.) at the withers. A dog of either sex measuring under 10 inches (25 cm.) or over 12½ inches (32 cm.) shall be disqualified.

Coat and Colour

Coat smooth, hard and short, straight, and lustrous, closely adhering to and uniformly covering the body. Colour: a) Solid red or stag red. b) Lustrous black with sharply defined tan, rust-red markings on cheeks, lips, lower jaw, throat, twin spots above eyes, and chest, lower half of

Can. Ch. Juddawood Eric von Baron Rouge, owned by Lorraine Lyons, finished his championship under noted judge, Michele Billings. Shown with handler, Jim Campbell.

forelegs, inside of hind legs and vent region, lower portion of hocks and feet. Black pencil stripes on toes. c) Solid brown or chocolate with rust or yellow markings.

Faults: Thin, too long, dull coat; upstanding coat; curly coat; dry coat; area of various thickness or bald spots. Any colour other than listed; very dark or sooty spots.

Head

In correct proportion with the body. From top: Tapering, narrow with well-fitted but not too prominent foreface which should balance with the skull. No indication of coarseness. From front: Skull appears flat, tapering forward towards the muzzle. Muzzle itself strong rather than fine and delicate, and in proportion to the head as a whole; cheeks and lips small, taut and closely adherent to each other. Teeth in perfect alignment and apposition. From side: Well balanced with only a slight drop to the muzzle, which should be parallel to the top of the skull. Nose black only (with the exception of chocolates, which may have a self-coloured nose). Eyes full, slightly oval, almost round, clear, bright and dark, even to a true black; set wide apart and fitted well into the sockets. Ears well set and firmly placed, upstanding (when cropped, pointed, and carried erect in balance with the head).

Faults: Too large or too small for the body, too coarse or too refined, pinched and weak in foreface, domed in skull, too flat and lacking in chiselling, giving a vapid expression. Nose any colour other than black (with the exception of chocolates which may have a self-coloured nose). Jaws and teeth overshot or undershot. Eyes too round and full, too large, bulging, too deepset or set too far apart; or too small, set too close (pig eyes). Light-coloured eyes are not desirable. Ears poorly placed, low-set hanging ears (lacking in cartilage) which detract from head conformation. (Poorly cropped ears if set on the head properly and having sufficient cartilage should not detract from head points, as this would be a man-made fault and automatically would detract from general appearance.)

Neck

Proportioned to head and body. Slightly arched, gracefully curved, clean and firm, blending into shoulders, length well balanced, muscular and free from a suggestion of dewlap or throatiness.

Faults: Too straight or too curved; too thick or too thin; too long or short; knotty muscles; loose, flabby or wrinkled skin.

Forequarters

Shoulders clean, sloping with moderate angulation, coordinated to permit the true action of the

Above: Can. Ch. Equinox Meant T'B Gold Fabert, multiple Best Puppy in Show winner, with Group wins and placements. Bred by Judy Bohnert and owned by Françoise Allard, Robert Brousseau, and Myriam Ruel, of Quebec.

Left: Can. Ch. Frontenac's Firefox, bred and owned by Armand and Jacline Gratton.

Can. Ch. Equinox Metric Exquisite Gold V Bezee, bred by Judy Bohnert and owned by Sandra Dunham. Winner of Best Puppy in Show and multiple Group wins and placements.

Can. Ch. Equinox Mesure Metric V Fabert, bred by Judy Bohnert and owned by Françoise Allard, Robert Brousseau, and Myriam Ruel.

Can. Ch. Equinox Metric Xplosion V Harr, bred by Judy Bohnert and owned by Dianne Bailey. Multiple Best Puppy in Show winner and multiple Group wins and placements.

Can. Ch. Patapin Next Episode, the Number 3 Miniature Pinscher in Canada in 2003. Bred by Patricia Gauthier and owned by Judy Bohnert.

Hackney pony. Strong bone development and small clean joints. As viewed from the front, straight and upstanding; elbows close to body, well knit, flexible yet strong with perpendicular pasterns.

Faults: Shoulders too straight, too loose, or too short and overloaded with muscles. Forelegs bowed or crooked, weak pasterns, feet turning in or out, loose elbows.

Body

From top: Compact, slightly wedge-shaped, muscular with well-sprung ribs. From side:

Back level or slightly sloping towards the rear. Length of males equals height at withers. Females may be slightly longer. Forechest well developed and full, moderately broad. Depth of brisket, the base line of which is level with the points of the elbows; short and strong in loin with belly moderately tucked up to denote grace in structural form. From rear: High tail set; strong, sturdy upper shanks, with croup slope at about 30 degrees; vent opening not barreled.

Faults: From top—too long, too short, too barreled, lacking in body development. From side—too long, too short, too thin, or too fat, hips higher or considerably lower than the withers, lacking depth of chest, too full in loin, sway back, roach back or wry back. Forechest and spring of rib too narrow (or too shallow and underdeveloped). From rear—quarters too wide or too close to each other, overdeveloped, barreled vent, underdeveloped vent, too sloping croup, tail set low.

Hindquarters

Well-knit muscular quarters set wide enough apart to fit into a properly balanced body. All adjacent bones should appear well angulated with well-muscled thighs or upper shanks, with clearly well-defined stifles, hocks short, set well apart turning neither in nor out, while at rest should stand perpendicular to the ground and upper shanks, lower shanks and hocks parallel to each other. Feet cat-like, toes strong, well arched and closely knit with deep pads and thick, blunt nails.

Faults: Too narrow, undermuscled or over-muscled, too steep in croup. Too thick or thin bone development, large joints, spreading flat feet. Thin underdeveloped stifles, large or crooked hocks, loose stifle joints.

Tail

Set high, held erect, docked to ½ to 1 inch (1 to 3 cm.).

Faults: Set too low, too thin, drooping, hanging or poorly docked.

Disqualifications

Thumb marks or any area of white on feet or forechest exceeding ½ inch (1 cm.) in its longest dimension. A dog of either sex measuring under 10 inches (25 cm.) or over 12½ inches (32 cm.) shall be disqualified.

Scale of Points

General appearance and movement	30
Skull	5
Muzzle	5
Mouth	5
Eyes	5
Ears	5
Neck	5
Body	15
Feet	5
Legs	5
Colour	5
Coat	5
Tail	5
Total:	100

Can. Ch. Harr's 24KT Brat V Equinox, the Number 1 Miniature Pinscher in Canada in 2005. He has won multiple Best in Specialty Show and Best Puppy in Show awards, as well as Group wins and placements. Bred by Dianne Bailey and owned by Judy Bohnert, both of British Columbia.

This Miniature Pinscher, called the *dværgpinscher* in Denmark, poses with his larger cousin, known as the *mellempinscher*. Both dogs are owned by Herbert and Jytte Baumkirchner.

HISTORICAL DEVELOPMENT AROUND THE WORLD
23

AUSTRALIA

The Miniature Pinscher was unknown in Australia prior to 1958, when George Byron imported the dog, Brazen of Tavey, and bitch, Kanoon of Tavey, from the Curnows' kennel in England. The male, nicknamed Tiny, won Best of Breed four times in England, including the 1956 and 1957 Crufts Southern Counties Dog Show. The female, Poppett, was not shown in England, but a litter brother was the winning dog at Crufts in 1958. Poppett's pedigree included one International and eight American champion ancestors. Although the quality of Byron's Min Pins was excellent, the difficulty in competing against the more popular toy breeds and locating homes for the puppies led him to discontinue breeding.

The Min Pin might have faded from Australian history at that point, except for the interest of the late Harold R. Spira, B.V.Sc., M.R.C.V.S., H.D.A., a well-known veterinarian, writer, and all-breed dog judge, and his

Ch. Roepin Bronze Prince, owned by Mike and Helen Towell. Photos by T. Dorizas.

These three Min Pins are from the Zwergpin kennel. Note the variation of ear-stance development.

Left: Ch. Roepin Naaram, Miniature Pinscher of the Year for 1979 and 1980, is owned by Mrs. M. Rose's Roepin kennel.

Below left: Ch. Hayclose Heritor, from Hayclose kennel, is owned by Dora Hay.

Below: Ch. Khanrae Smart Leigh, owned by Mrs. M. Rose, is a Best in Show winner and Miniature Pinscher of the Year for 1987 and 1988. Photo by Trafford.

wife Margaret. The Spiras, who learned about the breed from English judge MacDonald Daly, founded Pindom kennel with a pair of Byron's dogs: Tasso Simba and Tasso Little Red Eva.

The most serious problem facing Australian breeders has been the lack of consistent size and type. Some of the early dogs, though structurally sound, were large and somewhat coarse. Smaller dogs, brought in to modify size, tended to produce Min Pins that resembled tiny Chihuahuas. Breeders have worked hard to eliminate the domed head, prominent round eyes, and weak hindquarters often found in such undersized dogs.

Michael and Helen Towell, from New South Wales, who breed under the Zwergpin kennel name, discuss the dog's progress in Australia:

"The Min Pin reached a peak in popularity and quality from the mid-1970s to early 1980s. Australia had many breeders during this period, and many dogs were introduced from the United Kingdom. The breed still is very popular as a pet, due to his agility, sharp sense of hearing, and will to protect his home and owner.

"Over the last 25 years, breeders have seen many changes in the Min Pin's general appearance—all for the better. Today, dogs are taller (11 to 12 inches), with longer legs, greater depth of body and forechest development, and more-elongated heads. With the introduction of foreign bloodlines, the hindquarters have strengthened and dogs are getting more turn of stifle. This produces a better driving movement. Breeders have their likes and dislikes on the hackney gait, and have bred accordingly. Some prefer the shorter-stepping hind movement, which compensates with more of a hackney action.

"In the show ring, the red color tends to dominate, although occasionally we have seen quality black-and-tan dogs. The black and tan

Above: Ch. Wichita Melody is owned by Margaret Holmes. Photo by T. Dorizas.

Left: Ch. Lylac Le Grand Onyx UD was the first Min Pin champion to earn an Australian obedience title.

seems to be most popular among pet buyers, as this color gives the impression of a small Doberman. The chocolate and blue colors have never really taken in popularity. This may be a result of Australia's harsh climate. The chocolate fades to a patchy color, whereas the blue suffers from skin problems that may cause the dog to become bald when he is only two to three years old."

A few dedicated individuals have ventured into the fields of obedience training and Agility trials. Mrs. Rae Galea's Aust. Ch. Lylac Le Grand Onyx UD qualified in obedience 57 times and placed 39 times. One of Minnie's best tricks was to jump through a hoop of fire. Another Miniature Pinscher, Aust. Ch. Whypin Lawson Lad, has scored well in the popular sport of Agility. Mrs. Galea also trained the Miniature Pinscher that appeared in several episodes of the Australian television show, *A Country Practice*.

Australian kennels, past and current, include Calgary (Audrey and Ben Swanston), Daunton (George Tucker), Haycoss (Dora Hay), Pindom (Dr. and Mrs. Spira), Reechelar (Tess Henderson), Rockwood (Frank Longmore), Roepin (Marilyn Rose), Tasso (George Byron), Wichita (Margaret Holmes), Zandor (Colin and Judy Weaver), and Zwergpin (the Towells).

Above: Ch. Wildeshan Tiger Eye, Miniature Pinscher of the Year for 1982 and 1983.

Above right: Ch. Zwergpin Sweetn Spicy, a deep-red Min Pin, free stacks for owners Mike and Helen Towell.

Right: Ch. Hayclose Handyman, bred by John and Peggy Stott's Hayclose kennel, in England, was imported by Dora Hay. Shown with two future champions, Haycoss Helio Bronze and Haycoss Helio Russette.

COLOMBIA

Information on the Miniature Pinscher in Colombia is provided by Sonia Guarin Zambrano, a dog breeder and veterinarian:

"Until recently, show-quality dogs in Colombia were not as popular as pet quality. This may have been due to the fact that a pet Miniature Pinscher was much less expensive (about $80 to $100 U.S. compared to $350 to $400), and many dogs that looked like Min Pins actually were not purebred.

"The rules for showing in the Asociación Club Canino Colombiano (ACCC) are very similar to the American Kennel Club's rules. However, we also depend on the standard of the Fédération Cynologique Internationale (FCI). Breeding regulations vary quite a bit from those in the United States. In Colombia, owners can't breed a male or female under 18 months of age in small breeds or under 24 months in large breeds. In order for the puppies to have an ACCC pedigree, both the sire and dam must have been shown at least twice and they must have won Best of Class two times. When the bitch is in season, the owner goes to the ACCC office and asks permission to breed her. An experienced breeder/owner can choose the male he wants to use, but an inexperienced breeder is told which dog(s) he can use for mating. The owner must breed the female with that particular male in order to register the puppies.

"Line breeding (breeding bloodlines) is normally done. Close line breeding (half-brothers/half-sisters) or inbreeding are only permitted by experienced breeders and they must explain why they are breeding those dogs and what they expect from it. When the puppies are six to eight weeks of age, the breeder takes them to the ACCC office for individual registration. There, the puppies are examined for correct bites, testes, breed faults and disqualifications, colors, and number of dogs in the litter (only nine puppies per litter can be registered). Although these rules are good for

Above: Merlin de la Trojita is owned by Sonia Guarin of Bogotá, Colombia.

Below: Ch. Festival de Cannes Blas, also owned by Sonia Guarin, is shown placing second in Group and winning Best Puppy in Group.

Three blue-and-rust Miniature Pinschers, bred by Rigmor Andersen, include Danni Sofia, Danni Blue Boy, and Danni Barbette Stardust. Grey Cavalier Mimi De La Praga, from the Netherlands, and Barb's Red Strejker, from the United States, formed the foundation for Kennel Danni's blue line of Miniature Pinschers.

new, inexperienced breeders, veteran kennel owners don't want to take their puppies out at such an early age, to places where other dogs may not have been inoculated. For the good of breeding and quality, this method is very positive. However, for the health of the puppies it's absurd."

The success of the breed in Colombia is a direct result of the interest shown by several individuals. Miss Ligia Maya Sanín, one of the earliest enthusiasts, started her Santa Ana kennel in the early 1960s. Adding dogs from Jay-Mac and Bo-Mar, in the United States, to her kennel's own bloodlines, Miss Maya is credited with breeding the first Colombian Miniature Pinscher to win Best in Show. Mr. Guillermo Castaño bought Miss Maya's kennel in the late 1970s, when she retired from showing and moved to the United States. His El Troncal kennel has produced several fine Min Pins. One of these, Colombian and Ecuadorian Champion Pupe de El Troncal, was purchased and shown by Mr. Victor Daniel Cajiao. Mr. Cajiao also imported several dogs from the Von Enztal kennel in the United States. Girls Sweet Dream von Enztal won Best Puppy in Show three times and became the second Min Pin in Colombia to win Best in Show. Dynamite Red von Enztal was another promising female, placing a number of times in Group competition.

Several individuals have been actively promoting the Min Pin in Colombia. Mrs. Magdalena Gutierrez was quite successful with Bonnie Blue de Santa Catalina. Bonnie won Best in Show as a 6-month-old puppy, her first time in the ring. Her sire is Ch. Bu-Bic's Big Bird, a U.S. import owned by Mr. Hernán Castrillón. Sonia Guarin's kennel, Festival de Cannes, features red, black-and-rust, and chocolate-and-rust dogs. A lifelong owner of pet Min Pins, she did not begin showing until 1981, when she received Ch. Trosky de Santa Ana. By carefully introducing quality dogs from the United States to current Colombian lines, Ms. Guarin has produced Festival de Cannes Blas, Festival de Cannes Britta (Bonnie's dam), and Festival de Cannes Fergie.

Right: Pinschergården's Grete.

Far right: Pinschergården's Grete, a 9-week-old puppy, is shown with her sire, Pinschergården's Fritjot.

Above: Ch. Muddi belongs to Rigmor Andersen's Kennel Danni.

Above right: Pinschergården's Alberte is owned by Herbert and Jytte Baumkirchner.

Right: Ch. Rødkildes Musse and Ch. Stolz are owned by Inge Hansen.

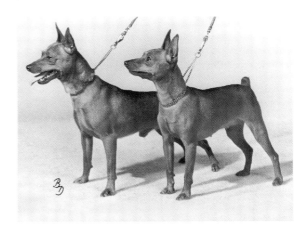

DENMARK

Inge Hansen, whose Kennel Rødkilde has bred 11 champions, to date, including International Ch. Pinschergårdens Andy, discusses the breed called the *dværgpinscher:*

"Miniature Pinschers have been bred in Denmark since the beginning of the 20th century. They were first exhibited in Copenhagen, in 1905, with an entry of four males and two females. By 1922, the number of entries had grown to 20, half of them imported from Germany—the home of the Miniature Pinscher. Today, breeders can trace their dogs' family lines back to the big stars of the 1920s, such as Stern von Affentor and Darling Exelcior. (Stern v. Affentor had a descendant in this country in the 1930 German champion Konig Heinzelmennchen, owned by Mrs. H. Proctor Donnell. He appeared on Konig's pedigree in the fourth generation of both the sire and dam.) In Denmark, ear cropping has been forbidden for many years. Through selective breeding, we have been able to achieve very good, well-placed standing ears."

Rosedell Tassen, born in 1937, shared his home with founders of the Norwegian Miniature Pinscher Club, Bergljot and Lyder Jensen.

Mr. K. Johansen, one of the country's outstanding early breeders and author of the first Miniature Pinscher breed book, *Dværg Pinscheren*, founded his Ajas kennel in 1920. He utilized several top bloodlines from Germany, including Herzhof, von der Lichtweishöhle, and von Gretelheim, which he bred with dogs from Norway, Sweden, and the Netherlands. Ajas dogs were known worldwide for excellence and were exported to many European countries, as well as the United States. Ch. Ajas Sheik, a Best in Show winner, and Ch. Ajas Flyver, called the best Miniature Pinscher in Scandinavia by a Swedish judge, were two of Mr. Johansen's most distinguished dogs.

Today, more than a dozen fanciers belong to a Miniature Pinscher breeding club, with about half involved in exhibiting. Ten to 20 dogs compete at most shows. Current and past kennels of note include Ajas (K. Johansen), Akva (Magda Christoffersen), Danni (Rigmor Andersen), Pinschergården (Jytte and Herbert Baumkirchner), Rødkilde (Inge Hansen), and Vedhauge (Jytte Pedersen).

NORWAY

One of Norway's earliest Min Pins of merit was Rosedell Tassen, born in 1937. He was owned by Bergljot and Lyder Jensen, who started the Norwegian Miniature Pinscher Club in 1946. In 1979, this organization joined the Schnauzer Club and is now called the Norsk Schnauzer Pinscher Bouvier Klubb. Olga Tjugum and Else Hegbom are two of Norway's long-time Min Pin breeders. Mrs. Tjugum started her kennel, in 1959, when she imported several dogs from Denmark, Finland, and England. Else Hegbom began, in 1961, with a dog from Denmark and a bitch, Amber's Mink, from Mrs. G. Linington of Canada. Ch. Mink's Rodi, born in 1987, is a seventh-generation descendant of the original pair. She provides the following information on the breed:

"The quality of our Miniature Pinschers has improved, due to some good imports, and we think the breed is quite sound. A dog from Israel [in the 1990s] has improved the head and bone.

Amber's Mink, bred by Mrs. G. Linington of British Columbia, was imported to Norway by Else Hegbom.

Ch. Mink's Rodi, also owned by Else Hegbom.

Our standard allows a height of 25 to 30 centimeters, but most of the show dogs measure 29 to 30 centimeters—some even more. Fortunately, illness or other problems are rare in this breed."

In July 1988, Norway became the first country to ban tail docking. (Sweden followed in 1989). Fifty-six breeds are affected by the ruling, which prohibits dogs with docked tails from competing in the show ring. The ruling also affects imported dogs because their tails already would be docked. However, imported dogs could successfully be used in breeding programs.

Among the Miniature Pinscher kennels listed by Norway's breed club are: Begi (Berit Stokkvin), Mink (Else Hegbom), and Olgum (Olga Tjugum).

SOUTH AFRICA

The earliest Miniature Pinschers in South Africa were English dogs imported during the 1950s. Mr. de la Chanaie, stationed with the French Embassy, is credited with introducing the breed. His de la Chanaie kennel can be found in the pedigrees of many South African dogs. Mrs. Arlene Kriel also took an early interest in the Min Pin. Foundation stock for her Bonne kennel came from Mr. Lionel Hamilton Renwick's world-famous Birling line in England.

Breeders in South Africa have achieved excellent results by combining English and American bloodlines. American dogs brought a racy, elegant appearance, superior topline and tail placement, and deep, rich color to the breed. Dogs imported from England helped to introduce very attractive, naturally erect ears. Although drop-eared dogs are

Ch. Bo-Mar's Vagabond is held by owner Colleen Flight.

Above: Colleen Flight with Jay-Mac's The Baroness and Ch. Whitnel Mr. Happiness.

Above right: Ch. Jay-Mac's Scarlet Ribbon.

Below: American Ch. Whitnel Mr. Happiness.

permitted to compete, they tend to lack the bright, alert expression typical of the Miniature Pinscher.

Mrs. Colleen Flight's Eureka kennel has excelled in both breeding and showing. With a limited breeding program, Eureka has produced multiple Group and Best in Show winners. She relates her experience with the Min Pin in South Africa:

"In 1969, I started my breeding program with two Min Pins—Ch. Bo-Mar's Vagabond and Bo-Mar's Pink Champagne—imported from Dr. Buris Boshell. I then imported Ch. Jay-Mac's Jezebel (Ch. Rebel Roc's Jackpot x Ch. Jay-Mac's Ramblin Rose) from Mr. John McNamara. Jezebel's ears were cropped, unfortunately, and I was unable to show her. However, she produced superb puppies when bred with Ch. Jay-Mac's Song and Dance Man (Ch. Jay-Mac's Pat Hand x Ch. Jay-Mac's Caroline).

"In 1973, I visited Mr. McNamara in the United States and returned home with South Africa's well-known Ch. Jay-Mac's Scarlet Ribbon (Ch. Bo-Mar's Road Runner x Ch. Jay-Mac's Miss Michigan). Scarlet Ribbon was a credit to all concerned and she flung herself wholeheartedly into everything. She was our top Miniature Pinscher, winning numerous Groups and Bests in Show under such respected judges as Frank

Sabella (U.S.) and Joe Cartledge (England). She also proved to be a fantastic dam, with champions in every litter. To date, without a doubt, there has not been a Miniature Pinscher like her."

Another noteworthy South African breeder was Mr. Louis Loubser. Mr. Loubser, who obtained his doctorate in animal husbandry, started his Vergelegen kennel with Colleen Flight's Ch. Eureka's Concerto. Combining his knowledge of animals with a selective breeding program, Mr. Loubser produced Min Pins of superior quality. In 1981, Vergelegen Solo Sue won Best in Show under Vera Halpin Bistrim, a Toy Group judge and Min Pin breeder from the United States.

Currently South Africa has only a few exhibitors. During the period from 1977 to 1983, an average of 1,000 Min Pins were registered annually with the Kennel Union of Southern Africa. Miniature Pinscher kennels and breeders of the past and present include Bonne (Arlene Kriel), Eureka (Colleen Flight), Mr. and Mrs. Henry Stephens, and Vergelegen (Louis Loubser).

SWEDEN

Miniature Pinschers in Sweden date to the turn of the 20th century when enthusiasts imported foundation stock from the leading kennels of Germany. During the 1920s and 1930s, several breeders, including Mrs. H. Gerhard (Kennel Lilltorpet), Mr. O. N. Holmstrom (Kennel av Oscaria), Mr. Gunnar Christersson (Kennel Acostis), Mrs. Olga Edqvist and Mrs. Ebba Moller (Kennel Tjustorp), achieved quality results in both breeding and showing. Mrs. Ellen Lindeblad's Kennel Assartorp produced the first Miniature Pinschers to earn their Swedish championships. Her kennel gained additional recognition when Mona av Assarstorp (imported and owned by Mr. and Mrs. K. J. Hedengren) became the first breed champion in the United States.

The Min Pin reached a peak in popularity during the 1950s and 1960s. In addition to the German kennels, von Gretelheim and Siegerland, quality dogs were imported from Denmark's Kennel Ajas and the Dutch kennel, Trouwe Vriendjes. Mrs. Agneta Rätz exhibited many top Min Pins, such as Ch. Bobo v.d. Trouwe Vriendjes, Ch. Kicki, and Ch. Tjustorps Troll. Strangely, Troll, a black and tan, whelped a gray male with yellow markings (possibly blue and tan) in 1966 and two years later whelped a gray female. These were the only gray (or blue) dogs known to exist in Scandinavia.

Nini Hermansson of Kennel Arrica relates the breed's progress:

"The Miniature Pinscher is not very common in Sweden, although it was once one of the most popular toy breeds. The number of new registrations with the Svenska Kennelklubben is rather low and most shows have five or fewer entries. Despite the breed's rarity, the quality is very good. Red is the most common color, but black and tan also is seen. Breeders have succeeded in obtaining an elegant, wedge-shaped head. On occasion, falling ear crops and too-low tail sets still appear."

Swedish kennels include Ajbis (B. J. Johansson), Hunnebo (Ruth Bergman), Lulobos (Marina Lundberg), Arrica's (Nini Hermansson), and Musicantens (Greta Ericson).

Right: Ch. Arrica's Nemo Cubanboy is owned by Nini Hermansson's Kennel Arrica.

Below: Arrica's Naranja Cubana, also owned by Nini Hermansson, is pictured after winning Best in Show at a 1988 Specialty Show.

Ch. Flashfires Pretty Boy Floyd is shown with judge Michele Billings (left) and owner Kim Swilling. Floyd has received three Best in Show awards and a Best in Specialty Show before retiring. He was bred by Rocky and Kim Swilling.

WINNERS' GALLERY
24

When founding members organized the Miniature Pinscher Club of America, in 1929, their objective was to form an association of fanciers interested in promoting the owning, breeding, and showing of Miniature Pinschers, and to conduct dog shows featuring this dignified little breed. Mrs. D. E. Van Buskirk, past secretary of the MPCA, presented the following analysis of the club's best-known event—its annual Specialty: "What is the purpose of an annual Specialty show? What part does it play in the general pattern of dog shows and showing Miniature Pinschers? It is our Annual Statement. It presents at an annual gathering the best dogs owned and bred by Miniature Pinscher fanciers. It is the visual proof of the progress we have made each year in promoting our breed and the bettering of breed type.

"Most of us are not geographically situated or financially able to attend shows throughout the country. We can participate only in the shows in our immediate area and, through reports and pictures, share in the others. Yet, we realize that if we do not gather at some particular place with our dogs, compare them, and talk over our problems, we can never intensify breed type, which is, after all, the main purpose for which our club was organized so many years ago. We leave the campaigning and promoting of our breed to a few. It is true that our breed sells itself; however, there must be a 'salesman' or 'saleslady' to display our breed. These [canine] salesmen present themselves as the ideal of the breed, or breed type, but are the outstanding winners in the East, the South, the Midwest, and the West actually the same type? For this purpose we hold our annual Specialty show, that these dogs may meet."

MPCA National Specialty shows were held in conjunction with all-breed events until 1964, when the club sponsored its first independent Specialty. In 1972, MPCA members decided to hold two national shows—spring and fall—at two different show sites. This was discontinued in 1987, when organizers returned to the practice of one annual Specialty.

Ruth H. Norwood's Ch. Sunbrook Buckskin Gal.

The quality of a person's life is in direct proportion to his commitment to excellence, regardless of his chosen field of endeavor.
Vince Lombardi

MPCA SPECIALTY SHOW
BEST OF BREED WINNERS

2007 MPCA National Specialty winner, Ch. Marlex Mister Chips. Bred by Armando Angelbello and Salina Bailey and owned and handled by Armando Angelbello, Chip's show career also includes an all-breed Best in Show award. Shown with breeder-judge David Krogh and MPCA President Sandee White.

Ch. Marlex Mercedes, the 1997 winner, was bred by Armando Angelbello, Ann Dutton, and L. Munoz and owned and handled by Armando Angelbello. Shown with judge Elaine Mathis and MPCA President Sharon Krogh.

**Miniature Pinscher Club of America
National Specialty
Best of Breed Winners**

2008 Ch. Altanero Barnstormer
Owners: Susan P. Goldman, Joanne Wilds,
and Kim Byrd
Breeders: Susan P. Goldman and Joanne Wilds

2007 Ch. Marlex Mister Chips
Owner: Armando Angelbello
Breeders: Armando Angelbello and Salina Bailey

2006 Ch. Wannabee Nancy Nagsalot
Owners: Eddie and Pam Dziuk, Anne Hendler
Breeders: Ken and Carole Rerko

2005 Ch. Windwalker Cool Hand Luke
Owner: Roberta Mills
Breeders: Deborah Long, Barbara Stamm,
and Roberta Mills

2004 Ch. Roadshow's Just Cuttin Up
Owners: Bunny Kimsey and Paula Gibson
Breeder: Paula Gibson

2003 Ch. Labell High Speed Chase
Owners: Leona Riley and Laurie Chism
Breeders: Angela Sanders and Laurie Chism

2002, 2000 Ch. Winters The Red Pony
Owner: Katie Winters
Breeders: Katie Winters and Pam Stevenson

2001 Ch. Nicolerins Front Paige News
Owner: Sandee White
Breeder: Sandee White

1999 Ch. Roadshow Steppin on the Edge
Owners: Terrie and Jerry Crawford
Breeders: Randy and Paula Gibson

1998 Ch. Whitehouse's Hot Damm Here I Am!
Owner: Judith A. White
Breeder: Judith A. White

1997 Ch. Marlex Mercedes
Owner: Armando Angelbello
Breeder: Armando Angelbello, Ann Dutton,
and L. Munoz

1996 Ch. Lulin Jerry Lee
Owners: Susan Goldman and Dr. Antonio Cusi
Breeders: Luis Colarte and Linda Johnson

1995 Ch. Hackberry Syrus
Owner: Gretchen S. Hofheins
Breeders: Dan and Carol Greenwald

1994 Ch. Chateau Acres Flackey Jake
Owner: Richard Sufficool
Breeder: Gloria Knapp

1993, 1992 Ch. Redwings On The Cutting Edge
Owners: Helen Chrysler Greene
and Paula Gibson
Breeders: Irvine Stevens, Belle Hunt,
and Sally Strickland

1991, 1989, 1988 Ch. Sanbrook Silk Electric
Owner: Armando Angelbello
Breeder: Ann Dutton

1990 Ch. Sunbrook Buckskin Gal
Owner: Ruth H. Norwood
Breeders: Ruth H. Norwood and Linda Stevens

1987 Ch. Pevensey's Cash Dividend
Owners: Pam Ruggie and Marcia Tucker
Breeder: Pam Ruggie

1986 (Fall National)
Ch. Bee Jay's Photo Finish
Owners: Bob and Billie Jean Shuler
Breeder: Billie Jean Shuler

1986 (Spring National), 1979 (Fall National)
Ch. Pine Hollow's Peter Pan
Owners: Linda Kazan (Stevens)
and W. L. Aston
Breeders: Leon Duffer and W. R. Ptomey, M.D.

1985 (Fall National)
Ch. Sunsprite Saxon of Carlee
Owners: Tom Baldwin and Marcia Tucker
Breeders: Carol Garrison and Marcia Tucker

1985 (Spring National), 1983 (Spring National), 1980 (Spring National), 1978 (Spring National), 1977 (Fall National), 1976 (Fall National)
Ch. Mercer's Desert Dust Devil
Owner: Irene Kloeber
Breeder: Kay Bergeron

1984 (Fall National)
Ch. Sanbrook Sahara
Owner: Ann Walker
Breeder: Ann Dutton

1984 (Spring National)
Ch. Sanbrook Simplicity
Owner: Nancy Gwynne
Breeder: Ann Dutton

1983 (Fall National), 1982 (Fall National), 1982 (Spring National)
Ch. Carlee Nubby Silk
Owner: Marcia Tucker
Breeders: Ann Dutton and Carol Garrison

1981 (Fall National)
Ch. Shajawn Semi Tough
Owners: Dorothy Hazel and Betty Moore
Breeder: Linda Talbot

1981 (Spring National)
Ch. Fillpin's Serendipity
Owners: Dave and Judy Fillpot
Breeders: Dave and Judy Fillpot

1980 (Fall National)
Ch. Onlyone Chocolate Bon Bon
Owners: Tom Baldwin and B. Bushey
Breeder: Tom Baldwin

1979 (Spring National)
Ch. Shinyas Pipe Dream
Owner: Sue Neville
Breeder: Sue Neville

1978 (Fall National)
Ch. Joy's Lady Ginger
Owners: Al and Dee Stutts
Breeders: John and Helen Yarwood

1977 (Spring National)
Reh-Mont's I Got Rhythm
Owners: Mr. and Mrs. Harmon Montgomery
Breeders: Mr. and Mrs. Harmon Montgomery

1976 (Spring National)
Ch. Jay-Mac's Dream Walking
Owners: Jack Phelan and John McNamara
Breeders: Mr. and Mrs. John McNamara

1975 (Fall National), 1974 (Fall National), 1973 (Spring National)
Ch. Jay-Mac's Impossible Dream
Owners: Dorothy Turco (1973)
and Dorothy DeMaria (1974, 1975)
Breeders: Mr. and Mrs. John McNamara

1975 (Spring National)
Ch. Top Hat Arabella
Owners: Juanette Woodie
and Jeanne Crutchfield
Breeders: Neal Tadlock and A. Schomber

1974 (Spring National)
Ch. Jay-Mac's Pat Hand
Owners: Jack Phelan and John McNamara
Breeders: Mr. and Mrs. John McNamara

1973 (Fall National)
Ch. K-Roc's Black Doubloon
Owners: David and Sharon Krogh
Breeders: David and Sharon Krogh

Winners' Gallery   245

1972 (Fall National)
Jay-Mac's Candy Man
Owners: Mr. and Mrs. John McNamara
Breeders: Mr. and Mrs. John McNamara

1972 (Spring National)
Star-M Trace of Scarlet
Owners: Don and Shirley Meyers
Breeders: Don and Shirley Meyers

1971 Ch. Allens Brandy Snifter
Owners: Bill and Sue Allen
Breeders: Bill and Sue Allen

1970 Ch. Jay-Mac's Jacqueline
Owners: Mr. and Mrs. John McNamara
Breeder: Mrs. Madeline Condon

1969 Ch. Helm's Nero
Owners: Bill and Sue Allen
Breeders: Maynard W. and Joyce Helms

1968, 1967 Ch. Rebel Roc's Star Boarder
Owner: Dr. Buris Boshell
Breeder: Mrs. E. W. Tipton, Jr.

1966 Ch. Rebel Roc's Jackpot
Owner: Mrs. Madeline Condon
Breeder: Mrs. E. W. Tipton, Jr.

1965 Ch. Bo-Mar's Drummer Boy
Owner: Dr. Buris Boshell
Breeder: Dr. Buris Boshell

1964 Ch. Shieldcrest Cinnamon Toast
Owner: Mrs. Boyce Bailes
Breeder: Claire C. Curtin

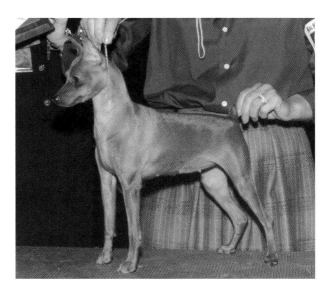

Top: Ch. Onlyone Chocolate Bon Bon, owned by Thomas W. Baldwin and B. Bushey. She is the only chocolate-and-rust Min Pin to win the National Specialty, to date.

Middle: Ch. Joy's Lady Ginger CD, owned by Al and Dee Stutts.

Bottom: Ch. Sanbrook Sahara, owned by Ann Walker.

MPCA SPECIALTY SHOW BEST OF BREED WINNERS

Ch. Windwalker Cool Hand Luke, owned by Roberta (Bobbie) Mills and bred by Deborah Long, Barbara Stamm, and Bobbie Mills. Luke also won Best of Breed at the 2004 Westminster Kennel Club and the January 2006 AKC/Eukanuba National Championship dog shows. According to his owner, "Luke loves his toys and can empty a toy basket in a matter of minutes to find just the right one."

Ch. Roadshow Steppin on the Edge finished his championship quickly. He was the 1993 Winners Dog at the MPCA National Specialty and won Best of Breed at the 1999 National Specialty from the Veterans Class. His owners, Terrie and Jerry Crawford, remember, "Stretch was always a showman up to the very end. He truly loved it!"

MPCA SPECIALTY SHOW
BEST OF BREED WINNERS

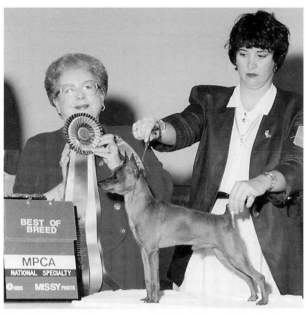

Ch. Hackberry Syrus, owned by Gretchen S. Hofheins-Wackerfuss and bred by Dan and Carol Greenwald. After winning the National Specialty, in 1995, Russell returned to the Specialty the following year to receive the first Award of Merit. He also won the Stud Dog Class, having sired the 1996 Winner's Dog and Winner's Bitch.

Ch. Chateau Acres Flackey Jake, who won in 1994, was bred by Gloria Knapp and handled by Joe Waterman. Jake moved to Japan as a young dog, where he was the Number 1 Toy Dog for several years before retiring. Gloria Knapp said, "Jake had a wonderful temperament and was a show dog extraordinaire."

Ch. Sanbrook Simplicity, bred by Ann Dutton and owned by Nancy Gwynne, won the 1984 MPCA Spring National Specialty in Tampa, Florida.

MPCA SPECIALTY SHOW
BEST OF BREED WINNERS

Top left: Ch. Lulin Jerry Lee, owned by Susan P. Goldman and Dr. Antonio Cusi and bred by Luis and Linda Colarte.

Middle left: Ch. Sanbrook Silk Electric, owned by Armando Angelbello and bred by Ann Dutton.

Bottom left: Ch. Sunsprite Saxon of Carlee, owned by his breeder Marcia Tucker and Thomas W. Baldwin.

Top right: Ch. Pine Hollow's Peter Pan, owned by Linda Kazan Stevens and W. L. Aston.

Bottom right: (Ch.) Star-M Trace of Scarlet, owned by Don and Shirley Meyers.

MPCA SPECIALTY SHOW
BEST OF BREED WINNERS

Above: Ch. K-Roc's Black Doubloon, owned by David and Sharon Krogh, also was a Best in Show winner in the early 1970s.

Left: Ch. Bee Jay's Photo Finish, owned by Bob and Billie Jean Shuler.

Ch. Shajawn Semi Tough, owned by Dorothy Hazel and Betty Moore.

Ch. Mercer's Desert Dust Devil, owned by Irene Kloeber.

Westminster Kennel Club
Best of Breed Winners 1960-2008

2008, 2007 Ch. Kimro's Toy Soldier

2006 Ch. Wannabee Nancy Nagsalot

2005 Ch. Maraven Pop Secret

2004 Ch. Windwalker Cool Hand Luke

2003 Ch. Nicolerins Front Paige News

2002, 2001 Ch. Kimro's Rocket Man

2000 Ch. Winter's The Red Pony

1999, 1997 Ch. Carovels Jacobs Ladder

1998 Ch. Sunsprite Absolutely Sable

1996 Ch. Seville's Unchained Melody

1995 Ch. Madrics Life of the Party

1994 Ch. Seville In Tempo With Madric

1993 Ch. Elan's Shiloh von Whitehouse

1992, 1990 Ch. Sunbrook Buckskin Gal (Group 4, 1992; Group 2, 1990)

1991 Ch. K-Phil's Ace In The Hole

1989 Ch. Sanbrook Silk Electric

1988 Ch. Sanbrook Smooth Operator

1987 Ch. Fillpin's Beautiful Dreamer

1986 Ch. Fillpin's Red Raider

1985, 1984 Ch. Sanbrook Silk Trader

1983, 1982 Ch. Carlee Nubby Silk

1981 Ch. Kloeber's I'm A Superman

1980 Ch. Pine Hollow's Peter Pan

1979 Ch. Mercer's Desert Dust Devil

1978 Ch. Jay-Mac's Fanfare

1977 Ch. Jay-Mac's Dream Walking (Group 3)

1976, 1975, 1974 Ch. Jay-Mac's Impossible Dream (Group 1, 1975; Group 2, 1974)

1973 Ch. Allens Brandy Snifter

1972 Ch. Ric-Lor's Running Wild

1971, 1969 Ch. Bo-Mar's Drummer Boy

1970 Ch. Bo-Mar's The Spoiler

1968 Ch. Sparkles of Craighill

1967 Ch. Bo-Mar's Brandy of Jay-Mac

1966 Ch. Sanbrook Sentry v. Spritelee

1965 Ch. Rebel Roc's Fiesta

1964 Ch. Spritelee Reddy Teddy v. Bimbo

1963, 1962, 1961, 1960 Ch. Rebel Roc's Casanova v. Kurt (Group 1, 1963; Group 3, 1962; Group 2, 1961 and 1960)

Note: The photographs shown in this section represent only a partial illustration of MPCA National Specialty and all-breed Best in Show winners. See Bibliography for additional sources of both historical and current show winners.

Facing page:

Top left: Ch. Carlee Nubby Silk, owned by Marcia Tucker.

Top right: Ch. Ruffian's Starbuck, owned by Larry and Penny Dewey.

Middle left: Ch. K-Phil's Ace In The Hole, bred and owned by Edd and Kay Phillips.

Middle right: Ch. JJ's Red Eric v Chateau Acres, owned by Jean Schroll.

Bottom left: Ch. Jay-Mac's Impossible Dream, owned by Dorothy Turco and Dorothy DeMaria.

Bottom right: Ch. Bentwater American Pie, owned by Sherry Bernard.

ALL-BREED
BEST IN SHOW WINNERS

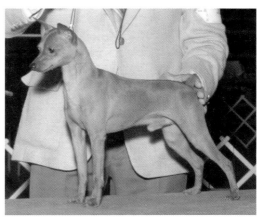

ALL-BREED
BEST IN SHOW WINNERS

Four generations of all-breed Best in Show winners are shown above. Ch. Sunsprite Absolutely Sable (top left), her son Ch. Kimro's Rocket Man (top right), grandson Ch. Kimro's Space Cowboy V Edgewind (bottom right), and great grandson Ch. Kimro's Toy Soldier (bottom left). Breeders and owners of these four top winners include Marcia Tucker, Robin Greenslade, Kimberly Pastella, Howard Schwell, Mary Curtin, and Anthony Calvacca.

ALL-BREED BEST IN SHOW WINNERS

Ch. Altanero Barnstormer, bred and owned by Susan P. Goldman and Joanne Wilds and co-owned by her handler Kim Byrd.

Just weeks after winning Best of Breed at the MPCA National Specialty Show, in 2007, Ch. Marlex Mister Chips won an all-breed Best in Show award. Chip was bred by Armando Angelbello and Salina Bailey and is owned and handled by Armando Angelbello.

Ch. Flashfires Pretty Boy Floyd, bred and owned by Rocky and Kim Swilling. At eight months of age, Floyd won his first of three Best in Show awards, making him one of the youngest Miniature Pinschers to earn that honor. He also won a Best in Specialty Show before retiring.

Ch. Sunbrook Indian Lullaby, bred by Ruth H. Norwood and owned by Luis M. Colarte and Linda J. Colarte. Annie, named for noted dog judge Anne Rogers Clark, also has three full sisters who have won all-breed Bests in Show: Ch. Sunbrook Buckskin Gal, Ch. Sunbrook Dances With Wolves, and Ch. Sunbrook Montauk Daisy.

ALL-BREED BEST IN SHOW WINNERS

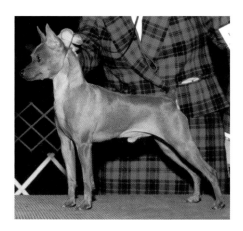

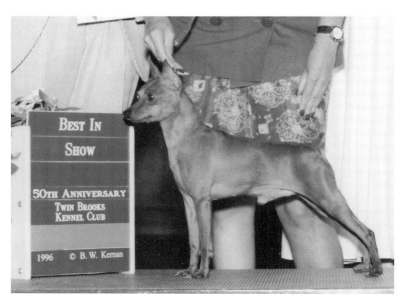

Top left: Ch. Madric's Motown Magic, owned by Sue E. Shore.

Middle left: Ch. Sanbrook Smooth Operator, owned by Ruth H. Norwood.

Bottom left: Ch. Elan's Shiloh v Whitehouse, owned by Debra Farhnbruch, Judith A. White, and Bobbie Stout.

Top right: Ch. Carovels Jacobs Ladder, owned by Jeffrey and Philip Helming.

Bottom right: Ch. Wil-B's Spicer Hi-Steps v. MC, bred, owned, and handled by Bernard and Wilma Griffith.

ALL-BREED
BEST IN SHOW WINNERS

Above left: Ch. Zellmat's Whiff of Kloeber, bred by Irene Kloeber and Linda Talbot, and owned and handled by Nancy Mathieu, set the record of youngest bitch (all breeds) to win Best in Show, in 1982, at Idaho Capital City Kennel Club. At six months and eight days of age, she won her title from the Six-to-Nine Month Puppy Class. Said Nancy Mathieu, "Many a night I woke up giggling over that!"

Above right: Ch. Sunsprite Tigereye, owned by Marcia Tucker.

Below: Ch. Dynasty's Spirit Of The West, bred and owned by Helen Chrysler Greene and handled by Sue Shore, is a current "special" in the show ring and is Number 4 in the country, in 2007.

Ch. Dynasty's Speaking of Him, bred and owned by Helen Chrysler Greene and handled by Joe Waterman, was the Number 1 Miniature Pinscher for several years. He is shown winning one of his multiple Best in Show awards.

ALL-BREED BEST IN SHOW WINNERS

Ch. Whitehouse's Oh Danny Boy, bred by Judith A. White and owned by his breeder and Sandee White. According to Judith White, Ms. Dorothy Nickles gave Danny Boy his Best in Show award. "She has to have a show dog asking for it, and well-trained. When she pulled him to the middle of the ring, Danny walked around me, planted, and I backed up to the end of the lead. She walked all the way around him—he did not move—and the win was his."

Ch. Marlex Mercedes is shown winning one of her two all-breed Best in Show awards. Mercy also won 11 Best in Specialty Shows and many Groups. Owned by Armando and Xio Angelbello.

ALL-BREED BEST IN SHOW WINNERS

Ch. Allens Brandy Snifter, owned by Al and Betty Krause.

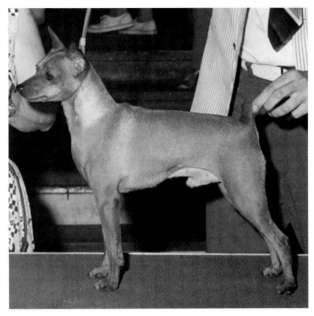

Ch. K-Roc's Kopper Kidd, owned by David and Sharon Krogh, also is an Honor Roll Sire with 18 champion offspring.

Ch. Rebel Roc's Casanova von Kurt, one of the top-winning show dogs of the 1960s, retired with 75 all-breed Best in Show awards. He was bred and owned by Mr. and Mrs. E. W. Tipton, Jr. and always was handled by Mr. Tipton.

What Is A Miniature Pinscher?
By Penny Craft

A short, stubby tail,
which wags incessantly at the slightest provocation
Bright, dark eyes,
shining with intelligence and the light of love
Little cat-like paws,
that dance for years through your life,
and forever on your heart
Long, erect ears,
never missing a sound, not a sigh nor a footstep,
nor a word of praise
A glossy coat,
always groomed to perfection,
rubbed to a high shine by an owner's loving hands
Personality,
that overwhelms friend and stranger alike,
and wins hearts over right and left
A soul,
as sweet and pure as an angel's,
existing only for love
A mind,
quick and sharp,
always one step ahead of the person he owns
A heart,
that keeps this little bundle of energy bouncing through your life,
spreading love and excitement
to even the farthest corner of your soul
That is a Min Pin,
and if you've never been blessed with one,
you've missed an awful lot in your life.

© *Pure-Bred Dogs/American Kennel Gazette,* May 1975.

APPENDICES

This illustration by R. Scholz originally was published in the 1960s by a newspaper in Berlin, Germany. It was part of a series of 52 dog prints, featuring a variety of German animal artists.

1929 MINIATURE PINSCHER BREED STANDARD

General Appearance—From muzzle to stern, trim and clean in outline with well-distributed, flexible muscles that must not be knotty or bunchy. Quick in movement, proud in carriage, alert and watchful in manner, denoting eagerness and intelligence.

Head—Moderately long and in correct proportion to body and not thick nor cumbersome. Cheeks and lips to be firm and tight and in no way pendulous. Head should have pronounced slope from occiput to the muzzle and to have appearance of ruggedness, rather than too much refinement. Entire head to be well balanced and without distortions. Jaws to be of even length, formed for clean bite, neither overshot nor undershot.
Nose—To be black on the blacks and red-blacks; on the brown and spotted ones, the nose may be lighter. Flesh-colored and spotted nose not to disqualify on the brown and spotted dogs.
Eyes—To be of size to conform to head, neither too full and round, nor too small and slanting. Color of eye to be dark—nearly black, or black.
Ears—Well set on, pointed and stubby.
Head Faults—Heavy skull, short and snipy muzzle, apple head, large or protruding eyes, uneven jaws.

Neck—Strong and muscular, slightly arched and sloping smoothly into the shoulders without throatiness or loose skin.

Body—Compact and muscular, length to equal height, except in bitches when body may be somewhat longer. Topline to form straight slope from shoulders to hips. Chest to be deep with well-sprung ribs, to taper back to clean loin giving free movement to quarters.
Body Faults—Higher at hips than at shoulders, sway back or roach back, low stern, too-sloping rump, hollow chest, too-wide chest, or too slab sided.

Legs and Feet—Front legs and hind legs to have good bone formation, strong and firm pasterns, toes to be strong, close together, well arched and black toenails. Well-bent stifles with strong, short hock joints and wide, flat quarter muscles. From side view, the front and hind legs are to stand at slight angle to body giving appearance of being ready to spring.
Leg Faults—Light bone, weak pasterns, crooked pasterns or hocks, crooked legs, loose shoulders or elbows, cow-hocked, or legs bowed out.

Tail—Short and strong, set high on the rump pointing upward, docked short.

Coat—Short and thick lying close to the body, which must be evenly covered. Coat must have a healthy, glistening appearance.

Color—(1)Bright black, with rusty-red to yellow markings on cheeks, lips, under jaw, a spot over each eye, two spots on the chest, also markings on the throat, on pasterns, and inside of hind legs and around vent. (2)Solid yellow, solid red, or solid stag red. (3)Brown, blue or blue-toned with red or yellow markings the same as for (1) above. (4)Spotted on white body, flecked, mostly gray, with black spots and red or yellow markings the same as for (1).
Color Faults—White on pasterns, chest, eye brows, or on parts as indicated for (1). White markings not to disqualify on (1). If yellowish white or grayish white, to be counted as faults on (1).

Height—Ideal shoulder height 11 inches, but moderate variations not to disqualify.

This German breed standard, courtesy of the Pinscher-Schnauzer Klub, guided early Miniature Pinscher breeders and exhibitors in the United States, prior to the creation of the MPCA's first standard.

Early post card, from the author's collection.

1935 MINIATURE PINSCHER BREED STANDARD

General Appearance–A miniature of the Doberman Pinscher, having on a modified scale most of its physical qualifications and specifications, viz., symmetrical proportions, sturdy though slim, pert, lively, attentive, with well-distributed muscle formation and a carriage suggestive of an active and lively temperament.

General Faults–Heavy set, coarse, poor quarters, too long or short coupled, knotty muscles, lethargic, timid or dull.

Head–The head should be in correct proportion to the body. As viewed from the side–elongated and tapering, with only a slight drop to the muzzle, which should be parallel to the top of the skull. As viewed from the top–narrow with well-fitted but not too prominent foreface. As viewed from the front–the skull appears flat, tapering forward to the muzzle. Muzzle itself strong, rather than fine and delicate, and in proportion to the head as a whole; cheeks and lips small, taut and closely adherent to each other. Teeth in perfect alignment and apposition.

Faults–Too big or too small for body, too short or coarse, too long or fine or distorted, top too broad, foreface too prominent, skull too round or hollow with too much stop, poor teeth, jaws undershot or overshot.

Eyes–Full, slightly oval, almost round, clear and bright, dark, even to a true black, set wide apart and fitted well into the sockets.

Faults–Too round and full, too small or large, too bulging or deep set, too close or far apart.

Ears–Well set and placed, firm, upstanding (or when legal, cropped short, pointed and upstanding).

Faults–Poorly set, placed low, weak or hanging, or poorly cropped.

Nose–Black in black and tan, red, or stag red.

Faults–Brown or spotted in black and tan, red, or stag red.

Neck–Slightly arched and gracefully curved, blending into the shoulders, relatively short, muscular, and free from throatiness. Length from occiput to withers equal distance from nose to occiput.

Faults–Too straight or too curved. Too thick or too thin. Too long or short, knotty muscles, loose, flabby or wrinkled skin.

Body–Compact, wedge shaped, muscular with well-sprung ribs, the base line of which is level with the points of the elbows; well-knit muscular quarters set wide apart, with back level or slightly sloping towards the rear. Length of males equals height, females may be slightly longer.

Faults–Chest too narrow or barrel shaped, quarters too wide or too close to each other, too thin or too fat, sloping rump, swayback, roach back, wry back, hips higher or considerably lower than shoulders.

Legs and Feet–Straight and upstanding as viewed from the front or rear with strong bone development and small joints; viewed from side–all adjacent bones should appear well angulated with well-muscled stifles, short well-developed hocks, well-knit flexible pasterns, strong, well-arched and closely knit toes with thick blunt nails.

Faults–Bow or X-legs–too thick or too thin bone development, large joints, thin stifles, large or crooked hocks, floating kneecaps, weak pasterns, spreading flat feet, feet turning in or out.

Tail–Set high, broad, held erect and cropped one to two inches.

Faults–Set too low, too thin, drooping, hanging, or poorly docked.

Coat–Thick, hard, short, straight, and lustrous, closely adhering to and uniformly covering the body.
Faults–Thin, too short, dull, upstanding, curly, dry, areas of various thickness, or bald spots.

Color–(1)Lustrous black with tan, rust-red or yellow markings on cheeks, lips, lower jaw, throat, above eyes, twin spots on chest, lower half of forelegs, inside of hindlegs and vent region. Black pencil stripes on toes. (2)Solid yellow. (3)Solid red or stag red. (4)Solid brown or brown with red or yellow markings. (5)Solid blue or blue toned with red or yellow markings.
Faults–Light colored or white, very dark or sooty spots in listed markings.

Height–Approximately 11½ inches at the shoulder or withers, with a slight variation permissible.
Faults–Too small or too large.

Weight–Five to 10 pounds.

VALUE OF POINTS	
General appearance and movement	25
Nose	5
Mouth	5
Eyes	5
Ears	5
Neck	5
Body	15
Feet	5
Color	10
Coat	15
Tail	5
Total number of points	100

UKC MINIATURE PINSCHER BREED STANDARD

MINIATURE PINSCHER
Official U.K.C. Breed Standard
Revised May 1, 2008
Companion Dog Group
© Copyright 1992, United Kennel Club, Inc.

HISTORY
Well-known as the "Min-Pin," the Miniature Pinscher has been bred in Germany for hundreds of years. One theory is that it was developed by breeding the German Pinscher to Dachshunds and Italian Greyhounds to obtain a smaller-sized dog. It was one of the breeds included in the Pinscher-Schnauzer Club formed in Germany in the 1890s.
The Miniature Pinscher was recognized by the United Kennel Club in 1936.

GENERAL APPEARANCE
The Miniature Pinscher is structurally well balanced and sturdy. It is compact and short coupled. The breed is smooth coated and naturally well groomed. Characteristic of the breed is its hackney-like gaiting action.
Fault: Structurally lacking in balance.

CHARACTERISTICS
In character the Miniature Pinscher is proud, vigorous and alert. It shows fearless animation and complete self-possession, accompanied by a spirited presence.

HEAD
The narrow, tapering, well-balanced head is in proportion to the body. The length of the muzzle should be equal to the length of the skull. There is a slight stop as the muzzle transitions into the skull. The head shows no indication of coarseness.
SKULL–The skull appears flat and tapers in width toward the muzzle.
MUZZLE–The muzzle is strong, rather than fine and delicate. The top line of the muzzle is parallel to the top line of the skull. The

cheeks are smooth and well chiseled. The lips are taut and closely adherent to the muzzle.
TEETH–Meet in a scissors bite. A full complement of teeth is preferred, but a few missing teeth are acceptable.
EYES–The full, slightly oval eyes are clear, bright and dark, almost a true black. Black dogs have black eye rims. Chocolate, blue, and fawn (Isabella) dogs may have a lighter eye pigment and have self-colored eye rims.
NOSE–The nose is black, except in chocolate-colored, blue, and fawn dogs, which have self-colored noses.
EARS–The ears may be cropped or uncropped. They are set high and stand erect from the base to the tip.

NECK
The slightly arched, clean, muscular, gracefully curved neck blends smoothly into the shoulders. It is in proportion to the head and body.

FOREQUARTERS
The clean, sloping shoulders have moderate angulation, coordinated to permit the hackney-like action.
FORELEGS–The forelegs have strong bone development, and small, clean joints. When

Early post card, from the author's collection.

viewed from the front, they are straight and upstanding. The elbows are close to the body. The pasterns are strong and perpendicular. Dewclaws should be removed from the forelegs.
Fault: Weak pasterns.

BODY
The muscular, compact body is slightly wedge shaped. The ribs are well sprung. The forechest is well developed. The base line of the brisket is level with the point of the elbows. Whether gaiting or standing, the backline is level or slopes slightly. The croup is level with the backline. The loin is short and strong. The belly is moderately tucked up. In proportion, males appear square, measured from the breastbone to the back of the thigh and the top of the withers to the ground. Females may be slightly longer.

HINDQUARTERS
HIND LEGS–Viewed from the rear, the hind legs are straight and parallel. Viewed from the side, they present a well-angulated appearance. The thighs are well muscled. The stifles are well defined. The rear pasterns are short and set well apart. Dewclaws should be removed from the hind legs.

FEET
The small, catlike feet have strong, well-arched, closely-knit toes. The pads are deep. The nails are thick and blunt.

TAIL
The tail is set on high and held erect. It is generally docked in proportion to the size of the dog.

COAT
The short, smooth coat is hard, straight and lustrous. It closely adheres to, and uniformly covers, the body.
Faults: Thin, too long, dull coat.

COLOR
Acceptable colors include:

- Solid clear red.
- Stag red, which is red with an intermingling of black hairs.
- Black, with sharply defined rust-red mark-

ings on the cheeks, lips, lower jaw, throat, twin spots above the eyes and chest, on the lower half of the forelegs, inside of the hind legs and vent region, on the lower portion of the rear pasterns and on the feet. Black pencil stripes are found on the toes.
- Chocolate, with rust-red markings found as specified for the Black dogs, except that brown pencil stripes are found on the toes.
- Blue, with rust-red markings found as specified for the Black dogs, except that blue/gray pencil stripes are found on the toes.
- Fawn (Isabella), with rust-red markings found as specified for the Black dogs, except that fawn pencil stripes are found on the toes.

In the Solid Red and Stag Red, a rich, vibrant medium to dark shade is preferred.

Disqualifications: Any color other than those listed. A thumb mark, which is a patch of black hair surrounded by rust on the front of the forelegs between the foot and the wrist. On chocolate dogs, the thumb mark is chocolate. On blue dogs, the thumb mark is blue. On fawn dogs, the thumb mark is fawn. White on any part of the dog that exceeds one-half inch in its longest dimension.

HEIGHT & WEIGHT
The acceptable height range is from 10 inches to 12½ inches. Weight is in proportion to the build, neither too fat nor too thin.

Disqualifications: Height under 10 inches or over 12½ inches.

GAIT
The fore- and hind legs move parallel, with the feet turning neither in nor out. The hackney-like action is a high-stepping, reaching, free and easy gait in which the front leg moves straight forward and in front of the body, and the foot bends at the wrist. There is a smooth, strong drive from the rear. While gaiting, the head and tail are carried high.

DISQUALIFICATIONS
Unilateral or bilateral cryptorchid. Viciousness or extreme shyness. Any color other than those listed. A thumb mark, which is a patch of black hair surrounded by rust on the front of the forelegs between the foot and the wrist. On chocolate dogs, the thumb mark is chocolate. On blue dogs, the thumb mark is blue. On fawn dogs, the thumb mark is fawn. White on any part of the dog that exceeds one-half inch in its longest dimension. Height under 10 inches or over 12½ inches.

FCI Standard N° 185 / 18.04.2007/ GB

MINIATURE PINSCHER
(Zwergpinscher)

FÉDÉRATION CYNOLOGIQUE INTERNATIONALE
MINIATURE PINSCHER STANDARD

FCI Standard N° 185 / 18.04.2007/ GB

TRANSLATION: Mrs C. Seidler.

COUNTRY OF ORIGIN: Germany.

DATE OF PUBLICATION OF THE ORIGINAL VALID STANDARD: 06.03.07.

UTILISATION: House and Companion Dog.

CLASSIFICATION FCI:
Group 2–Pinscher and Schnauzer-Molossian breeds–Swiss Mountain and Cattle Dogs and other breeds.
Section 1–Pinscher and Schnauzer type.
Without working trial.

BRIEF HISTORICAL SUMMARY: Miniature Pinschers were kept in large numbers around the turn of the century already and the Stud Book for 1925 records no less than 1,300 entries. Like with the German Pinscher, from the numerous colour variations, only the colours black with lighter markings and solid red to red-brown were thoroughbred.

GENERAL APPEARANCE: The Miniature Pinscher is a reduced image of the German Pinscher without the drawbacks of a dwarfed appearance. His elegant square build is clearly visible due to his short smooth coat.

IMPORTANT PROPORTIONS:
- The ratio from length to height shall make his build appear as square as possible.
- The length of the head (measured from the tip of the nose to the occiput) corresponds to half the length of the topline (measured from the withers to the set on of the tail).

BEHAVIOUR/TEMPERAMENT: Lively, spirited, self assured and evenly tempered. These qualities make him an agreeable family and companion dog.

HEAD
CRANIAL REGION
  Skull: Strong, elongated without markedly protruding occiput. The forehead is flat without wrinkles, running parallel to the bridge of nose.
  Stop: Slight, yet clearly defined.

FACIAL REGION
  Nose: Nose leather well developed and black.
  Muzzle: Ending in a blunt wedge. Bridge of nose straight.
  Lips: Black, smooth and tight-fitting to the jaw. Corners of lips closed.
  Jaws/Teeth: Strong upper and lower jaw. The complete scissor bite (42 pure white teeth according to the dentition formula) is strong and firmly closing. The chewing muscles are strongly developed without pronounced cheeks interfering with the smooth outline.
  Eyes: Dark, oval, with black pigmented close fitting eyelids.
  Ears: Prick ears; drop ears, set high, V-shaped with the inner edges lying close to the cheeks, turned forward towards temples. Folds parallel, should not be above the top of the skull.

NECK: Nobly curved, not too short. Blending smoothly into the withers without any marked set on. Dry without dewlap or throatiness. Throat skin tight-fitting without folds.

BODY
  Topline: Slightly sloping from withers towards rear.

Withers: Forming the highest point in topline.
Back: Strong, short and taut.
Loins: Strong. The distance from last rib to hip is short to make the dog appear compact.
Croup: Slightly rounded, imperceptibly blending into tail set on.
Chest: Moderately broad, oval in diameter, reaching to elbows. The forechest is distinctly marked by the point of the sternum.
Underline and belly: Flanks not too tucked up, forming a nicely curved line with the underside of the brisket.

TAIL: Natural; a sabre or sickle carriage is sought after.

LIMBS
FOREQUARTERS: Seen from the front, the front legs are strong, straight and not close together. Seen from the side, the forearms are straight.
Shoulders: The shoulder blade lies close against the ribcage and is well muscled on both sides of the shoulder bone, protruding over the points of the thoracic vertebrae. As sloping as possible and well laid back, forming an angle of approximately 50° to the horizontal.
Upper arm: Lying close to the body, strong and well muscled, forming an angle of 95° to 100° to the shoulder blade.
Elbows: Correctly fitting, turning neither in nor out.
Forearm: Strongly developed and well muscled. Completely straight seen from the front and the side.
Carpal joint: Strong and firm.
Pastern: Strong and springy. Seen from the front, vertical; seen from the side, slightly sloping towards the ground.
Forefeet: Short and round, toes well-knit and arched (cat feet), pads resistant, nails short, black and strong.
HINDQUARTERS: Standing obliquely, when seen from the side, standing parallel but not close together seen from the rear.
Upper thigh: Moderately long, broad, strongly muscled.
Stifle: Turning neither in nor out.
Lower thigh: Long and strong, sinewy, running into a strong hock.
Hock: Markedly angulated, strong, firm, turning neither in nor out.
Metatarsus: Vertical to the ground.
Hind feet: Somewhat longer than forefeet. Toes well-knit and arched. Nails short and black.

GAIT/MOVEMENT: The Miniature Pinscher is a trotter. His back remains firm and rather steady in movement. The movement is harmonious, sure, powerful and uninhibited with good length of stride. Typical of the trot is a ground covering, relaxed, fluent movement with strong drive and free front extension.

SKIN: Tight fitting over the whole body.

COAT
HAIR: Short and dense, smooth, close and shiny without bald patches.

COLOUR
- Self coloured: Deer red, reddish-brown to dark red brown.
- Black and Tan: Lacquer black with red or brown markings. The aim is for markings as dark, as rich and as clearly defined as possible. The markings are distributed as follows: Above the eyes, at the underside of the throat, on the pasterns, on the feet, at the inside of the hind legs and under the root of the tail. Two even, clearly separated triangles on the chest.

SIZE AND WEIGHT
Height at withers: Dogs and bitches: 25 to 30 cm.
Weight: Dogs and bitches: 4 to 6 kg.

FAULTS: Any departure from the foregoing points should be considered a fault and the seriousness with which the fault should be regarded should be in exact proportion to its degree.

Particularly:
- Clumsy or light in build. Too low or too high on leg.
- Heavy or round skull.
- Wrinkles on forehead.
- Short, pointed or narrow muzzle.
- Pincer bite.
- Light, too small or too large eyes.
- Ears set low or very long, unevenly carried.
- Throatiness.
- Too long, tucked up or soft back.
- Roach back.
- Croup falling away.
- Long feet.
- Pacing movement.
- Hackney gait.
- Thin coat.
- Roans; black trace on the back, dark saddle and lightened or pale coat.
- Over- or undersize up to 1 cm.

SERIOUS FAULTS:
- Lack of sexual type (*i.e.,* doggy bitch).
- Light appearance.
- Apple head.
- Lines of head not parallel.
- Elbows turning out.
- Hindlegs standing under the body.
- Straight or open hocked hindlegs.
- Hocks turning out.
- Over- or undersize by more than 1 cm but less than 2 cm.

DISQUALIFYING FAULTS:
- Shy, aggressive, vicious, markedly suspicious, or nervous behaviour.
- Malformation of any kind.
- Lack of breed type.
- Faults in mouth, such as over- or undershot or wry mouth.
- Severe faults in individual parts, such as faults in structure, coat or colour.
- Over- or undersize by more than 2 cm.

Any dog clearly showing physical or behavioural abnormalities shall be disqualified.

NB: Male animals should have two apparently normal testicles fully descended into the scrotum.

Early post card, from the author's collection.

MINIATURE PINSCHER ANATOMY

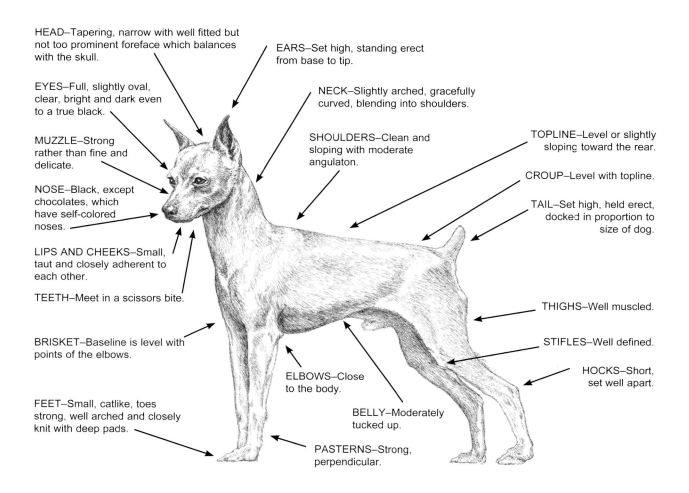

CANINE TERMINOLOGY

AKC–American Kennel Club.

Angulation–The angles formed by a meeting of the bones; mainly, the shoulder, upper arm, stifle, and hock.

Apple head–A distinct roundness of the topskull, undesirable in the Miniature Pinscher.

Balance–Symmetrical, individual parts (head, body, etc.) in proportion to whole.

Bat ear–An erect ear, broad at the base, rounded in outline at the top, with the opening directly to the front.

Best in Show (BIS)–The dog judged to be the best of all breeds.

Bilateral cryptorchid–An adult dog with neither testicle descended in the scrotum.

Bitch–Female dog.

Bite–The manner in which the teeth meet when the mouth is closed.

Breeder–The person who owns the dam of a litter. One who selectively breeds dogs.

Brisket–The region below the chest, between the forelegs, closest to the ribs.

Brood bitch–A female used for breeding.

Castrate–Surgical removal of the testicles of a male dog.

Cat foot–A round, compact foot, with well-arched toes, tightly bunched or close cupped. This is correct for the Miniature Pinscher.

Champion (Ch.)–A prefix used with a dog's name, designating that he defeated a certain number of dogs in AKC-licensed shows.

Cheeky–Cheeks prominently rounded; thick and protruding. A fault in the Miniature Pinscher.

Chiseled–Clean-cut in head, particularly beneath the eyes.

Cobby–Short-bodied, compact in build.

Companion Dog (CD)–The Novice title in obedience training awarded by the AKC.

Companion Dog Excellent (CDX)–The intermediate (Open) obedience title awarded by the AKC.

Conformation–A dog's appearance as it compares to its breed standard.

Coupling–The part of the body between the ribs and pelvis.

Cow-hocked–When the hocks turn toward each other.

Crabbing–Often due to greater angulation in the rear than the front, the dog moves with his body at an angle to the line of travel. (Crabbing also may occur when the dog turns to watch his owner when heeling.)

Cropping–Trimming of the ear leather to help the ears stand erect.

Croup–The dog's rear, from the loin to tail.

Dam–The mother dog.

Dewclaw–An extra claw or toe on the inside of the leg. Should be removed when puppy is three to five days old.

Dewlap–Loose, pendulous skin under the throat.

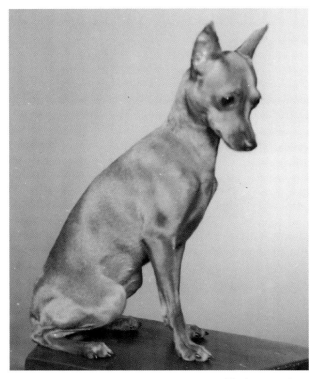 

Photos courtesy of Mauriene Pierce.

Dock—To shorten the tail by cutting. Done at same age as dewclaws.

Dog—The male dog. Or, may be applied to either sex.

Dome head—See Apple head.

Drive—A solid thrusting of the hindquarters, denoting sound locomotion.

Drop ear—The flaps of the ear folded or drooping forward as in young Miniature Pinscher puppies.

Entire—A dog that has not been spayed or neutered.

Expression—The general appearance of the face, dependent upon the eyes, ears, head shape, and temperament.

Fiddle front—Forelegs out at elbows, pasterns close, and feet turned out.

Foreface—Muzzle.

Front—The forepart of the body as viewed head on, including forelegs, chest, brisket, and shoulder line.

Gait—The dog's locomotion in the show ring.

Goosestep—The forearm is extended straight in front without any bend at the wrist.

Hackney-like—A high-stepping, reaching, free and easy gait in which the front leg moves straight forward and in front of the body and the foot bends at the wrist. The correct movement for the Miniature Pinscher.

Hare foot—A long, flat foot. Undesirable in the Miniature Pinscher.

Harlequin—An early Miniature Pinscher color, now a disqualification, characterized by gray, brown, or tan body color with black, tan, or brown patches or spots.

Haw–A third eyelid or membrane in the inside corner of the eye.

Heat–The female's breeding season.

Heel–The dog's proper position at the handler's left side.

Height–The vertical measurement from the withers to the ground.

Hock–The tarsus, or collection of bones of the hind leg forming the joint between the second thigh and the metatarsus; the dog's true heel.

Hocks well let down–Hock joints close to the ground.

Inbreeding–The mating of two closely related dogs, such as father/daughter, mother/son, or brother/sister.

Incisors–The six upper and six lower front teeth between the canines.

Iris–The colored membrane surrounding the pupil of the eye.

Isabella–Fawn or light bay color. An early Miniature Pinscher color, now an AKC disqualification.

Kennel–A building, crate, run, or enclosure used to house dogs. An establishment involved in keeping or breeding dogs.

Layback–The angle of the shoulder blade to vertical.

Lead–Leash.

Leather–The flap of the ear.

Level bite–When the front teeth of the upper and lower jaws meet exactly edge to edge.

Line breeding–The mating of dogs that are related to a common ancestor. Also, the mating of dogs that are related more distantly than in inbreeding.

Lippy–Pendulous lips or lips that do not fit tightly.

Litter–Puppy or puppies from one whelping.

Loin–The portion of the body from ribs to croup.

Loose Shoulders–Often shows excessive up-and-down motion in the shoulders. The chest drops low in front and the upper shoulder blades rise abnormally high above the withers.

Mate–To breed a dog and bitch.

Milk teeth–The first set of teeth.

Muzzle–Foreface: nasal bone, nostrils, and jaws.

Nick–A breeding that produces desirable puppies.

Open bitch–A bitch that can be bred.

Out at elbows–Elbows turning out from the body as opposed to being held close.

Outcrossing–The mating of unrelated individuals within the same breed.

Overshot–The top teeth protrude beyond the lower teeth.

Padding–A compensating action to offset constant pressure that occurs when a straight front is subjected to overdrive from the rear. The front feet flip upward in a split-second delaying action to coordinate the stride of the forelegs with the longer stride from behind.

Paddling–Also called "tied at the elbows," this restrictive movement stems from pinched-in elbows and shoulder joints, which cause the dog to swing the front legs in a stiff outward arc.

Pastern–The lower portion of the front legs; the wrist.

Miniature Pinschers have been honored on postage stamps around the world.

Pedigree—Chart denoting a dog's ancestors.

Pencil stripes—Black lines dividing the rust-red on the toes.

Premium list—An advance-notice brochure sent to prospective exhibitors, containing information on an upcoming show.

Prepotent—The ability of a dog or bitch to transmit traits to most or all offspring.

Put down—To be left unplaced at a show. Also means to euthanize a dog.

Put up—To place a dog in competition.

Racy—Trim, sleek, and refined in appearance.

Roach back—A curvature of the back in which the rear is higher than the shoulder.

Scissors bite—The top teeth overlap the bottom teeth and touch on the inside edges. Correct bite for the Miniature Pinscher.

Set up—Pose, so as to make the most of the dog's appearance for the show ring.

Snipy—A pointed, weak muzzle.

Soundness—Physical and temperamental health.

Spay—To surgically remove reproductive organs from the female.

Square body—A dog whose height, measured from withers to the ground, equals his length, from the point of shoulder to the rearmost projection of the upper thigh.

Stack—To position a dog's feet squarely in a show stance.

Stag red—Red with intermingling of black hairs. One of the acceptable colors of the Miniature Pinscher.

Stifle—The dog's knee (hind legs).

Stop—The step up from muzzle to skull; indentation between the eyes where the nasal bone and skull meet.

Stud book—A written record of breeding information.

Stud dog—A male used for breeding purposes.

Tail set—How the base of the tail sits on the rump.

Thumb mark—Patch of black hairs (chocolate in chocolate-colored dogs) completely surrounded by rust on the front of the foreleg between the foot and wrist. Disqualification in the Miniature Pinscher.

Toeing In—Dog turns the front feet inward while moving.

Toeing Out–Associated with the "east-west front," toeing out results from incorrectly positioned pasterns that cause the feet to turn outward; usually occurs with a narrow front.

Topline–The dog's outline from just behind the withers to the tail set.

Type–The characteristic qualities distinguishing a particular breed.

Unilateral cryptorchid–One testicle descended in the scrotum.

Utility Dog (UD)–The most advanced obedience degree awarded by the AKC.

Vent–The anal opening.

Weaving–Also called "crossing over" or "knitting and purling," this gait occurs when the dog twists the elbows outward, crisscrosses the pasterns, and toes out.

Whelping–The birth of a litter.

Whelps–Newborn puppies.

Winners–An award given at dog shows to the best dog (Winners Dog) and bitch (Winners Bitch) competing in regular classes. The dog or bitch that takes points toward his or her championship at a show.

Withers–The point of the shoulder blade on the topline.

Lalarookh Eros Aus Dem Ziverge (1955).
Photo by Thomas Fall.

Illustration by Nancy Ross.

BIBLIOGRAPHY

PUBLICATIONS
Miniature Pinscher Books

Bagshaw, Margaret R. *Pet Miniature Pinscher*. Fond du Lac, WI: All-Pets Books, Inc., 1956.

Bagshaw, Margaret R., revised by Mary L. Booher. *Pet Miniature Pinscher*. Fond du Lac, WI: All-Pets Books, Inc., 1958.

Boshell, Buris R., M.D. *Your Miniature Pinscher*. Fairfax, VA: Denlinger's Publishers, Ltd., 1969.

Burgess, Daphne. *A King Amongst Toys*. Cheshire, England: Onyx, 1999.

Coile, D. Caroline, Ph.D. *Miniature Pinschers: Everything About Purchase, Care, Nutrition, Breeding, Behavior, and Training (A Complete Pet Owner's Manual)*. Hauppauge, NY: Barron's Educational Series, Inc., 1996, 2006.

Dunbar, Ian and Radel, Rose J. *The Essential Miniature Pinscher*. New York: Howell Book House, 2000.

Edmondson, Sue. *British Miniature Pinscher*. Lancashire, England: Mayfields, 2007.

Hungerland, Jacklyn E. *The Miniature Pinscher: Reigning King of Toys*. New York: Howell Book House, 2000.

Jones, Chips. *The Miniature Pinscher That You May Know*. Privately published, 1969.

Krogh, David M. *The King of Toys Champion Book (1931-1993)*. Gresham, OR: Garvin Lazertype, 1994.

Krogh, David M. *Miniature Pinschers in America (series)*. Privately published, 1971, 1980, 1983.

Land, Bobbye. *The Miniature Pinscher*. Neptune City, NJ: T.F.H. Publications, Inc., 2006.

Linzy, Jan. *Miniature Pinscher Champions, 1969–1994*. Camino Books, Inc., 2002.

Linzy, Jan. *Miniature Pinscher Champions, 1995–2002*. Camino Books, Inc., 2003.

Miller, Evelyn. *How to Raise and Train a Miniature Pinscher*. Neptune City, NJ: T.F.H. Publications, Inc., 2000.

Miller, Evelyn. *Miniature Pinschers*. Neptune City, NJ: T.F.H. Publications, Inc., 1996.

Miller, Madeline. *Miniature Pinschers...as pets*. Jersey City, NJ: T.F.H. Publications, Inc., 1958.

O'Neil, Jacqueline F. *A New Owner's Guide to the Miniature Pinscher*. Neptune City, NJ: T.F.H. Publications, Inc., 1997.

O'Neil, Jacqueline F. *Guide to Owning a Miniature Pinscher*. Neptune City, NJ: T.F.H. Publications, Inc., 1997.

Radel, Rose J. *The Miniature Pinscher: An Owner's Guide to a Happy, Healthy Pet*. New York: Howell Book House, 1998.

Ricketts, Viva Leone. *The Complete Miniature Pinscher*. Middleburg, VA: Denlinger's Publishers, Ltd., 1957.

Ricketts, Viva Leone. *The Complete Miniature Pinscher*. New York: Howell Book House, Inc., 1972.

Schlintz, Irene C. Khatoonian. *The Top Producers, Top Ten Group and Breed Winners: Miniature Pinschers*. Fresno, CA: H.I.S. Publications, 1979.

Schwartz, Charlotte. *Miniature Pinscher: A Comprehensive Guide to Owning and Caring for Your Dog*. Allenhurst, NJ: Kennel Club Books, Inc., 2003.

Tietjen, Sari Brewster. *The New Miniature Pinscher*. New York: Howell Book House, Inc., 1988.

Tucker, Marcia P. *Miniature Pinscher*. Allenhurst, NJ: Kennel Club Books, Inc., 2005.

Zagrodnick, Barbara. *Miniature Pinscher Champions*. Privately published, 1989.

Foreign Language Miniature Pinscher Books

Blineau, R. *Les Pinschers*. Paris, France: Editions Bornemann, 1983. (France)

Johansen, K. *Dværg Pinscheren*. J.Fr. Clausens Forlag, 1949. (Denmark)

Klub Chovatelu Hladkosrstych Pincu 1979-1989. (Czechoslovakia)

Schnauzer & Pinscher. Club Français du Schnauzer et du Pinscher. (France)

General Dog Books

American Kennel Club. *The Complete Dog Book*. New York: IDG Books Worldwide, 2007.

Berman, Kathleen and Bill Landesman. *Caring for Your Older Dog*. New York: Arco Publishing, Inc., 1978.

Carlson, Delbert G., D.V.M. and James M. Giffin, M.D. *Dog Owner's Home Veterinary Handbook*. New York: Howell Book House, 2007.

Christiansen, Ib J. *Reproduction in the Dog and Cat*. Philadelphia, PA: Baillière Tindall/W.B. Saunders Co., 1984.

Collins, Donald R., D.V.M. *The Collins Guide to Dog Nutrition*. New York: Howell Book House, Inc., 1987.

Elliott, Rachel Page. *The New Dogsteps*. New York: Howell Book House, Inc., 1973.

Ganz, Sandy and Boyd, Susan. *Tracking Dog Excellent*. St. Louis, MO: Show-Me Publications, 1989.

Goldston, Richard T., D.V.M., M.S. and Hoskins, Johnny D., D.V.M., Ph.D. *Geriatrics & Gerontology of the Dog and Cat*. Philadelphia, PA: W.B. Saunders Co., 1995.

Handler, Barbara. *Successful Obedience Handling: The New Best Foot Forward*. Loveland, CO: Alpine Blue Ribbon Books, 2000.

Kalstone, Shirlee. *The Kalstone Guide to Grooming All Toy Dogs*. New York: Howell Book House, Inc., 1976.

Kalstone, Shirlee and Walter McNamara. *First Aid For Dogs*. New York: Arco Publishing, Inc., 1980.

Koehler, William R. *The Koehler Method of Training Tracking Dogs*. New York: Howell Book House, Inc., 1996.

Lehman, Patricia F. *Your Healthy Puppy*. Neptune City, NJ: T.F.H. Publications, Inc., 1998.

Lewis, Lon D., D.V.M, Ph.D., *et al*. *Feeding Dogs and Cats: A Commentary on Nutritional Management of Small Animals*. Topeka, KS: Mark Morris Associates, 1988.

Lewis, Lon D., D.V.M., Ph.D., *et al*. *Small Animal Clinical Nutrition IV*. Topeka, KS: Mark Morris Institute, 2000.

Little, Clarence C. *The Inheritance of Coat Color in Dogs*. New York: Howell Book House, Inc., 1957.

McDonald, L. E., D.V.M., Ph.D. *Veterinary Endocrinology and Reproduction*. Philadelphia, PA: Lea & Febiger, 1989.

Migliorini, Mario. *Secrets of Show Dog Handling*. Loveland, CO: Alpine Publications, Inc., 1995.

Nicholas, Barbara. *The Portable Pet*. Boston, MA: The Harvard Common Press, 1983.

Nichols, Virginia Tuck. *How To Show Your Own Dog*. Neptune City, NJ: T.F.H. Publications, Inc., 1969.

Onstott, Kyle. Revised by Philip Onstott. *The New Art of Breeding Better Dogs*. New York: Howell Book House, Inc., 1970.

Robinson, Roy. *Genetics for Dog Breeders*. Elmsford, NY: Pergamon Press, Inc., 1990.

Walkowicz, Chris and Wilcox, Bonnie, D.V.M. *Successful Dog Breeding: The Complete Handbook of Canine Midwifery*. New York: IDG Books Worldwide, 1994.

Willis, Malcolm B., B.Sc., Ph.D. *Genetics of the Dog*. New York: Howell Book House, Inc., 1989.

Dog Magazines
AKC Gazette
American Kennel Club
260 Madison Avenue
New York, NY 10016
www.akc.org

Dog Fancy
P. O. Box 6050
Mission Viejo, CA 92690-6050
www.dogchannel.com/dog-magazines/
dogfancy/default.aspx

Dog Owner's Guide (Online magazine)
www.canismajor.com/dog/

Dog & Kennel
Pet Publishing, Inc.
7-L Dundas Circle
Greensboro, NC 27407
www.petpublishing.com

Dog World
P. O. Box 6050
Mission Viejo, CA 92690-6050
www.dogchannel.com/dog-magazines/
dogworld/default.aspx

Dogs In Canada
Apex Publishing, Ltd.
89 Skyway Avenue
Etobicoke, Ontario, Canada M9W 6R4
www.dogsincanada.com

Good Dog! Magazine Online
www.gooddogmagazine.com

Pinscher Patter
5031 Plover Road
Wisconsin Rapids, WI 54494-9705

The Whole Dog Journal
P. O. Box 1349
Oroville, CA 95965
www.whole-dog-journal.com

Top Notch Toys
Doll-McGinnis Enterprises, Inc.
8848 Beverly Hills Road
Lakeland, FL 33809-1604
www.dmcg.com

CLUBS AND ORGANIZATIONS
Miniature Pinschers
Canadian Miniature Pinscher Club
RR3, Site 1, Box 7
Rocky Mountain House, AB
Canada T4T 2A3
www.cdn-miniaturepinscherclub.com

Internet Miniature Pinscher Service, Inc.
www.minpinrescue.org

Miniature Pinscher Club of America, Inc.
www.minpin.org

National Miniature Pinscher Breeders
Association (United Kennel Club)
www.nmpba.org

Operation Blue Prints
(Blue Miniature Pinschers)
www.operationblueprints.com
pets.groups.yahoo.com/group/Operation
BluePrints

Pinscher-Schnauzer-Klub 1895 e.V.
Barmer Str. 80
42899 Remscheid, Germany
www.psk-pinscher-schnauzer.de

Miscellaneous
American Dog Owners Association, Inc.
P. O. Box 186
Castleton, NY 12033
www.adoa.org

American Kennel Club (AKC)
260 Madison Avenue
New York, NY 10016
www.akc.org

Canadian Kennel Club (CKC)
89 Skyway Avenue, Suite 100
Etobicoke, Ontario, Canada M9W 6R4
www.ckc.ca

Canine Good Citizen Program
American Kennel Club
8051 Arco Corporate Drive, Suite 100
Raleigh, NC 27617-3390
www.akc.org

Fédération Cynologique Internationale (FCI)
13, Place Albert 1er
B-6530 Thuin, Belgium
www.fci.be

National Association of Dog Obedience
Instructors (NADOI)
729 Grapevine Highway, PMB 369
Hurst, TX 76054-2085
www.nadoi.org

National Dog Groomers Association of
America, Inc.
P. O. Box 101
Clark, PA 16113
www.nationaldoggroomers.com

Pet Food Institute (PFI)
2025 M Street, NW, Suite 800
Washington, DC 20036
www.petfoodinstitute.org

United Kennel Club, Inc. (UKC)
100 East Kilgore Road
Kalamazoo, MI 49002-5584
www.ukcdogs.com

United States Dog Agility Association (USDAA)
P. O. Box 850955
Richardson, TX 75085-0955
www.usdaa.com

DOG SHOW SUPERINTENDENTS
BaRay Event Services, Inc.
www.barayevents.com

Bob Peters Dog Shows, Ltd.
www.bpdsonline.com

Garvin Show Services
www.garvinshowservices.com

Jack Bradshaw Dog Shows
www.jbradshaw.com

Jack Onofrio Dog Shows
www.onofrio.com

Jim Rau Dog Shows
www.raudogshows.com

Kevin Rogers Dog Shows
www.rogersdogshows.com

MB-F Dog Shows (Infodog)
www.infodog.com

McNulty Dog Shows, Inc.
www.mcnultydogshows.com

Newport Dog Shows
www.newportdogshows.com

Sleeper Dog Shows (Roy Jones)
www.royjonesdogshows.com

DOG PHOTOGRAPHERS
DogAds
Chris & Tom Halvorson
5798 Tonawanda Creek Rd.
Lockport, NY 14094
www.dogads.com

Mark Raycroft Photography, Inc.
256 Broatch Road, R. R. #3
Trenton, Ontario, Canada K8V 5P6
www.markraycroft.com

SOURCES
Cruise Lines
Cunard Cruise Line
6100 Blue Lagoon Drive
Suite 400
Miami, FL 33126
www.cunardline.com

Kennel Suppliers
Drs. Foster & Smith, Inc.
P. O. Box 100
Rhinelander, WI 54501-0100
www.drsfostersmith.com

PetEdge
P. O. Box 1000
Beverly, MA 01915-0700
www.petedge.com

Recreational Vehicles
The Good Sam Club
P. O. Box 6888
Englewood, CO 80155-6888
www.goodsamclub.com

Winnebago Industries, Inc.
P. O. Box 152
Forest City, IA 50436-0152
www.winnebagoind.com

Travel
American Boarding Kennels Association
1702 East Pikes Peak Avenue
Colorado Springs, CO 80909
www.abka.com

Fresh Pond Travel
344 Boston Post Road
Marlboro, MA 01752
www.dogshowtravel.com

Pet Sitters International
201 East King Street
King, NC 27021
www.petsit.com

Veterinary Products, Services, and Organizations
AKC Canine Health Foundation
P. O. Box 37941
Raleigh, NC 27627-7941
www.akccfh.org

American Heartworm Society
P. O. Box 667
Batavia, IL 60510
www.heartwormsociety.org

Canine Eye Registration Foundation, Inc. (CERF)
VMDB/CERF
P. O. Box 3007
Urbana, IL 61803-3007
www.vmdb.org/cerf.html

Canine Inherited Disorders Database
The University of Prince Edward Island
Charlottetown, PE, Canada
www.upei.ca/~cidd/

Dr. Urs Giger
Department of Clinical Studies–Philadelphia
University of Pennsylvania
School of Veterinary Medicine
3900 Delancey Street
Philadelphia, PA 19104-6010
giger@vet.upenn.edu

Institute for Genetic Disease Control
P. O. Box 177
Warner, NH 03278
www.gdcinstitute.org

Prof. Dr. Tosso Leeb
Research Project Color Dilution Alopecia
Universität Bern

Institute of Genetics
P. O. Box 8466
CH-3001 Bern, Switzerland
www.genetics.unibe.ch/content/e2353/e2694/index_eng.html

OptiGen, LLC
767 Warren Road,
Suite 300
Ithaca, NY 14850
www.optigen.com

The Orthopedic Foundation for Animals, Inc.
2300 E. Nifong Boulevard
Columbia, MO 65201-3856
www.offa.org

Seager Canine Semen Bank, Inc.
4544 Beacon Drive
Sarasota, FL 34232
www.seagercaninesemenbank.com

Synbiotics Corporation
12200 N.W. Ambassador Drive,
Suite 101
Kansas City, MO 64163
www.synbiotics.com

VetGen
3728 Plaza Drive,
Suite 1
Ann Arbor, MI 48108
www.vetgen.com

Early post card, from the author's collection.

Early post card, from the author's collection.

REFERENCES

BREEDING AND REPRODUCTION

"10,000 Dog Zinc Gluconate Study in Mexico." *ACC & D*. Alliance for Contraception in Cats & Dogs. 11 Mar. 2007.
<http://www.acc-d.org/News>

"Australian Biotechnology Company Peptech Animal Health Has Launched a Novel Animal Contraceptive Suprelorin® in Australia." *The Veterinarian*. 14 Mar. 2007.
<http://www.theveterinarian.com.au/industry info/article498.asp>

"Breeding Soundness Examination in the Male," *American Animal Hospital Association's 1985 Scientific Proceedings*. Shirley D. Johnston, D.V.M., Ph.D. 1985, pp. 603–605.

"Canine Ovulation Timing." *American Rottweiler Club*. Veterinary Referral Center. 23 Mar. 2007. Melissa Goodman, D.V.M.
<http://www.amrottclub.org/ovultime.htm>

"Companion Animal Product Suprelorin®." *PEPTECH*. 14 Mar. 2007.
<http://www.peptech.com/HTML/Animal_Health/Superlorin_general.html>

"Diagnosing and Managing Dystocia in the Bitch," *American Animal Hospital Association's 1985 Scientific Proceedings*. Shirley D. Johnston, D.V.M., Ph.D. 1985, pp. 600–602.

"First Neutering Drug for Puppies Gains FDA Approval." *AllOurPets.com*. 19 May 2003. 11 Mar. 2007.
<http://www.allourpets.com/canine/neuterpuppy.shtml>

"GonaCon™ New GnRH Single Shot." *National Wildlife Research Center*. 23 Jan. 2007. United States Department of Agriculture Animal & Plant Health Inspection Service Wildlife Services. 13 Mar. 2007.
<http://www.aphis.usda.gov/ws/nwrc/research/reproductive_control/gonacon.html>

"Gonadotropin-Releasing Hormone Immunocontraception in Mammals." *National Wildlife Research Center*. 15 Feb. 2006. United States Department of Agriculture Animal & Plant Health Inspection Service Wildlife Services. 13 Mar. 2007.
<http://www.aphis.usda.gov/ws/nwrc/research/reproductive_control/gnrh.html>

"Hormone Levels: Determining Breeding Times and Whelping Dates." *PetEducation.com*. 2006. Doctors Foster and Smith. 23 Mar. 2007. Veterinary & Aquatic Services Department, Drs. Foster and Smith.
<http://www.peteducation.com/article.cfm?cls=2&cat=1627&articleid=3201>

"Mastitis in Dogs & Cats." *PetStyle*. 2007. 28 Mar. 2007. Roger Ross, D.V.M.
<http://www.petstyle.com/dog/health_well_article.aspx?id=487&ion=Health%20 amp%20Safety>

"Part 1: Reproduction and the Bitch." *Wing-N-Wave Labradors*. 2000. 23 Mar. 2007. Pamela A. Davol.
<http://www.labbies.com/reproduction1.htm>

"Paternity Testing," *icg News*. Andrew Kuniyuki, Ph.D. and Shirlee O'Neill. 1989, Volume 3, pp. 2, 5.

"Pharmacological Approaches to Pregnancy Termination in Dogs and Cats Including the Use of Prostaglandins, Dopamine Agonists, and Dexamethasone." *IVIS*. 13 Aug. 2002. 23 Mar. 2007. M. M. Wanke, S. Romagnoli, J. Verstegen III, and P. W. Concannon.
<http://www.ivis.org/advances/Concannon/wanke/chapter_frm.asp?LA=1>

Physiology and Clinical Parameters of Pregnancy in Dogs. 27 WSAVA Congress, 2002, Cornell University, Ithaca, NY, USA. 28 Mar. 2007. Patrick W. Concannon, M.S., Ph.D.
<http://www.vin.com/proceedings/Proceedings.plx?CID=WSAVA2002&PID=2681>

Pregnancy Management in Dogs and Cats. 29th World Congress of the World Small Animal Veterinary Association, Oct. 2004, Cornell University, Ithaca, NY, USA; Univ. of Florida, Gainesville, FL, USA. 28 Mar. 2007. Patrick W. Concannon, M.S., Ph.D., and John Verstegen, D.V.M., Ph.D.
<http://www.vin.com/proceedings/Proceedings.plx?CID=WSAVA2004&PID=8746&O=Generic>

"Pregnancy Termination." *Marvistavet.com*. Mar Vista Animal Medical Center. 23 Mar. 2007.
<http://www.marvistavet.com/html/pregnancy_termination.html>

Reproduction in the Dog and Cat. Ib J. Christiansen. Philadelphia, PA: Baillière Tindall/W. B. Saunders, 1984.

"Reproductive Physiology–Understanding the Bitch's Cycle," *icg News*. Melissa F. Goodman, D.V.M. Volume 5 (n.d.) pp. 1, 3, 5.

"Reproductive Problems of the Breeding Bitch," *icg News*. Vicki Meyers-Wallen, V.M.D., Ph.D. July 1990, Volume 4, pp. 1, 2, 4.

"Status of Current Approaches." *ACC & D*. Alliance for Contraception in Cats & Dogs. 13 Mar. 2007.
<http://www.acc-d.org/News>

"Update on Suprelorin®." *ACC & D*. 11 July 2006. The Alliance for Contraception in Cats and Dogs. 14 Mar. 2007. Joyce Briggs.
<http://www.acc-d.org/ACCD%20docs/Suprelorin%20Interview%20July%202006>

"Use of Commercial Luteinizing Hormone and Progesterone Assay Kits in Canine Breeding Management." *IVIS*. 24 May 2001. Department of Small Animal Clinical Sciences, College of Veterinary Medicine, University of Minnesota, St. Paul, MN. 23 Mar. 2007. M. V. Root Kustritz.
<http://www.ivis.org/advances/Concannon/root2/chapter_frm.asp?LA=1>

"Use of GnRH Agonists and Antagonists for Small Animal Contraception." *Proceedings of the Third International Symposium on Non-Surgical Contraceptive Methods for Pet Population Control*, 2006, Cornell University, Ithaca, N.Y., and International Veterinary Information Service, Ithaca, N.Y., USA. 13 Mar. 2007. P. W. Concannon.
<http://www.acc-d.org/2006%20Symposium%20Docs/2Concannon.pdf>

Veterinary Endocrinology and Reproduction. L. E. McDonald. Philadelphia, PA: Lea & Febiger, 1989, pp. 293–294.

COAT COLOR

"B/B, E/E, and Beyond: a Detailed Examination of Coat Color Genetics in the Labrador Retriever." *Wing-N-Wave Labradors*. 1999. 1 Dec. 2007. Pamela A. Davol.
<http://www.labbies.com/genetics2.htm>

"Blue Miniature Pinschers–Operation Blue Prints–Blue and Rust Min Pins." *Operation Blue Prints*. 2007. 1 Dec. 2007.
<http://www.operationblueprints.com/>

"Canine DNA Testing." *HealthGene*. 1 Dec. 2007.
<http://healthgene.com/canine/>

"Canine Genetics Primer." *Dog Colour Genetics Primer & FREE Canine Genetics Software*. 2003. Tenset Technologies Ltd. 1 Dec. 2007.
<http://www.tenset.co.uk/doggen/indexus.html>

"Color Dilution Alopecia." *Canine Inherited Disorders Database*. 2 Feb. 2004. Sir James Dunn Animal Welfare Centre, at the Atlantic Veterinary College, University of Prince Edward Island, and the Canadian Veterinary Medical Association. 15 Dec. 2007.
<http://www.upei.ca/cidd/Diseases/dermatology/colour%20dilution%20alopecia.htm>

"Color-Dilution Alopecia in Dogs." *Journal of Veterinary Science* 6 (2005): 259–261. 1 Dec. 2007. Jae-Hoon Kim, Kyung-Il Kang, Hyun-Joo Sohn, *et al*.
<http://www.miniature-pinscher.info/download/ColourDilutionAlopecia.pdf>

"Color Genetics in the Dog," *Pure-Bred Dogs/American Kennel Gazette*. Gail Knapp, Ph.D. June 1992, pp. 47–52.

"Genes affecting coat colour and pattern in domestic dogs: a review." *Animal Genetics* 38 (2007): 539–549. S. M. Schmutz, and T. G. Berryere.

"Genetics of Coat Color and Type in Dogs." *Dog Coat Color Genetics*. University of Saskatchewan. 1 Dec. 2007. Sheila M. Schmutz, Ph.D., Professor.
<http://homepage.usask.ca/~schmutz/dogcolors.html>

"Information on the Blue-Coated Miniature Pinscher (Reprint from the 1995 minutes)," *Pinscher Patter*. June 1999, pp. 38–42.

"Miniature Pinscher Diseases." 2007. 1 Dec. 2007.
<http://www.miniature-pinscher.info/diseases.htm>

"Polymorphisms Within the Canine MLPH Gene are Associated with Dilute Coat Color in Dogs." *BioMed Central Ltd*. 16 June 2005. 1 Dec. 2007. Ute Philipp, Henning Hamann, Lars Mecklenburg, Seiji Nishino, Emmanuel Mignot, Anne-Rose Günzel-Apel, Sheila M Schmutz, and Tosso Leeb.
<http://www.biomedcentral.com/1471-2156/6/34>

"Standard Accepted Coat Color Genetics in Dogs." *Chromadane*. 2007. 15 Dec. 2007. J. P. Yousha.
<http://www.chromadane.com/standardcoat.htm>

The Inheritance of Coat Color in Dogs. New York: Howell Book House, Inc., 1957. Clarence C. Little.

"Variation in Hair Coat and Skin Texture in Blue Dogs," *Nordisk Veterinaermedicin*. Rikke Langebaek. 1986, 38:383–387.

"VetGen DNA CHROMAGENE Coat Color Testing." *VetGen: Veterinary Genetic Services–Canine–List of Services–Coat Color*. VetGen. 1 Dec. 2007.
<http://www.vetgen.com/canine-coat-color.html>

EARS
"A brochure on Ear cropping: an effective means of improving communications with clients," *Veterinary Medicine/Small Animal Clinician*. Glenn K. Miller, D.V.M. and Alice Martel, B.S., M.S. Feb. 1979, pp. 183–186.

"Ear Cropping: a technique," *Veterinary Medicine/Small Animal Clinician*. Thomas J. Rogers, V.M.D. May 1977, pp. 893–904.

"Let's Break a Tradition," *Dog World*. Lerae Britain. January 1983, pp. 124–125.

FEEDING AND NUTRITION
"BARF World–What We are All About." *BARF World*. 6 Mar. 2007.
<http://www.barfworld.com/html/barfworld/about.shtml>

"Dr. Billinghurst's BARF Diet™ Biologically Appropriate Raw Foods." *BARF World*. 6 Mar. 2007.
<http://www.barfworld.com/html/learn_more/what_is_barf.shtml>

"How Safe is a Raw Diet? Not Very–and the Facts are Chilling: Ann Martin Has Spent Her Career Taking on the Pet-Health Establishment." *LookSmart, Ltd.* June 2005. Better Nutrition, PRIMEDIA Intertec. 8 Mar. 2007. Ann N. Martin.
<http://www.findarticles.com/p/articles/mi_m0FKA/ is_6_67/ai_n13788104/pg_2>

"Raw Feeding." *Wikipedia*. 4 Mar. 2007. 6 Mar. 2007.
<http://en.wikipedia.org/wiki/Raw_feeding>

"Raw Meat Debate–Should You Feed It to Your Dog?" *PetPlace.com*. Intelligent Content Corp. 8 Mar. 2007. Alex Lieber.
<http://dogs.about.com/gi/dynamic/offsite.htm?zi=1/XJ/Ya&sdn=dogs&cdn=homegarden&tm=27&gps=383_565_1076_868&f=20&tt=14&bt=0&bts=0&zu=http%3A//www.petplace.com/articles/artShow.asp%3FartID%3D3723>

"Raw Meat Diets Spark Concern." *American Veterinary Medical Association*. 15 Jan. 2005. 8 Mar. 2007. Kate O'Rourke.
<http://www.avma.org/onlnews/javma/jan05/050115ww.asp>

Small Animal Clinical Nutrition III. Lon D. Lewis, et al. Topeka, KS: Mark Morris Associates, 1989, pp. 1-1 to 1-25; 3-1 to 3-32.

The Collins Guide to Dog Nutrition. Donald R. Collins, D.V.M. New York: Howell Book House, Inc., 1989, pp. 207–222.

GENERAL HEALTH
"Auburn Develops Revolutionary New Canine Kidney Transplant Procedure." *Auburn News*. 21 June 2004. Auburn University. 25 Aug. 2007. Charles Martin.
<http://www.ocm.auburn.edu/news_releases/canine.html>

"Azodyl: Treatment for Dogs and Cats Chronic Kidney Disease." *AC the People's Media Company*. 2007. 12 Aug. 2007.
<http://www.associatedcontent.com/article/204934/azodyl_treatment_for_dogs_and_cats.html>

"Campus Helps Expand Pet Dialysis Availability." *U.C. Davis News & Information*. 3 May 2002. U.C. Davis School of Veterinary Medicine. 25 Aug. 2007. Amy Agronis.
<http://www.dateline.ucdavis.edu/dl_detail.lasso?id=7063>

Canine Brain Aging: From Diagnosis to Management. 27 WSAVA Congress, 2002. 31 July 2007. Karen L. Overall, M.A., V.M.D., Ph.D.
<http://www.vin.com/proceedings/Proceedings.plx?CID=WSAVA2002&PID=2566>

Canine Dementia–Its Diagnosis, Treatment and Medical Differentials. 29th World Congress of the World Small Animal Veterinary Association, 6 Oct. 2004. 31 July 2007. Sarah Heath, B.V.Sc., M.R.C.V.S.
<http://www.vin.com/proceedings/Proceedings.plx?CID=WSAVA2004&PID=8576&O=Generic>

"Canine Kidney Disease." *VCA Animal Hospitals*. 12 Aug. 2007.
<http://www.petshealth.com/dr_library/caninekidney.html>

"Canine Oral Health Continues to Make Significant Advances." *Medical News Today*. 17 Nov. 2006. 11 Feb. 2007.
<http://www.medicalnewstoday.com/medicalnews.php?newsid=56910>

"Canine Osteoarthritis–the Roles of the Veterinarian and Veterinary Technician in Companion Animal Rehabilitation." *IVIS*. 7 Jan. 2006. College of Veterinary Medicine, North Carolina State University and Animal Rehabilitation and Wellness Hospital, Raleigh, NC. 1 Apr. 2007. Dr. Denis J. Marcellin-Little.
<http://www.ivis.org/proceedings/navc/2006/SAE/329.pdf?LA=1>

"Canine Renal Transplantation." *University of California, Davis, Veterinary Medical Teaching Hospital*. 5 Jan. 2007. U.C. Davis School of Veterinary Medicine. 25 Aug. 2007.
<http://www.vmth.ucdavis.edu/vmth/clientinfo/info/sasurg/k9rentrans.html>

"Chronic Renal Disease and Failure (CRD, CRF)." *Washington State University College of Veterinary Medicine*. 12 Aug. 2007.
<http://courses.vetmed.wsu.edu/vm552/urogenital/crf.htm>

Clinical Perspectives on Canine Joint Disease. 17 Jan. 2001, IAMS Company. 2 Apr. 2007.
<http://www.eukanuba-scienceonline.com/download/slibraryCanineJoint%202001TNAVC.pdf>

"Cognitive Dysfunction Syndrome in the Dog." *ThePetCenter.com*. Sept. 1998. DVM Newsmagazine. 31 July 2007. Pfizer Animal Health.
<http://www.thepetcenter.com/imtop/cds.html>

"College Performs Successful Kidney Transplant Operation in Client-Owned Dog." *UF: Vet School: Fall 2002 Florida Veterinarian*. 2002. University of Florida's Veterinary Medical Teaching Hospital. 25 Aug. 2007. Sarah Carey.
<http://www.vetmed.ufl.edu/pr/news_ext/Fall_02/KIDNEY.HTM>

"Coming to the Ryan Veterinary Hospital in January: Hemodialysis." *Penn Veterinary Medicine*. Fall 2003. University of Pennsylvania School of Veterinary Medicine. 25 Aug. 2007. Susan I. Finkelstein.
<http://www.vet.upenn.edu/schoolresources/communications/publications/bellwether/58/hemodialysis.html>

"Degenerative Arthritis in Dogs." *PetPlace.com*. 1 Apr. 2007. Dr. Robert Parker.
<http://www.petplace.com/article-printer-friendly.aspx?id=92>

"Dialysis: Is It for Your Pet?" *Marvistavet.com*. Mar Vista Animal Medical Center. 25 Aug. 2007.
<http://www.marvistavet.com/html/body_dialysis.html>

"Dietary Protein and the Kidney." *IAMS*. 12 Aug. 2007.
<http://iams.com/en_US/jhtmls/vet_section/sw_VeterinariansFaq_page.jhtml;jsessionid=OBUF2F3RE QTYFQFIAJ1YYCQ?li=en_US&bc=I&vetqi=40 098&pti=VN>

"Dog Health: Urinary Incontinence." *Vet 4 Petz*. 2002. 7 Apr. 2007.
<http://www.vet4petz.com/articles/urinary_incontinence.htm>

"Effect of Fermentable Fiber Blends on Nitrogen Repartitioning in the Feline." *The Iams Company Nutrition Library*. 2004. The Iams Company. 12 Aug. 2007. Gregory D. Sunvold, Ph.D., R. Jason Vickers, M.S., and Gregory A. Reinhart, Ph.D.
<http://www.iamscompanybreeders.com/bronline/en_US/jhtmls/nutrition_library/BO_NutritionLibrary_Detail_Page.jhtml?li=en_US&pti=NL&sc=C&articleID=233>

"Focus Products: Azodyl™" *Vétoquinol Azodyl*. 2005. 12 Aug. 2007.
<http://www.vetoquinolusa.com/pages/global_06.html>

"Identity Theft: When Senior Dogs Forget." *Veterinary Forum*. Feb. 2007. Veterinary Forum. 31 July 2007. Marie Rosenthal, M.S.
<http://www.forumvet.com/pdf/VF_COVER%20story_0207%20FNL.pdf>

"Kidney Transplantation in the Dog." *ThePetCenter.com*. Published in the March, 2002 Issue of Dog World Magazine. 25 Aug. 2007. Dr. Dunn.
<http://www.thepetcenter.com/imtop/kt.html>

Laboratory Procedures for Animal Health Technicians. Paul W. Pratt, V.M.D. Goleta, CA: American Veterinary Publications, Inc., 1985, pp. 454–457.

"Medical Management of Urinary Incontinence." *This Manuscript is Reproduced in the IVIS Website with the Permission of WSAVA.* 2006. Clinic for Reproductive Medicine Vetsuisse-Faculty, University of Zurich. 7 Apr. 2007. Dr. Susi Arnold, Dr. Madeleine Hubler, and Dr. Iris Reichler.
<http://www.ivis.org/proceedings/wsava/2006/lecture27/Arnold2.pdf?LA=1>

"News." *Penn Animal Hospital.* 2006. Pfizer Animal Health. 11 Feb. 2007.
<http://www.pennanimal.com/news.htm>

"Pain Management for Canine Osteoarthritis." *IVIS.* 7 Jan. 2006. Hill's Pet Nutrition, Inc. 1 Apr. 2007. Philip Roudebush, D.V.M.
<http://www.ivis.org/proceedings/navc/2006/SAE/355.pdf?LA=1>

"Pain Medications for Dogs." *About.Com.* 20 Sept. 2006. 1 Apr. 2007. Carol Eustice and Richard Eustice.
<http://arthritis.about.com/od/dogarthritis/a/painmedications.htm>

"Senior Pets: The Importance of Behavior Signs in Diagnosis and Treatment." *Michigan Veterinary Medical Association.* 31 July 2007. Gary Landsberg, B.Sc., D.V.M., D.A.C.V.B.
<http://www.michvma.org/documents/MVC%20Proceedings/Landsberg5.pdf>

"Support Your Pet's Kidneys...with Azodyl!" *Kibowbiotech.com.* 25 Aug. 2007.
<http://www.kibowbiotech.com/PDF/vetbro.pdf>

"Surgery of the Coxofemoral Joint," *American Animal Hospital Association's 1985 Scientific Proceedings.* Don Hulse, *et al.* 1985, pp. 518–520.

The Diagnosis and Treatment of Chronic Renal Failure in the Dog & Cat. 29th World Congress of the World Small Animal Veterinary Association, 6 Oct. 2004. 12 Aug. 2007. Hein P. Meyer, D.V.M., Ph.D.
<http://www.vin.com/proceedings/Proceedings.plx?CID=WSAVA200>

Treating Canine Kidney Disease: An Evidence-Based Approach. 2006 North American Veterinary Conference: Small Animal and Exotics Section—Orlando, Florida, USA, 7 Jan. 2006. 13 Aug. 2007. D. Polzin, D.V.M., Ph.D.
<http://www.ivis.org/proceedings/navc/2006/SAE/239.asp?LA=1>

"Understanding Canine Arthritis." *Rimadyl.* 2007. Pfizer Animal Health. 1 Apr. 2007.
<http://www.rimadyl.com/display.asp?country=US&lang=EN&drug=RC&species=CN&sec=110>

Veterinary Hemodialysis: State-of-the-Art. 28th World Congress of the World Small Animal Veterinary Association, 24 Oct. 2003. 25 Aug. 2007. Larry D. Cowgill, D.V.M., Ph.D.
<http://www.vin.com/proceedings/Proceedings.plx?CID=WSAVA2003&PID=6606&O=Generic>

GENETICS

"An Introduction to Genetics." *CyberPet.* 12 Nov. 2007. Betsy O. Davison.
<http://www.cyberpet.com/dogs/articles/general/genetics.htm>

"Boxer is First Dog to Have Full Genome Revealed." *NewScientist.* 7 Dec. 2005. 12 Nov. 2007. Rowan Hooper.
<http://www.newscientist.com/article/dn8430.html>

"DNA." *Wikipedia.* 12 Nov. 2007. 12 Nov. 2007.
<http://en.wikipedia.org/wiki/DNA>

"Dog Genome Assembled." *National Human Genome Research Institute/National Institutes of Health.* Feb. 2007. 12 Nov. 2007.
<http://www.genome.gov/12511476>

"Dog Genome Exposed." *BARK.* 7 Dec. 2005. 14 Nov. 2007. Mark Derr.
<http://thebark.typepad.com/barking/2005/12/dog_genome_expo.html>

"Dogs Really are Man's Best Friend—Canine Genomics Has Applications in Veterinary and Human Medicine!" *Oxford Journals.* July 2005. Henry Stewart Publications. 14 Nov. 2007. Mike P. Starkey, Timothy J. Scase, Cathryn S. Mellersh, and Sue Murphy.
<http://bfgp.oxfordjournals.org/cgi/reprint/4/2/112>

"Genetics and the Shape of Dogs." *American Scientist Online.* Sept.–Oct. 2007. 14 Nov. 2007. Elaine A. Ostrander.
<http://www.americanscientist.org/template/AssetDetail/assetid/55869?fulltext=true&print=yes>

"Genetics for Breeders," *Pure-Bred Dogs/American Kennel Gazette.* Olive Lombard. February 1988, pp. 68–79.

Genetics Principles. 30th World Congress of the World Small Animal Veterinary Association, 11 May 2005. 12 Nov. 2007. Lowell Ackerman, D.V.M., D.A.C.V.D., M.B.A., M.P.A.
<http://www.vin.com/proceedings/Proceedings.plx?CID=WSAVA2005&PID=11051&Category=1553&O=Generic>

"Genome Sequence, Comparative Analysis and Haplotype Structure of the Domestic Dog." *Nature International Weekly Journal of Science*. 11 Oct. 2005. Broad Institute of Harvard and MIT. 14 Nov. 2007. Kerstin Lindblad-Toh, *et al*.
<http://www.nature.com/nature/journal/v438/n7069/full/nature04338.html>

"How are Defects Inherited?" *Canine Inherited Disorders Database*. 15 Dec. 2000. Joint Initiative of the Sir James Dunn Animal Welfare Centre At the Atlantic Veterinary College, University of Prince Edward Island, and the Canadian Veterinary Medical Association. 12 Nov. 2007.
<http://www.upei.ca/~cidd/howare.htm>

"James Watson, Francis Crick, Maurice Wilkins, and Rosalind Franklin." *Chemical Heritage Foundation*. 2005. 13 Nov. 2007.
<http://www.chemheritage.org/classroom/chemach/pharmaceuticals/watson-crick.html>

"MAF [Morris Animal Foundation] funds unprecedented genetic study," *Dog World*. Darlene Arden. September 1990, pp. 28–29, 61–62.

"Sequencing the Genome of the Domestic Dog *Canis Familiaris*." *National Human Genome Research Institute*. Fred Hutchinson Cancer Research Center and Whitehead/MIT Center for Genome Research. 14 Nov. 2007. Elaine A. Ostrander, Kerstin Lindblad-Toh, *et al*.
<http://www.genome.gov/Pages/Research/Sequencing/SeqProposals/CanineSEQedited.pdf>

"Tasha Offers Up the Genetic Secrets of Man's Best Friend." *Telegraph.co.uk*. 12 Aug. 2005. 14 Nov. 2007. Roger Highfield.
<http://www.telegraph.co.uk/news/main.jhtml?xml=/news/2005/12/08/ndog08.xml&sSheet=/news/2005/12/08/ixhome.html>

"The FHCRC Dog Genome Project." *Fred Hutchinson Cancer Research Center*. 12 Nov. 2007.
<http://www.fhcrc.org/science/dog_genome/>

"World's First Sex-Selected Puppies Prove Again XY Inc. Technology Works." *XY Inc*. 6 Mar. 2007. 31 July 2007. Melissa Katsimpalis.
<http://www.xyinc.com/news/releases/07_0306_puppies.php>

GROOMING
"Periodontal Disease in Pets: The pathogenesis of a preventable problem," *Veterinary Medicine*. Edward R. Eisner, D.V.M. January 1989.

HEREDITARY DISEASES
"CERF: Better Eyes, Better Dogs." *Pure-Bred Dogs/American Kennel Gazette*. Hilary Freer. July 1988, pp. 48–50.

"General Patellar Luxation Information." *Orthopedic Foundation for Animals*. 2007. 12 Nov. 2007.
<http://www.offa.org/patluxgeninfo.html>

"Helen Chrysler Greene Instrumental in Funding Orthopedic Disease Study." *American Kennel Club Canine Health Foundation*. 28 Feb. 2003. 13 Nov. 2007.
<http://www.akcchf.org/news/index.cfm?article_id=76>

Inherited Eye Disease in Purebred Dogs. Lionel F. Rubin, V.M.D., M.Med.Sci., Baltimore, MD: Williams & Wilkins. (n.d.), pp. 200–201.

"Legg-Calvé-Perthes Disease," *Pinscher Patter*. Virginia Brookings, D.V.M. June 1995, p. 24.

"Legg-Calvé-Perthes Disease in Dogs," *Bones and Joints*. Paul C. Gambardella. (n.d.) pp. 625–629.

"Linkage Analysis and Comparative Mapping of Canine Progressive Rod-Cone Degeneration (Prcd) Establishes Potential Locus Homology with Retinitis Pigmentosa (RP17) in Humans." *NCBI, U.S. National Library of Medicine*. 17 Mar. 1998. James A. Baker Institute for Animal Health, College of Veterinary Medicine, Cornell University; Fred Hutchinson Cancer Research Center; Department of Molecular and Cell Biology, University of California, Berkeley, CA. 13 Nov. 2007. Gregory M. Acland, Kunal Ray, Cathryn S. Mellersh, Weikuan Gu, Amelia A. Langston, Jasper Rine, Elaine A. Ostrander, and Gustavo D. Aguirre.
<http://www.ncbi.nlm.nih.gov/sites/entrez?db=pubmed&uid=9501213&cmd=showdetailview&indexed=google>

Long-term Results of Excision Arthroplasty of the Canine Hip," *The Veterinary Record.* R. Duff and J. R. Campbell. September 3, 1977, Vol. 101(10), pp. 181–184.

"Mode of Inheritance of Perthes' Disease in Manchester Terriers." Privately published. Philip B. Vasseur, *et al.* (n.d.), 19 pages.

"Mucopolysaccharidosis (MPS) Type VI." *Penn Veterinary Medicine.* 2007. 13 Nov. 2007. <http://w3.vet.upenn.edu/research/centers/penngen/services/deublerlab/mps6.html>

"Mutation Causing Storage Disease in Miniature Pinschers Identified." *American Kennel Club Canine Health Foundation.* 19 Aug. 2003. 13 Nov. 2007. <http://www.akcchf.org/news/index.cfm?article_id=65>

"New DNA Test for MPS VI in Miniature Pinscher." *BellWether.* Summer 2003. Penn Veterinary Medicine. 13 Nov. 2007. <http://www.vet.upenn.edu/schoolresources/communications/publications/bellwether/57/bellwether57-summer2003.pdf>

"New Mutation Test for Prcd PRA is Now Available." *OptiGen, LLC.* 1 June 2005. 13 Nov. 2007. <http://www.optigen.com/opt9_prcdpramutation.html>

"Patellar Luxation." *IVIS.* 1 Jan. 1985. 12 Nov. 2007. D. M. Nunamaker. <http://www.ivis.org/special_books/ortho/chapter_81/81mast.asp>

"Perthes' Disease in Rabbits and Puppies," *Clinical Orthopaedics and Related Research.* H. B. S. Kemp, M.S., F.R.C.S. August 1986, Number 209, pp. 139–159.

"PRA and Genetics–Myth and Truths," *Poodle Variety.* Candy Lobb. December 1988/January 1989, pp. 54, 72.

"PRA–The Specialists' View," *Poodle Variety.* Dr. Keith Barnett and Dr. Roger Curtis. December 1987/January 1988, p. 22. (Reprinted in P.V., courtesy of England's Dog World. September 11, 1987.)

Progressive Retinal Atrophy: an Overview. 28th World Congress of the World Small Animal Veterinary Association, 24 Oct. 2003, Department of Small Animal Clinical Sciences, Michigan State University. 13 Nov. 2007. Simon M. Petersen-Jones, D.Vet.Med., Ph.D. D.V.Ophthal. <http://www.vin.com/proceedings/Proceedings.plx?CID=WSAVA2003&PID=6687&O=Generic>

"Progressive Retinal Atrophy/Degeneration." *PetEducation.com.* Drs. Foster and Smith. 13 Nov. 2007. Marty Smith, D.V.M., and Holly Nash, D.V.M, M.S. <http://www.peteducation.com/article.cfm?cls=2&cat=1606&articleid=343>

"Progressive Retinal Atrophy (PRA) in Dogs." *Animal Eye Care, LLC.* 13 Nov. 2007. <http://www.animaleyecare.net/diseases/pra.htm>

"Treatments for Patellar Luxations in Dogs and Cats," *American Animal Hospital Association's 1990 Scientific Proceedings.* Joseph Harari. 1990, pp. 287–289.

"Update from the Poodle Club of America Genetic Anomalies Committee," *Poodle Variety.* Diann Ellis. June/July 1990, p. 12.

INFECTIOUS DISEASES

"Canine Influenza–Background for Professionals." *American Animal Hospital Association.* 3 Oct. 2005. 19 Mar. 2007. <http://www.aahanet.org/index_adds/canine_flu_background.html>

"CDC: West Nile Virus–QA: West Nile Virus and Dogs and Cats." *CDC.* 22 Dec. 2003. Centers for Disease Control and Prevention. 16 Feb. 2007. <http://www.cdc.gov/ncidod/dvbid/westnile/qa/wnv_dogs_cats.htm>

"Control of Canine Influenza in Dogs–Questions, Answers, and Interim Guidelines." *American Veterinary Medical Association.* 1 Dec. 2005. 19 Mar. 2007. <http://www.avma.org/public_health/influenza/canine_guidelines.asp>

"Ehrlichia Infection in Dogs." *VeterinaryPartner.com.* 15 Aug. 2005. Veterinary Information Network, Inc. 18 Feb. 2007. Wendy C. Brooks, D.V.M. <http://www.veterinarypartner.com/Content.plx?P=A&S=0&C=0&A=2103>

"Ehrlichiosis (Canine)." *Wikipedia.* 2007. 18 Feb. 2007. <http://en.wikipedia.org/wiki/Ehrlichiosis>

"Experimental Infection of Cats and Dogs with West Nile Virus." *CDC*. Jan. 2004. Centers for Disease Control and Prevention. 16 Feb. 2007. Laura E. Austgen, *et al*.
<http://www.cdc.gov/ncidod/eid/vol10no1/02-0616.htm>

"Fast Facts About Canine Influenza." *American Animal Hospital Association*. 19 Mar. 2007.
<http://www.aahanet.org/graphics/pdf/canine_influenza.pdf>

"The Threat of Canine Brucellosis: Myth or Menace?" *Wildside Kennels*. 1995. 23 Mar. 2007. Ed and Chris Faron.
<http://www.wildsidekennels.com/articles/brucellosis.html>

"World-Famous Scientists Donate Services to the Rabies Challenge Fund Charitable Trust." *The Rabies Challenge Fund*. 14 Mar. 2007.
<http://www.rabieschallengefund.org/files/press%20release.pdf>

JUDGING

"Evaluating the Miniature Pinscher." *Miniature Pinscher Club of America, Inc.* 1 Feb. 2007. Madeline K. Miller.
<http://www.minpin.org/judges_ed_files/jec_articles/evaluating_min_pin.pdf>

Guidelines for Dog Show Judges and Provisional Breed Judging Requirements, American Kennel Club, 5580 Centerview Drive, Suite 200, Raleigh, NC 27606.

"MPCA Judges' Education–Illustrated Standard." *Miniature Pinscher Club of America, Inc.* 11 Feb. 2007. Madeline K. Miller, Marcia P. Tucker, and Gloria Knapp.
<http://www.minpin.org/ ill_stand.htm>

MISCELLANEOUS

"For the Record," *Pure-Bred Dogs/American Kennel Gazette*. Jenny Drastura. November 1991, pp. 71–76.

"Miniature Pinscher" breed columns, *Pure-Bred Dogs/American Kennel Gazette*. May 1931, pp. 40–41; September 1931, pp. 38–39; October 1935, p. 45; November 1935, p. 51; February 1936; September 1936; March 1938, p. 54; November 1939, pp. 32–33; December 1939, pp. 59–60; January 1940, pp. 29–30; February 1948, p. 49; August 1966, pp. 72–73; April 1967, p. 68; April 1973, p. 95; September 1975, pp. 107–108; April 1977, p. 111; April 1988, p. 134.

"MPCA–Hall of Fame (ROM) Sires & Dams." *Miniature Pinscher Club of America, Inc.* 1 May 2007.
<http://www.minpin.org/honors_files/ROM_list.html>

"Round the World Flights." *WingNet*. 1 Feb. 2007. 26 Feb. 2007.
<http://www.wingnet.org/rtw/ rtw002aa.htm>

OBEDIENCE AND TRAINING

Canine Good Citizen, American Kennel Club, 5580 Centerview Drive, Suite 200, Raleigh, NC 27606.

"Min Pins and Agility," *Pinscher Patter*. Karen Egbert. March 1994, pp. 70–71.

Obedience Regulations, American Kennel Club, 5580 Centerview Drive, Suite 200, Raleigh, NC 27606.

"The Miniature Pinscher in Obedience, A Survey," *Pinscher Patter*. Gretchen S. Hofheins. December 1993, pp. 68–70.

"Tracking Events," *Dog Fancy*. Liz Palika. March 1996, pp. 94–95.

PARASITES

"2005 Guidelines for the Diagnosis, Prevention and Management of Heartworm (*Dirofilaria Immitis*) Infection in Dogs." *American Heartworm Society*. 2005. 14 Feb. 2007. Executive Board Of The American Heartworm Society.
<http://www.heartwormsociety.org/AHS%20Guidelines-Canine 2005PF.htm>

"Companion Animal Parasite Council." *CAPC Companion Animal Parasite Council*. 2006. 12 Feb. 2007.
<http://www.capcvet.org/?p=Guidelines_Fleas&h=0&s=0>

"Demodectic Mange." *VeterinaryPartner.com*. 20 Feb. 2006. Veterinary Information Network, Inc. 20 Feb. 2007. Wendy C. Brooks, D.V.M.
<http://www.veterinarypartner.com/Content.plx?P= A&S=0&C=0&A=630>

"Demodex–the Mighty Mite," *Dog World*. Edward Baker, V.M.D. October 1988.

"Dog Tip: Fleas, Ticks, Mosquitoes–Prevention and Treatment." *Partnership for Animal Welfare*. 2006. 2 Feb. 2007. Robin Tierney.
<http://www.paw-rescue.org/PAW/PETTIPS/DogTip_Insect Prevention.php>

"Evaluation of Five Popular Methods for Tick Removal," *Pediatrics*. G. R. Needham. June 1985, 75(6), pp. 997–1002.

"Flea Problems: Flea Removal and Treating Fleas." *Doctors Foster and Smith*. 12 Feb. 2007. Drs. Foster & Smith Educa.
<http://www.drsfostersmith.com/pic/article.cfm?dept_id=0&siteid=12&acatid=176&aid=60>

"General Heartworm Disease Information." *American Heartworm Society*. 2007. 14 Feb. 2007.
<http://www.heartwormsociety.org/CanineHeartwormInfo.htm>

"Heartworm Treatment." *VeterinaryPartner.com*. 28 Nov. 2005. Veterinary Information Network, Inc. 14 Feb. 2007. Wendy C. Brooks, D.V.M.
<http://www.veterinarypartner.com/Content.plx?P= A&A=610>

"Immunoglobulin-Binding Proteins in Ticks: New Target for Vaccine Development Against a Blood-Feeding Parasite." *Cellular and Molecular Life Sciences (CMLS)* 56 (1999): 286–295. 14 Feb. 2007. H. Wang and P. A. Nuttall.
<http://www.springerlink.com/content/rxcfpkw53qfnkl04/fulltext.pdf>

"PROGRAM® Flavor Tabs® for Dogs Product Information." *Novartis*. 2004. 12 Feb. 2007.
<http://www.program.novartis.us/dog/en/label.shtml>

"Taking the Bite out of Fleas and Ticks," *FDA Consumer Magazine*. U.S. Food and Drug Administration. Linda Bren. July–August 2001.

"Treatment for Demodex in Dogs." *VetInfo.com*. 2002. 20 Feb. 2007. Michael Richards, D.V.M.
<http://www.vetinfo.com/ddemotreat.html>

"UNL Entomology–Tick Images." *Department of Entomology, University of Nebraska-Lincoln*. 15 Feb. 2007.
<http://entomology.unl.edu/images/ticks/ticks.htm>

"West Nile Virus." *Healthypet.com*. 2006. American Animal Hospital Association. 16 Feb. 2007.
<http://www.healthypet.com/library_view.aspx?id=43>

"What are the Best Methods to Control Fleas on My Pet and in My House?" *About: Veterinary Medicine*. 12 Feb. 2007. Janet Tobiassen Crosby, D.V.M.
<http://vetmedicine.about.com/od/parasites/f/FAQ_fleacontrol.htm>

PUPPY CARE
"Feeding the Puppy," *Nutrition and Management of Dogs and Cats (looseleaf)*. D. M. Bebiak, Ph.D. St. Louis, MO: Ralston Purina Co., 1987, Section F-2, pp. 1–3.

"Feeding of Orphan Puppies," *Nutrition and Management of Dogs and Cats*. William J. Monson, Ph.D. Section F-3, pp. 1–6.

Tube Feeding Puppies (pamphlet). Dennis F. Lawler, D.V.M. St. Louis, MO: Ralston Purina Co., 1987.

SHOWING
How to Show Your Own Dog. Virginia Tuck Nichols. Neptune City, NJ: T.F.H. Publications, Inc., 1976.

"MPCA–National Specialty." *Miniature Pinscher Club of America, Inc*. 1 May 2007.
<http://www.minpin.org/nat_spec.htm#nat_results>

TRAVEL
"Canine Travelers From Fashion-Craft Products Inc." *Fashion-Craft Products Inc*. 2006. 3 Mar. 2007.
<http://caninetraveler.com>

"Choosing a Boarding Kennel." *The Humane Society of the United States*. 2006. 1 Mar. 2007.
<http://www.hsus.org/pets/pet_care/choosing_a_boarding_kennel.html>

"For Pets Crossing the Atlantic Aboard Queen Mary 2, the Luxuries Abound." *Cruiseline.Co.uk*. 16 Feb. 2006. 19 Apr. 2006.
<http://www.cruiseline.co.uk/news.php?&newsid=13541>

"How to Select a Pet Care Facility." *ABKA*. 1 Mar. 2007.
<http://www.abka.com/abka/findAFacility/Find_A_Facility.pdf>

"ON THE ROAD: RVing with Your Pet." *CyberPet*. 2001. 3 Mar. 2007. Lexiann Grant.
<http://www.cyberpet.com/dogs/articles/lexi/rvsandpets.html>

"Showing in Style," *Pure-Bred Dogs/American Kennel Gazette*. Jo Campbell. December 1989, pp. 76–82.

ACKNOWLEDGMENTS

Why read dog books? Why write them? Although the roots of the modern dog book lie as deep as a buried bone, *cynogetica*, or the literature of the dog, began to achieve prominence among the general public in 19th-century England. Through classic commentaries, such as *The Dogs of the British Islands*, by Stonehenge; *Dogs: Their Points, Whims, Instincts, and Peculiarities*, by Henry Webb; and *Illustrated Book of the Dog*, by Vero Shaw, early enthusiasts could trace the history and development of their chosen breeds, as well as apply a new level of scientific knowledge to their kennel's breeding practices. Today's books, in the tradition of their predecessors, offer a peek into the dog's past, and supply up-to-date information on general care, health, feeding, genetics, and reproduction. Dog books not only provide a forum for the exchange of ideas, but also a method of preserving such knowledge for future generations.

Thus, one of my purposes in writing *The Miniature Pinscher: King of Toys* was to bring together in one source as much breed-specific information as possible for both the newcomer and veteran fancier. To accomplish this, I sent questionnaires to members of the Miniature Pinscher Club of America, to foreign breed clubs and breeders, and to handlers, trainers, judges, and veterinarians. I received quite a few interesting responses—from Australia to South Africa, the Czech Republic to Scandinavia. Another reason for writing this book was to update readers on the progress of the Miniature Pinscher, by emphasizing fanciers of the last decade. Photographs of dogs, past and current, will allow students of the breed to put a "face" to many of the names in their dog's background.

To all who participated in this project—the owners, breeders, handlers, judges, and veterinarians who answered my call for assistance with a generous outpouring of photographs, kennel records, training tips, and veterinary information—I offer a collective "thank you."

In particular, I want to express my appreciation to the late Marie Munson, of Gilmer, Texas. Although Marie operated her Tay-Mar kennel on a limited scale in breeding and showing, she truly loved her Min Pins. Marie provided background material for this book and, through our correspondence, instilled in me a deep regard for the breed. Unfortunately, Marie did not live to see the publication of this work. However, I hope she would approve of my efforts.

Recognition also goes to Lorraine Lyons, of Gillies Bay, British Columbia. Not only did Lorraine answer my questions about the Min Pin, she also supplied a personal video showing the birth of two "Pawznplay" litters of puppies. Most important, though, Lorraine acted as liaison among Canadian breeders, garnering support for my project in the form of photographs, kennel history, genetic information, and health records.

Other Min Pin owners and breeders who have played key roles in providing material for this book include Armando Angelbello, Thomas W. Baldwin, Michele L. Basye, Sherry Bernard, Dr. Buris R. Boshell, Lerae Britain Bush, Norma D. Cacka, Laurie Chism, Luis M. and Linda Colarte, Terrie Crawford, Georgette Curran, Ann Dutton, Valerie Edwards, Amy Fields, Mark S. Fiorentino, Susan P. Goldman, Burt and Lonnie Gordon, Helen Chrysler Greene, Robin Greenslade, Bernard and Wilma Griffith, Kathy Helming, Gretchen S. Hofheins-Wackerfuss, Amy Putnam Issleib, Juanita L. Kean, Sharon Krogh, Joan Krumm, Paula A. Lacker, Rhonda Ludwig, Cherie McDaniel, Cindy McNeal, Sandra J. Mestyanek, Ellen Michel, Roberta (Bobbie) Mills-Bowhay, Ruth H.

Norwood, Kimberly Pastella, Hal and Patsy Pawley, Virginia Priest, Edward and Rose Radel, Sue E. Shore, Judy Smay, Catherine E. Smith, Susan Souza, Barbara Stamm, Kim Swilling, Linda Talbot, Robyn Thomason, Marcia P. Tucker, Ann Walker, Judith White, Joanne Wilds-Snell, and Barbara Zagrodnick.

A particular interest of mine is obedience training and competition. Whereas some dog books have given this activity short shrift, I am pleased to offer an in-depth look at the accomplishments of this small yet highly intelligent dog. As you will note, the Miniature Pinscher was the first of any toy breed to earn the title, Companion Dog, and continues to succeed in Utility, Tracking, and Agility. I appreciate the help of Dee Stutts, recognized by her peers as the "first lady" of Min Pin obedience training, along with Karen Egbert, Martha Fair, Rae Galea, Velma Janek, Velda Pearson, Mary Silfies, Merlin Van De Kinder, Doralyn Wheatley, John Yarwood, Barbara Zagrodnick, and Sandra A. Hill, who provided tracking information and photos.

I would like to express my gratitude to supporters from foreign countries, as well, who contributed so abundantly. From Canada: Dianne Bailey, Mary Bates, Judy Bohnert, Patricia Gauthier, Armand and Jacline Gratton, Gerona MacCuaig, Edris Matulock, Winnifred Wartnow, and Judith Wellwood. From Scandinavia: Rigmor Andersen, Inge Hansen, Jytte Pedersen, Herbert and Jytte Baumkirchner, Else Hegbom, and Nini Hermansson. From Australia: Rae Galea, Dora Hay, Marilyn Rose, and Michael and Helen Towell. From Colombia, Sonia Guarin Zambrano, and from South Africa, Colleen Flight.

Judges and handlers who assisted with this book include Thelma R. Brown, Melbourne T. L. Downing, David and Sharon Krogh, Ellen Michel, Madeline K. Miller, Herbert Rosen, Alfred E. Treen, Darryl Vice, Sue A. Lackey, and Patricia (Patti) L. Proctor. Veterinarians and scientists who provided support include Edward Baker, V.M.D., Edward R. Eisner, D.V.M., Elaine A. Ostrander, Ph.D., and, from Denmark, Rikke Langebaek.

In addition, I would like to recognize illustrator, Nancy Ross; dog book dealer, Kathy Darling, who generously loaned me a set of early German stud books for my research; and the late Joan Klepac (one of the few post card dealers able to locate Miniature Pinscher cards), who provided many of the post cards that appear throughout the book. And finally, no dog book acknowledgment would be complete without recognizing Roberta Vesley, retired librarian of the American Kennel Club. Roberta not only tracked down early photographs, but also supplied copies of *AKC Gazette* breed columns, along with a list of AKC champions and obedience title holders.

"The farther back you can look, the farther forward you are likely to see," said Winston Churchill. As a researcher and writer, as well as dog book collector, I understand the importance of assembling and preserving historical data, kennel records, pedigrees, and photographs of dogs for future generations. Through the "literature of the dog," all fanciers are brought closer to those early canine supporters whose understanding, perseverance, and vision brought us the many dog breeds we know today.

Patricia F. Lehman

Can. Ch. Patapin Next Episode, with Mojo, her feline friend. This pair shares their home with Judy Bohnert.

INDEX

A
accommodations, travel, 46
acute metritis, 190
agility, 206–212, 215
agouti series, genes, 139
air travel, 43–44
Airlane, 219–221
AKC Canine Good Citizen® Program, 32–33
Amateur-Owner-Handler Class, 107
American-Bred Class, 107
anal glands, 36–37
anestrus, 176
arthritis, 97–98
artificial insemination, 171
artificial respiration, 92
attitude, 126–127
Australia, development, 229–232

B
BAER hearing test, 67
BARF diet, 80
barking, 28–29
bathing, 35
begging, 29
Bel-Roc, 12–13
Berta, Josef, 6–7, 49, 121
Best of Breed Class, 108
Best of Opposite Sex, 108
Best of Winners, 108
birth control, 179–180
black-and-rust coat color, 141
black-brown pair, genes, 140
bleeding, 92
blue-and-rust coat color, 145
Bo-Mar, 13, 113, 238
boarding kennels, 47
bottle feeding, 192–193
Brace Class, 109
bracing, ear, 71
Bred-by-Exhibitor Class, 107
breech delivery, 189
breed standard, AKC, 51–57
breed standard, Canadian, 224–227
broad jump, 204
Brockhaus *Konversation Lexikon*, 6
brood bitch, 173–179

Brood Bitch Class, 109
brucellosis, canine, 167–168, 178
Bruette, Dr. William A., 9
brushing, 35
Bungartz, Jean, 2–3
bus travel, 44
buying, 21–24
Byron, George, 114, 229

C
Caesarean section, 189–190
canine genome, 136–137
canine influenza, 86
canned food, 80
car travel, 44
carbohydrates, 76
Carlee, 13
cataracts, 103
championship, AKC, 108–109
championship, Canadian, 223–224
chewing (destructive), 29
chocolate-and-rust coat color, 142
choking, 92–93
choosing dog (obedience), 199
chromosomes, 130–131
chromosomes, sex, 133
chronic renal failure, 100–102
classes, regular, conformation, 106–109
clear red coat color, 142
coat, 54–55
coat color, 55–56, 139–146
coat problems, senior, 98
cognitive dysfunction syndrome, 98–100
Colombia, development, 233–234
color dilution alopecia, 147
colostrum, 191
come command, 30–31
Companion Dog title, 202–204
Companion Dog Excellent title, 204
constipation, 90
corona virus, 86
coughing, 90
CPR, 93
crate training, 28
cropping, ear, 68–70
cryptorchidism, 166

299

D

Day, Mr. & Mrs. Charles Healy, 9, 43
deafness, 67
dehydration, 90
demodectic mange, 39
Denmark, development, 236
dental care, 37–38
dental vaccine, 38
dewclaw removal, 195
dialysis, 101–102
diarrhea, 90
dilution pair, genes, 140
disorders, genetic, 133–136
disqualifications, 57
distemper, 86–87
DNA, 130
Doberman Pinscher, 6, 50
dog shows, Canadian, 222–223
down command, 31
dry food, 78–79

E

ear bracing, 71
ear cropping, 68–70
ear diseases, 65–67
ear mites, 65–66
eclampsia, 190–191
Ehrlichiosis, 41
estrous cycle, 174–176
estrus, 175
evaluating show puppies, 113–114
excusals, 124
extension pair, genes, 140–141

F

fat, dietary, 76–77
fawn coat color, 145
feeding, 75–83
feeding, adults, 81–82
feeding, amount, 78
feeding, puppies, 80–81
feeding, seniors, 95–96
feeding, stress, 82
feeding, weight loss, 82–83
first aid, 92–93
first impressions, judging, 121
fleas, 38–39
flea allergy dermatitis, 39
foundation bitch, 155–159
fractures, 93

Fresh Pond Travel, 47
Fritz von Arnowtal, 11–12
Futurity Stakes, 111

G

gait, 56–57, 59–63
gaiting, show, 123
genes, 130–131
genes, coat color, 139–141, 152–153
genetic disorders, 133–136
genome, canine, 136–137
Graham, Sheilah, 9
grooming, show, 116–117
growth, feeding, 80–81, 194

H

hackney-like gait, 56–57, 59–63
Hall of Fame Dams, 181
Hall of Fame Sires, 171
harlequin coat color, 146
heart disease, 100
heart massage, 93
heartworms, 39–40
heat exhaustion, 93
heat stroke, 93
Hedengren, K. J., 11, 50–51, 59, 239
heel command, 31
hormone tests, breeding, 179
housebreaking, 27–28

I

identification, 26–27
inbreeding, 160–161
incontinence, 102–103
infection, ear, 65
infectious canine hepatitis, 87
infectious diseases, 86–88
insect stings, 90–91
Internet Miniature Pinscher Service, 25

J

Jay-Mac, 14, 238
judging, show, 121–127
jump heights, 204
jumping up, 29
Junior Showmanship, 111

K

kennel cough, 87
kidney disease, 100–102

kidney transplantation, 101–102
King Eric v Konigsbach (Ch.), 12
Konig Heinzelmennchen (Ch.), 11

L
labor, 185–188
lactation, 191–192
lead training, show, 117–118
Legg-Calvé-Perthes disease, 133–134
leptospirosis, 87–88
limited registration, 26
line breeding, 161–162
Lo-Bob, 221
Lyme disease, 41

M
maintenance, feeding, 81
major points, show, 108–109
mastitis, 190
mating, timing, 179–180
measurements, 123–124
medication, giving, 85–86
meiosis, 132–133
Mendel, Gregor, 129–130
metestrus, 175–176
minerals, 77
misalliance, 180
mites, 39, 65–66
mitosis, 132
Mona av Assarstorp (Ch.), 11, 239
mosquitoes, 39–40

N
natural ears, 72–73
neutering, 88–89
No Tape Ear Bracing Method, 71
nonsurgical sterilization, 89–90
Norway, development, 236–237
Novice Class, conformation, 107
Novice Class, obedience, 202–204

O
obedience achievements, 197–198
obedience, choosing a dog to train, 199
Obedience Trial Champion, 206
obesity, 82–83
Onlyone, 14–15
Open Class, conformation, 107
Open Class, obedience, 204
Operation Blue Prints, 147

orphaned puppies, rearing, 191
osteoarthritis, 97–98
outcrossing, 162–163

P
paper training, 27
parvovirus, 88
patellar luxation, 134–135
pedigrees, understanding, 159
periodontal disease, 37–38
Pinscher-Schnauzer Klub, 5, 49
postwhelping care, 190–191
pre-breeding exam, bitch, 178
pre-breeding exam, stud dog, 167–168
pregnancy, danger signs, 187
pregnancy, detecting, 183–184
pregnancy, feeding, 184–185
Proctor Donnell, Henrietta, 11
proestrus, 175
progressive retinal atrophy, 135–136
protein, 75–76
pseudopregnancy, 180
puberty, 176–177
pulse rate, checking, 85
puppies, large, whelping, 189
Puppy Class, 106
puppy proofing, 25
puppy supplies, 25

Q
Queen Mary 2, 45–46

R
rabies, 88
raw food, 80
Rebel Roc, 15–16
red coat color, 141
registration, 26
reproductive hormones, 178
rewards of training, 201
rules and regulations, obedience, 201
recreational vehicle travel, 45

S
Sanbrook, 16–17
sarcoptic mange, 66
sex chromosomes, 133
shampoo, 36
ship travel, 45–46
shock, 93

show puppy, purchasing, 113–116
show training, 117–119
showing, Canada, 222–223
sit command, 30
size, 52
skin problems, senior, 98
skunk odor, 91
soft-moist food, 79–80
South Africa, development, 237–239
stag red coat color, 141
standard, AKC, 51–57
standard, Canadian, 224–227
stay command, 31
Strebel, Richard, 3
stress, feeding, 82
stud dog, 165–171
stud dog, choosing, 160
Stud Dog Class, 109
Sunsprite, 17
supplemental feeding, newborn, 192–193
Sweden, development, 239
Sweepstakes, 111

T
tail docking, 195
tan coat color, 142
Team Class, 109
temperament, 57
temperature, taking, 86
ticks, 40–41
toenail clipping, 35–36
Torfspitzgrupe, 2
touring, 47
tracking, 213–214

train travel, 44
training classes, 199–200
tube feeding, 193–194
tumors, 103
Twelve-to-Eighteen Month Class, 106

U
uncropped ear, 72–73
uterine inertia, 188
Utility title, 205–206
Utility Dog Excellent, 206

V
Vanderbilt, Mrs., 11
Veterans Class, 109
vision problems, 103
vitamins, 77
vomiting, 91
von der Kammer-Brugger, Hertha, 2, 4, 146

W
water, 77–78
weaning, 194
West Nile Virus, 40
whelping, 185–189
whelping, preparations, 185
whelping problems, 187–190
whelping supplies, 185
Winners Class, 108
Wolphofer, Bernardt, 5
worms, 91

Z
Zwerg pinscher, 5

ABOUT THE AUTHOR

Patricia F. Lehman is a freelance writer and photographer, specializing in the topic of dogs and their care. Her work has appeared in a variety of canine magazines, newspapers, and newsletters. Her books include *Your Healthy Puppy* and *Cairn Terriers (A Complete Pet Owner's Manual)*, which was named "Best Short Book Under 100 Pages" by the Dog Writers Association of America, Inc. A member and former treasurer of DWAA, she also served, from 1991 to 2003, as treasurer of the Dog Writers' Educational Trust, an organization that granted scholarships to students with a special interest in dogs. She won The Iams Company's *Eukanuba Nutrition Award* for "Best Article on Canine Nutrition," as well as four DWAA Honorable Mention certificates for excellence in dog writing. She is a member of the Miniature Pinscher Club of America, and holds the designation, Small Animal Dietitian, from Hill's Pet Products. A graduate of the University of Delaware, the author lives with her family in Wilmington, Delaware.